Love and Globalization

LOVE AND GLOBALIZATION

Transformations of Intimacy in the Contemporary World

Mark B. Padilla, Jennifer S. Hirsch,
Miguel Muñoz-Laboy, Robert E. Sember,
and Richard G. Parker

Vanderbilt University Press
Nashville

11 10 09 08 07   1 2 3 4 5

This book is printed on acid-free paper
made from 50% post consumer recycled paper.
Manufactured in the United States of America

Library of Congress Cataloging-in-Publication Data

Love and globalization : transformations of intimacy in the contemporary world /
Mark B. Padilla ... [et al.]. — 1st ed.
    p. cm.
Includes bibliographical references.
ISBN 978-0-8265-1584-1 (cloth : alk. paper)
ISBN 978-0-8265-1585-8 (pbk. : alk. paper)
1. Intimacy (Psychology)—Cross-cultural studies.   2. Sex—Cross-cultural
studies.   3. Love—Cross-cultural studies.   4. Interpersonal relations—Cross-
cultural studies.   5. Globalization—Social aspects—Cross-cultural studies.
I. Padilla, Mark, 1969–
HQ16.L68 2007
306.701--dc22   2007023101

Contents

Acknowledgments

We gratefully acknowledge the support of key institutions and individuals who made important contributions to the preparation of this volume.

The initial meeting that provided a point of departure for this book was held at Columbia University in April 2004, with support provided by the Ford Foundation through its grant for the project Sexuality, Culture, and Society (Grant #1020–148103; Principal Investigator Richard G. Parker, PhD), based in the Center for Gender, Sexuality, and Health and the Department of Sociomedical Sciences of the Mailman School of Public Health at Columbia University. At Columbia University, we especially want to thank Mayra Pabon for her help in organizing that meeting, and Raul Angeles for his assistance with the initial preparation of the text for this volume.

Finalization of the text took place at the University of Michigan, where we want to thank Danya Keene and Lisa Lapeyrouse in the Department of Health Behavior and Health Education, the School of Public Health, for their assistance in meticulously editing and reformatting the chapters.

Special thanks to Michael Ames at Vanderbilt University Press for his enthusiasm and support for this book.

Introduction
Cross-Cultural Reflections on an Intimate Intersection

Mark B. Padilla, Jennifer S. Hirsch,
Miguel Muñoz-Laboy,
Robert E. Sember, and Richard G. Parker

What is love? A virtue? A form of knowledge? An instinct? And what does the contemplation of love illuminate about fundamental human experiences, such as intimacy, sexual and marital bonding, gender relations, kinship, consumption, and pleasure? Love, in the framing of Jacques Derrida, is the original and central question of philosophy, providing a basis for the development of the fields of ethics, ontology aesthetics, and epistemology (Dick and Kaufman 2002). In a range of different social science disciplines, a growing number of detailed and highly specific ethnographies have similarly begun to recognize—largely as a result of the influence of feminist analysis and cross-cultural studies of gender and sexuality—that love is a particularly useful lens for social analysis, providing as it does a glimpse onto the complex interconnections between cultural, economic, interpersonal, and emotional realms of experience. Love, in a word, is holistic. As a master trope as pervasive as it is variable, love is highly productive as a tool for social analysis, revealing some of the most basic ways that human societies organize social life, meaning, and intimate experience, as well as how individuals enact, resist, or transform social discourses of love within specific cultural and historical contexts. As Naomi Quinn (1992) has argued in her studies of American constructions of marriage, examining how love is constructed necessitates an analysis of how narratives of love connect conceptually to other domains of experience, such as work, family, and gender relations. Like cultural constructions of gender, love is often "naturalized"—made to appear natural, essential, and immutable through its representation and reproduction in cultural systems of meaning (Yanagisako and Delaney 1995). This naturalization makes it all the more powerful in its ability to shape the most fundamental characteristics of social organization. Because of this productive quality, cross-cultural examinations of love permit the analyst a privileged position from which to consider the power and function of cultural, economic, and social forces in shaping what is often described—at least in the Euro-American West—as one of the most personal of human experiences.

While studies of gender and sexuality have begun to document the enormous range of variation in social constructions of love, the discipline is only beginning to grapple with how these constructions are changing in the context of contemporary processes of globalization. By the very nature of their ethnographic grounding in specific times and places, ethnographic accounts of experiences of love have often been particularist—describing in great detail the local operation of systems of gender and sexuality but attending less to the ways that these systems are embedded within and transformed by the escalating insertion of the local in the global (Jankowiak 1995; Sobo 1995). Conversely, while some recent works have pointed to the crucial importance of grounding analyses of gender and sexuality within a self-consciously global framework, the broad theoretical lens employed by such an approach often fails to capture the microsociological, interpersonal, and emotional responses of individual actors to the broad changes that are occurring as a consequence of globalization (see Altman 2001; Manalansan 2003; Parker 1999). Because theoretical discussions of globalization are concerned with political, economic, technological, and cultural transformations on a broad scale—such as the increasing flexibility of global capital, neoliberal state policies, the rise of global media and communications technologies, and escalating population mobility—they have frequently failed to articulate how these large-scale processes are embodied and experienced, or how they come to influence the most intimate aspects of one's life. For example, what new vocabularies for friendship, sexual intimacy, or romance emerge from the creative recombination of cultural forms from different places—processes that are facilitated by communications technologies such as the Internet? How do desires, pleasures, and emotions circulate as commodities in the global marketplace? In what ways do the economic processes characteristic of contemporary economies shape the acceptability of both public and private expressions of sexual intimacy and the ways that sexuality is depicted and reproduced in global media?

This volume is premised on the belief that sophisticated theoretical engagements with globalization can be productively combined with deeply local, intensely ethnographic considerations of love. It brings together the work of researchers trained in social science disciplines such as anthropology and sociology who have conducted long-term ethnographic research on love and intimacy in specific cultural contexts, addressing the question of how contemporary shifts in late modern economies and the forces of globalization influence intimate experiences—even, perhaps, "love," that most sacred and elusive of modern expressions of bonding. Drawing on ethnographic and social scientific research in a wide variety of cultural contexts—ranging from Indonesia to Egypt to Mexico—each chapter in this volume examines local expressions of love and intimacy within a theoretical framework that seeks to further our understanding of the linkages between intimacy and the various processes that have come to be called "globalization." Questions that orient the work presented here include: How are experiences of love and intimacy changing in response to globalization? What global or regional tendencies can be perceived in these transformations? What are the cultural bases of their specific variations? Further, we explore how we might theorize the various manifestations of love as affect, as subjective experience, as interpersonal relationship, and as the expression of historically contingent political-economic structures.

Throughout this volume, contributors refer to, borrow from, and extend some of the arguments developed in the foundational work on globalization and culture by authors such as Arjun Appadurai (1996), who theorizes globalization as unfolding in the unstable tension between cultural homogenization and cultural heterogenization, and producing both continuities and disjunctures along the lines of economy, culture, and politics. To track these disjunctures and continuities, Appadurai defines five dimensions of global cultural "flows"—ethnoscapes, mediascapes, technoscapes, financescapes, and ideoscapes—each representative of fluid, irregularly shaped "landscapes" that characterize the movement of global capital, populations, ideas, styles, and so forth. Contributors to this volume use ethnographic case studies to map how affects and subjectivities travel these landscapes of globalization, inflected by economies, cultures, and politics and organized within the constant tension between homogenization and heterogenization. Again, the topic of love grounds and tests Appadurai's framework. As a master trope, love traverses many of the conceptual levels of globalization Appadurai describes, allowing researchers to examine how various kinds of global scapes intersect to shape local and global meanings and practices of intimacy. Indeed, our consideration of love in this volume suggests that love is a unique cultural domain in that it is both particularly sensitive to globalizing processes and it takes its shape at the juncture of multiple intersecting cultural flows. The ethnographic case studies in the following chapters illustrate the incredible ethnographic variation that is generated by love's position within this highly productive global intersection.

In this chapter, we provide a brief overview of the theoretical concerns that organize the ethnographic analyses in this volume, highlighting the intersections between love and globalization that have shaped our analytical approach. These reflections fall within three general theoretical junctures: love and political economy; love, kinship, and gender/sexuality; and love and modernity. While, to repeat, we use these categories for the sake of conceptual organization, a fundamental argument is that the intersections of love and globalization can be fully captured only if they are viewed at the juncture of multiple simultaneous global flows.

Love and Political Economy

As cross-cultural social research has developed in the past decade, political economy —or an approach that foregrounds a structural vision of the ways that social and economic inequalities influence the meanings, practices, constraints, and vulnerabilities of individuals on the ground—has become an increasingly important interpretive framework for ethnographic analysis. Such approaches have been crucial in refocusing attention on the ways that changing political-economic structures shape the cultural meanings and social patterns that anthropologists seek to understand (Farmer 1992; Parker 2001; Parker and Easton 1998). However, most considerations of political economy, because they privilege large-scale structures at the levels of nations or global systems, tend to lose sight of the interaction between these systems and the personal and emotional experiences of real people, that is, the subjectivity, emotion, and agency of people who struggle within these constraints to establish emotional connections and intimacy with others. An alternative approach, which we might gloss here as the *political economy of love*, is one that would seek to trace large-scale shifts in political economy to the lived experiences and practices of love and intimacy, while continually listening to the voices of people themselves, their subjective understandings of intimate relationships and interactions, and their struggles to establish and maintain intimacy within the shifting terrain of globalizing processes.

This volume contributes to a new approach to globalization by foregrounding a dualistic theoretical framework in which macro-level political-economic transformations are seen to interact with the various cultural and psychosocial meanings of love, intimacy, and sexuality for the actors themselves. There is much at stake in the development of such an analytic approach.[1] First, while theories of globalization have done much to describe in broad terms the macro-structural trends that characterize the contemporary "globalized world"—including such phenomena as "flexible" accumulation, acceleration of migration, and the growth of travel and information technologies (Appadurai 1996; Castells 1996; García Canclini 1995; Harvey 1990)—they have less often sought to explicate the linkages between these phenomena and the subjective experiences and local meanings of actors in specific cultural settings. In the present volume, the social processes described within each chapter are seen as necessarily embedded within larger processes of globalization, but the ethnographic evidence clearly demonstrates that the various configurations of gender, sexuality, and identity expressed in such processes are not simply reducible to the material "condition of postmodernity" (Harvey 1990). That is, we cannot predict the social expressions of love and intimacy solely on the basis of the material structures within which they operate. Such a presumption would lead us to conclude that the inevitable outcome of globalization is the homogenization of human experiences of love, a position that has been rightly challenged in both theoretical and ethnographic analyses of globalization (Clifford 1994; Kearney 1995; Marcus 1995).

In addition to ensuring that structural analyses include considerations of subjectivity, a political economy of love requires that intimacy be understood as fundamentally linked to social and economic inequalities, and—as a corollary—that marginalities in sex and gender be seen as crucial means by which such inequalities are maintained. In other words, the direction of interaction between political-economy and intimacy is two-way; the ways that love and intimacy are socially and emotionally organized on the ground also influence how resources, hierarchies, and power are distributed at the level of political-economic systems. So, for example, in the chapters by Elizabeth Bernstein, Sealing Cheng, and Katherine Frank—which consider the intersection of sexual consumption in the global marketplace—it is clear that individual experiences of sexual exchanges are not simply emerging as an epiphenomenon of the economic organization of societies but rather are also linked to how intimate desires and experiences of sexuality are constructed by individuals and groups. From this perspective, subjective experiences of desire and longing for particular kinds of intimacy, for example, are seen to be the creative force behind certain expressions of consumption and economic exchange systems. Thus, our theoretical approach to the intersection of love and political economy in this volume seeks to depict a two-way, mutually constitutive relationship between structure and the intimate experiences of love, such that each of these phenomena can never be analyzed as entirely independent of its counterpart.

This dualistic approach avoids the problematic tendency in much of the globalization literature to exclude subjective experience from analysis in preference for the creation of master narratives about processes of globalization. Despite the analytic utility of frameworks such as Appadurai's (1996) "scapes," essentialized depictions of global processes tend to focus attention away from the rich descriptions of local meanings and practices that would advance the cross-cultural literature on the effects of globalization on human experience. What, after all, is a "technoscape" if it remains at the level of theory with no grounding in how individuals in specific cultural settings actually engage with specific technological transformations in the global sphere? In Inhorn's chapter in this volume, for example, we see the surprising tensions and appropriations that occur in the Middle East with the introduction of global reproductive technologies. Framed within rich ethnographic narratives gathered from two decades of research on Muslim women and men seeking assisted reproductive technologies, these technologies can be seen not as part of a reified cultural flow but as creating new opportunity structures that individuals are actively negotiating, appropriating, and transforming on interpersonal, familial, and spiritual levels. Thus, the rich descriptions that anthropology has made its own have enormous potential for the development of new theories of globalization that highlight the agentive aspects of social engagement with globalizing processes, rather than essentializing global systems in ways that do not reflect behavioral reality in most cultural contexts.

By placing the political economy of love in dialogue with the now-expansive social science literature on globalization, we also seek to ensure that contemporary approaches to globalization within anthropology do not neglect the political-economic structures, inequalities, and social hierarchies that shape globalizing processes and their consequences on the ground. For example, while a growing number of cross-cultural studies have addressed the issue of how Euro-American notions of identity or sexuality are being appropriated and transformed in local settings—including the influence of gay tourism, international networks, migration, and global media on the dissemination of cultural knowledge about love and intimacy[2]—most of these analyses have focused on the flow of ideas or social categories of intimacy rather than the stark differences in race, class, and nationality through which these notions are often transmitted. A political-economic analysis of love emphasizes the importance of situating our analyses within a global context that is not only "hybrid" and highly interactive but also cross-cut by entrenched political-economic differences and social inequalities related to factors such as race/ethnicity, class, gender, and sexuality. This book intentionally brings these differences into relief, highlighting how globalization unfolds within a contemporary political economy of love.

Love, Kinship, and Gender/Sexuality

Particularly in anthropology, but also in comparative sociology, kinship has long been a key area in which intimate relationships have been examined. For the most part, however, early research on kinship focused on cross-cousin marriage and dowry and bride price, as well as the broader descriptions of the social organization of family relationships, to mark difference between the West and the rest of the world. While this work generated important foundational knowledge in areas such as social organization and cross-cultural variations in the construction of the family, Euro-American family structures tended to be normalized and rendered invisible through this early period of kinship studies, in which anthropology largely focused on the "exotic" and sociology on the "familiar."[3] The analysis of kinship was primarily concerned with descriptive taxonomies of kinship structures rather than with the subjectivity of the relationships they represented and therefore did not fully elaborate the human emotional bonds that cohere and maintain kinship systems.

Simply put, love brings subjectivity back into kinship studies. And, we might argue, it has been a long time coming. While feminist research provided the basis for focusing analytical attention on gender and kinship as potential sites of inequality and exploitation (Dwyer and Bruce 1998), this very focus has occasionally led analysts to marginalize the nuances of subjectivity and the experiential aspects of love. It was feminist analysis, of course, that first posed questions within our field about how families and "compulsory heterosexuality" (Rich 1980) reproduce gender inequality. These questions were asked throughout the social sciences (Chodorow 1978; Fausto-Sterling 1985; Gallop 1982; Haraway 1991; Scott 1986), as women who were involved in the political aspects of the women's movement turned their newly gendered lens onto their own work, with the hope of finding intellectually grounded political solutions.[4] A central concern in this early research on gender (at that time, framed primarily as women's studies) was the extent to which the organization of social and biological reproduction was the "cause" of gender inequality (Chodorow 1978; Ortner and Whitehead 1981; Reiter 1975; Rosaldo and Lamphere 1974). This concern led to a great focus on these topics within the subfield of the anthropology of gender. But, ironically, at the same time that early work on gender might have obscured the love that women felt for their supposedly exclusively or at least primarily oppressive mates, the very same anthropology of gender—through its insistence on the theoretical importance of the personal and the private—opened the door for an anthropology of love.

More broadly, a turn to love seems a product of the increasing theoretical reach and sophistication of the study of gender, which has moved beyond exploring families and kinship systems as the sites for the negotiation and reproduction of gendered inequalities. In part, this move beyond a portrait of men and women as structural antagonists is a product of a certain discomfort with seeing families only as the sites for negotiation and reproduction of inequalities. Consequently, a number of scholars, including many of the contributors to this volume (Brennan 2004; Hirsch 2003; Rebhun 1999; Smith 2002; Wardlow 2006; Yan 2003), have come to think about families as simultaneously sites of pleasure, intimacy and sharing *and* exploitation, oppression, and inequality. The increasing interest in love may also grow from the realization that for many women around the world, gender inequality is not necessarily the most virulent form of inequality they face; this awareness points to the importance of an intersectional perspective and opens the door for a consideration of the ways in which disenfranchised men and women in diverse contexts may be allies and may provide mutual sources of comfort, pleasure, or love. These were not questions of direct concern in the first-wave feminist-inspired approaches, which focused on developing a social critique of the inequalities that structure gender relations at all levels. Unfortunately, while this crucial critique was being developed, love was entirely lost.

This volume has grown out of our belief that the comparative study of love provides an important opportunity to revitalize the field of kinship through consideration of the idea that, around the world, people seem increasingly committed to the idea that love makes a family. A growing literature has emerged in recent years that collectively depicts a global—if uneven—trend away from "traditional" notions of family that emphasize the role of social obligation in the reproduction of kinship systems and toward globalizing models of family that are increasingly based on a "love" that is chosen, deeply felt, "authentic," and profoundly personal. We might articulate this global transition as one that increasingly privileges a notion of people deliberately using love both as an ideal for which to strive and as the means through which they constitute their families. Yet as the chapters in this volume demonstrate, this transition is not unitary, nor does it express itself in predictable ways when we turn the ethnographic lens to the wide range of societies and groups considered here. For example, while the discourses of "love" and "choice" may increasingly structure the meanings and practices of families, global capitalist interests and patterns of consumption may lead to a proliferation of commercialized experiences of "love." Elizabeth Bernstein epitomizes this possibility in her important consideration of the growing demand for the services of "temporary love"—the "bounded" or constrained experiences of love that have found a particularly willing market niche in the context of late capitalist economic restructuring. Thus, while the meanings of love in the context of globalization increasingly center on notions of intimacy that are emotionally authentic and personal, the ways that global markets are responding to these changes can produce patterns of intimate commodification that are not necessarily predictable. Indeed, as the growing literature on marginal genders and sexualities has illustrated (Carrillo 2002; Herdt 1994; Kulick 1998; Lumsden 1996; Murray 1996; Padilla 2007; Parker 1999), the cultural changes that have followed from the globalization of notions of chosen or "authentic" love are tied to broader transformations in the ways that sexual and gender identities are conceptualized. This emerging literature on marginal genders and sexualities provides evidence that the widespread emphasis on desire and choice has profoundly reconfigured contemporary families (Weston 1993, 1995), broadening the range of culturally available family formations in ways that have implications far beyond the heteronormative family.

Ironically, sexuality may be one of those rare areas in which the intersection of public health and social science has been productive for theory development. For those who were interested in using social research methods and theory to explore situations in which people made choices that appeared irrational from a public health point of view—such as having "unintended pregnancies" or not pressing for condom use in situations in which they might reasonably be believed to be at risk—work as early as Sobo's (1995) on the importance of love for understanding the strategic value of risky behavior opened the way to a new consideration of subjectivity as part of culturally specific rationalities. Indeed, this work is what led several of the editors of this volume to consider love ethnographically, since the applied work in which we engage necessitates an ethnographic understanding of how the meanings of intimacy and love influence sexual practices and reproductive health choices. In fact, the global expansion of the HIV/AIDS epidemic has brought renewed energy to sexuality studies, as well as new weight to the examination of the ways that desires and experiences of love shape trends in patterns of HIV transmission. In an era in which heterosexual marriage is rapidly becoming one of the primary "risks" associated with HIV infection among women in many global areas, there is an urgent need to understand how the meanings of love shape individual situational vulnerabilities.

Finally, the growth of sexuality studies also allows us to consider the ways that global practices of consumption have reorganized kinship and family structures by providing a growing diversity of alternative forms of intimacy. For example, Katherine Frank's chapter discusses the emergence of Lifestyles, an international organization centered on the creation of a global community of heterosexually identified couples dedicated to nonmonogamous forms of sexual play. The social spaces created by the organization's international parties not only provide the physical places through which dispersed "virtual communities" can come together for sexual exploration but also provide rules and the performative environments that enable the creation of alternative cultural definitions of love and partnership. Thus, as several of the contributions in this volume attest, globalizing constructions of love and intimacy are increasingly inseparable from the consumptive practices and market forces that commodify certain kinds of sexual and relational intimacy. What is crucial about the contributions in this volume, as they relate to this juncture of sexuality and consumption, is that they demonstrate that the kinds of intimacy that are emerging from global forms of consumption are not limited to what might be considered traditional forms of sex work. Rather, several of these chapters trace the connections between love and erotic consumption among groups that represent indirect, emerging, or alternative forms of sexual commerce. This work both benefits from and extends the growing ethnographic literature that analyzes the intersections between late modern forms of capitalism and the meanings and practices of gender and sexuality (Freeman 2000; Hirsch 2003; Manalansan 2003; Parker 1999).

Love and Modernity

It is impossible, furthermore, to discuss the increasing frequency with which people in very diverse contexts use the language of love to talk about how they build their families without addressing the lure of modernity—of which love has become a critical element. There are several aspects to this intersection of love and modernity. To begin, there is the historical fact—which makes us a bit uncomfortable for the way it could be distorted as proof of a sort of evolutionary or linear approach to culture—that in 19th-century western Europe and North America, demographic and economic factors such as urbanization, gains in life expectancy, the rise of wage labor, extended schooling, and fertility decline created the conditions within which marriage increasingly became viewed as an arena for self-realization and pleasure rather than a strategy for survival, social reproduction, and the fulfillment of kin obligations (Coontz 2005; D'Emilio 1983; Gillis, Tilly, and Levine 1992; Skolnik 1991). This does not mean that marriage ceased to be a critical element of social reproduction but only that love and pleasure gained increasing prominence as key criteria for the evaluation of a successful marriage. This companionate marital ideal, which arose later in some parts of Europe than others (Bott 1971; Stone 1977; see also Cole 1991; Collier 1997), emphasizes the critical role that emotional intimacy and satisfaction play in building the bonds of marriage. As is made clear in Hirsch and Wardlow's (2006) recent volume, *Modern Loves*, there is a great deal of diversity around the world in how people actually interpret this globally available ideology and in how it intersects with gender inequality and local constructions of sexuality. This volume extends that landmark comparative portrait of emerging modern loves by locating it more firmly within a political-economic perspective and by challenging the intense heteronormativity that undergirds the ideology responsible for the global rise of Valentine's Day as a frenzied moment of affectively oriented consumption. Indeed, marketing, advertisements, and movies have been key factors promulgating this trend, but we must also acknowledge the way it has been deliberately promoted through government-sponsored family-planning ideologies (Thornton 2005; see also Hirsch and Wardlow 2006; Kanaaneh 2002). Because of the global dissemination of this ideal of the love-based family—which became marked as a product of the cosmopolitan West—when regions of the developing world encountered these new (to them) ideas at the same time they were undergoing transformations in their demographic and economic circumstances, people experienced the shifting marital project as a moment of becoming more Western.[5] At the very least, they conceived of the possibility of love-based relationships in terms that were framed by the intertwining of geography and history: Rebhun, for example, found that her informants in Northeastern Brazil "speak as if each city generates its own figurative temporal wheel, forming the proudly modern center of a circle that grows more old-fashioned the further out you travel from it" (1999:2), so that they could love in a way that was not just more modern but more urban—or, pushing this somewhat more broadly, in a way that was more Western.

Part of what is simultaneously engaging and discomforting about research on globalization, however, is the ways in which the cultural and economic gears of the globalization machine may move in ways that are not exactly in sync. Although perhaps it originally came to prominence in a cultural moment in which it was a reflection of or response to underlying social, demographic, and economic changes, love has now, as it were, taken on a life of its own, so that rather than being complementary ideology that helps people make sense out of and respond to the fact that the world they face is not the same one their parents faced, love is now something for which people strive—or at least a phenomenon in reference to which people build their sexual and intimate strategies—under conditions that bear little resemblance to those of rapidly modernizing 19th-century North America (Erickson 2006; Gregg 2006; Junge 2002; Reddy 2006). For example, although urbanization and industrialization are the primary political-economic conditions framing love in certain settings (Collier 1997; Pashigian 2002; Yan 2003), people still strive for love-based marriages in areas with strikingly different economic and demographic changes (Ahearn 2001; Inhorn 1996; Parikh 2005; Rebhun 1999; Smith 2006). In other words, love—and the practices of affective consumption that surround it—has become a strategy for affective mobility, and a very individually oriented technique for framing oneself as a modern subject.[6]

There is an irony to all of this, which is that even in the rich developed world the idea of entirely love-based relationships is a fiction: in regimes of choice (as opposed to arranged marriage) most people still tend to marry people much like themselves; and the notion that modern conjugality is only about affect contrasts sharply with actual demographic data on extramarital sex and gendered effects of divorce, which show that sex is much more prevalent outside of marriage and money much more important within it than the ideology of pure relationships (Giddens 1993) would have us think. This is a sort of hint that even current theories of kinship may be more culture-bound than they would appear at first glance. (A critical reading of this concept of pure relationships suggests that it is in some way an ideological maneuver by Giddens through which the material aspects of current Euro-American kinship systems are deliberately obscured.)

Together, the chapters that follow help us to reframe these questions about love, social and economic change, and modernity in a number of ways. First, they go beyond being simply comparative in terms of collecting parallel material from a variety of contexts by pressing us to consider how the very inequalities, relationships, and interconnections that exist between these contexts—whether between mail-order brides and those who send for them or between travelers who arrive in the Dominican Republic seeking to buy sex and women who sell sex there in order to leave the Dominican Republic—are themselves a critical part of the landscape of love. Moreover, through their very variety—beyond heteronormativity, beyond a purely "developing" or "developed" world context—these chapters argue both for the centrality of love in understanding the intimate sides of globalization and for the diversity of ways in which that intimacy is experienced. Finally, through the juxtaposition of ethnographic work on love in the context of marital, extramarital, and commercial sexual contexts, this work conclusively decenters Euro-American conceptions of love as natural, normal, or inevitable.

Love and Globalization IS DIVIDED INTO THREE PARTS to highlight three general domains within which the authors in this volume engage the intersection of love and globalization: "Love and Inequality"; "Love, Sex, and the Social Organization of Intimacy"; and "Fantasy, Image, and the Commerce of Intimacy."

Part I, "Love and Inequality," focuses on social inequalities, with respect to both their proliferation and their instrumental uses within global processes. Social inequalities are central to this volume, because one of its key goals is to underline how political-economic inequalities and social hierarchies shape the subjective experiences of love and intimacy. This approach to love is a crucial contribution of the volume; most considerations of love and globalization have failed to address adequately the connection between social inequalities—such as class, race, gender, and sexuality—and the micro-level practices of intimacy in specific ethnographic contexts. The three chapters in this part, each taking different approach to love and inequality, examine the globalization of love within an analytical framework that highlights the reverberations of large-scale structural processes in the lives of men and women variously positioned in the world system.

Chapter 1, "Neoliberalism, Respectability, and the Romance of Flexibility in Barbados" by Carla Freeman, focuses on the ways in which entrepreneurship in the context of globalization—with all of its associated reconfigurations of labor, consumption practices, and capital flows—has been promoted as an untapped engine of economic growth in much of the developing world. On the small island of Barbados in the Caribbean, those increasingly drawn into entrepreneurship represent a changing face of middle-class business ownership, an arena once believed to be the privileged preserve of a small handful of white-minority elite families. Freeman interprets the expansion of entrepreneurial discourse and practice through the experiences of male and female entrepreneurs in Barbados as a commentary on the embrace of neoliberalism by the state and private sectors. In particular, she examines the ways in which the Caribbean cultural model of "reputation and respectability" gives a distinctive shape to these entrepreneurial ventures in a neoliberal era. Her study helps to recast the "master paradigm" of reputation and respectability in Caribbean studies in ways that allow us to examine changing dynamics of class, gender, and race and the specificities of "neoliberalism" as it is enacted in this part of the world.

In Chapter 2, "Tourism and Tigueraje: The Structures of Love and Silence among Dominican Male Sex Workers," Mark B. Padilla discusses men who exchange sex for money in the informal tourism economy in the Dominican Republic, and the influences of this industry on heterosexual relationships and household economies. Drawing on extended ethnographic research in two Dominican cities, he describes how men's growing participation in the informal tourism economy intersects with men's notions of masculinity, "tigueraje" (a local notion of masculine behavior and sexuality), and the negotiation of gender roles in the household. Through the analysis of in-depth interviews and ethnographic data, he argues that the social expression of male sexual exchange depends fundamentally on cultural notions of appropriate expressions of masculinity and the asymmetric gender norms that enable and maintain sexual commerce between local men and foreign tourists.

In Chapter 3, "'If there is no feeling . . . ': The Dilemma between Silence and Coming Out in a Working-Class Butch/Fem Community in Jakarta," Saskia E. Wieringa explores the tension between silence and rational speech in the lives of a group of "butch/fem" women on the brink of being consumed by the new "rights discourse" that globalization has brought to this Indonesian community. These women are members of the largest women's organization in Indonesia, which disseminates a globalizing discourse about feminism and women's rights (including sexual rights). Nevertheless, because of their marginal position in relation to normative notions of gender and sexuality, these butch/fem women have survived by blending in with the environment, fighting a desperate battle for acceptance in a culture in which the marginal can be incorporated only because of their silence. The chapter eloquently describes how these women negotiate love and sexuality in this liminal situation.

The chapters in Part I expand upon and extend theoretical literature on the globalization of intimacy as articulated by theorists such as Dennis Altman and Anthony Giddens. From Giddens's (1991) perspective, for example, the state's efforts at the regulation of love are nearly always in tension with the new possibilities for the exercise of love and intimacy that are enabled by globalizing processes. Thus, even in the context of the state's attempts at surveillance—that is, its frequently articulated mandate to police the borders of a "perverse" love that has "gone global"—local populations draw on a range of global resources in reforming their identities, altering their practices, or resisting dominant regimes of gender and sexuality. As Giddens describes them, globalizing expressions of love are inherently porous and slippery; while they can provoke conservative local responses that seek to contain "traditional" forms of intimacy or reverse their insertion into the global sphere, the polymorphous nature of globalizing intimacies often defies its absolute containment. For example, while the local moral-sexual worlds in places such as the Dominican Republic and Indonesia are resistant to non-normative expressions of gender and sexuality, the increasingly outward-looking posture of what we might cautiously describe as "local" sex/gender systems and the global linkages to phenomena such as the tourism industry, neoliberal policies, and international sexual rights movements enable alternative strategies and visions for intimacy. Part I therefore offers a unique opportunity to examine ethnographically the tensions between neoconservative responses to global intimacies and the inherent "porousness" and flexibility of love in a globalizing world.

Part II, "Love, Sex, and the Social Organization of Intimacy," examines how processes of globalization, including transformations in patterns of mobility and the global dissemination of alternative conceptions of intimacy, influence the meanings of love and the patterns of marital bonding in three very different world areas: Mexico, Greece, and the Middle East. These chapters contribute to the analysis of love and globalization by moving beyond the simple generalizations that tend to dominate much of the theoretical literature on globalization, demonstrating that the global circulation of contemporary notions of "modern" love does not lead to the simple homogenization of conceptions of intimacy but rather are in continual conversation and occasionally in tension with traditional, local ideas of love and bonding. This part calls attention to how patterns in the globalization of love may relate to changes in the social organization of intimate relationships under different cultural and historical conditions.

In Chapter 4, "'Love Makes a Family': Globalization, Companionate Marriage, and the Modernization of Gender Inequality," Jennifer S. Hirsch explores the implications of global shifts to a companionate marital ideal. She draws on ethnographic research on love and marriage in a Mexican transnational community to describe transformations in the Mexican marital ideal from one of *respeto* (respect) to one of *confianza* (intimacy or trust), exploring how in Mexico these changes are—and are not—related to economic and cultural aspects of globalization. She then links this discussion with a broader analysis of modern love around the world, using comparative, cross-cultural material to sketch out commonalities and tensions in local interpretations of this increasingly prominent affective ideal. The final section of this chapter closes with three sets of queries (or provocations) about love and globalization. First, it explores how questions about love and globalization intersect with various kinds of social and economic inequalities—including, in particular, the gendered implications of these changing affective ideals. Second, it raises some questions about what these explorations about love and globalization can teach us about globalization and cultural transformation. Third, it sketches out some of the key policy issues to be considered by those who conduct research on these new, very fragile, kinship forms.

In Chapter 5, "The Strange Marriage of Love and Interest: Economic Change and Emotional Intimacy in Northeast Brazil, Private and Public," L. A. Rebhun focuses on how rapid urbanization, political opening, and the expansion of an unstable, globalized economy have transformed discourses of emotional relationships in Northeast Brazil. Describing how older people prize marriages of *consideração* (considerateness) while younger couples emphasize the importance of *paixão* (passion), she examines the ways in which shifts in expectations with regard to both intimate and public transactions modify power relations among generations, social classes, and genders. Drawing on fieldwork in the interior of Pernambuco state in Northeast Brazil, Rebhun highlights the rapidly changing concepts of love, romance, and patronage in what has been characterized as one of the most traditional and conservative regions of the country. The chapter has broader implications, though, for the way that it traces out the importance of studying love to understand kinship; Rebhun shows us, for example, how the growing importance of affect as a source of social relations intertwines economic transformation to make people see friends rather than cousins as more central to their social worlds.

Chapter 6, "A Fluid Mechanics of Erotas and Aghape: Family Planning and Maternal Consumption in Contemporary Greece," by Heather Paxson, explores the impact of globalizing forces on middle-class women's gendered subjectivity in Athens, Greece. Paxson describes how Greek women's modern subjectivity is largely realized through sexual and maternal relationships, which often elicit conflicting subjective stances. Love—*erotas* and *aghape*—lies at the heart of women's ambivalent visions of a modern, liberated subjectivity that remains recognizably Greek. *Erotas*, passionate, physical love, is distinct from *aghape*, enduring love epitomized by maternal love. Whereas *erotas* eclipses the self, *aghape* subordinates self to other. Greek romantic ideology suggests that *erotas*, to be valued because it defies human will, may mature into *aghape*. Through NGO- and state-sponsored family planning initiatives and media advertising of prophylactics, modernizers exhort women, in particular, to think differently about sexual intimacy—to prepare for prophylactic sex. Paxson describes how women, asked to bring *erotas* under the penumbra of rational action, are promised that they will derive a new kind of sexual pleasure from the knowledge that, by looking out for themselves, they are in fact looking out for their loved ones. Family planners attempt to bring *aghape* to bear on *erotas*, creating a "love" whose moral object is the self. This analysis focuses on how these women reconcile their desire to be good mothers and good women in the context of these competing discourses and the changing exigencies of modern womanhood.

In Chapter 7, "Loving Your Infertile Muslim Spouse: Notes on the Globalization of IVF and Its Romantic Commitments in Sunni Egypt and Shia Lebanon," Marcia C. Inhorn explores the ways in which in vitro fertilization (IVF) and other assisted reproductive technologies to overcome infertility are spreading rapidly around the globe. Inhorn underlines the impact of globalization processes on reproductive practices in the nations of the Muslim Middle East, where IVF centers have opened in small, petro-rich Arab Gulf countries as well as in the larger but less prosperous nations of North Africa and the Levant. In these clinics, high-tech reproductive medicine is practiced according to Islamic guidelines. However, since the late 1990s, divergences in opinion over third-party donation have occurred between Sunni and Shia Muslims, with Iran's leading ayatollah permitting both egg and sperm donation under certain conditions. Inhorn's analysis, based on field research carried out in Sunni Egypt and mixed Sunni-Shia Lebanon, explores the implications of IVF and third-party donation for Muslim marriages in a part of the world that is described by some Middle Eastern feminist theorists as "one of the seats of patriarchy." She shows that although the Sunni Muslim ban on third-party donation may particularly disadvantage women—as some infertile men begin to divorce their reproductively elderly wives to try the newest variant of IVF with younger, more fecund women—couples in Shia clinics in Lebanon are signing up on donor-egg waiting lists, regarding donor eggs as a "marriage savior." Indeed, despite widespread expectations within the Middle East that infertile marriages are bound to fail, with men blaming women for the infertility and divorcing them if they do not produce children, especially sons, such expectations may represent stereotypes rather than lived reality. The tremendous growth of IVF clinics in this region might be seen to demonstrate deep feelings of love, loyalty, and commitment experienced by many couples that Inhorn explores from both male and female perspectives. She theorizes and interrogates the potential of love to shape the IVF experience, as well as the potential of IVF and donor technologies to transform notions of love, companionate marriage, and gender relations in the Middle East.

The five chapters in Part III, "Fantasy, Image, and the Commerce of Intimacy," develop analyses of how fantasies of love and intimacy intersect with the particular market forces that characterize postindustrial forms of commodity exchange and fantasy formation. As a growing body of political-economic research has shown, late capitalist changes in the structures of global commerce have led to qualitatively different and more flexible forms of production, consumption, and distribution. Less understood is how these transformations influence the subjective construction of fantasies or the generation of market demands for particular kinds of intimacy. This part of the book addresses these concerns through a variety of ethnographic case studies that explore how the structures of late capitalism influence the commodification and consumption of love and sex.

In Chapter 8, "Playcouples in Paradise: Touristic Sexuality and Lifestyle Travel," Katherine Frank explores the commodification of intimacy through "sex play" (as opposed to "sex work") by investigating the leisure events sponsored by the international tourist agency Lifestyles. Lifestyles International sponsors swingers' (also known as lifestyle or playcouple) conferences and events at tourist destinations in several countries (though especially in well-known tourist locales like Mexico or the Caribbean). Though the sexual practices of attending couples vary, playcouples generally engage in or support nonmonogamous behaviors and encounters at the same time they remain "coupled" (a requirement for attendance for every individual and a personal value for many). While many attending couples are from the United States, couples also hail from Eastern and Western Europe, South America, Asia, and the host countries. Most are of a fairly homogeneous middle-range social class, however, because conference and event fees are quite steep. Through ethnographic fieldwork, the chapter examines the experiences of playcouples themselves, and sheds light on conceptualizations of love, sex, and intimacy in an ever-changing global context. Because the events at the Lifestyles conferences are geared to legitimizing certain kinds of sexual and intimate lifestyle choices through "expert" talks and seminars, and the evening events (such as dances or parties) are often themed to encapsulate fantasies of wealth, glamor, and power, the conferences are an important site for exploring ethnographically how global capitalism can support and commodify particular expressions of intimacy and reproduce, as well as recreate, particular fantasies, desires, and pleasures.

Chapter 9, "Buying and Selling the 'Girlfriend Experience': The Social and Subjective Contours of Market Intimacy" by Elizabeth Bernstein, explores a shift in the social and cultural construction of commercial sexual exchange under conditions of capitalist globalization in the late 20th and early 21st centuries. Social historians have typically linked the expansion of large-scale, commercialized prostitution in the West to modern industrial capitalism and its attendant features in the late 19th-century: urbanization, the expansion of wage labor, and the decline of the extended-kin-based "traditional family." These structural transformations brought with them new cultural ideologies of gender and sexuality and new symbolic boundaries between public and private life. For both prostitutes and their clients, the commercial sex transaction came to be conceptualized in terms of an expedient and emotionally contained exchange of cash for sexual release—the ideological antithesis to private sphere romance and love. This chapter argues that late-capitalist transformations of social life have brought about a shift away from modern-industrial paradigms of commercial sexual exchange to intimate relations that are imbued with meaning. What is bought and sold within the commercial context is increasingly contingent on the sex-worker's performance of emotional as well as physical labor, with successful commercial transactions dependent on the fact or semblance of authenticity and mutual desire. Yet the attachment of a monetary fee to the transaction remains crucial for both worker and client. As with other forms of service work that have proliferated in late capitalist societies, the market basis of the exchange provides an important emotional boundary, but one that can also be temporarily subordinated to clients' desires for authentic interpersonal connection.

In Chapter 10, "Love Work in a Tourist Town: Dominican Sex Workers and Resort Workers Perform at Love," Denise Brennan examines the practices and meanings of "love" within the Dominican community in Sosúa, the Dominican Republic, that have emerged alongside the growing tourist and sex-tourist trades. Brennan focuses on how resort workers and sex workers try to parlay their access to foreign tourists into marriage proposals and visa sponsorships. At the discos, bars, and beaches, it is possible for any Dominican to meet—and perhaps to marry—a foreigner. Love takes on multiple meanings in this tourist setting, and marriage has specific uses. Marriage in a tourist economy—especially in an internationally known sex-tourist destination—often has nothing to do with emotion-driven love or romance. After all, why waste a marriage certificate on romantic love when it can be transformed into a visa? In the process, no relationship between foreigners and Dominicans escapes scrutiny. In this context of transnational desires and economic ambitions, these relationships become fodder for the gossip mill. Sosuans understand—indeed expect—that many relationships in their town are strategic performances on the part of Dominicans. Their skepticism about love results from the fact that they know that many sex workers and resort workers are hard at work selling romance along with the other goods and services they deliver.

Chapter 11, "Romancing the Club: Love Dynamics between Filipina Entertainers and GIs in U.S. Military Camp Towns in South Korea," by Sealing Cheng, focuses on female sexual services for U.S. military personnel stationed in South Korea. Cheng notes that the deployment of female sexual services for military men has typically been analyzed as an effect of aggressive male sexuality legitimized by military hypermasculinity. Studies by political scientists and concerned critics on U.S. military prostitution are premised on exposing how masculinist state projects rely on the mobilization of women's bodies. These analyses constitute a powerful criticism of the military and war as institutionalized gender violence for the reproduction of state and capital. Viewed in this light, the image of burly young men in uniforms sexually overpowering helpless women makes the notion of love—with its connotation of romance and mutuality—unthinkable. This chapter builds on these cogent analyses of gender ideology and violence in military institutions. However, it departs significantly from this body of research by looking at the actual interactions on an everyday level between military men and women entertainers in an R&R (rest-and-recreation) industry since the late 1990s. Specifically, it explores romantic love as a discourse of emotion between Filipina entertainers and their regular GI patrons who meet in their displacement in South Korea between 1998 and 2000. Within this particular setting, Cheng examines the importance of love as a discursive and emotional site for the exercise of individual agency and the interactive creation of social reality.

Finally, in Chapter 12, "Love at First Site? Visual Images and Virtual Encounters with Bodies," Nicole Constable builds on earlier work criticizing existing studies, popular media images, and antitrafficking representations of so-called mail-order brides for their superficial depictions of foreign women as commodities who, desperate for opportunities that are unavailable in their impoverished homelands, are said to "sell" themselves to first world men who seek to "buy" wives (Constable 2003). She argues that such stereotypical views overlook ways in which political economy is intertwined with cultural constructions of love and desire and therefore pay little attention to women's and men's experiences, choices, and desires. Building on research on correspondence courtship and marriage among Chinese women, Filipinas, and U.S. men, Constable turns to the role of Internet technology in relation to romantic and marital desires. She examines how women's and men's bodies are depicted in virtual space at various stages of the correspondence process, how photographic images are presented and (mis)read by women and men, and how women's and men's intimate imaginings, fantasies, and experiences differ across virtual and real space. Technologically mediated bodily images and global intimacies often expand the bounds of what is considered acceptable or appropriate in "real life"—and the Internet undoubtedly provides expanded opportunities for men and women to meet and marry across borders. But the Internet also reinscribes social markings of gender and race on "invisible" bodies, and there are important structural and cultural difficulties in translating virtual bodily experiences and fantasies into actual relationships on the ground. The "global technological democracy" thus works at certain cross purposes with the desires of those who seek to create better lives for themselves in the real world.

The chapters in this final part illustrate the performative dimensions of love as an experience with both cultural and material salience that can be used to foster the production of sexual or erotic "commodities." Its rich ethnographic analyses also caution against a simple conceptual separation between "authentic" and "inauthentic" love. These contributions are unique in their emphasis on the ambivalences and unpredictability of moments of intimate "performance" in the context of global capitalism. While the performative metaphor is in many ways quite apt in describing certain aspects of the "love work" that these chapters explore, the approach used by these ethnographers is to couch the phenomena of study within a deeper theoretical discussion in which the performance of intimacy does not necessarily equate to less genuine or less "real" subjective experiences; indeed, it may be precisely those moments of tension between deep feelings of attachment and the material and other interests that shape intimate "performance" that is the most revealing of the globalizing projects we seek to elucidate in this book. Questioning easy presumptions about the inherent dehumanizing features of commodified love, these analysts eschew ideological binaries in favor of more nuanced, ethnographically informed examinations of the fluid and dynamic boundaries that often exist at the nexus of love and commerce.

Taken together, the detailed explorations of love in diverse cultures and contexts that compose this volume provide an overview of at least some of the ways in which emotional intimacy has begun to be transformed and re-imagined in the rapidly changing, globalized world of the late 20th and early 21st centuries. In particular, they fill a void in much recent research on gender and sexuality, which has often ignored the complex, subjective motives underlying sexual practices and relationships—and they do so by relentlessly reminding us that subjective motives are always constructed and constituted in the wider world of intersubjective cultural meanings and collective social processes. They may only begin to scratch the surface of such a complex subject—leaving unaddressed many of the myriad forms of love that characterize life in the modern world. Think, for example, of patriotism and love for one's country, of religious passion or devotion, or maternal/paternal love for one's children—all of which might well be described as forms of love for which many are quite literally willing to risk their lives. Yet even if they fail to characterize the full breadth of such a complex emotion, these essays take an important first step in developing what we have describe as a political economy of love within the context of globalization. They illuminate one of the most important forms of intimate human experience and provide a lens for understanding the most basic ways in which social life is organized and cultural meanings are expressed in the contemporary world.

Notes

1. This discussion benefits from the work by Altman (2001) on "sex and political economy," as well as ethnographic analyses by anthropologists such as Hirsch (2003), Lancaster (1992), Padilla (2007), and Parker (1999)
2. For a concise review of the literature, see Parker 1999 and Parker and Cáceres 1999.
3. Similarly, early studies of gender and sexuality within anthropology frequently focused on these phenomena as expressed outside of the Euro-American West, while rendering Western sexuality—and particularly heterosexuality—undertheorized.
4. These dialogues between early feminist social scientists may, in turn, have something to do with the lack of complexity regarding affect between men and women at this specific historical moment; it was, ironically but not accidentally, a moment at which pioneering work was done by historians such as Smith-Rosenberg (1975) on the history of emotional intimacy between women.
5. As Skolnik (1991), Stone (1977), and others describe at great length, the shift to a more intimacy-oriented family ideal occurred in the United States and Europe at a historical moment in which the combination of declining fertility and gains in life expectancy meant that there were suddenly many years of married life during which couples were not raising

children. This change, along with urbanization and the literacy gains that underlie the rise of Stone's "affective individualism," are the critical structural changes that accompanied this shift in the cultural center of gravity to a more companionate model of love. While Brazil, the Caribbean, East Asia, and the other regions of the developing world in which the chapters that follow are situated did experience somewhat similar shifts in demographic structure in the post–WWII era (Population Reference Bureau 2004), a striking difference in the two broad historical processes is that the developing world faced and experienced these shifting grounds of love and family structure in the historical shadow—and thus almost inevitably in reference to—these changes having already taken place elsewhere first.

6.   Indeed, the idea that people use love-based relationships as a means through which to perform a modern self can hardly be understood without reference to the emergence of new concepts of the self and the individual. Stone (1977), for example, discusses "affective individualism," which Collier (1997) ties to the emergence of wage labor and the ways it remade the self. In the modern world, love, and the exchange of purchased gifts through which it is negotiated, expresses and sometimes is consummated (as in the exchange of rings) as a cultural product not just of modernity but of the modern self.

References

Ahearn, Laura
   2001   Invitations to Love: Literacy, Love Letters, and Social Change in Nepal. Ann Arbor: University of Michigan Press.
Altman, Dennis
   2001   Global Sex. Chicago: University of Chicago Press.
Appadurai, Arjun
   1996   Modernity at Large. Minneapolis: University of Minnesota Press.
Bott, Elizabeth
   1971   [1957] Family and Social Network: Roles, Norms and External Relationships in Ordinary Urban Families. New York: Free Press.
Brennan, Denise
   2004   What's Love Got to Do With It? Transnational Desires and Sex Tourism in the Dominican Republic. Durham: Duke University Press.
Carrillo, Hector
   2002   The Night Is Young: Sexuality in Mexico in the Time of AIDS. Chicago: University of Chicago Press.
Castells, Manuel
   1996   The Rise of the Network Society. Oxford: Blackwell.
Chodorow, Nancy
   1978   The Reproduction of Mothering. Berkeley: University of California Press.
Clifford, James
   1994   Diasporas. Cultural Anthropology 9(3):302–338.
Cole, Sally
   1991   Women of the Praia: Work and Lives in a Portuguese Fishing Community. Princeton: Princeton University Press.
Collier, Jane Fishburne
   1997   From Duty to Desire Remaking Families in a Spanish Village. Princeton: Princeton University Press.
Constable, Nicole
   2003   Romance on a Global Stage: Pen Pals, Virtual Ethnography, and "Mail Order" Marriages. Berkeley: University of California Press.

Coontz, Stephanie
  2005   Marriage, a History: From Obedience to Intimacy or How Love Conquered Marriage. New York: Viking.
D'Emilio, John
  1983   Capitalism and Gay Identity. *In* Powers of Desire: The Politics of Sexuality. Ann Snitow, Christine Stansell, and Sharon Thompson, eds. Pp. 100–113. New York: Monthly Review Press.
Dick, Kirby, and Amy Ziering Kaufman, dirs.
  2002   Derrida. 85 minutes. New York: Jane Doe Films, Inc., and Zeitgeist Films Ltd. DVD.
Dwyer, Daisy, and Judith Bruce, eds.
  1998   A Home Divided: Women and Income in the Third World. Stanford: Stanford University Press.
Erickson, Pamela
  2006   Romantic Love, Sexual Initiation, and the Transition to Parenthood among Immigrant and U.S. Born Latino Youth in East Los Angeles. *In* Modern Loves: The Anthropology of Romantic Love and Companionate Marriage. Jennifer S. Hirsch and Holly Wardlow, eds. Pp. 118–134. Ann Arbor: University of Michigan Press.
Farmer, Paul
  1992   AIDS and Accusation: Haiti and the Geography of Blame. Berkeley: University of California Press.
Fausto-Sterling, Ann
  1985   Myths of Gender: Biological Theories about Women and Men. New York: Basic Books.
Freeman, Carla
  2000   High Tech and High Heels in the Global Economy: Women, Work, and Pink-Collar Identities in the Caribbean. Durham: Duke University Press.
Gallop, Joan
  1982   The Daughter's Seduction: Feminism and Psychoanalysis. New York: Macmillan.
García Canclini, Néstor
  1995   Hybrid Cultures: Strategies for Entering and Leaving Modernity. Minneapolis: University of Minnesota Press.
Giddens, Anthony
  1991   Modernity and Self-Identity, Self and Society in the Late Modern Age. Stanford: Stanford University Press.
  1993   The Transformation of Intimacy: Sexuality, Love and Eroticism in Modern Societies. Stanford: Stanford University Press.
Gillis, John R., Louis A. Tilly, and David Levine, eds.
  1992   The European Experience of Declining Fertility, 1950–1970: The Quiet Revolution. Cambridge: Blackwell.
Gregg, Jessica
  2006   "He Can Be Sad Like That": *Liberdade* and the Absence of Romantic Love in a Brazilian Shantytown. *In* Modern Loves: The Anthropology of Romantic Love and Companionate Marriage. Jennifer S. Hirsch and Holly Wardlow, eds. Pp. 157–173. Ann Arbor: University of Michigan Press.
Haraway, Donna
  1991   Simians, Cyborgs, and Women: The Reinvention of Nature. New York: Routledge.
Harvey, David
  1990   The Condition of Postmodernity. Cambridge: Blackwell.
Herdt, Gilbert, ed.
  1994   Third Sex, Third Gender. New York: Zone Books.
Hirsch, Jennifer
  2003   A Courtship after Marriage: Sexuality and Love in Mexican Transnational Families. Berkeley: University of California Press.

Hirsch, Jennifer S., and Holly Wardlow
  2006   Introduction. *In* Modern Loves: The Anthropology of Romantic Love and
         Companionate Marriage. Jennifer Hirsch and Holly Wardlow, eds. Pp. 1–34. Ann
         Arbor: University of Michigan Press.
Inhorn, Marcia
  1996   Infertility and Patriarchy: The Cultural Politics of Gender and Family Life in Egypt.
         Philadelphia: University of Pennsylvania Press.
Jankowiak, William, ed.
  1995   Romantic Passion: A Universal Experience? New York: Columbia University Press.
Junge, Benjamin
  2002   Bareback Sex, Risk and Eroticism: Anthropological Themes (Re)Surfacing in the
         Post-AIDS Era. *In* Out in Theory: The Emergence of Lesbian and Gay Anthropology.
         William Leap and Ellen Lewin, eds. Pp. 186–221. Urbana: University of Illinois Press.
Kanaaneh, Rhoda A.
  2002   Birthing the Nation: Strategies of Palestinian Women in Israel. Berkeley: University of
         California Press.
Kearney, M.
  1995   The Local and the Global: The Anthropology of Globalization and Transnationalism.
         Annual Review of Anthropology 24:547–565.
Kulick, Don
  1998   Travestí: Sex, Gender and Culture among Brazilian Transgendered Prostitutes. Chicago:
         University of Chicago Press.
Lancaster, Roger N.
  1992   Life Is Hard: Machismo, Danger, and the Intimacy of Power in Latin America.
         Berkeley: University of California Press.
Lumsden, Ian
  1996   Machos, Maricones, and Gays: Cuba and Homosexuality. Philadelphia: Temple
         University Press.
Manalansan, Martin
  2003   Global Divas: Filipino Gay Men in the Diaspora. Durham: Duke University Press.
Marcus, George E.
  1995   Ethnography in/of the World System: The Emergence of Multi-Sited Ethnography.
         Annual Review of Anthropology 24:95–117.
Murray, Stephen O.
  1996   American Gay. Chicago: University of Chicago Press.
Ortner, Sherry B., and Harriet Whitehead
  1981   Sexual Meanings: The Cultural Construction of Gender and Sexuality. New York:
         Cambridge University Press.
Padilla, Mark
  2007   Caribbean Pleasure Industry: Tourism, Sexuality, and AIDS in the Dominican
         Republic. Chicago: University of Chicago Press.
Parikh, Shanti
  2005   Bifurcating Risk and Pleasure: The Commercialization and Medicalization of Sexuality.
         In The Moral Object of Sex: Science, Development and Sexuality in Global Perspective.
         V. Adams and S. Pigg, eds. Pp. 125–158. Durham: Duke University Press.
Parker, Richard
  1999   Beneath the Equator: Cultures of Desire, Male Homosexuality, and Emerging Gay
         Communities in Brazil. New York: Routledge.
  2001   Sexuality, Culture, and Power in HIV/AIDS Research. Annual Review of Anthropology
         30:163–179.

Parker, Richard, and Carlos Cáceres
  1999 Alternative Sexualities and Changing Sexual Cultures among Latin American Men. Culture, Health, and Sexuality 1(3):201–206.
Parker, Richard, and Delia Easton
  1998 Sexuality, Culture, and Political Economy: Recent Developments in Anthropological and Cross-Cultural Sex Research. Annual Review of Sex Research 9:1–16.
Pashigian, Melissa
  2002 Conceiving the Happy Family: Infertility and Marital Politics in Northern Vietnam. *In* Infertility around the Globe: New Thinking on Childlessness, Gender, and Reproductive Technologies. Marcia Inhorn and Frank Van Balen, eds. Pp. 134–151. Berkeley: University of California Press.
Population Reference Bureau
  2004 Transitions in World Population. Population Bulletin: A Publication of the Population Reference Bureau. 59(1):1–43.
Quinn, Naomi
  1992 The Motivational Force of Self-Understanding: Evidence from Wives' Inner Conflicts. *In* Human Motives and Cultural Models. Roy D'Andrade and Claudia Strauss, eds. Pp. 90–126. Cambridge: Cambridge University Press.
Rebhun, L. A.
  1999 The Heart Is Unknown Country: Love in the Changing Economy of Northeast Brazil. Stanford: Stanford University Press.
Reddy, Gayatri
  2006 The Bonds of Love: Companionate Marriage and the Desire for Intimacy among Hijras in Hyderabad, India. *In* Modern Loves. Jennifer S. Hirsch and Holly Wardlow, eds. Pp. 174–192. Ann Arbor: University of Michigan Press.
Reiter, Rayna, ed.
  1975 Towards an Anthropology of Women. New York: Monthly Review Press.
Rich, Adrienne
  1980 Compulsory HeteroSexuality and Lesbian Existence. Signs: Journal of Women in Culture and Society 5:631-60.
Rosaldo, Michelle Zimbalist, and Louise Lamphere
  1974 Women, Culture and Society. Stanford: Stanford University Press.
Scott, Joan
  1986 Gender as a Useful Category of Historical Analysis. American Historical Review 91(5):1053–1075.
Skolnik, Arlene
  1991 Embattled Paradise: The American Family in an Age of Uncertainty. New York: Basic Books.
Smith, Daniel J.
  2002 "Man No Be Wood": Gender and Extramarital Sex in Contemporary Southeastern Nigeria. Ahfad Journal 19:4–23.
  2006 Love and the Risk of HIV: Courtship, Marriage and Infidelity in Southeastern Nigeria. *In* Modern Loves: The Anthropology of Romantic Love and Companionate Marriage. Jennifer S. Hirsch and Holly Wardlow, eds. Pp. 135–156. Ann Arbor: University of Michigan Press.
Smith-Rosenberg, Carroll
  1975 The Female World of Love and Ritual: Relations between Women in Nineteenth-Century America. Signs 1(1):1–29.
Sobo, Elisa J.
  1995 Choosing Unsafe Sex: AIDS-Risk Denial among Disadvantaged Women. Philadelphia: University of Pennsylvania Press.

Stone, Lawrence
  1977 The Family; Sex and Marriage in England, 1500–1800. New York: Harper & Row.
Thornton, Arland
  2005 Reading History Sideways: The Fallacy and Enduring Impact of the Developmental Paradigm on Family Life. Chicago: University of Chicago Press.
Wardlow, Holly
  2006 Wayward Women: Sexuality and Agency in a New Guinea Society. Berkeley: University of California Press.
Weston, Kath
  1993 Lesbian/Gay Studies in the House of Anthropology. Annual Review of Anthropology 22:339–367.
  1995 Forever Is a Long Time: Romancing the Real in Gay Kinship Ideologies. *In* Naturalizing Power: Essays in Feminist Cultural Analysis. S. Yanagisako and C. Delaney, eds. Pp. 87–110. New York: Routledge.
Yan, Yunxiang
  2003 Private Life under Socialism: Love, Intimacy and Family Change in a Chinese Village, 1949–1999. Stanford: Stanford University Press.
Yanagisako, Sylvia, and Carol Delaney
  1995 Naturalizing Power. *In* Naturalizing Power: Essays in Feminist Cultural Analysis. S. Yanagisako and C. Delaney, eds. Pp. 1–22. New York: Routledge.

Part I
Love and Inequality

1

Neoliberalism and the Marriage of Reputation and Respectability
Entrepreneurship and the Barbadian Middle Class

Carla Freeman

For increasing numbers of Barbadians today the pursuit of middle-class livelihood and status and the desire for new paths of creative self-invention and economic "success" are being sought through entrepreneurship. Many critics see this phenomenon in developing countries as evidence of the manipulations and ever-expanding reach of capitalist globalization enabled through neoliberal policies that emphasize economic flexibility and place the responsibility for economic growth on individual actors as states whittle down their public sector payrolls and structures of support (Chomsky 1999; Giddens 1991; Harvey 1989). As such, the entrepreneur has been viewed as the quintessential neoliberal actor (Bourdieu 1998), "freed" from traditional class structures and labor contracts, self-made and self regulated within the expanding global marketplace. At the same time one might also read this expansion of independent businesses and the pursuit of upward mobility through entrepreneurship in the small island of Barbados as a flourishing new expression of a long tradition of a Caribbean cultural model known as "reputation," a formulation of cultural practices understood to be rooted in African tradition and associated with "creole" or new world enactments of creativity and ingenuity among Caribbean peoples, especially the lower classes. Just as capitalism, modernity, and globalization are always articulated through the specific cultural and economic contours of local people and contexts, neoliberalism, for all of its abstraction as a model of economic structure, has a local face. My aim in this chapter is to "localize" our understanding of the embrace of entrepreneurship as a key dimension of neoliberalism and to explore some of its more intimate and subjective dimensions. If the entrepreneur is a quintessential neoliberal subject, how, in the context of a small Caribbean island long enmeshed in the web of global capitalism, is neoliberal subjectivity enacted and understood by those who embrace some of its most visible forms? By focusing on contemporary middle-class entrepreneurs in Barbados, I hope to show that notions of "flexibility"[1] that are demanded by a neoliberal economy (e.g., with a retrenchment in the public sector and a decline in the power of trade unions) and actively sought by social actors emanate from multiple contemporary and historical sources that are both "global" and deeply local. Further, the entrepreneurial quest, generally portrayed as evidence of liberal individualism, is among many of these middle-class Bajans often intriguingly coupled with what appears to be a recent local formulation of "partnership marriage." In Barbados, the conjoining of "flexibility" and "marriage" has an ironic ring, because "adaptability" and "flexibility" are qualities long associated with nonmarried, lower-class family forms, and the institution of marriage has been an idealized but less common form of union associated with the values of patriarchy, rigid order, and British colonial tradition (Alexander 1977; Barrow 1988; Senior 1991; Smith 1956, 1988; Wilson 1973).[2] How, then, are patterns of marriage and entrepreneurship dialectically engaged in this era of neoliberalism, and how might their entanglement sharpen our understandings of the nuances and local subjectivities of neoliberalism itself?

Middle-class entrepreneurs in Barbados today signal intriguing historical shifts both in the demographics of and ideologies about business. While petty traders, higglers, and hawkers are well-established historical icons of the lower classes, middle- and upper-class businesses of larger size and profits have been positioned in complex and somewhat fraught ways within Barbadian society and its cultural imagination. And while the higgler is a proud symbol of lower-class female strength, the middle-class entrepreneur occupies a space of increasing political optimism, but of relative scholarly avoidance. On one hand, business has been stigmatized as a "nonrespectable" path for the Afro-Barbadian majority who have historically favored higher education as the route to upward mobility through the professions and an extensive civil service.[3] On the other hand, business has been seen as the privileged preserve of a small, white family elite long seen as nepotistic and impenetrable (Barrow and Greene 1979; Beckles 1990; Karch 1982; Ryan and Barclay 1992). Today, however, business is becoming a significant realm of economic growth for a new and aspiring fraction of the Barbadian middle class, and I would argue, represents a critical subject for ethnographic inquiry.

Several recent ethnographies have richly analyzed the links between political economy, sentiment, and the cultural logics of love and marriage in ways that elucidate the culturally specific idioms of these emotions and structures as well as their particular relations to capitalism and modernity (Collier 1997; Constable 2003; Hirsch 2003; Lipset 2004; Rebhun 1999). I was first inspired by the organizers of the April 2004 Columbia workshop to pursue these links of "love" and "globalization" among Barbadian middle-class entrepreneurs, and I was awed to discover not a single reference in my original field notes and interview transcripts to "love" or "romance." Sometimes it is precisely such absent categories that can be particularly instructive in our research endeavors. The absence of love as an explicit referent has lead me to return to what Appadurai (1986) describes as regional "gate-keeping concepts," those powerful conceptual preoccupations that have anchored certain analytical topics or questions in world areas, while simultaneously precluding others. The primacy of the economic as the linchpin of social and cultural life, advanced by a long tradition of structural functionalism and Marxism in Caribbean social science, has also reinforced a scholarly ambivalence toward dimensions of identity and experience beyond the economic and the social—love, and sentiment in general, as both internal states and as individually and socially meaningful experiences (Freeman and Murdock 2001).

Reputation and Respectability: Rethinking a Caribbean Conundrum

As an organizing frame, my discussion invokes what has been one of the Caribbean region's most powerful (and controversial) gate-keeping concepts, reputation/ respectability, first developed by the anthropologist Peter Wilson (1964) writing in the 1960s about the island of Providencia, a tiny English-speaking Afro-Caribbean island off the Colombian coast. By giving this paradigm greater ethnographic scope, my hope is to broaden its analytical strength. Wilson argued that Providencia and the wider Afro-Caribbean could be understood as steeped within the structures and ideologies of two competing but dialectically related value systems or cultural models: respectability (the inescapable legacy of colonial dependence through which patterns of social hierarchy are upheld and reproduced) and reputation (a set of responses to colonial domination and the elusiveness of respectability, through which people achieve a social leveling or "communitas") (1973:9). In Wilson's model, these competing value systems are enacted by particular groups of social actors, in particular spaces, and through particular forms, practices, and institutions that might be summarized very briefly as follows: Respectability is a middle-class ideological framework subscribed to largely by women (and old men), encoding ideals of domesticity, propriety, enacted through formal marriage, participation in the church, and associated with the formal, hierarchical world of bureaucratic institutions, and with the private domain of the home. Reputation, by contrast, is described as a lower-class and masculine sphere of public performance, enacted in such venues as street corners, the political platform, the rum shop, and the market, and on the musical stage; it is also demonstrated through sexual prowess, verbal wit, and economic guile. Central to reputation is a kind of improvisational adaptability—or flexibility—displayed in realms of performance as well as economy, and the salience of these appears particularly pronounced under the conditions of economic stress. Where Wilson understood reputation to embody what is most authentic in Caribbean culture, respectability was for him the essence of false consciousness and colonial oppression. "Respectability, . . . living right, is conforming to a pattern of behavior [and] . . . having certain social skills and graces which are 'modern' and 'cosmopolitan'—and white, . . . where proper English is spoken, where manners come naturally, where a house is immaculate and furnished in the best taste to the utmost convenience, where sophistication has its roots and modernity its zenith, where God and the church are an integral part of daily life, and where morality is impeccable!" (1973:114–115).[4] The deep absorption of these values by Barbadians of all walks of life would have been cause for utmost regret for Wilson. Indeed, if any of the Caribbean islands is associated with the realm of respectability, it is Barbados, coined both critically and fondly, "Little England," as the only territory to remain solely in British hands under colonialism (Lewis 1968).

The strong influence of the reputation/respectability paradigm on works of Caribbean ethnography cannot be overstated (see Besson 1993; Brana-Shute 1979; Burton 1997; Douglass 1992; Freeman 2000; Miller 1994; Pyde 1990; Sobo 1993; Sutton 1974; Wardle 2000; Yelvington 1995). Many feminist critiques (Barrow 1986a, 1986b; Besson 1993; Freeman 2000; Pyde 1990; Sutton 1974; Yelvington 1995) have taken issue with the limits of its parameters, noting that reputation, in all of its creative and resistant forms, is not off-limits to women. However, by staking such heavy claims on the ways in which women engage in reputation too, anthropologists and other scholars have also often unwittingly lost the richness of the dialectic and further reinforced a preoccupation with the lower classes, masculinity, sex, and the female-headed household (Cooper 1995; Miller 1994). All this has left less well examined ethnographically the "middling" groups and the lived enactment of marriage.[5] In Wilson's paradigm, reputation encodes promiscuity and virility (in which love is either irrelevant or merely instrumental for getting sex or money), and respectability maps neatly onto the elusive institution of marriage, the moral commitment to monogamy and restraint, and sentiment/love is implicitly equated with duty. However, following several anthropologists whose work engages emotion as individual and social, internal and cultural, (e.g., Abu-Lughod 1987; Lutz 1988; Lutz and White 1986; Rebhun 1999; Yanagisako 2002) I propose here that we briefly reread the cultural model of reputation/respectability not as a survival from the region's colonial past but as a living dialectic of dynamic sentiments, cultural forces of production that are constitutive of social actors themselves. And in particular, by turning our lens on marriage within the realm of the entrepreneurial middle class, we open up a space for analyzing the changing and intimate relationships between economy and sentiment implicit but seldom ethnographically explored in Caribbean studies.

A large body of scholarship on kinship in the region has asserted that the Afro-Caribbean "matrifocal" family has been an adaptive response to the legacies of plantation slavery and colonialism. As Christine Barrow says, "In Caribbean circumstances of poverty and economic marginality, rigid nuclear family structures with specified roles and relationships were unrealistic and unworkable. If people were constrained by nuclear family expectations they would not be able to leave their marriages, delegate responsibilities to others and shift their children in order to take advantage of economic opportunities at home and abroad" (1996:460). In essence then, visiting unions, and nonmarital, nonnuclear family forms in the Caribbean were not aberrant, as they had formerly been construed, but rather logical adaptations; "no longer a problem but a solution" (460). Flexibility has long been understood to be opposed to marriage as a social structure. In her review of recent kinship studies, Barrow notes, "conjugal co-residence, especially marriage, is culturally defined as a segregated relationship, . . . a difficult relationship to manage and therefore best postponed until the partners are more mature and they have undergone a period of testing. Marriage may be more respectable, but visiting relationships are easier to handle. They allow more personal autonomy and ensure an escape from conjugal violence" (460). What then might we make of the fact that among my sample of

Barbadian entrepreneurs, a group for whom flexibility and economic adaptability are key, a majority were discovered also to be married?

While the terms *reputation* and *respectability* are not frequent in common Bajan parlance, the cultural practices they denote are intimately familiar to virtually all West Indians and were referenced by many of the entrepreneurs in my study. For instance, Suzanne, a successful public relations entrepreneur I interviewed, expressed the essence of the dialectical tension when she said, "You have to understand the Barbadian psyche; . . . we have a proverb that says, 'share and share alike,' that means there's that unconscious thing between Barbadians that we are to help each other. But it also unconsciously reflects that *you must not step ahead of each other either.* In other words, if you step ahead you in some way would have violated the code that if you were 'sharing and sharing alike' you would not have enough to step ahead." Wilson (1973) likened this "psyche" as Suzanne calls it, to "crab antics"—the inclination on one hand to rise up and climb socially and economically but the accompanying threat that success is predicated on the simultaneous pulling down of the next person attempting the same upward feat—much like the dynamics of crabs in a barrel struggling to make their way out. Mintz (1971) and others have attributed a heightened individualism to the legacy of slavery, its destruction of social ties and the prevention of strong community institutions among the majority of Caribbean populations. Wilson, however, observed that in the public, largely masculine realm of reputation, a greater sense of social "communitas" was fostered, and he saw this set of cultural values as pointing the way forward for the region, in opposition to the false and hierarchical values associated with the opposite pole of respectability. What I want to suggest is that the contemporary neoliberal agenda has given support to the very individualism that has been so fraught with historical and analytical tension. For recent entrepreneurs, individualism is enacted in ways that have allowed some to negotiate this fundamental dialectic, for instance, through an intimate connection between marriage and self-employment. Whereas Wilson saw the realms of reputation and respectability as oppositional and enacted largely by different groups (young men on one hand, and women and older men on the other), increasingly within the entrepreneurial middle class, and in the "partnership" marriages of many of the entrepreneurs I have studied, the two cultural dynamics are performed and embraced simultaneously.

I turn particular attention to the realm of marriage for several reasons. Unlike many other regions of the world where marriage is normative not merely ideologically but practically, in Barbados and the Anglophone Caribbean generally a range of union formations, and in particular the female-headed household and "visiting union," have been more prevalent in practice even while marriage and the nuclear family continue to be idealized. The Caribbean literature is rich with descriptions of lower-class women's capacity (slave and freewomen, and market women past and present) to traverse public spaces, assert acute business acumen, and challenge ideological conventions for feminine respectability, in particular the notion that women should be relegated to the private sphere (Freeman 2001; Katzin 1959; Mintz 1955; Ulysse 1999). The analytical preoccupation with the origins and implications of these alternative family forms and a longstanding association of marriage with a legacy of British colonialism and its emphasis on "respectability" has lead social scientists largely to avoid the empirical study of marriage and of middle-class life with which it is associated.[6]

Marriage has also been understood to be a seldom realized ideal for the majority, in a society in which 46 percent of households are headed by women. The most recent Barbados census (2000) lists only 23 percent of the adult population as married, and 68 percent as "never been married." Yet in my recent study sample of 75 entrepreneurs, 45 (60 percent) are married, and only 11 (15 percent) are female headed households. This finding is especially intriguing, since marriage has been a vital part of Barbadian associations with middle-class "respectability," whereas entrepreneurship has been associated more with the realm of "reputation." "Flexibility" figures prominently (albeit in uneven ways) for married entrepreneurs as they straddle the dialectic of respectability/reputation. How these entrepreneurial marriages straddle the simultaneous demands of "respectable," private, domesticity and public, "reputation-oriented" entrepreneurial endeavors, where these demands and desires converge, and what these challenges demonstrate about the gendered dimensions of Barbadian neoliberalism are fascinating entanglements of the contemporary moment. These couplings, of marriage and entrepreneurship, reputation and respectability, are especially charged for mothers. Just as entrepreneurship offers married women greater "flexibility" to juggle their responsibilities as mothers and wives with their economic and professional goals, so too does marriage offer female entrepreneurs the social prestige and emotional and economic stability associated with feminine respectability. In the process, what had formerly been understood to be subaltern practices and values of reputation (e.g., the flexible and highly public economic strategies associated with entrepreneurship) have become particularly adaptive strategies under neoliberalism and are hailed by economic and political leaders alike. In turn, these are redefining cultural institutions and their associated meanings (e.g., marriage) in ways that present a new idealization of an economic/romantic partnership as opposed to patriarchal hierarchy. Reputation, in the vein of entrepreneurship therefore, has become a critical and adaptive mode not just for lower classes "making do" but also for those achieving and enhancing their middle-class livelihood, status, and sense of self. And simultaneously, formal marriage (one of the key markers of respectability) provides for many a new space of vital emotional and material support.

To develop these connections, I begin with the political-economic landscape in which neoliberalism and "flexibility" are central discursive themes in Barbados and the wider Caribbean. I then engage the narratives of several entrepreneurs currently attempting to enact these goals of middle-class entrepreneurial livelihood. Through their stories I show the intimate ways in which the dialectics of public/private life, reputation/respectability, and entrepreneurship/marriage are entangled, and central to these entanglements is the desire for "flexibility."

Situating Neoliberalism and the Celebration of "Flexibility" in Barbados

The trope of flexibility within neoliberal discourse is ubiquitous in both utopian and critical representations (i.e., flexibility is presented as idealized goal or pernicious force) among popular and academic analysts alike.[7] From one vantage point, "flexibility" connotes instability, changes in temporal and spatial frameworks, and changes in economic and social commitments. Flexibility has been associated with vulnerable conditions of labor for an increasingly disempowered body of low-skilled employees, as it was, in many ways, for the off-shore data processors I studied in the region (Freeman 2000). From another vantage, flexibility engenders the possibilities for new realms of self-invention, social mobility, and self-powered stability in the face of economic flux and change. These qualities are well illustrated by the contemporary figure of the entrepreneur.

A new "cult" of the entrepreneur and a discourse of entrepreneurship that emphasizes individual motivation, drive, and self-determination are now on the lips of Barbadian educators, development officers, government officials, and religious leaders alike. Sermons adopting power-point saleslike motifs are on the rise, and Ernst and Young's "Entrepreneur of the Year" competition nearly rivals in media exposure events surrounding the local Calypso King and Queen competition. Business ownership is increasingly seen as a viable path to financial success and esteem for white as well as black Barbadians.[8]

As a local cultural value, creative flexibility has been hailed as key to survival for female heads of households just as it is equated with the multiple endeavors Caribbean peoples have historically managed within and across formal and informal economies in piecing together their livelihoods. "Flexibility" in sexual relationships, however, has been bemoaned but endured by women caught in a sexual double standard that permits men "outside" relations and has lead lower-class women to employ another model of "flexibility" through which they gamble for economic and loving support from different fathers for their children (Barrow 1996; Senior 1991). As Barrow has pointed out, by the 1970s an analytical shift had occurred in the realm of kinship from the negative and pathologizing rhetorics of "family instability" and the "aberrant" matrifocal family (i.e., "denuded, dysfunctional, unstable") to one that redefined Caribbean family forms as adaptive and flexible to suit economically marginal conditions of life (1996:459).[9] Marital or union flexibility, and the ability to "shift" or move children to different households for their upbringing has been a critical dimension of lower class Caribbean survival.[10]

Carnegie (1987) has argued that "strategic flexibility" operates as a general cultural model with which West Indians approach most aspects of life. It is rooted in a history of movement and expressed in numerous ways across the life course, for instance, in circuits of labor migration and the dispersed networks of kin (regionally as well as transnationally) through which families often "foster" their children and maintain enduring transnational kin relations. In the economic realm, the salience of "occupational multiplicity," the "simultaneous or sequential engagement in a number of economic activities" by which people demonstrate their ability to "cut and contrive" (to make a living) is a time-honored tradition (Carnegie 1987; Comitas 1963:41–50; Katzin 1971; Trouillot 1992:23).[11] As Trouillot says, "Caribbean peoples seem to have fewer problems than most in recognizing the fuzziness and overlap of categories *and multiplicity is not confined to the economic realm or to the poor*" (1992:33). However, it is increasingly evident that movement, and expressions of flexibility more generally, are social practices that are ascribed gendered meanings.

Indeed, the new entrepreneurs I have studied are evidence that increasingly reputation-oriented practices are vital to middle-class livelihoods and a growing middle-class idealization of economic autonomy, even as respectability continues to be sought and romanticized in the realms of marriage. However, if flexibility is bound up with the Caribbean cultural model of reputation, as I describe it, its pursuit by male and female entrepreneurs also bears the marks of gendered difference. The entrepreneurs in my recent study vigorously embrace "flexibility" and autonomy (using these terms often, as well as highlighting their various meanings). They describe the often passionate desire to break out of and move beyond the limits set for them by other bosses (public or private sectors) or institutional frameworks, seeking self-realization, greater economic rewards, and for women, the ability to manage competing demands of work and family life—in many ways the quintessential goals of rugged individualism so often associated with modernity.

At the national and regional levels of official discourse and policy, *flexibility* is among the most frequently heard catch terms. Certainly the most ambitious region-wide effort to create economic flexibility is the recently ratified Caribbean Single Market and Economy (CSME). Right Honorable Owen Arthur, Prime Minister of Barbados, outlined CSME's rationale in a speech delivered in July 2003 in Kingston, Jamaica. Modeled directly on the European Union, the "CSME brings together 14 separate and distinct markets and economies, each governed by their own rules and divided from each other by formidable barriers, to be organized and to be made to operate in the future effectively as *one* market and *one* economy, free of restrictive barriers, and governed by common rules, policies and institutions." Arthur's regional free market mantra departs intriguingly from the Marxist-inspired dependency critiques of the postindependence era, which were often tied to the nationalization and protection of major industries (e.g., bauxite, sugar). The creation of a regional market, he argues, provides little island nations such as Barbados a "larger market and a wider set of options." And adds, the "liberalizing of services especially offers us an opportunity for expanded productivity that can compensate for any loss in commodity production." What he is referring to here is the dramatic decline in manufacturing industries as well as sugar, the island's historical economic base that in recent years has been taken over by foreign interests and yielded to tourism as the island's economic linchpin.[12] The language of neoliberalism encoded in Arthur's speech—the reign of the free market flexibility—has become so mainstream in Barbados and the wider Caribbean, that the association of sugar and protectionism with an old and unsuccessful model of globalization has been squarely replaced by an assumed equation of services (tourism, off-shore banking, and an array of off-shore back-office work) and, perhaps especially, new entrepreneurial enterprises, with the rationality and flexibility of a new global era.

This neoliberal vision has given rise to regional free-trade initiatives and, at the national level, to a host of private sector and government-sponsored programs, such as the Small Business Development Center and the Youth Entrepreneurial Scheme, and to a subtly changing profile for upward mobility in contemporary Barbados. The Honorable Lynette Eastmond, senator, and minister of commerce consumer affairs and business development, summarized the growing emphasis well in a 2003 speech in honor of the launching of the National Innovation Competition of the Enterprise Growth Fund Ltd.[13] Asserting the need for innovation and creativity, and the hampering effect of a tradition of conservatism, Senator Eastmond said:

> What I urge in this context is a maximum degree of *flexibility*. . . . The strength of a new economy must be in a structure where there are more opportunities for more people in every area; and therefore more flexibility for those persons. . . . I often wonder if there is not a Bill Gates or Michael Dell in Gall Hill that does not have access to a computer, a Venus Williams somewhere in St. Patrick's that does not have access to a tennis court, a Tiger Woods somewhere in St. Martin's that does not have access to a golf course [and] . . . an Oprah Winfrey in Baxter's Road or Bathsheba that never got the opportunity to dream just a little. . . . It is my wish that this initiative should signal that Barbados wishes to move in a direction where there is a place for the proper evaluation of every idea, the granting of an opportunity to as many people as possible, the *liberation of a mindset that restricts us to a sameness and a dullness*. One thing of which I am sure is that *there must be a change in attitude. We must believe that we are an innovative people.* We must believe that we are a creative people and we must show support for creativity—we must not stifle it. . . . *And it starts in the home—it is still the wish of most parents that their children should get a job—and if they are lucky a Government job*—no matter the ability of the child or the inclination—unless of course their child could become a lawyer or a doctor. (Italics added)

Senator Eastmond's calling upon these icons of American success (many of them African American) signals a pointed shift away from a tradition of British colonial order (embodied in the robust structure of the civil service, and the possibility of a scholarship to Oxford or Cambridge) to one of American ingenuity and self-invention. The modern Caribbean citizen conjured in these assertions is creative as well as industrious, independent, and keenly attuned to a growing and changing market. The cultural tensions Senator Eastmond alluded to when she called for the "liberation of a mindset" that stifles creativity and referred to the historically ambivalent inclination toward entrepreneurship are well illustrated in the generational conflicts endured by many of the entrepreneurs I interviewed. With the following narratives of Barbadian middle-class entrepreneurs, I am venturing an inroad into the lived sentiments and enactments of reputation and respectability as a way to examine the manifestations of neoliberalism in this small Caribbean island. In particular, these stories of entrepreneurial marriages help to elucidate the ways in which flexibility is demanded, sought, enacted, and constrained in the lives of contemporary men and women in this expanding fraction of the middle class, and how these sentiments and practices are deeply gendered. By probing the dual engagements of entrepreneurship and marriage, reputation and respectability, we see as well the ways in which marriage for some provides a buttress against the demands and stresses of their businesses, while for others it continues to impose gendered conventions that are restrictive and burdensome and that actively preclude the flexibility their lives as entrepreneurs demands. And through the idioms of support and security, we gain a window into the realm of love and sentiment.

Narratives of Entrepreneurial Marriage: Partnerships of Reputation and Respectability

Suzanne

Suzanne started a corporate public relations firm several years ago, choosing to leave a well-paying position with an established private firm. She describes the struggle she continues to face with her mother, a "conventional Bajan women" in her sixties who is troubled by her daughter's giving up a "good job" with well-known company to strike out on her own. Despite the fact that there were other entrepreneurs in her family (including a grandfather who ran a rum-shop, and who was, according to Suzanne, the first black man to private label his own rum), Suzanne says, within her family conservative expectations for education and upward mobility through the civil service or employment by an established company reigned supreme.

> My family has a civil service mentality and for the first three years of my business my mother was showing me ads in the paper, "Look, they want an HR manager; you don't want to apply?" I say, "I'm employing people, paying my bills, and running my house . . . [and] I have a car," and she says, "You *sure* you don't want a look?" You would think I was doing badly or something.

Coming from a long line of teachers, the very core of respectable Barbadian society, Suzanne says that entrepreneurship has been viewed in her family and among her family's friends as a last resort in the absence of a better, more secure, and more respectable option. Mocking the assertions of her parents' friends, she quotes them as follows: "Why does that girl not go and get a job? This girl is bright, she is talented, she did well at school [and] . . . she had good jobs! She give up all these good jobs and now look what she gone and do!" In essence, the view she expresses reflects a critical ideological distinction Barbadians have drawn in their minds between paths of reputation and respectability—entrepreneurship belongs in the realm of reputation, and as a vehicle for "making do" can be a strategic survival mechanism. But, in terms of status, the ideal path, for an older generation especially, involves the conventional trajectory of education and the recognized realm of corporate or public sector employment. As Suzanne says, "Starting your own business is seen as something to fall back on," not a goal to pursue. For Suzanne, the struggle to maintain "respectability" among her family and family friends has been achieved in part through her marriage and her involvement in her church.

Though marriage and the church are the cornerstones of traditional "respectability," the particular form of these institutions in Suzanne's life are departures from the conventional model Wilson might have envisioned. She and her husband met through "Abundant Life," the popular "mega church" originating in Bradford, England, whose appeal has grown in recent years to include a wide cross-section of lower- and middle-class Barbadians, many of whom have migrated from the Anglican Church. Together, they have developed a group of friends and business contacts through church as well. Their marriage is a self-defined "partnership," like their business, in which Suzanne is "more the front person" and "he is behind the scenes." "While I had the skills," Suzanne explained, "the driving force and the strategic positioning and so on really came from him, . . . like when you have a singer, they have a manager who grooms the career." Her analogy to a singer is apt, because the public domain in which Suzanne operates is similar to the reputation-oriented sphere of the stage. As the visible "people person" she must secure business contracts and give formal public presentations, while her husband quietly manages the accounts and keeps the business going in their private home-based office, "back stage."

Suzanne has a busy working life, which includes membership on the boards of several national organizations and a recent senatorial appointment. Her descriptions of the time and energy her husband commits to the business, his sensitivity to her emotional states and needs, and the private and safe mooring he provides reveal the supportive role her marriage plays in their joint entrepreneurial endeavor. When she describes her marriage as a unique partnership, she is referring not only to the practical and flexible partner who shares in the management of their business and domestic lives but to the man with whom she is emotionally in synch, and whose love is expressed in these ways. "Partnership" in such couples is inextricably about the structural and emotional demands of their marriages and their entrepreneurial endeavors. Hirsch (2003) illustrates with rich detail the efforts to achieve companionate marriage among Mexican transmigrants. In her study, marriage is a critical context in which to explore gender and sexual experience/selfhood, since these identities typically unfold within the realm of marriage. Similarly, Inhorn (1994) has written about the development of companionate and loving marriages among Egyptian couples whose marriages were often arranged, and who developed new and affectionate marriages in the face of infertility. In contrast to other cultural contexts, such as Mexico and Egypt, however, in Barbados marriage is not the normative union formation, and gender relations have long been structured by a legacy of plantation slavery whereby the dual roles of motherhood and paid labor have been expected of women, regardless of formal marriage. As mentioned earlier, less than one-quarter of the adult population recorded in the 2000 census reported being married. Further, the high valuation associated with female autonomy and economic participation, illustrated by the life story of another female entrepreneur, Yvonne, whose father, as she said, repeatedly emphasized that she should always be able to take care of herself and not depend on anyone else, frames relationships including marriage in a radically different light than in many other parts of the world. As such, the Barbadian case of middle-class entrepreneurs provides an intriguingly different angle on the enactment of "modern" marriage relationships.

In Barbados, the language of "partnership" that figured so prominently in my interviews appears intimately connected to the entrepreneurial pursuits of these middle-class couples. This is not to imply, however, that love is not integral to these marriages but rather to suggest that sentiment is often framed in ways to emphasize the importance of shared responsibilities and mutual support. The emphasis on trust and emotional as well as more applied forms of support must be understood as local idioms of love and not, somehow, evidence of its absence. Indeed, "love" is often described and alluded to in what appears to be utilitarian terms. For instance, the degree to which a spouse is helpful and makes sacrifices economically or through volunteering time and skills to the business is evidence of his or her love and caring. While the portrayal of marriage as important to Caribbean women not for love but for security is a persistent theme in popular calypsos and social science literature alike, I would argue that this oppositional and mechanistic understanding has been implicitly furthered by a narrowly dualistic reading of Wilson's reputation/respectability paradigm (Barrow 1986b; Senior 1991:87).

Far from presenting women's interest in security as an expression of love itself, the two are more commonly presented at odds—women are condemned for mercenary approaches to relations with men, trading sex and affection for material rewards, while men are presented as having no choice in the matter but to "offer up the goods." In this matrix, sex is invariably presented as men's goal and economic security or the acquisition of material "goodies" as women's goal. Only discussions of a mother's sense of duty toward her children approximate the notion that support is itself an idiom of love. As Elisa Sobo writes about Jamaica, "to look love is to search for sex" (1993:187), and as R. T. Smith elaborates, "sexual relations are conceived as 'giving' one to the other rather than as the joint activity of a couple. Intense affect is not necessary" (1988:142). In Trinidad, Birth and Freilich (1995) describe this tradition of men "begging" for sex in exchange for material rewards as part of the "smart rules" operative in village life in the mid 20th century. However, they observe these patterns changing (in the 1990s) with the expansion of economic opportunities for women. With greater economic autonomy, as well as the threat of AIDS, the increased difficulty of sexual secrecy, and the influences of American television and popular culture, they argue that a new set of "smart rules" of romantic love has begun to supplant the "sex and begging system" to one of "sex and romance" (269–270). Again, the interpretive anchoring of relationships (especially sex, since little mention is actually made of love) in terms of economic interests, and the definitively nonemotional, manipulative associations of this economic interest has been a strong theme in Caribbean ethnography, especially of lower-class life (Rodman 1971; Wilson 1964). What is interesting is that economic idioms for love and commitment are strong among the married middle classes as well as the lower classes, whose union formations are more fluid (Alexander 1977; Douglass 1992; Smith 1988). For both men and women of the middle classes, the formality of marriage is bound up with the expectation of economic stability and support.[14] What I would like to suggest, very simply, is that the persistent emphasis on a desire for support and material security be read not as an absence of romance and love but as the particular idioms through which love and romance are expressed. In an examination of masculinity in the Caribbean, Christine Barrow (1998) reads the narrow interpretation of love and affect (as primarily expressed in terms of obligation and economic survival) as an outgrowth of the dominance of functionalist analyses in Caribbean social science, much as I have tended to attribute the region's framing of social analysis in terms of an economic base to its Marxist intellectual and political traditions (Freeman and Murdock 2001). However, the middle-class entrepreneurs I am studying, for whom the ideals of, "western romance" and companionate marriage are strongly imaginable, reveal that love as the desire for and provision of "support" and material as well as emotional security is prevalent just as it has been among struggling poor or working classes. The following case of Yvonne bears the marks of longstanding traditions for the pursuit of upward mobility for the Afro-Barbadian majority and at the same time signals the rise of entrepreneurship as an unconventional dimension of middle-class femininity, focusing our attention on some of the particular challenges faced by women to realize their desires as well as their sense of domestic duty amid businesses that are thriving and growing.

Yvonne

At 40, Yvonne appears by all middle-class standards to "have it all." She is married, has a two-year-old son, owns a modern suburban house, employs a full-time nanny/housekeeper, and is a member of the Moravian Church. She studied in Europe, Australia, and the Caribbean, earning advanced degrees culminating in a Ph.D. After years of government employment, Yvonne now runs her own consultancy firm, which she started in 1998. These successes are all the more striking considering her modest roots—her father worked as a contracted seaman for many years, and then in the maintenance department of a foreign oil company, while her mother was consumed by caring for a severely disabled younger child. Yvonne describes her family as "not very poor, but definitely not middle class" and the most important lesson she learned as a child was "you must always be able to look after yourself, you must never depend on anyone, take nothing from anyone; you always must be able to support yourself." In contrast to the gendered ideologies described in Hirsch's (2003) study of Mexico or Inhorn's (1994) study of Egypt, this admonition by a father toward his daughter is evidence of the push toward autonomy and independence for women above that of making "the right" marriage.

Unlike the many entrepreneurs I interviewed whose fathers had deserted the family and whose desire for both independence and distinction was frequently fueled by a sense of early paternal abandonment, Yvonne grew up "at her father's hip." "He saw the value in education. . . . I try to figure out why it is that . . . I am here . . . in the socioeconomic class that I'm in and [my schoolmates] are there . . . and I've put it down to the fact that I had a different home environment. . . . I went to the same rural primary school where you walked a mile to it and you sat on the hard bench and you came back . . . We took the same exam, . . . and this is where it starts to look different. . . . What made the difference had to be the fact that my dad would sit with me on evenings and we'd do homework and make fun of it and make games out of it and we'd do little tests and he'd make fun out of learning things in the kitchen and the house . . . [and gave me] lots of books to read." Yvonne was the only child from her rural primary school she could think of who had gone to university; "half of" the others," she said, "are now grannies." "They had their kids very, very young." One of four children, Yvonne has a brother who is also an aspiring entrepreneur with a new spiritual bookshop he is struggling to keep afloat amid stiff competition from larger chains. Another brother, alcoholic and bitterly ostracized from the family, lives in New York, where he has been unemployed for many years.

In many respects, Yvonne's profile conforms closely to Wilson's model of feminine middle-class respectability. Married with one small child, she manages the domestic life of her family efficiently, goes to church, and has pursued advanced education as a path to upward mobility. Her husband, a successful actuary with his own firm, is the primary breadwinner of their nuclear household. However, Yvonne's decision not only to work outside the home but, like Suzanne, to leave a secure government job to pursue the path of entrepreneurship reflects an assertion of the values of "reputation," her primary desire being independence, self-actualization, and, most important—flexibility.

> When I started . . . I was . . . looking at a part-time consultancy type thing that I could juggle with the family— [but] I've grown now into a full-fledged business that has commitments to its staff and has started now to look at something that is Caribbean[wide] and big— and that's a definite shift in goals I hadn't seen when I first started because I didn't know the potential that it could grow to.

Yvonne's success and the growth of her business have far exceeded her expectations, and ironically perhaps, have introduced an unexpected conundrum. The flexibility she sought in running a business that would allow her to accommodate her marriage, young family, and professional aspirations has become more illusory as her business has flourished, requiring her to travel, manage staff, and take on a wider range of responsibilities. And as her husband's company too has grown, Yvonne's primary responsibility for the domestic realm has led her to enlist a full-time nanny and a second helper at times to pick up the slack in the evenings and weekends when her nanny is off duty. Because Yvonne delayed childbearing in favor of pursuing an advanced education and career, the extended-family safety net that has historically provided child care in Barbados is unavailable to her (her mother has died and her other relatives are too old). As such, like that of a majority of the other entrepreneurs in the study, Yvonne's respectability as a mother and wife are predicated on the paid services of others to maintain the domestic sphere, again, a typical marker of middle-class status, even for the stay-at-home housewife.

While traveling was always an exciting prospect for Yvonne, and the expansion of her company into regional contracts a dream, now the reality of these pursuits carries a sense of conflict and burden. She has often brought her toddler and a nanny with her on business trips, but it is becoming more difficult to manage. Meanwhile, her husband's company is entering the "big times" and he has been "begging off" more nights at home than usual to work late. While the demands of her husband's work and travel means more household juggling for Yvonne, she also insists that her husband's support and practical help in her business has been unparalleled.

> My husband [is] one hundred and ten percent [supportive]. He's very, very, very busy, make no bones, he's involved in like 20 different things that are at the same very demanding level, but if I need something he'd be there. I've been fortunate that I can take . . . risks, because my husband is employed and makes a good salary so I can take the risk knowing that if things are not doing well this month or this year with the company I'll still be able to eat but if he were not so umm securely employed perhaps I may rethink.

The marital partnership Yvonne describes is difficult to disentangle from the businesses that she and her husband own and run. With the exception of beach outings with their young child, their social life revolves around client entertaining, and each is intimately involved in the nuances of the other's business. The fact that her husband's breadwinner status and economic success insures her own capacity to venture into entrepreneurship is accompanied by the subtle but unquestioned assumption that the domestic domain is Yvonne's to manage. She is responsible for all of the conventionally feminine domestic duties, but her entrepreneurial strategy is to manage them more than to provide them all herself, and she is grateful that her husband "doesn't mind" that she picks up take-out food for dinner and orchestrates their toddler's care with a stable pair of nannies whose salaries are paid for through Yvonne's business. For Yvonne, the desire for flexibility is a practical desire to juggle home and work along with a more existential desire to imagine herself outside the professional and personal confines set by government (in the case of her former job), or social convention (in the case of motherhood and raising her child).

The kind of flexibility sought by emergent female entrepreneurs like Yvonne represents a complex union of reputation and respectability—the desire to go into business for oneself to insure financial security and professional success, self-actualization, creative expression, and a sense of adventure (reputation) not afforded by the rigid state bureaucracy is coupled with the desire to preserve the sanctity of family and home (respectability) and develop a mutually supportive, "partnership" marriage. Like the entrepreneurial ventures themselves, these entrepreneurial marriages involve a complex matrix of sentiments and relationships in which reputation and respectability are structurally and symbolically intertwined. Love and commitment are conveyed through efforts to "back each other up" in their businesses, to offer tangible assistance (accounting help, financial support) as well as less tangible but equally important support in the form of gentle counsel and encouragement, and more flexible understandings of how household divisions of labor are performed. This "flexibility" surrounding basic services within the home, in turn, relates back to the broader neoliberal economy in which formerly private, domestic services are increasingly available for sale on the expanding market.

Where middle-class women might once have been expected to sew, cook, clean, and arrange family and social gatherings, many of these household activities have been transformed by the increasing availability of "take away" food and gourmet catering and premade clothes purchased from boutiques, from the Internet, or from overseas stores visited during business travel, and a host of other services. In the realm of cleaning, laundry, and child care, entrepreneurial wives are relying heavily on domestic services provided by paid nannies and helpers, a longstanding tradition for all middle-class Caribbean households but one on which women's businesses critically hinge. These middle-class business women continue to be held responsible for the bulk of domestic duties, though their manner of enacting them has changed and now relies more heavily on paid, non-kin, providers, as well as the flexibility of their employees and partners at work who cover for them when, for instance, they must pick up children at school. To the extent that women as entrepreneurs and wives/mothers are able to combine these roles, and to the extent that they are able to employ talented "nanny/housekeepers" or their husbands enter into the domestic arena from which their active participation has long been exempt, they are in the process of enacting a new formulation of "marital partnerships."[15] We see in each of the cases of Suzanne, Yvonne, and in a moment, Sheila, varying degrees to which this new model is achieved. In Suzanne's case, the absence of children and of frequent business travel eliminates what appear to be key dimensions of the struggles in Yvonne's marriage. However, others' efforts to meld marriage and entrepreneurial ventures are not always so fruitful.

Sheila

Sheila is the 25-year-old owner of Red Carpet Express, a small company she started in 1999 after having worked as a marketing manager of a business software company. While traveling across the region marketing software for hotels, she realized that the vagaries of travel and the fact that delays, poor service, or any number of other bad experiences can deter repeat tourism and spoil a vacation for a valued tourist or investor. "Travel," she explains, "is very difficult."

> It can either make or break your vacation, . . . and that's what the hotels are realizing. [For instance,] if a man loses his luggage . . . he had a hard day in

customs, and he comes in . . . and then you don't have his room ready, . . . you know it just ruins at least three days of his holiday, so that's what we deal with in Red Carpet; we meet and greet the passenger (it's an airport service) we let the hotel know . . . he's lost his luggage or whatever we want. We send him down to the hotel, . . . arrange the transportation, . . . make sure that there is something extra in his room for him; . . . maybe he lost his luggage, so they'll probably put like a toothbrush, a t-shirt, swimming trunks, . . . whatever. 'Cause the only hotels we deal with are four- and five-star . . . and villas, so they . . . can do that. I bring in clients like . . . Mariah Carey . . . and, well, . . . Mick Jagger and Prince Andrew.

Unlike the numerous registered tour operators in Barbados, however, who now are required by airport regulations to abide by certain rules and regulations, Sheila has a special arrangement for meeting VIP visitors that exempts her guests from some of the red tape of arrival and departure. Having secured contracts with all of the island's most expensive hotels, using excellent self-promotion skills, and then allowing one contract to snowball into several, she has gained the cooperation of an otherwise dense and notoriously rigid bureaucracy. She is also grossing BDS$20,000 a month—US$10,000 (more than a well paid doctor would earn)—and her only overheads are BDS$3,000 a month for her two full-time employees and her cell phone bills.

Sheila is an attractive and vivacious Afro-Barbadian woman. Signaling her explicit enactment of "reputation," she admits that she uses her good looks and flirting acumen to her advantage, saying, "I didn't have a hard time getting myself through the door when it came to men but I had a very hard time keeping it above board, I would say. It became a little easier when [I was married]. . . . So you'd put on as many rings as you [can, to say,] 'I'm married' and it became a little easier. . . . At least they have a little more respect for you when you're married." Her entry into this line of work and its relation to the rest of her life, family background, and modes of femininity are full of contradiction.[16] At every turn, Sheila signals her negotiation of the boundaries of reputation and respectability. Like Suzanne, Yvonne and most of the women I interviewed, Sheila describes her mother's reaction to her leaving a "good—read secure—job" in a private foreign-owned marketing firm in favor of self-employment as one of bemusement and chagrin. Her family is steeped in many of the most valued signs of respectability, especially that of education—her father a doctor, her mother a secretary in the Ministry of Education, an aunt who is a professor, another a secretary in the Prime Minister's Office. Sheila is the only one in the extended family who owns her own business. Like many others I interviewed (men and women alike), she describes herself as a maverick—a rebel in the conservative Barbadian context in which education is emphasized above all else as the route to a profession or government job.

Sheila's family's solid middle-class base offered her opportunities that she acknowledges were integral to fostering her entrepreneurial success—even as they marked her failures in the conventionally valued realm of academic achievement.

Originally, like Yvonne, Sheila started the business as a way of creating flexible hours that would allow her to care for her young daughter and a nephew she is raising as her own, and now that the business has grown, she employs a nanny/housekeeper and enlists the occasional help of her mother to juggle her busy work schedule with school pick ups, dinner preparation, and so on.[17] In fact, she described her business as the best form of birth control—because of the long hours and the attractive (sexy) and professional impression she must make. ("In my line of business," she says, "how are they going to take you serious with a [pregnant] belly?") Her active social life helped her gain the social contacts she has needed to make her way, inventing from scratch a new entrepreneurial niche within the tourism sector. These, in turn, have earned her privileged access in this sector, and speak to her reputation—garnered during long nights in the public space of the airport.

By marrying young and then (in that order) having one child, and also through employing a domestic worker, Sheila upholds some key indicators of respectability that were in delicate balance in her own upbringing. Though in the professional realm, education and occupational status brought respectability to her mother and aunts, her father deserted her mother when she was only three months old, and Sheila grew up without any relationship with him. Entrepreneurship, however, and especially involving a business like hers that is so public, is deeply imbued with the marks of reputation. Now Sheila is separated from her husband and is careful not to let people know. She described, with tremendous emotion, the process of going to two banks to apply for a mortgage for a house, to be financed entirely by herself, another of the primary signs of middle-class respectability. "Don't tell any of them that you're separated!" she said.

> We were still living under one roof but we knew we were going to separate so the plan was that when I bought the house, I would just move out and go into my new home. He signed the document saying he has no claim on the house. . . . He has not contributed anything to the house, he doesn't want the house, whatever, and [the bank managers] would not accept it. They would not accept it . . . [even though] I gave them my contracts from my hotels. . . . My hotels are *very* good hotels, *well-known* hotels, and they said, . . . "Well, who's to say that they're going to renew next year?" . . . Well . . . there's nothing called certain, but I went back anyway and I got my GMs to write her a note saying well we have all intention of this long-term relationship with Red Carpet and whatever, and I carried it back to her . . . and she was like, "You know what, . . . we will feel safer if your husband was guarantor." Fine, I said, alright. They went through. And then, to find out when the mortgage papers came through that they had on . . . my husband's name. . . . My name was not even on the damn mortgage. . . . I got my lawyer to write them back and they had to change it then . . . but up to this day when I go to pay my mortgage, it is not even in my name.

With her repeated attempt to claim respectability in her own name, Sheila's story embodies a struggle that is at once about changing configurations of gender, class, marriage, and local capitalist relations. Her story highlights the dialectical struggle between reputation and respectability, and the lengths to which entrepreneurs, and women in particular, must go to offset their participation in the realm of reputation with the signs and symbols of respectability. She has used her well-honed reputation to generate contacts, enhance her business, and secure her own economic base with the respectable goals of home ownership and economic and emotional security for her children. Her encounters with not one but two female bank managers—themselves iconic gatekeepers of respectability—remind us, however, of the complex ways in which the moral codes and boundaries of respectability can be enforced to serve the interest of an older patriarchal order. Her struggle over her marriage is fraught with tension over maternal duty and a model of companionship and love that eludes her. Instead, she enjoys dinners out with a highly placed and older male "friend" and describes her separated status as her choice for now.

> Well, . . . I don't have to rush home to cook, I pick up something quick on the way for my kids or my mom would give them something to eat, but ummm when you have a husband then you have to think of quality time, what time am I spending with this husband . . . and it's hard for a woman, a mother, and being an entrepreneur and a mother and a wife you just don't have that. . . . It's hard, you just can't break yourself away. . . . My husband used to travel all the time with his business and he would just come and he would say, "Well, you know, Sheel, . . . I'm goin' . . . I'm going to be away from Thursday to Saturday. He would not have to make provisions for [the baby], what to do with her, whatever. When I'm going away, it's like . . . I have to start contacting the nanny, I have to make sure somebody picks her up and somebody washes her clothes, somebody does this, somebody does that, make sure *he* knows what he's to do . . . but when he's traveling he just comes and says, "Well, you know, I'm traveling. . . . I'm going to be out of the island." Now, she is with me, and I obviously have to make all these provisions, how she's going to get to school, how she's gonna get home and men just don't seem to do it that way. . . . Men always think, well you know, . . . you have to arrange the children . . . the children are *your* responsibility so you have to work around these children. . . . Nobody seems to realize , "Well hey, they're half yours too," but we always have to make [all the arrangements]. . . . Next time I want to come back as a man.

Sheila's juggling of social, duty-filled, domestic, maternal, and wifely, as well as individual, desire-filled entrepreneurial agendas signals her efforts to achieve flexibility in combining elements of reputation and respectability, and the limits to her doing so. For Sheila, the flexibility to invent herself as an entrepreneur and as a partner in marriage is hampered by the competition between her business and her husband's. Like Yvonne, her marriage partnership could be sustained as long as she continued to absorb the traditional emotional and domestic labors, including arranging meals, child care, and "quality time" with her husband. The uneven division of labor in the home was the crux of the conflict, and it was exacerbated by the absence of shared emotional labor; Sheila was expected to carry the exclusive burden for "quality" marital time. When their marriage no longer conformed to the "partnership" she desired, Sheila chose separation, described in emotionless terms like a business deal gone bad, and divorce and shared custody were the logical solution. The fact that she is not beholden to her husband as a primary breadwinner gives her the flexibility to end her marriage and pursue other romantic and business relations while continuing to rely on the paid services of nannies and maids and her extended family to sustain her single-household headship and business.

For Sheila, like several other divorced or single entrepreneurial mothers I interviewed, and like the lower-class women described by Senior (1991) and Moses (1981), a "traditional" or patriarchal husband may offer financial support but be seen as an impediment to the flexible livelihood, sentiment, and partnered relationship they seek. For middle-class entrepreneurial women, risk taking, innovation, travel, adopting changing market niche specializations, and other aspects of "flexibility" become entwined with those practices more frequently associated with conventional respectability (saving, re-investing in the company, relying on family networks and support, and in the household realm, responsibility for all of the domestic and child-care duties). They use modes of reputation to gain economic resources with which to procure some of the key markers of respectability, but in some cases, like that of Sheila, the ability to realize these desires through a combination of business success with marital partnership fails. The female bank manager's capacity to deny her hard-won economic independence without the sanction of marital status is powerfully expressed through a denial of her very name. And as Peter Wilson cautions, "a concern for respect, for one's good name, is always smoldering. . . . 'He who steals my purse steals trash, but he who steals my good name steals everything'" (1973:19).

Despite the remarkable successes demonstrated by increasing numbers of women in the realm of entrepreneurship, sexual double standards associated with reputation and respectability continue to frame their experiences of these successes. For successful men, the expectation that they juggle economic advancement/respectability with other enactments of reputation goes almost without comment—from outside relationships to the necessity of travel, late working days, and absence from the home is well documented in the narratives of middle-class entrepreneurs I have gathered, as well as in the wider literature (Alexander 1977, 1984; Douglass 1992; Sobo 1993). For men, positive status can be gained, for instance, by fathering "outside" children and being an active participant "outside" on the street, while women must generally make up in the respectable domain for any forays she makes in the realm of reputation. The very fact that a middle-class woman pursues entrepreneurship generally demands that she compensate in some way for her breech of respectability within other (mainly domestic) realms of life, whereas for a man, even one who rejects some of the key markers of respectability (i.e., marriage, church), respectability is derived from successful business in its own terms and can be easily melded with "flexible" domestic and parenting arrangements. Patrick is a case in point. Unlike most of the male entrepreneurs I interviewed who are married (22 of 35, or 63 percent), who are affiliated with churches, and who maintain "respectable" domestic lives, Patrick is especially interesting for his defiance of these key conventions of respectability and his embrace of reputation in his family and business lives.

Patrick

A shrewd and driven businessman, Patrick is a partner in a successful accountancy firm and also owns real estate across the island and a car rental company. His business model bears the marks of many dimensions of the global, neoliberal economy. The employer of 40 full-time staff, he employs only those younger than himself and adopts a flexible approach with a deliberately "short ladder of promotion," reminiscent of the foreign-owned off-shore sector, in which he expects to retain them only up to two years. The son of two lawyers and a family "choc-a-block with professionals," he describes his success as facilitated in large part by his mother's model of determination and support. "My mother's . . . competitive nature, argumentative nature, and her boldness about just about everything in life— some of it passed on to me." Like the female entrepreneurs I cite, Patrick, an athletic-looking man of 38, also described being confronted by his parents' and their associates' worries when he broached leaving employment in a secure and established firm to go out on his own. "My brothers didn't have too much to say. . . . They all have their own respectable lives to think about; but my mother is a little bit of an ultraconservative and umm when it comes to taking chances, she was [nervous]." However, she supported his living at home without the expectation that he contribute financially, allowing him to save for the initial investment he needed to start his company. Further, "she's always allowed us to date who we wanted and do what we want [but] . . . the one thing she's asked us to do is to stay out of drugs, alcohol, and umm . . . becoming criminals." Patrick is the father of three children, two of exactly the same age by different mothers, a fact that he muttered with some apparent embarrassment. "I got into a lot of hot water for that," he added. He remains unmarried but devoted to his live-in girlfriend, and to all of his children. He visits his former girlfriend and child most evenings in time to give his toddler her bath. And he says decisively, "Marriage is more important to women than to men." While his current girlfriend is also an entrepreneur, now that she has young children she is devoted to running their household. She runs a "small boutique half day because she prefers to spend her . . . well . . . *I prefer her* to spend her time with my daughter, and she also wanted to do that." Patrick adds with some apparent relief, "She's not the overly demanding type for time" and the children "keep her so busy that . . . it keeps her mind away from sitting and worrying about me. I mean, I still try to make a dinner a week and a night out. Saturday nights we go out together and probably once during the week we go out for dinner. . . . Sunday's we just lounge around and go to the beach." His narrative of reputation—fathering children out of wedlock by two different mothers, combining several business ventures, and even relying on the meals and support of his mother—is combined with expectations that are reminiscent of a conventional patriarchal household (a male breadwinner, a largely stay-at-home wife devoted to raising children).

Patrick's narrative is full of referents to flexibility. His business model adopts a neoliberal thrust of individualism, dominated by a policy of and hiring and firing at will. His story illustrates some of the ways flexibility and multiplicity operate in the public and private realms of Caribbean life and reveals that reputation is not limited to the lower classes. His unmarried status and concurrent relationships with two women appears to transgress the expected mores of middle-class respectability. However, as Wilson argued, especially for politicians and other public figures, indeed for men of all classes, the well-acknowledged and expected multiplicity of sexual partners is another realm of adaptive "flexibility."[18] Jack Alexander notes that what distinguishes middle-class Jamaican men from working-class men is "that the middle class male operates on two tracks at the same time. The middle class male has both a 'responsible' legal family and an 'irresponsible' illegitimate, 'outside' relationship" (1984:162). And it is precisely his economic success that culturally demands this romantic multiplicity. As Sobo says, "Only the poor man concerns himself solely with reputation, for the very good reason that he has no chance of ever gaining 'respect'" (1993:176–178), and by extension, according to Wilson, "those having prestigious occupations . . . cannot automatically enjoy respect. . . . A schoolteacher, however learned he may be, will carry little authority unless he fathers children, mixes freely with other men in the rum shop, and can compete with them when challenged"(1973:100). The "hot water" Patrick refers to, for fathering two children by different mothers simultaneously has had little if any consequence for his business success, and as long as he maintains these intact. By contrast, as Sheila's case shows, middle-class femininity allows for reputation, but the expectation for compensatory enactments of traditional respectable domesticity continues.

There is no question that the expansion of entrepreneurship within the Barbadian middle class has broadened the boundaries and social conventions for reputation, and that the neoliberal economy is encouraging these pursuits. The cases I cite show the greater latitude and determined efforts men and women have made to define new identities for themselves and create new economic niches more generally. They have also shown some of the limits especially for women in melding reputation and respectability sentiments and economic practices. These limits are not merely the sexual double standard of outside relationships, as in Patrick's case, but also a sexual double standard surrounding "outside" space itself. For both Yvonne and Sheila, juggling business travel with family responsibilities is a critical challenge, and one that in many ways led to the unraveling of Sheila's marriage. The taken-for-grantedness of husbands' "absences," whether they are actually away from home because they are working late in the office or traveling outside the island, or they are simply emotionally remote with regard to the intricacies of domestic life, is a common theme in the reports by male and female entrepreneurs alike.

Kate Mulholland (2003:6) suggests that within business families in Britain, "male partners absent themselves emotionally from the domestic sphere in order to transform their emotional energy into creativity and business formation, and whilst simultaneously abdicating their patriarchal responsibilities to their partners, draw on wifely emotional labor." In constructing their relations through "engagement in public sphere activities and non-engagement with private sphere emotional work," she says, men reproduce a model in which breadwinning is construed as an economic task of rationality, distinctly opposed to sentiment. While among Barbadian entrepreneurial husbands a wife's responsibility for the domestic sphere remains a vital ingredient in affluent masculine reputation, these women are radical departures from Veblen's (1953) early 20th-century businessman's "idle wife" (or Mulholland's [2003] contemporary "trophy wife"). Within the entrepreneurial marriages I have studied, men tend to provide a great deal of support (material as well as emotional) for their wives' businesses at the same time they expect their wives to continue managing the household and family. Again, flexibility as a foundational desire on the part of these entrepreneurs is charged with gendered sentiment and expectations and is far from a generic/rational economic strategy.

Mary Chamberlain (1998) notes in her study of Caribbean migrants to London that men's narratives of migration are embedded in discourses of autonomy while women's are articulated within the frame of family responsibilities. Similarly, Coughlin (2002:109) asserts that Canadian female entrepreneurs' primary concern in running businesses is to balance their work and family duties with the effect that they are less likely than male entrepreneurs to envision expansion and growth. But what is critical to the entrepreneurial story of Caribbean neoliberalism I aim to convey is the dialectic. Barbadian men's and women's narratives of entrepreneurship are imbued with goals of flexibility that are framed around autonomy (the desire to be one's own boss, to dictate the direction, growth, and development of the business oneself and not answer to a boss), and a sense of duty (the effort to juggle one's duty to support one's family, to attend to the needs of children and spouses). And these sentiments of self-realization and obligation, of economy and love are intertwined. Becoming an independent and successful entrepreneur is understood by the majority of those I interviewed to be simultaneously about creating a distinct self and creating a particular sort of relationship/marriage and way of life.

The emphasis on "partnership" as a model for middle-class marriage opens up new spaces of possibility for many entrepreneurial couples. For some, like Suzanne, the model embraces a neoliberal ideal of flexibility and self-invention in ways that she and her husband find mutually rewarding. By devising their own divisions of entrepreneurial and domestic labor in ways that place Suzanne center stage and her husband behind the scenes, they invert some of the gendered conventions of a traditional model of respectability and yet uphold the high valuation on marriage that in turn makes their entrepreneurial rejection of bureaucratic hierarchy more socially palatable. For others, like Sheila and Patrick, the neoliberal mandate for flexibility and their hard-won economic successes allow them to eschew the conventions of marriage, a decision not without costs to Sheila but ultimately one she prefers to the failed marital "partnership" she attempted. She is more comfortable dispensing with her disappointing marriage in favor of her thriving business and attempting to juggle her domestic and family duties through the paid help of her children's nanny, and occasionally, her extended kin network. In this sense her insistence on marriage as a "partnership" and not a reiteration of a traditional patriarchal order lead her to rely on another traditional Caribbean household form in which as single, female household head, she can fall back upon the support of other female kin as well as the marketplace to juggle her family duties and entrepreneurial goals.

In the realm of Barbadian popular culture this emergent model of partnership marriage coupled with entrepreneurship figures prominently in a new series of romance novels, Caribbean Caresses. In this series, written for a West Indian market by Caribbean authors, Jane Bryce (1998) notes that deliberate efforts have been made to portray gender and romance in ways that counter persistent stereotypes and acknowledge romance, family. and class as dynamic relations. Since, as Bryce asserts, "representation is not only a matter of 'reflecting reality' but also an act of reclamation for these West Indian audiences," the heroes and heroines of these romances promise each other, for instance, "gender equality rather than swooning submission" (325). These authors attempt to subvert the traditional idealization of domesticated, submissive, pure, nurturing, virginal, or maternal femininity presented in European-derived notions of respectability, as well as the sometimes simplistic profile of the autonomous and tough Afro-West Indian woman who shoulders the responsibility of family and economy out of sheer grit and determination.

Where the entrepreneurial couples of my study and the lovers in the Caribbean Caresses romances are intriguing is in their deliberate counterimage to both the subservient and passive mythological feminine "ideal" from the colonial past and the portrait of Caribbean woman as mercenary, manipulative, and dominating/emasculating. The male heroic figures are also cleverly redrawn, departing from male profile described in Senior (1991:166) as almost irretrievably unreliable, unfaithful, and prone to drunkenness and violence. These romances are largely devoid of the common referents of "outside woman" teenage pregnancy and male violence and instead present an "ideal man" who is sensitive, trustworthy, and domesticated (Bryce 1998:329). Even the case of Patrick, in his insistence on demonstrating that he can provide economic support along with nurturing care for his "outside" girlfriend and child, whom he bathes and readies for bed each night en route to his residential family, is an indication of changing gendered relations. Most significant in the novels are lovers who attain the highly sought fidelity and affection they mutually desire. The heroines of these stories, like many of the entrepreneurs in my study, are usually professional, independent women who are financially self-sufficient (Bryce 1998:334).

Is it any surprise, then, that entrepreneurs figure prominently in these new romance novels? The protagonists are typically Caribbean men and women of "ordinary families" who have propelled themselves upward socially as well as economically. Giselle, the dress designer, in "*Sun Valley Romance*, for instance, is forced to give up her university career when her family can no longer support her, and though she falls back on her own artistic talent, dressmaking is also a traditional feminine skill inherited from her mother" (Bryce 1998:324). "Betty of *Heartaches and Roses* is attracted to the hero, who runs a hotel in Tobago, partly because like her, he is a businessperson. His proposal of marriage is entwined with a discussion of how much money Betty would lose if she didn't go back to her flower-shop, and part of what brings them together finally is her skill as an accountant, which enables her to keep the hotel going when he is in hospital after an accident" (335). Suzanne, the public relations entrepreneur I interviewed, describes her business success as due in part to the quiet involvement of her husband, who handles the accounts, a role frequently performed by spouses engaged in business ventures. Indeed, nearly half of all women entrepreneurs I interviewed describe their husbands as significantly involved in their businesses, both emotionally and pragmatically. The partnerships they envision are simultaneously economic and romantic, and their desires for marriage like their drive toward entrepreneurship are permeated by the language of responsibility and self-realization that is at once "rational" and sentimental, about duty and love. These alternative visions of femininity and masculinity, of work and family, romance and love allow not only for fantasy but for the possibility of refashioning their own self-understandings, relationships, and practices, and are indication that many of these dimensions of middle-class life in Barbados are in states of flux. Entrepreneurship, in fiction, as we see from these romances, and in real life as my research demonstrates, provides new mechanisms for some, for tapping into local and global, traditional and neoliberal mechanisms of flexibility, and for engaging and reworking the contours of reputation and respectability.

Conclusions

The Barbadian middle-class entrepreneur occupies an important place in this neoliberal era as a figure imbued with local historical significance that also embodies contemporary global capitalist transformations. On one hand, the entrepreneur is a local economic actor whose roots go back to the early days of the Caribbean marketplace in which slaves and freed-persons engaged in vibrant systems of trade and are credited with establishing a robust internal marketing system. On the other hand, today's entrepreneurs are demonstrating the capacity to thrive within economic realms that were largely considered off-limits to them as women or as Afro-Barbadians without family connections or that were considered "non-respectable" domains for pursuing upward mobility (Karch 1982). Race is also significant in these transformations in redefining business as an increasingly attractive and achievable pursuit among Afro-Barbadian men and women and in presenting a new realm of economic opportunity and independence for a minority of white Barbadian women as well.[19] Whereas self-invention and upward mobility are celebrated aspects of these transformations, the capacity for these enactments in the present era of neoliberalism is increasingly a burden borne by the individual. As critics have noted, the "reflexive project of the self" (Giddens 1991) or "entrepreneur of the self" (du Guy 1996) increasingly mandated by "late-modernity" demands "the flexible and autonomous subject . . . to be able to cope with constant change in work, income, and lifestyle and with constant insecurity. It is the flexible and autonomous subject who negotiates, chooses, succeeds in the array of education and retraining forms that form the new 'lifelong learning' and the 'multiple career trajectories' that have replaced the linear hierarchies . . . of the old economy" (Walkerdine 2003:240). Walkerdine discusses the intricate complex of psychological services that now play a central role in "propping up" this neoliberal, self-invented subject. Interestingly, in Barbados one can trace similar reliance among middle-class entrepreneurs on very new services aimed to salve the stresses and pain of contemporary life. New businesses that offer "holistic" healing, iridology, nutritional counseling, and psychological and spiritual counseling, along with yoga studios, spas, gyms, personal trainers, and spiritual bookshops are all evidence of the increasing emphasis on self-mastery in the face of the uncertainties that come with flexibility. They operate simultaneously as services provided to the middle classes to stave off the burdens of flexibility and as a growth field of new entrepreneurial niches. And while these services are not exclusively feminine domains, their most visible clients are women, and a striking number of these business owners are women as well. Ironically, Walkerdine notes, the subject of neoliberalism "is actually produced as multiple, having to cope with existing in a number of different discourses and positions: the subject who is supposed to be able to choose who they are from a myriad offerings, who can make themselves. But, this subject is actually also supposed to be sustained by a stable centre, an ego capable of resilience" (2003:241). In Barbados along with the "props" mentioned above, marriage, and in particular, a partnership-marriage, that elusive marker of respectable middle-class life, appears to be sought by a majority of entrepreneurs, as a safe harbor in the face of the shifting neoliberal tides.

The local inscription of neoliberalism fits neatly into Caribbean traditions of flexibility in the domain of reputation and opens up spaces of opportunity and mobility that also transform the contours of respectability for the Barbadian entrepreneur, but there are economic limits and constraints in the formation of new subjectivities. And because these limits are especially pronounced along gendered lines, they present unsettling contradictions.[20] Downsizing and job losses in economic sectors that are enmeshed in neoliberal pressures to create flexible labor open up avenues for middle-class livelihoods to groups formerly excluded from these domains. At the same time, however, they tap mechanisms of patriarchal exclusion, a sexual double standard, and the critical reliance on lower-class female labor to subsidize the flexibility enjoyed by the emergent middle class.

By rethinking the dialectic of reputation and respectability as a lens through which to examine the changing meanings and practices of social, cultural, and economic life, and ethnographically engaging this emergent entrepreneurial middle class, we can examine the changing dialectics of public and private, material and sentimental enactments of neoliberalism. On one hand are structural retrenchments and waning ideological privilege surrounding the public sector, long the bedrock of the middle class. On the other, are reconfigurations and expectations of *partnership* marriages, not simply the "respectable" nuclear patriarchal family of duty, but a "partnership" in love and in labor. Just as entrepreneurship is envisioned increasingly as a new realm of possibility, of self-invention and success, this model of middle-class "partnership" marriage is, intriguingly, sought not in a static replica of some European/Victorian ideal of the "respectable" nuclear patriarchal family of duty but amid other creolized dimensions of interpersonal and social life. Together the narratives of entrepreneurs, whose desires for entrepreneurial flexibility are both convergent and distinct, provide a window on some of the various strategies and sensibilities of this fraction of the Barbadian middle class and their local enactment of neoliberalism. In so doing, they also remind us that just as no abstract theory of capitalism can adequately explain the subjectivities and desires of specific class groups, so too are the articulations of social class/gender/race being re-formulated in and through contemporary capitalism in its flexible, neoliberal guise.

Acknowledgments

Parts of this paper were presented at the Society for the Anthropology of North America meetings in Atlanta, the American Anthropological Association meetings in Chicago, the Women's Studies Department at Georgia State University, and an International Symposium on Gender and Class at Emory University. Many thanks to the participants in each of those gatherings and especially to the following individuals whose comments have sharpened my thinking about the relationships between gender and class, the cultural specificities of "neo-liberalism" and the particularly vexing ambivalence in anthropology toward the non-western middle class as worthy ethnographic subjects: Kate Browne, Allaine Cherwonka, John Clarke, Virginia Dominguez, Robert Goddard, Ema Guano, Jennifer Hirsch, Carla Jones, Aisha Khan, Cory Kratz, Viranjini Munasinghe, Gul Ozyegin, Mark Padilla, Roger Rouse, Louisa Schein. The fieldwork for the entrepreneurship study was conducted in Barbados in 1999 and 2001–2002 as part of a comparative study conducted in collaboration with Katherine Browne (Martinique) and Moira Perez (Puerto Rico), and generously funded by the National Science Foundation. I wish to acknowledge the support of Emory University's Institute for Comparative and International Studies and Office of Research for funding phases of data preparation and analysis, and the Center for Humanistic Inquiry for providing me with time and a quiet perch to puzzle and write. My research with middle class entrepreneurs and their families in Barbados is ongoing (2004–present) with the support of Emory's Alfred P. Sloan Foundation–funded Center for Myth and Ritual in American Family Life (MARIAL). Thank you to Diane Cummins for her assistance in the field, and to all of the entrepreneurs whose accounts of struggle and pleasure, rebellion and respectability have shed invaluable light on the changing permutations of marriage, class, gender, and race in contemporary Barbados.

Notes

1. Anchored in both Marx and Foucault, Aihwa Ong describes the dialectics of flexibility and its simultaneously repressive and creative manifestations, whereby contemporary globalization allows, on one hand, for freer movement and, on the other, for strict state interventions through which "political rationality and cultural mechanisms (which) continue to deploy, discipline, regulate, or civilize subjects in place or on the move" (1999:19).

2. Citing Fernando Henriques, R. T. Smith outlines this ideal as the "'Victorian patriarchalism' of much of rural Jamaican family life." He adds, "The ideal model of domestic life, with a strong capable father, a respectable, respectful, pious and submissive mother, and clean, well-behaved, obedient children, is widespread in the West Indies. It is sometimes referred to as 'middle class' and acts as a pattern for the upwardly mobile" (1988:163)

3. This changing cultural association of businesses as "non-respectable" is cited in India, another former British colony steeped in a complex bureaucratic state system. Thanulingom notes, "Many respectable and qualified people are running towards an entrepreneurial career. This shift reflects a changing attitude towards business, even though most people seem to believe that businessmen by and large are all black marketers. Families still prefer to marry their daughters to Government servants or to those holding clerical jobs rather than to businessmen. Mothers discourage their sons from joining business" (2000:79).

4. Although "crab antics" (Wilson's name for the dynamic, as well as the title of his book) has elicited a great deal of criticism, few have argued with the general ingredients of "respectability" or "reputation" or refuted these domains as powerfully gendered. Domesticity, for instance, the primary domain of respectability, is associated with order, cleanliness, and modesty—clearly a feminine preserve. Lace doilies covering sofa arms and backs, dresser tops, and television sets, echo the layering of modest clothing—the nylon stockings and slips worn underneath dresses, and in earlier times, the corsets, long undergarments, and petticoats, vests, starched shirts, and formal outer coats worn by the plantation elite when dressed for dinner—propriety never giving way to the tropical heat. Likewise, the main ingredients of reputation—verbal banter, sexual promiscuity, musical or other modes of public performativity—are seen predominantly as masculine pursuits (the calypsonian, the storyteller, the political pundit, the "crews" or groups of young men one sees in virtually every Caribbean island, gathered around rum-shops, or in other public settings, generally with alcohol to be consumed). Critiques of the paradigm have mainly focused upon the boundaries and exclusivity of the domains themselves, arguing, for instance, that women too engage in the realm of reputation (Besson 1993; Pyde 1990; Sutton 1974; Yelvington 1995).

5. Jean Besson (1993:21) has argued that the destruction of African marriage traditions by the harshness of plantation slavery gave rise to new, "Creole transformations of European legal marriage and social stratification based on Eurocentric respectability." These adaptive creole forms included "a dynamic conjugal complex, bilateral kinship networks, and cognatic family lines." Each, she argues, "is a continuance of proto-peasant cultural resistance." Her discussion is helpful in rethinking the boundaries of reputation and respectability and demonstrating later on that through market higglering and other entrepreneurial ventures, women in Martha Brae "earn reputation too." Where Caribbean research needs to go even further is in exploring how these processes are enacted in contemporary life. My aim is to link Besson's historical note that "in the 19th century when slaves were allowed to enter legal Christian marriage, they transformed this European institution to symbolize proven conjugal commitment among the oldest slaves" to contemporary attempts among middle-class entrepreneurs to arrive at new articulations of "respectability" that may include marriage but are dialectically engaged with other signs of flexibility (i.e., reputation).

6. Indeed, the avoidance of the middle class as a subject of analysis in the Caribbean was

noted in the 1940s by C. L. R. James who asked, "Who and what are our middle classes? What passes my comprehension is that their situation is never analyzed in writing, or even mentioned in public discussion. That type of ignorance, abstinence, shame, or fear, simply does not take place in a country like Britain. There must be some deep reason for this stolid silence" (1984:80). Jack Alexander (1977) observed this lacuna in the 1970s, and more recently Michel-Rolph Trouillot (1992) noted the same. What is most significant about this gap, however, is that it has given tacit reinforcement to respectability as pure, unchanging, and inauthentic ideology mapped onto, in particular, middle-class women, while reputation has retained the flesh, blood, and vibrancy of what is construed as authentic, and highly masculinized, Caribbean culture. Alexander 1977, 1984; Douglass 1992; and Sobo 1993 are notable exceptions to this avoidance of marriage and the Caribbean middle classes as ethnographic subjects, each providing fascinating discussions about marriage arrangements within elite (Douglass), middle-class (Alexander), and lower-class life (Sobo). The work of Sherry Ortner (1998, 2006) has been especially powerful in foregrounding the middle class as an intriguing and particular ethnographic subject in the United States. In the "non-West" the middle class is increasingly the empirical subject of ethnographic inquiry and being theorized as a particular entity whose interests and identities are taking particular shape in new ways in the neoliberal context of globalization (e.g., Fernandes 2006; Gewertz and Errington 1999; Leichty 2003; O'Dougherty 2002).

7.   Bourdieu (1998) asserts that the "essence of neoliberalism" is its "absolute reign of flexibility," "the easy hiring and firing of employees, constant corporate restructurings, internal competitions established within as well as between firms, and most dramatically, the internalization of these tactics at the level of the individual him/herself." "[S]imple wage labourers [are] in relations of strong hierarchical dependence, are at the same time held responsible for their sales, their products, their branch, their store, etc., as though they were independent contractors. This pressure toward "self-control" extends workers' "involvement" according to the techniques of "participative management" considerably beyond management level. All of these are techniques of rational domination that impose over-involvement in work (and not only among management) and work under emergency or high-stress conditions. And they converge to weaken or abolish collective standards or solidarities."

8.   It is notable that the negative valuation of business as nonrespectable, even among the elite white community, is still alive and well. For instance, as one of the Afro-Barbadian male entrepreneurs I interviewed told me, entrepreneurship/business is the path for the "dummies." He proceeded to point out that several of the island's richest and best-known businessmen had not completed school (secondary) or had been known to be "dumb" when it came to "book learning." The ideal route, even for white elites with family-business backing, was and continues to be today, to a lesser degree, the path of higher education and the professions. As in many other parts of the world in which the public sector has experienced retrenchment (either by forced IMF restructuring measures or otherwise), government jobs offer neither the stability nor prestige they once did, and as such the shift in ideology to the private sector as the reservoir of creativity and success appears to be a growing phenomenon (Birdsall et al. 2000).

9.   This flexibility has been most powerfully demonstrated in the formally recognized relationship of the "visiting union"—a fluid romantic union in which partners do not share permanent residence but whose relationship is recognized and often long lasting, bearing the fruit of offspring.

10.   As some have noted, significantly, this historical characterization of the Caribbean family referred exclusively to the Afro-Caribbean populations and tended to leave unexamined other groups (e.g., Indo-Caribbean, Chinese) (Barrow 1996; Reddock 1994).

11.   Politicians who are also historians or writers, the fisherman who keep a rum-shop storefront

that also rents video tapes, successful Cambridge-educated medical doctors who also keep kitchen gardens and raise pigs, office workers who spend their weekends buying fashions and household wares in Miami for resale in living room marketplaces are all well-known and prized examples of occupational multiplicity in the Caribbean.

12. Arthur makes explicit the connection between the contemporary regional single-market initiative and earlier efforts of regionalism by invoking the Federation period statesman Norman Manley of Jamaica.

13. The Barbados government provided support to the Enterprise Growth Fund Ltd. in conjunction with contributions from the private sector, such that its capitalization rose from $4.7 million to $10 million in 2003. The fund provides financing and technical assistance to entrepreneurs. Senator Eastmond's speech was delivered Tuesday, November 11, 2003, *www.commerce.gov.bb/FYI/news00p.asp?artid=86.*

14. This desire for economic stability and support is the reason that for working-class couples, marriage often still postdates the arrival of children. A couple will host a big wedding, with their children in the ceremony, once they can afford it and can demonstrate to the community that they have the economic means to support their family under the respectable rubric of formal marriage.

15. Many scholars, such as Chaney and Castro (1989) and Ozyegin (1993), have pointed out the integral relationship between middle-class women's enactment of professional and feminist goals and their employment of paid domestic workers who absorb responsibility for their "double shift" at home. This pattern is certainly not new in Barbados, though the increasingly indispensable role of domestic workers and nannies in the lives of entrepreneurs has heightened a longstanding dependency on lower-class women to perform this hidden labor.

16. This enactment of coquettishness or "pussy power" as it is often locally called, implies flirtation without actually having sex—flattery and a chase that is all about sex without actually performing the acts. In essence these expectations are well known among women as a way of deploying sexuality in a reputation-like manner to enhance their power in otherwise constrained contexts.

17. Employing a domestic worker is also an important sign of middle-class status (Greenfield 1966).

18. Though seldom acknowledged and socially taboo, the common practice of covert bisexuality is yet another dimension of "flexibility," as opposed to stasis, in the private or sexual sphere. Widespread male sexual promiscuity, according to an explanation men frequently give, reflects a demographic imbalance of men to women in the Barbadian population that is due to the out-migration of male labor and "the need for men to have more than one woman." Interestingly, though this demographic imbalance existed during the building of the Panama Canal, when many men migrated temporarily, the population has long since stabilized to a roughly equal proportion of men and women. Nonetheless, the rationale persists, and was offered to me on numerous occasions by lower- and middle-class men alike as a matter of fact.

19. The implications for white women in Barbados entering entrepreneurship is a theme I explore in the longer work in process. These women's stories and those of nonheterosexual Barbadian women, which have been missing from the scholarly record of the Caribbean, provide a window on the intersections and contradictions of race, gender, and class.

20. Michel-Rolph Trouillot has said so aptly for this part of the world, "What appears to some as divided political, economic, or social loyalties has a long history on the frontier" (1992:33).

References

Abu-Lughod, Lila
 1987   Veiled Sentiments: Honor and Poetry in a Bedouin Society. Berkeley: University of
        California Press.
Alexander, Jack
 1977   The Role of the Male in the Middle-Class Jamaican Family: A Comparative Perspective.
        Journal of Comparative Family Studies 8(3):369–389.
 1984   Love, Race, Slavery, and Sexuality in Jamaican Images of the Family. In Kinship
        and Ideology in Latin America. Raymond T. Smith, ed. Pp. 147–180. Chapel Hill:
        University of North Carolina Press.
Appadurai, Arjun
 1986   Theory in Anthropology: Center and Periphery. Comparative Studies in Society and
        History 28:356–361.
Barrow, Christine
 1986a Autonomy, Equality and Women in Barbados. Paper presented at the 11th Annual
        Meeting of the Caribbean Studies Association, Caracas, Venezuela, May.
 1986b Male Images of Women in Barbados. Social and Economic Studies 35(3):51–64.
 1988   Anthropology, the Family and Women in the Caribbean. In Gender in Caribbean
        Development. Patricia Mohammed and Catherine Shepherd, eds. Pp. 156–169. Mona,
        Jamaica, Cave Hill, Barbados, St. Augustine, Trinidad: University of the West Indies
        Women and Development Studies Project.
 1996   Family in the Caribbean: Themes and Perspectives. Kingston, Jamaica: Ian Randle.
 1998   Caribbean Masculinity and Family: Revisiting "Marginality" and "Reputation." In
        Caribbean Portraits: Essays on Gender Ideologies and Identities. Christine Barrow, ed.
        Pp. 339–358. Kingston, Jamaica: Ian Randle.
Barrow, Christine, and J. E. Greene
 1979   Small Business in Barbados: A Case of Survival. Cave Hill, Barbados: Institute of Social
        and Economic Research, University of the West Indies, Eastern Caribbean.
Beckles, Hilary
 1990   A History of Barbados: From Amerindian Settlement to Nation-State. Cambridge:
        Cambridge University Press.
Besson, Jean
 1993   Reputation and Respectability Reconsidered: A New Perspective on Afro-Caribbean
        Peasant Women. In Women and Change in the Caribbean. Janet Momsen, ed.
        Bloomington: Indiana University Press. Pp. 15–37.
Birdsall, Nancy, Carol Graham, and Stefano Pettinato
 2000   Stuck in the Tunnel: Is Globalization Muddling the Middle Class? Center on Social
        and Economic Dynamics, Working Paper no. 14.
Birth, Kevin, and Morris Freilich
 1995   Putting Romance into Systems of Sexuality: Changing Smart-Rules in a Trinidadian
        Village. In Romantic Passion: A Universal Experience? William Jankowiak, ed. Pp.
        262–276. New York: Columbia University Press.
Bourdieu, Pierre
 1998   The Essence of Neo-liberalism. Le Monde Diplomatique, December. www.en.monde-
        diplomatique.fr/1998/12/08bourdieu
Brana-Shute, Gary
 1979   On the Corner: Male Social Life in a Paramaribo Creole Neighborhood. Prospect
        Heights, IL: Waveland Press.

Bryce, Jane
   1998   Young 'ting is the name of the game': Sexual Dynamics in a Caribbean Romantic
          Fiction Series. *In* Caribbean Portraits: Essays on Gender Ideologies and Identities.
          Christine Barrow, ed. Pp. 320–338. Kingston, Jamaica: Ian Randle.
Burton, Richard D. E.
   1997   Afro-Creole: Power, Opposition and Play in the Caribbean. Ithaca: Cornell University
          Press.
Carnegie, Charles
   1987   A Social Psychology of Caribbean Migrations: Strategic Flexibility in the West Indies.
          In The Caribbean Exodus. Barry Levine, ed. Pp. 32–43. New York: Praeger.
Chamberlain, Mary
   1998   Caribbean Migration: Globalized Identities. London: Routledge.
Chaney, Elsa, and Mary Garcia Castro
   1989   Muchachas No More: Household Workers in Latin America and the Caribbean.
          Philadelphia: Temple University Press.
Chomsky, Noam
   1999   Latin America: From Colonization to Globalization New York: Ocean Press
Collier, Jane Fishburne
   1997   From Duty to Desire: Remaking Families in a Spanish Village. Princeton: Princeton
          University Press.
Comitas, Lambros
   1963   Occupational Multiplicity in Rural Jamaica. Proceedings of the American Ethnological
          Society. Seattle: University of Washington Press.
Constable, Nicole
   2003   Romance on a Global Stage: Penn Pals, Virtual Ethnography and "Mail Order"
          Marriages. Berkeley: University of California Press.
Cooper, Carolyn
   1995   Noises in the Blood: Orality, Gender and the "Vulgar" Body of Jamaican Popular
          Culture. Durham: Duke University Press.
Coughlin, Jeanne Halladay
   2002   The Rise of Women Entrepreneurs: people, Processes, and Global Trends. Westport,
          CT: Quorum Books.
Douglass, Lisa
   1992   The Power of Sentiment: Love, Hierarchy, and the Jamaican Family Elite. Boulder, CO:
          Westview.
Du Guy, Paul
   1996   Consumption and Identity at Work. London: Sage.
Fernandes, Leela
   2006   India's New Middle Class: Democratic Politics in an Era of Economic Reform.
          Minneapolis: University of Minnesota Press.
Freeman, Carla
   2000   High Tech and High Heels in the Global Economy: Women, Work, and Pink-Collar
          Identities in the Caribbean. Durham: Duke University Press.
   2001   Is Local:Global as Feminine:Masculine? Rethinking the Gender of Globalization.
          Special issue, "Gender and Globalization," Signs: Journal of Women, Culture and
          Society, 26 (4):1007–1037
Freeman, Carla, and Donna Murdock
   2001   Enduring Traditions and New Directions in Feminist Ethnography in the Caribbean
          and Latin America. Feminist Studies 27(2):423–458.
Gewertz, Deborah B., and Frederick K. Errington
   1999   Emerging Class in Papua New Guinea: The Telling of Difference. Cambridge:
          Cambridge University Press.

Giddens, Anthony
1991   Modernity and Self-Identity: Self and Society in the Late Modern Age. Oxford: Polity.
Greenfield, Sidney
1966   English Rustics in Black Skin: A Study of Modern Family Forms in a Pre-Industrialized
       Society. New Haven: College and University Press.
Harvey, David
1989   The Conditions of Postmodernity. Oxford: Blackwell.
Hirsch, Jennifer S.
2003   A Courtship after Marriage: Sexuality and Love in Mexican Transnational Families.
       Berkeley: University of California Press.
Inhorn, Marcia
1994   Quest for Conception: Gender, Infertility, and Egyptian Medical Traditions.
       Philadelphia: University of Pennsylvania Press.
James, C. L. R.
1984 [1962]   Party Politics in the West Indies. San Juan, Trinidad: Inprint Caribbean Ltd,
       C. L. R. James.
Karch, Cecilia A.
1982   The Growth of the Corporate Economy in Barbados: Class/Race Factors 1890–1977.
       In Contemporary Caribbean, a Sociological Reader, vol. 1. Susan Craig, ed. Pp. 213–
       241. Maracas, Trinidad and Tobago: College Press.
Katzin, Margaret
1971   The Business of Higglering in Jamaica. In peoples and Cultures of the Caribbean. M.
       Horowitz, ed. Pp. 340–381. Garden City, NJ: Museum of Natural History Press.
Katzin, Mary Fisher
1959   The Jamaican Country Higgler. Social and Economic Studies 8:421–440.
Leichty, Mark
2003   Suitably Modern: Making Middle-Class Culture in a New Consumer Society.
       Princeton: Princeton University Press.
Lewis, Gordon K.
1968   The Growth of the Modern West Indies. New York: Monthly Review Press.
Lipset, David
2004   Modernity without Romance? Masculinity and Desire in Courtship Stories Told by
       Yound Papaua New Guinean Men. American Ethnologist 31(2):205–224.
Lutz, Catherine A.
1988   Unnatural Emotions: Everyday Sentiments on a Micronesian Atoll and Their Challenge
       to Western Theory. Chicago: University of Chicago Press.
Lutz, Catherine, and Jeffrey M. White
1986   The Anthropology of Emotions. Annual Review of Anthropology 15:405–436.
Miller, Daniel
1994   Modernity: An Ethnographic Approach: Dualism and Mass Consumption in Trinidad.
       Oxford: Berg.
Mintz, Sidney W.
1955   Jamaican Internal Marketing Pattern: Some Notes and Hypothesis. Social and
       Economic Studies 4:95–103.
1971   The Caribbean as a Socio-cultural Area. In peoples and Cultures of the Caribbean.
       Michael M. Horowitz, ed. Pp. 17–46. Garden City, NY: Natural History Press.
1989 [1974]   Caribbean Transformations. New York: Columbia University Press.
Moses, Yolanda T.
1981   Female Status, the Family and Male Dominance in a West Indian Community. In The
       Black Woman Cross-Culturally. Filomina Steady, ed. Cambridge, Mass: Schenkman.
       Pp. 499–514.

Mulholland, Kate
  2003   Class, Gender and the Family Business. London: Palgrave Macmillan.
O'Dougherty, Maureen
  2002   Consumption Intensified: The Politics of Middle-Class Life in Brazil. Durham: Duke
         University Press.
Ong, Aihwa
  1999   Flexible Citizenship: The Cultural Logics of Transnationality. Durham: Duke
         University Press.
Ortner, Sherry B.
  1998   "Identities: The Hidden Life of Class. Journal of Anthropological Research 54(1):1–17.
  2006   Anthropology and Social Theory: Culture, Power and the Acting Subject. Durham:
         Duke University Press.
Ozyegin, Gul
  1993   Untidy Gender: Domestic Service in Turkey. Philadelphia: Temple University Press.
Pyde, Peter
  1990   Gender and Crab Antics in Tobago: Using Wilson's Reputation and Respectability.
         Paper presented at the meetings of the American Anthropological Association, New
         Orleans, November 28–December 2.
Rebhun, L. A.
  1999   The Heart Is Unknown Country: Love in the Changing Economy of Northeast Brazil.
         Stanford: Stanford University Press.
Reddock, Rhoda
  1994   Women, Labour and Politics in Trinidad and Tobago: A History. London: Zed Books.
Rodman, Hyman
  1971   Lower-Class Families: The Culture of Poverty in Negro Trinidad. Oxford: Oxford
         University Press.
Ryan, Selwyn, and Lou Anne Barclay
  1992   Sharks and Sardines: Blacks in Business in Trinidad and Tobago. St. Augustine,
         Trinidad and Tobago: Institute for Social and Economic Research, University of the
         West Indies.
Senior, Olive
  1991   Working Miracles: Women's Lives in the English-Speaking Caribbean. Bloomington:
         Indiana University Press.
Smith, R. T.
  1956   The Negro Family in British Guiana: Family Structure and Social Status in the Villages.
         London: Routledge and Kegan Paul.
  1988   Kinship and Class in the West Indies: A Genealogical Study of Jamaica and Guyana.
         Cambridge: Cambridge University Press.
Sobo, Elisa
  1993   One Blood: The Jamaican Body. Albany: SUNY Press.
Sutton, Constance
  1974   Cultural Duality in the Caribbean. Caribbean Studies 14(2):96–101.
Thanulingom, N.
  2000   Cultural Dimensions of Modern Entrepreneurship. In Women Entrepreneurship. K.
         Sasikumar, ed. Pp. 77–80. Chennai, India: Vikas.
Trouillot, Michel-Rolph
  1992   The Caribbean Region: An Open Frontier in Anthropological Theory. Annual Review
         of Anthropology 21:19–42.
Ulysse, Gina
  1999   Uptown Ladies and Downtown Women: Informal Commercial Importing and the
         Social/Symbolic Politics of Identities in Jamaica. PhD dissertation, Department of
         Anthropology, University of Michigan.

Veblen, Thorstein
  1953[1899]   The Theory of the Leisure Class. New York: NAL Penguin.
Walkerdine, Valerie
  2003   Reclassifying Upward Mobility: Femininity and the Neo-liberal Subject. Gender and
          Education 15(3):237–248.
Wardle, Huon
  2000   An Ethnography of Cosmopolitanism in Kingston, Jamaica. Caribbean Studies, vol. 7.
          Lewiston, NY: Edwin Mellen Press.
Wilson, Peter
  1964   Reputation and Respectability: A Suggestion for Caribbean Ethnography. Man
          4:70–84.
  1973   Crab Antics: The Social Anthropology of English-Speaking Negro Societies of the
          Caribbean. New Haven: Yale University Press.
Yanagisako, Sylvia
  2002   Producing Culture and Capital: Family Firms in Italy. Princeton: Princeton University
          Press.
Yelvington, Kevin
  1995   Producing Power: Ethnicity, Gender, and Class in a Caribbean Workplace.
          Philadelphia: Temple University Press.

2

Tourism and Tigueraje
The Structures of Love and Silence
among Dominican Male Sex Workers

Mark B. Padilla

Global markets and multinational corporations [are] key sites of the making and transformation of a global gender order. —R. W. Connell

On the popular radio programs that continuously emanate from the *colmados* (small corner stores) throughout the Dominican Republic, *bachateros* and *merengueros*[1] often sing of the comic-tragic strategies that men employ in their (variously successful) attempts to evade detection during extra-marital affairs. Men frequently gather around a dominoes game or a bottle of Brugal (a popular local rum) or Presidente (the pervasive local beer), listening to the newest hits from Raulin, or Zacarias, or Los Toros, and participating in what has become a rather significant global market for Dominican popular music. These men also reflect what has come to be an iconic—and somewhat essentialized—image of the Caribbean man "on the corner." During my fieldwork in two cities (Santo Domingo and Boca Chica) on the south coast, I was often struck by the ways that social interaction among groups of men is interwoven with the gendered meanings of the music that pervades homosocial masculine spaces. While there is much ethnomusicological work yet to be done on the gendered meanings embedded in Dominican popular music styles, scholars have noted the tendency to depict women as either entirely deceived by their *maridos/esposos* or as tragically martyred by their husbands' uncontrollable philandering. In one popular merengue by Luis Días, *Me Dejaste Sola* (You left me alone), for example, the female protagonist laments:

> *Te emborrachaste, pagué la cuenta,*
> *Y tú, de jumo, no [te] diste cuenta.*
> *Tenía[s] queri[d]as por todas partes.*
> *No te hice nada y me deshonraste.*

This chapter is adapted from sections of the author's book *Caribbean Pleasure Industry: Tourism, Sexuality, and AIDS in the Dominican Republic* (Chicago: University of Chicago Press, 2007).

You got drunk, I paid the bill,
In your stupor, you didn't even notice.
You had girlfriends all over the place.
I didn't do anything to you, and you degraded me.
    (Trans. Austerlitz 1997:118)

The cultural models that circulate through such popular *merengues* and *bachatas* are refractions of Dominican gender relations, even as they represent highly stereotyped notions of masculinity and femininity.[2] What is evident in the lyrics of these songs is a certain antagonism between men and women that is often rooted in infidelity, betrayal, and deceit. Frequently cast in a humorous tone, the gendered discourses that are promulgated by these musical forms reflect a characteristic feature of Dominican gender relations: the idea that men are incorrigible *mujeriegos* (womanizers) or *tígueres* (roughly, tigers) who are continuously deceiving their female partners. This complex notion of *tigueraje*, in its general form, is central to the construction of Dominican masculinity. Many of its primary features—such as its emphasis on sexual conquest and infidelity—are characteristic of what numerous classic analyses of Caribbean gender relations have referred to as the masculine notion of "reputation" among lower-class Caribbean men (Alexander 1984; Barrow 1996; Besson 1993; Olwig 1990; Press 1978; Wilson 1969). Nevertheless, as described by recent analyses of Dominican gender and sexuality (De Moya 2003; Krohn-Hansen 1996; Padilla 2007), the concept also incorporates meanings and practices that are particular to the Dominican Republic.

Tíguere seems to have its root in the Spanish word for "tiger" (*tigre*) and has been interpreted as a partially resistant response by urban men to the particular configuration of state repression under the Trujillo dictatorship (1930–1961) (Krohn-Hansen 1996). The term is central to the construction of masculinity for men of all social classes and embodies a set of polyvalent meanings that are associated with a particular gender identity. The *tíguere*, while stereotypically lower-class, is also a certain kind of man that is superficially similar to Wilson's man of reputation. In Santo Domingo, the term *tíguere* is often used to describe a man who regularly engages in a range of street behaviors, including drinking in all-male groups, carousing, womanizing, infidelity, aggression, and various kinds of delinquency. Yet the notion of *tigueraje* encompasses other qualities that are, perhaps, unique to Dominican gender constructions. In daily discourse, "*tíguere*" frequently indexes a kind of self-serving opportunism, deception, or avarice that is simultaneously disparaged and valorized. Men who take advantage of others for their personal gain are likely to be labeled *tígueres* by their social peers, a designation that can be both a social critique and an expression of admiration. *Tigueraje*, then, is associated in important ways with the ability to *aprovecharse de otros* (take advantage of others), whether the context be sexual, economic, or political. This parallels Krohn-Hansen's depiction of the Dominican *tíguere* as a "trickster," precisely because of his ability to "to resolve, in an acceptable way, the dilemmas which have to be faced as a consequence of a tough environment" (1996:121). The skill with which the *tíguere*, as trickster, confronts difficult situations—relying on verbal skills and a chameleon-like ability to convince—brings Krohn-Hansen to describe his essence as fundamentally ambiguous:

> The symbol of the *tíguere* (precisely because of its semantic and moral complexity) makes it possible to express what otherwise seems difficult to grasp and classify: paradoxes and ambiguities associated with the exercise of power in relationships. This is so because—according to people themselves—the essence of the image of the *tíguere* seems to be one of ambiguity. Being cunning but not a criminal, the *tíguere* stretches what is socially permissible and orthodox, but without losing moral balance. As the image literally suggests, the man who sees himself, and is seen by others, as a "tiger" is dangerous, tough, flexible and irresistible; even so, this man, this 'animal,' is not rejected by society—on the contrary, he often arouses others' admiration (1996:123).

These paradoxes and ambiguities are discernible in the erotic construction of the *tíguere*. Dominican women and gay-identified men, for example, often lament their relationships with *tígueres*, who are believed to embody two somewhat contradictory qualities: they are both the symbol of masculine (erotic) prowess and the frequent perpetrators of myriad abuses and *engaños* (betrayals). In my informal interviews with Dominican gay men, interviewees often described to me their frustration and dissatisfaction with the *tígueres* with whom they had developed intimate relationships but said they simultaneously felt a sexual compulsion for this "type" of man. While I did not directly study attitudes toward male partners among heterosexual Dominican women, informal conversations with numerous female friends—including many female sex workers at a local NGO—suggest a similar ambivalence toward the figure of the *tíguere*, who is seen as both a masculine ideal and an all-too-common prelude to unhappiness.[3] The normative construct of *tigueraje*, then, imbues the *tíguere* with both positive and negative masculine attributes, since he is simultaneously the pinnacle of manliness and the cause of considerable suffering on the part of his partners.

In this chapter, I draw on three years of ethnographic research with lower-class Dominican men who work in the informal sex industry to examine two fundamental questions. First, how does men's increasing activity in the global tourism economy—particularly their sexual-economic exchanges with tourists—intersect with existing notions of Dominican masculinity, such as the qualities associated with a *tíguere* identity? Second, how is the increasing insertion of Dominican masculinity into a global political economy through the tourism industry influencing intimate relationships between local men and their female partners (both wives and girlfriends)?

There is some precedent for such questions in the Caribbean, because of the growing literature on sex work from an anthropological or psychosocial analytical framework. Nevertheless, this literature is noticeably incomplete as regards a specific manifestation of Caribbean sex work that is of particular relevance to the research discussed here. The vast majority of anthropological or social scientific research on sex work in the region has either focused on female sex workers (Brennan 2004; Cabezas 1998; Castaneda et al. 1996; Kane 1993; Kempadoo 1999b; Pruitt and LaFont 1995) or analyzed male sex workers principally or solely in their roles as "gigolos" for female sex tourists (Phillips 1999; Press 1978; Pruitt and LaFont 1995). Yet what is so compelling about the case of Dominican men described here is that while they are in many ways quintessential examples of lower-class masculine *tigueraje*, they engage in regular—albeit usually elaborately hidden—sexual-economic exchanges with other men. As described in this chapter, this fact has profound consequences for the ways that they understand themselves and relate to others as gendered beings in the world.

The predominant focus in the existing literature on the heterosexual exchanges between male sex workers and female clients has meant that most studies in the Caribbean have tended to deemphasize the conflict between normative models of masculinity and engagement in sexual-economic exchanges. That is, several prior studies have reported that tourist-oriented male sex work in the Caribbean is not entirely antithetical to normative constructs of masculinity, as sex workers can enhance their masculine reputations through their (hetero)sexual conquests as well as draw upon rather conservative gender repertoires to improve their marketability to tourists. According to Pruit and Lafont, for example, the Jamaican phenomenon of the "rent-a-dread" or "rent-a-Rasta" demonstrates how male sex workers often draw on traditional notions of male dominance to establish relationships with foreign women (1995). Similarly, Phillips finds that a beach boy in Barbados is "able to demonstrate his 'skills of strength and knowledge' . . . in his role of tour guide and escort," since the female tourist "also allows him to be 'a man' and to adopt a dominant role in the relationship" (1999:197). This interpretation echoes Press's (1978) earlier study of Barbadian beach hustlers, which argues that men's exchanges with female tourists are a form of resistance to the restriction of economic options available to young men, as well as a way to enhance masculine esteem among their peers (see also Momsen 1994; Kinnaird et al. 1994:26). Kempadoo summarizes these interpretations as follows:

> In settings where young men are economically and racially marginalized, expressions of this type of heterosexuality allow them access to one of the few socially respected power bases available to them. Sex with a female tourist who holds the economic dominant position in the relationship appears not to threaten or disrupt this culturally approved expression of masculinity but rather to enable feelings of personal worth and self-confidence. Although perhaps shunned by 'decent' working men and women for their hustling activities, fundamental hegemonic constructions of Caribbean masculinity are not questioned or denied to the male heterosexual sex worker. An exchange of sex for material and financial benefits with a female tourist, instead, reaffirms conceptions of "real" Caribbean manhood, creating a space for . . . the liberation of a masculinity that, within the international context is subordinated to an economically powerful, white masculinity. (1999a: 24–25)

In the context of the Dominican sex workers with whom I conducted research, there is some evidence that men may gain access to certain avenues of masculine status through their participation in sex work. This is perhaps best evidenced by the use of sex work to gain access to global fashions and brand-name clothing—processes discussed in the larger ethnography upon which this chapter is based (Padilla 2007)—in order to project a particularly globalized masculine identity. Nevertheless, the unqualified notion that their participation in sex work does not pose any serious challenges to their status as men neglects entirely the commonality of discreet sexual exchanges with other men, the shame and homophobia that is often associated with these exchanges, and the ways that such exchanges are meticulously covered or veiled within intimate heterosexual and familial relationships. Indeed, this chapter argues that the case of gay-oriented male sex work in the Dominican Republic highlights how global political-economic structures and inequalities are beginning to restructure the ways that heterosexual intimacy is understood and enacted in the local setting, because they introduce a new set of largely clandestine social relations that must be managed by the sex worker. This analytical lens permits a more multifaceted discussion of the influence of global forces on Dominican masculinity and advances the theoretical project of placing the local meanings of masculinity within a global context in which tourists and local men experience very different social consequences as a result of their participation in sexual-economic exchanges. As Jasbir Puar (2002) has suggested, the connections between "queer tourism" and the social inequalities that sustain global capitalist enterprises, such as the tourism industry, have been almost entirely neglected in the nascent literature on queer travel, with most analyses viewing global mobility as having the potential to liberate individuals from oppressive, heteronormative local systems of gender and sexuality. In this chapter, I take a different approach, examining instead how involvement in commercial sexual exchanges with foreign gay men creates emotional and social challenges to heterosexual-identified Dominican men who use such sexual exchanges to make ends meet within the informal tourism economy. Rather than arguing that these exchanges unambiguously contribute to a masculine social reputation—the approach taken in most prior work in the Caribbean—I focus on how these men manage information about their participation in potentially stigmatizing sexual-economic exchanges in the context of their intimate relationship with women and family members. Drawing on data from surveys, ethnographic observations, and qualitative interviews with several hundred Dominican male sex workers from two cities (Santo Domingo and Boca Chica) on the south coast,[4] I argue that while the notion of *tigueraje* allows these men certain possibilities for mitigating the social stigma of their involvement in same-sex interactions and sex work, their masculine reputation is simultaneously endangered by these associations, resulting in the need to invoke numerous strategies to maintain a masculine social reputation.

Familial Discretions:
Sex Work and Silence in the Natal Household

During an interview, Miguel—a 32-year-old Dominican *bugarrón* (a local identity term roughly equivalent to "sex worker")[5] who has 20 years of experience in the Dominican sex trade—recalled events in his childhood that were anything but idyllic. Born in the eastern pueblo of La Romana, an area that would later be developed into one of the Dominican Republic's most lavish tourist zones, he remembered:

> My father was, as they say, an alcoholic. Everything he earned he drank, and he never gave a dime [*un chele*] to my mother, because everything was—everything he earned he drank. There were problems between them, so I decided to leave the house, and that way they avoided [another] problem. . . . The problem with me when I was little was that I was really mischievous [*travieso*] and my mother was always beating me, and I always had little problems. And between the beatings that she gave me, and the tormenting, what they did to me is tear me apart, and I got so that I didn't even want to *see* my house. When I looked at my family it was like looking at the devil, so when I left it was like fleeing. . . . At the end of it all, you have to leave the house and get by alone.

At age nine, Miguel left his family home and became, in his words, "a street kid" (*niño de la calle*): "I was raised in the street. Mainly I was raised with the tourists. I worked with them. Some were gays and I stayed with them, and that's how my life went. I raised myself alone." Two years after leaving home, he relocated from La Romana to Santo Domingo to try his luck in the city.

> Well, when I came to Santo Domingo the first time, I began working with a *triciculo* [tricycle][6] in the street . . . looking for bottles, looking for cardboard in the street. And I always stopped there in El Conde around a hotel that was called the Hotel Anastasia, and they [the tourists] always waved to me, and they started to give me things, and they said "Come," and from there I continued. I went every day, I passed by every day, since then I knew that they gave me—that they gave me a sandwich, they gave me 10 dollars, they gave me five pesos. . . . And I got a person, a guy, an American friend, and from the age of 12 I stayed almost—almost four or five years working with him in the hotel. I was the one who—who did it to him, who did it to him. And there I stayed.

Today, Miguel is a well-known sex worker in Santo Domingo with relatively lucrative connections to the international tourism trade, a success he attributes to his sociable personality and his English-language proficiency. "I learned [English] easily," he commented, "because aside from the fact that I don't know how to read or write, I'm very intelligent." These language skills have served him well, since they have allowed him to continue making a living in the sex industry despite competition with younger *bugarrones* who are often in higher demand. Now, as a well-connected *maipiolo* (roughly, a pimp) he has even been able to reduce his direct involvement in sexual exchanges without seriously compromising his income, since his networking services earn him regular *comisiones* (commissions).

> Basically, I don't have to be wandering around having sex with lots of people, because I always get something translating, or taking him [a tourist] to Boca Chica, or taking him to such and such a place to buy this or that. And they send for me if they need a person: "Hey! Get me that one." And I go and I look for him. In general, I don't have to have sex [*tener relaciones*], since now I almost don't use sex to, to get money.

Miguel's success with the tourists has allowed him to provide a relatively stable income for his common-law wife, Sonia, and their three children, the eldest of whom is now 12. The family has a small house in Los Mameyes, a lower-class barrio just across the Rio Ozama from the city's colonial zone. Miguel believes that the higher income one can attain through sex work has allowed him to provide a better life for his children. "I was a kid who suffered a lot on the street," he reflected, "and I know what that is like, and I don't want to throw kids out to suffer on the street because I can't take care of them." Sex work has also provided other benefits for his family, including a more flexible schedule, since "in my free time, I can be at home with my kids, sometimes playing Nintendo, sometimes we go to San Cristóbal to the river, to the beach, lots of things."

Nevertheless, he admits that when he is busy with tourists, he sometimes has "problems" with Sonia, who, while she is aware of his work and has even entertained tourist-clients in her home, is not wholeheartedly supportive of Miguel's occupation.

> You know how women are. They always want to have their husband beside them, so the problems always come because of that, because I have to go out to the street and sometimes I'm out until two, three o'clock in the morning, and those are, most of the time, the problems that we have. We've argued to the point of hitting each other.

Despite these arguments, Miguel feels that his wife has no grounds to criticize him for what he considers legitimate work that provides for his family's needs.

> The man always has to be in the street looking for money for the woman's food, and from that she eats. . . . You can't go on what everyone tells you in the street, because you know that I'm in this environment and, if you're my partner and we're living together, you're eating from what I bring here, you have to accept what—what I'm involved in.

Many of these tensions come to the fore when one of Miguel's regular clients, Larry—a North American executive in his early sixties—comes to Santo Domingo on his annual vacations. For the past 11 years, Larry has been traveling to the Dominican Republic to visit Miguel at least once a year, usually staying for two months at a time. Miguel recalls being introduced to Larry through another *bugarrón* who had established him as a regular client. When he was invited to accompany the couple to dinner, Miguel took the opportunity to impress the tourist.

> I took him a basket of fruit, and I got him with that, because when I went [to the hotel] I took him that present and he said to my friend, "Of the two or three years we've been seeing each other, you've never given me anything, I'm always giving you things. And look, yesterday I invited this boy to have dinner here and look what he came here with!" . . . And then we went on a trip to La Romana, with my friend driving and us in back, and he started falling in love with me. And that was when he told my friend that he didn't want to have anything to do with him anymore. . . . And later [from New York] he called me at my house and he told me that he was coming at such and such time and that I should wait for him. And that's when he started sending me money.

Larry now sends Miguel "a monthly payment of 150 dollars, and mainly with that I can get by."

During Larry's trips to Santo Domingo, Miguel has to spend significant amounts of time away from home to accompany him and serve as his tour guide and translator: "The problem when he's here is that I have to spend one night there [in the hotel] and one night in my house, one night there and one night in my house—because I have to divide myself." While Sonia complains about these absences, Larry is understanding when Miguel needs to spend time at home with his family. In fact, Larry "is the one who buys me what I need. If I need a fan, if I need a television, if I need a radio—it's always him that buys everything. He's bought almost everything I have in the house." Nevertheless, Larry is not accepting of Miguel's involvement with other male tourists, warning that "if [anybody] tells me that you're working I'm not going to Santo Domingo anymore." This is a tangible threat, since Miguel has come to depend on the regular remittances he receives from New York. When asked how he convinces Larry that he is not working with other tourists, Miguel shrugged and remarked, "No, it's not about convincing, because he's in the United States and I'm here; he doesn't know what I'm doing."

Despite his feeling that his career in sex work has provided him "easy money" (*dinero fácil*), Miguel is not quick to conclude that it is harmless.

> The foreigners come here and do a lot of damage. . . . How can I explain it? It's never really known because it stays with them, but the foreigners sometimes do a lot of damage to the boys. . . . They're the ones who get them used to it [*los acostumbran*], because if I'm a person who's making two hundred or

three hundred pesos a day [ten to fifteen dollars] and you come to me and say, "Look, come with me and I'm going to give you four thousand or five thousand pesos" . . . that boy will get used to it. That boy gets used to a life. And what life? Drinking every day, and drugs. And he gets accustomed to it. And that's where the problem comes from: when the boy doesn't have a dime, he has to rob the tourist.

However, he feels that this world of *vicios* (vices) in which he has spent most of his life has helped him to provide for his family, including his parents, whom he has always visited on occasion. Until his father's recent death, he had regularly supported both of his parents—who had been subsequently divorced and remarried—with whatever he could manage, despite the fact that he feels they neglected him as a child. He continued these contributions even though his father's new wife treated him very poorly and often objected openly to his occasional visits. Miguel feels that his father, though certainly a neglectful parent, suffered from a weakness and inability to control his drinking and his women. Indeed, Miguel seemed to find a certain poetic justice in the manner of his father's death, which—at least in Miguel's own imagination—was partially related to the old man's agonizing sense of guilt about his life-long neglect of his child.

That was something that tormented him a lot, and he started drinking, because he was saying, "Damn, I wasn't with my son when he was a boy." . . . And he started drinking, and drinking, and drinking, and then he fell off the bed and had a stroke.

In many ways, Miguel's story is typical of the life stories of many of the sex workers with whom I interacted in conducting this research. In talking about their childhood, these men frequently mentioned parental neglect, mistreatment, or alcoholism, often punctuated by memories of traumatic early ruptures from the natal household leading to a more vulnerable existence on the street. Miguel's sense that his departure from home was "like fleeing" provides a glimpse into the early context of childhood socialization—including regular beatings by his mother and his father's drunkenness and neglect—that contributed, at least partially, to his initiation into the world of the street. Nevertheless, these factors should not be viewed as simplistically as the cause of Miguel's being "raised with the tourists," if for no other reason than that he—and indeed most of the sex workers with whom I spoke—frames his departure from home as his own agentive decision. Phrases such as "so I decided to leave the house" are common in sex workers' narratives, but they are often used to describe the thought process of a child who is far too young to make an informed, rational decision about living on the streets. In general, then, there seem to be relatively strong push factors in the natal household leading to the rather extreme "choice" on the part of a young child to fend for himself on the streets, despite the fact that sex workers' narratives often emphasize their own agency in the decision to leave home.

While he does not say so directly, it is possible that Miguel's leaving home at the age of nine was motivated by certain messages from his family—whether implicit or explicit—that he should support himself economically. Indeed, his comment that "at the end of it all, you have to leave the house and get by alone" is similar to comments made by many sex workers concerning their early break with the family. Such comments are suggestive of a belief that male children of lower-class families should be more independent and self-supporting, especially as they approach adulthood. This is particularly true when there are many children in the family, when there is only one parent, or when a boy is considered old enough to cover part or all of his own expenses through formal or informal work. This expectation may explain why a significantly greater number of the sex workers surveyed in this study were among the older siblings in their natal families, suggesting that parents may prioritize younger children over older children, who are expected to be significantly more independent. As with Miguel, many of the men with whom I interacted had become street children by an early age, often working as *limpiabotas* (shoe-shiners) or *chiriperos* (street vendors)—occupations that tended to expose them to the opportunity, the vulnerability, and the temptation to engage in sex work. Indeed, a study of 30 homeless boys aged 14 to 17 who were living on the streets of Santo Domingo concluded that by age 15, 80 percent of these boys had already had experience exchanging sexual favors for money with adult gay men, most of whom were foreigners (Vásquez et al. 1990).

Despite the trauma that was associated with leaving home for some of the men in this study, these ruptures were often viewed ambivalently by sex workers. In some cases, such as Miguel's, "fleeing" the natal home was associated with independence from an abusive home life and was perceived as a kind of liberation that permitted one to engage more freely in certain sexual and economic activities, including sex work. In the Dominican Republic, this association of fleeing with independence is common when sex work begins while one is still residing with family, since co-residence with parents and siblings lends itself to the unavoidable indiscretions and questions about one's nocturnal activities that can be perceived as oppressive familial restrictions, often culminating in the decision to move away from home. Nevertheless, nearly half (43 percent) of the sex workers surveyed in this study were still living with one or both parents, and not surprisingly, those who were still living with their parents at the time of the survey were significantly younger than those who were not (p<.01). This figure increases to 52 percent living with family when we include those who resided not with parents but with siblings, aunts, uncles, or other extended family members—a scenario that is particularly common among rural-urban migrants (see Padilla 2007).

The effect of the commonality of co-resident family is that young men are subject to greater surveillance, leading many to seek an independent residence at the first opportunity. Martín explained to me how his decision to leave his father's house and rent a small room across the street had given him some relief from his father's constant surveillance of his activities.

Martín: I used to arrive late and [the neighbors] would tell [my father] that I was with so-and-so. . . . Since San Pedro is so little, they started to realize and people commented things. So, he told me he didn't want to see me with so-and-so, because sometimes [a regular client] took me nearby my house, and he would drop me off. . . . And I would go straight to my house and in 10 or 15 minutes it had already reached my father. And that had consequences. Problems. And so I had to move across the street.

Author: And now is the situation better?

Martín: Yes, now I practically don't have to depend on him, I depend on myself. What happens is that when you live with your parents and they put a roof over your head, you have to respect the—the example they want to give you. Now I can live my life the way I want to.

Similarly, Rafael explained how he had avoided problems with his family by distancing himself from them.

I am, as they say, separated from my family right now. At least, I decided to distance myself a little from my family, because they are really on the pulse of everything [*muy sobre el pulso*] and I can't depend on anyone. I'm in this and nobody knows. I mean, they know I'm a little crazy, I get home late, I'm out all night—stuff. But I tell them I'm with my friends.

While he had distanced himself from most of his family, Rafael was still living with his older brother when I interviewed him. When I asked whether his brother ever inquires about where he gets the money he brings home, he replied:

No, actually, he doesn't know about it. I mean, I don't show him the money. You understand? Instead, I say: "I'm doing a job [*una chiripa*], something around here. Here: Take 100 pesos. They gave me 200 pesos. You take half." I show him the money little by little, you see? And later I tell him, "I'm going to do another job. Here. You need 20 dollars? 40 dollars?"

Nevertheless, while many sex workers believe that engaging in sex work while living with family is both impractical and stressful, most of them are unable to become sufficiently economically independent to live alone. This reliance on family to meet living costs is demonstrated by survey data on the amount of economic support sex workers receive for specific household expenses. Participants were read a list of common household expenses and asked to indicate whether they alone paid for these expenses, whether they shared these expenses with another member of the household, whether someone else in the family paid for these expenses, or whether they did not have the indicated expense. Their responses demonstrated that a significant proportion of sex workers rely on members of their household to cover all or part of their routine expenses—one of the primary reasons that establishing a separate residence is out of reach for most *bugarrones* and *sankies*. Nearly half of those sex workers who paid rent for a house or apartment, for example, received help from other household members for all or part of this expense. Other expenses show a similar pattern.[8]

If we examine Rafael's statement more closely, we can observe a technique employed by many sex workers to mitigate the familial consequences of their engagement in stigmatized behavior. The methods Rafael uses to "cover" his involvement in the sex industry—for example, by inventing an unspecified *chiripa* (informal-sector sales job) to which he must urgently attend—is typical of the strategies used by many *bugarrones* and *sanky pankies* in their close kin relationships.[9] Indeed, much informal socializing among sex workers involves telling humorous stories about methods used to evade detection by family members, and friends often collude to create mutually beneficial alibis. During an interview, Humberto, 22, recalled the agreement he had made with a friend when he was just beginning to see clients several years earlier, while still residing with his aunt and uncle.

> Author: So your aunt and uncle didn't know anything about this work?
> Humberto: No. I told them that I slept at a friend's place.
> A: They didn't have any idea what you were doing?
> H: No. I told them, "I slept at a friend's."
> A: And they never said anything to you?
> H: Yeah, they said stuff, but my friend covered me [*me tapaba*].
> A: OK. And this friend knew what you were doing?
> H: Yeah.
> A: What did he think?
> H: Nothing. He didn't say anything to me because I gave him some of what I got so that he would cover me with my aunt.

In fact, it is quite common for sex workers to pay their peers to provide a credible explanation—always pre-arranged—for their absence from home, in the event of a more extensive inquiry by a suspicious family member. Thus, the need to cover one's involvement in sex work generates an additional demand for "alibi services," creating a niche for those who are *del ambiente* (in the know) to make a small amount of supplemental income by selling credible stories.[10]

Another covering technique employed by sex workers is to present themselves to their family as "*guías*" (tour guides), since this is a less stigmatizing explanation for extended or frequent absences from home and has the additional benefit of being a reasonable explanation for regular interaction with tourists. Miguel, whose story is summarized at the beginning of this chapter, described how his relationship with his mother had benefited from the cover provided by his self-presentation as a professional tour guide. When I asked him whether his mother knew about his involvement in sex work, he replied:

> Yes, because I've even taken tourists to her house. I mean, she doesn't know *exactly* what I do, because one thing doesn't necessarily have to do with the

other. Sometimes I go there with tourists who don't have anything to do with that [sex work], and sometimes I go there with tourists who have a lot to do with that. You understand? But you don't ever let your family know, even if they start to realize.

The ambiguity that Miguel describes is common in sex workers' relationships with family, since mutual pretense, rather than direct communication, is often preferred by all parties. The status of a tour guide thus provides just enough cover to avoid open conflict with family, permitting momentary denial to lapse into years of mutual pretense.[11]

Many sex workers believe that such techniques for avoiding detection are necessary because of the potential consequences if the true nature of their occupation were to be exposed to the family. Jaime, a 24 year-old student at the country's largest public university, described how he imagined his mother would react if she were to learn about his involvement in sex work:

If I tell her that I have sex with gays and all that, I know that she isn't going to understand. She'd tell me not to do it, and if she asks me why I do it I'm going to tell her, "Well, with that I get money," and then she'll tell me to get a job. She's not going to understand that there are no jobs that a person can make good money with because—For example, I study marketing. If I'm going to buy my materials for class and I take another job, I'm not going to have time to do the homework anyway. And she wouldn't understand those things.

Fears about discovery are reinforced by cases in which family members learn the truth about a sex worker's activity or develop strong suspicions about them. Edgar, 19, narrated his brother's recent discovery of his work and the conflict that resulted from this realization.

My brother and I had a fight [*un pleito*] near my house, because a client of mine, a homosexual, took me to my house in a Mercedes Benz. And my brother and some of his friends were watching, like, "Is it a man or a woman?" And I heard them. . . . And then one of them started to say that I was going around with a fag [*maricongo*], fucking around. I grabbed him and threw a couple of rocks at him. Later the police came by my house, but they couldn't send me to jail because you have to fight with a machete or a knife to go to jail.

Following this discovery, the family changed significantly in their treatment of Edgar.

They were ashamed that people would know that I was a relative of theirs, they were ashamed of me and that made me feel really bad. So, when I'm at home they bother me, and when I go out they bother me for going out or for not coming back. . . . But they don't worry about giving me money to leave—or to come back.

Concern about neighbors' suspicion and gossip is heightened by the fact that most sex workers live in lower-class barrios in which privacy is at a premium and surveillance is often intense. Like Martín, who described his father's network of neighbors who would inform him within minutes of any questionable behavior by his son, the men I interacted with were nearly always occupied with devising various schemes to evade their neighbors' curiosity. Neighbors are frequently the source of concern because they—rather than family members—are the ones who first witness potentially discrediting interactions with clients and later comment about them to family and friends. Cesar, 23, explained to me how his family was informed by curious neighbors of his involvement in sex work:

> Cesar: Of course, you know how the old people and women are in the barrios. They live to talk about, like, the guy who screws around with fags, that—that this is bad, since they think that fags are something from another world.
> Author: Did your family ever see you with anyone?
> Cesar: They never saw me, but with the neighbors—how should I say it?—I was always talked about. I was burned [*quemado*] in the *barrio* as a *bugarrón*. . . . I was with him [indicates a client across the street], and I always had money and was always buying clothes and going everywhere with him. So they deduced and did the calculations: "He's a *bugarrón* [*está bugarroniando*]."

Thus, being socially "burned" in the barrio was often a precursor to problems with family, both because neighbors might inform family members of questionable behavior and because families are frequently preoccupied with maintaining the respectability of the household in relation to their social peers.

Ricardo—a well-known *maipiolo* who founded what he described as the first sex work "agency" (*agencia*) specializing in brokering contacts between local *bugarrones* and foreign tourists—was unusually direct in his interactions with overly curious neighbors. He described his confrontational technique as follows:

> I live in a five-story building . . . so there are always two or three [neighbors] that you categorize as the newspaper *El nacional*, another as the newspaper *Hoy*. [Laughing] You know, like reporters, who don't have anything to do. Old ladies who spend their lives observing everything that happens in the *barrio*—the one who cheats, the one who fucks the fags [*maricones*], how you work, if you rob, sell drugs. So, I take care of those people. So a woman came to ask me questions and I said to her, "What I have in my house is an office of sex workers. Foreign guys come, we fuck them up the ass [*les damos por el*

culo]—excuse the phrase—they pay us. But there are also some women who call, so if you need anything let me know and I'll take care of you!" She turned her back to me and has never talked to me again! [Laughing]

The surprisingly direct style of Ricardo's dealings with neighbors is the exception that explains the rule. His unusual brazenness was undoubtedly related to the independence he has gained through his success as a professional *maipiolo*, and in a certain sense his apparent imperviousness to social criticism was required if he was to make his private home—where he lived with his wife and infant daughter—the headquarters for his sex work "agency."

Despite intense social pressures, some informants had managed to achieve some openness about their sex work with certain family members, and a handful had attained a degree of acceptance (or perhaps resignation) from their families regarding their "other life." Most often, sex workers understood this acceptance as the result of their economic contributions to the household, which tended to diffuse, in their view, any strong objections from family regarding their work. Indeed, financial contributions to the family were often constructed as a way of mitigating the potential consequences of engaging in stigmatized behavior, as illustrated by Rafael's reply to his brother's overly curious inquiries: "You need 20 dollars? 40 dollars?" This technique minimizes excessive curiosity by implicitly offering financial compensation in exchange for silence and complicity. Orlando, 27, made this logic explicit when I asked him whether his sister, with whom he was then living, had any suspicions about his sexual exchanges with tourists: "No, because she never sticks her nose in my life, and neither does my brother. I leave without a curfew. If I go out I come back the next day, and she doesn't ask me anything because I always give her a monthly payment [*una mensualidad*]." Orlando's last phrase makes clear the logic behind his conceptualization of his sister's silence: his provision of economic assistance—as well as his sister's acceptance of it—invalidates any presumed right to moral criticism about his sexual activities. As discussed in the following section, this logic is also evident in the ways that sex workers relate to their wives and girlfriends and is reinforced by conservative notions of male gender roles in the household.[12]

A few sex workers attributed the relative acceptance of their occupation by their family members to their recognition that sex work with men is a viable, if highly stigmatized, strategy for achieving upward mobility. Relationships with male tourists occasionally lead to sustained economic assistance by a client that can have a significant effect on a sex worker's ability not only to provide for basic needs but also to continue education and training that can improve long-term employability and salary. For example, a significant proportion of *bugarrones* pay either their own or their children's educational expenses with the money they make through sex work. I remember a conversation with Ernesto, a *bugarrón* in his mid-twenties, who described to me how difficult it is for him to pay his university tuition during the low tourist season. "You have to turn a trick to buy a book," he chuckled. "You think we don't have to study when the tourists stay home?"[13]

Many of the sex workers I spoke with said that family members who knew about and, to some degree, accepted their involvement in sex work also made relatively frequent references to the dangers of the occupation in terms of potential exposure to HIV and other sexually transmitted infections. Cesar, for example, explained that after his mother's initial shock and a series of difficult conversations about his career choice, "she started to leave me alone, except that she always says, 'Be careful you don't get AIDS.'" Similarly, Martín observed that in his relationship with his sister, with whom he now openly discusses his work, "she doesn't really give any opinions now. She just tells me to take care of myself, to use a condom and, in case anything happens, to talk to her about it first." Such comments suggest that family may provide a significant reinforcement of safer sex practices among those sex workers—generally the minority—who are able to be more open with their families about their engagement in sexual-economic exchanges with men. However, the contours of stigma and silence that surround male sex work, and homoeroticism more generally, place significant constraints on men's ability to safely disclose information about their involvement in sex work to their families, a point I discuss at length in Padilla (2007).

Finally, relationships with siblings were often quite strong in this study, and sex workers were generally more open about their activities with their brothers and sisters than they were with their parents, spouses, or partners. Particularly when informants did not have their own children, they often felt strong economic obligations toward their siblings, nieces, and nephews, and a significant proportion of sex workers who no longer had close relationships with their parents continued to live with or regularly visit their siblings. During semi-structured interviews, siblings were also the most common family members mentioned in replies to a question about the person to whom they feel the closest in the family.

This sense of closeness is at least partially related to the fact that often older brothers initiate their younger brothers into sex work, creating greater trust and openness with them regarding sexual exchanges. Jaime, for example, described his brother's role in socializing him into sex work when he was an adolescent:

> Well, I knew that he left home all the time, but I didn't really think anything. But then I saw that I was killing myself working and he would go, for example, one night to a disco and he came back with a lot of money. And he bought clothes and jewelry and stuff. And I thought, "But wait a second. How is it that this guy goes dancing at the disco and he comes back with money [*cuarto*], and I'm killing myself all week working and I'm completely broke [*en la olla*]?" And later he asked me if I wanted to go and I said, "Let's go," and so I went to see.

Jaime's story demonstrates one of the ways that some adolescents come into initial contact with the possibility of sex work, as they observe their older brothers' successes in displaying the material icons of the middle-class, including the prized designer fashions from abroad.[14] His story is also significant in that it demonstrates the ways that siblings can have a protective influence on those sex workers, particularly minors, who are just beginning and who lack the knowledge and experience to successfully navigate the social, physical, and emotional risks of sex work. As he later described to me, his brother eased the trauma of his transition to sex work—a trauma that is a common theme in sex workers' narratives of initiation—by taking him under his wing and patiently teaching him the best ways to select clients and negotiate exchanges. Thus, while he is partially responsible for Jaime's initiation into sex work, he also limited his younger brother's exposure to the dangers he would have encountered if he had attempted to discover this world on his own. This socialization role is often assumed by older *bugarrones* in their relationships with younger *bugarrones*, but the blood ties between brothers raise the stakes of these relationships and appeal to the older sibling's sense of familial obligation and fraternal care-taking. These relationships generally have a buffering effect on the subjective experience of younger sex workers such as Jaime, who can rely on advice, protection, and an understanding ear if they should require them.[15]

Wives, Girlfriends, and Evasion

On a late night in July 2001, I was drinking with Orlando across the street from Tropicalia, a gay disco on Santo Domingo's *malecón*, where sex workers frequently make contacts with clients. Orlando, while only 27, had considerable experience in the sex trade and was well-known and friendly with most of the *bugarrones* in the area—qualities that would serve him well as he approached an age at which his networking skills, rather than his direct sexual exchanges, would be his primary economic resource. He had joked with me on several previous occasions about the *lío* (big problem) that had developed as a result of his involvement with two women, as well as his somewhat ineffective attempts to prevent his sister, with whom he was then living, from learning about his sexual exchanges with men. Since we had chatted before, I asked him if I could audio-tape our conversation and he agreed. During the course of our conversation, we had the following exchange, which I quote here at length because of its vivid illustration of the cover *bugarrones* struggle to preserve amid the surveillance of their wives, girlfriends, family, and clients:

> Author: Do your girlfriends know that you "look for it" [*te la buscas*] with men?
> Orlando: No, because maybe if they knew they wouldn't be with me.
> A: You think they'd react badly?
> O: Yeah, because—Also if my friends [regular clients] knew that I had others, for example my friend the doctor, if he knew that I had others, he'd dump me [*me botaría*]. Or if he knew that I have a girlfriend, he'd think the same.
> A: He'd dump you?
> O: Yeah, because he says he would.
> A: So, is that difficult for you, to have, like, two lives, because you have your life with your girlfriend, and she doesn't know that you—

O: No.

A: And the doctor doesn't know anything either.

O: No.

A: Is that difficult for you?

O: [No response.]

A: Do you feel bad that you have to tell lies sometimes?

O: No.

A: No?

O: I sometimes have to tell little lies [*mentiritas*].

A: What kinds of lies?

O: Well, sometimes I even have to tell them [regular clients] that I have an uncle that's been feeling bad, that I have to go for a week to the country, but it's a lie because it's to be with my girlfriend. And sometimes I tell my girlfriends that I—I have a job, that I'm painting a house really far away and that I won't be back until really late, so I won't be able to go by their house, but it's a lie, since that's when I'm with my friends, right?

A: But that doesn't bother you, to tell those lies?

O: No.

A: Is it easy?

O: [Laughing] Yeah, because since the lie was invented, it hasn't betrayed anyone [*desde que se inventó la mentira, ya nadie queda mal*].

A: [Laughing] Oh! So they don't suspect anything?

O: No.

A: Are you a good liar?

O: [Long pause] No, because sometimes I make mistakes.

A: Give me an example of a mistake you've made.

O: Like, the other day I told the doctor that I was going to the country for a week, and the next day, or like two days later, he called my sister's house and it was me who answered the phone. But it was because I wanted to see my girlfriend, or to divide my time between my girlfriends.

A: And the doctor? What did he say when you answered?

O: Nothing. He came right over to my sister's house. He said, "Let's go drink some beers," and that's when we started to argue.

A: Did he get mad? What did he say?

O: [Laughing] Yeah! He was furious!

A: And you argued?

O: Yeah, of course. We had a bad argument, and he went like four days without calling, and later he called and said that he wanted to talk to me, and I said that I know I shouldn't have lied to him but that I did it because I wanted to hang out and relax at my sister's. He didn't know about my girlfriend.

A: What did he say? Did he believe that? Did he believe you?

O: I don't know if he believed it. I did it so he would relax [laughing]. I don't know if he believed it.

A: Sometimes they find out, and sometimes they have suspicions, I imagine.

O: I guess so. Sometimes he even calls my sister's house and he asks her about me, and sometimes I think that even my sister suspects.

A: Really?

O: Yeah.

A: But she never asks you anything?

O: No.

A: Why do you think she suspects then?

O: Because guys call me in the morning, in the afternoon, every day. She has a right to suspect something. And there are times when I'm not there and he [the doctor] just shows up at my sister's.

A: Really? He drives by in his car, or what?

O: No, there's an alley by my house, so he leaves the car around the corner and comes through the alley to my sister's.

A: How often does he do that?

O: Sometimes—almost every day.

A: Really? Oh, I can understand why your sister might suspect something.

O: Yeah, she might be suspecting something.

A: So, when you're at your sister's and he shows up, you go out with him then?

O: Yeah, because he's not obvious [*no se le nota nada*].

A: And do the neighbors have—Do they bother you or gossip in the neighborhood or anything?

O: No.

A: No?

O: No, because the neighbors have always seen me with lots of women.

A: Okay, so they don't have any idea—

O: No, and I sometimes—Like every once in a while I go by to, as they say, to "kill the bad thoughts" [*matar la mala mente*], or kill the bad tongues of the neighbors. I go to my sister's house with my girlfriend.

A: To avoid gossip [*evitar los chismes*].

O: Yeah. Because a few months ago my sister said to me, "Listen, you always used to bring girlfriends here, almost weekly, and now you're—it's been a long time since you introduced me to a girlfriend," and I said, "I have a girlfriend, but I didn't think you'd want me to bring women here." So later I showed up with my girlfriend.

Orlando's narrative is, in many respects, an apt example of the complex, multifaceted techniques that sex workers employ to manage information about their extrarelational sexual activities—including, but not limited to, their sexual-economic exchanges—with their wives, girlfriends, boyfriends, and clients. In many cases, these strategies are consciously employed to create the illusion of fidelity or to diffuse questions about involvement with men or with sex work. Some are used primarily to justify one's physical absence, as in Orlando's "little lie" to his girlfriend about a painting job that requires him to work until late at night. Others, such as his taking a girlfriend to his sister's house in order to "kill the bad thoughts" of the neighbors, are intended to dispel any suspicions about engagement in potentially stigmatizing behavior. In both of these examples, the strategies employed are "premeditated" in that they involve planning and coordination to create a convincing "scene." This premeditation is most dramatically illustrated by cases in which other sex workers or persons "in the know" are paid to buttress a particular alibi, usually by vouching for one's presence in a nonincriminating location. These techniques are therefore highly performative, requiring a continuous awareness of potential reactions and a talent for eliciting desired impressions.

These techniques are important for sex workers for two primary reasons. First, a substantial proportion of them are married, either legally or—more commonly—consensually (sometimes described colloquially as *casado sin papeles*, "married without papers"); nearly one-fourth (23 percent) of the sex workers in this study were married, either legally or consensually. Nevertheless, these numbers do not account for the commonality of relationships with *novias* (girlfriends), which were perceived as quite distinct from consensual wives. Generally, a woman was considered a *novia* rather than an *esposa* (wife, whether legal or consensual) when the couple was not co-habitating or when they had no children together. Most of the relatively stable *novia* relationships that did not yet include mutually recognized spousal obligations are therefore not represented in the survey data, or rather, would be categorized as "single." In fact, the vast majority of sex workers in this study were involved with one or more *novias* at any given time, ranging from casual visiting relationships to long-term engagements.

The commonality of relationships with women is linked to the second, and related, reason sex workers require strategies for covering their activities: most of their wives and girlfriends are unaware that they are involved in sex work or that they regularly have sex with men. The vast majority of these men did not engage in open conversations about their outside sexual activities with their significant others, and deception and covering were almost always preferred to open discussion or dialogue. Interestingly, when asked in in-depth interviews whether their wives or girlfriends "know about" their involvement in sex work, men often responded in the affirmative. This answer is corroborated by the survey data, in which slightly more than half of the participants (57 percent) answered yes to an opinion question about whether most sex workers' wives and girlfriends know about their partners' involvement in sex work with men. Nevertheless, when asked in the interviews whether they have "talked about" it specifically with their partners, very few men responded with an unequivocal yes. In fact, their responses were usually similar in form to the way that Miguel, quoted in the previous section, qualified his earlier assertion that his mother "knows" about his work: "Well, she doesn't know *exactly* what I do." The reality is that it is quite rare for explicit conversations to occur with spouses and girlfriends about sex work, with a few exceptions, such as when both partners are employed in the sex industry.[16] This is related to the fact that open communication about the details of one's private sex life—perhaps particularly with wives and girlfriends—is not a strong value in Dominican culture, especially when it involves highly stigma-tized sexual activity. Discussing non-normative sexual activities is generally taken as a more serious breach of social relations than engaging in them privately and discreetly.[17] Indeed, sex workers reported that when family members learned of their involvement in sex work, their primary concern was often the social consequences of any potential indiscretion, as illustrated by Orlando's summary of his mother's initial reaction upon discovering the nature of his work: "She just said for me to be careful because the people are talking a lot, that I should do my things discreetly." It is interesting to note in this context that the vast majority of gay-identified men with whom I regularly interacted had not explicitly "come out" as such to their families and often gave responses to my inquiries that paralleled those of sex workers: every-body *knows*, but we haven't *talked* about it. Thus, the cultural emphasis on discretion tended to reinforce sex workers' resolve to remain silent about their sexual activities, rather than discuss them explicitly with their families and partners.

The constant preoccupation with evasive techniques, however, demonstrates that sex workers are engaged in a passive game of mutual pretense with their partners and families while actively trying to deflect curiosity through the use of deception and "little lies"—described in Goffman's (1963) formulation as "stigma manage-ment techniques." The pervasiveness of these techniques begs the question of what partners and family really know about their activities and also suggests that the pre-sumption that family "already know" may function more as a justification for not speaking about extra-relational activities than as an accurate depiction of the family's awareness. Ironically, then, the notion that family members are already aware of one's engagement in sex work—whether or not this is actually true—may reinforce sex workers' noncommunicative stance, since there is no reason to discuss that which is presumably shared knowledge.[18] As discussed below, the silences that characterize sex workers' relationships with spouses and partners are also reinforced by the sexual permissiveness afforded to men in the Dominican sex-gender system, and the gen-dered expectation that most men are *tígueres*.

The centrality of these stigma management techniques for sex workers' psycho-social lives is perhaps best supported by the great lengths at which they spoke with me about them. Questions about these techniques sometimes resulted in highly emotional conversations about anxieties related to wives and girlfriends. For many sex workers, the ethnographic interview was the first time they had talked extensively about the various lives they were struggling to keep in balance, usually quite pre-cariously and often causing significant emotional stress about the potentially dam-aging consequences of their work for their intimate relationships with women. For example, Héctor, 27, became visibly anxious when I asked him about how his wife would feel if she knew about his sex work with men. "That's why I want to leave this [sex work] forever," he explained. "Because, you know, I have my woman now, you see? If my woman realizes that I have sex with men, maybe she'll leave me, you understand?" Similarly, Edgar, who had hurled rocks at his neighbor for spreading rumors about his involvement with *maricones*, described to me his fears about the fallout from this very public conflict.

My girlfriend will dump me, of course, because she's going to think that I don't love her and I don't respect her, and I can infect her with some strange disease. She loves me and she wants to marry me, and I'd like to marry her too, but if she finds out about this she's going to look for something—something better.

Sex workers' fears about the potential problems with their wives and girlfriends caused by their engagement in sex work seem to be borne out by stories of actual conflict in the household. Orlando, whose interview is quoted at length in an earlier discussion, had almost daily arguments with his girlfriend about his frequent absences from home and his late-night carousing. By the end of my fieldwork, he had decided that the conflicts had become too much for both of them. "It's because I practically don't dedicate the time I need to dedicate to her," he told me in our last interview.

> Orlando: Because a lot of the time, a guy will call me—to give an example—in the morning, and he says he's going to call me at 8 o'clock at night, and I have to be at my sister's waiting for the call. So, I have to call Elizabeth [his girlfriend] to tell her I have to go out, and that it won't be until the next day that we'll see each other.
> Author: And is that a problem for you?
> Orlando: Of course! That's why we've left each other so many times.

Humberto, who often commented to me, usually in the later hours of the night or early morning, that his wife "must be waiting up for me," said that the main problem in his relationship was the conflict generated by his late nights on the street. Things had gotten so intense of late that each night he feared that he would return in the early morning to find an empty house.

Fears about the end of relationships with women were often connected to larger concerns about raising a family and having children—highly valued goals for most *bugarrones* and *sankies*. Edgar's concerns about a public shaming, for example, were connected to his masculine reputation in the barrio, since he believed that *chismes* (gossip) about his alleged *bugarronería* could make it difficult for him to marry and raise children in the area.

> Edgar: It makes me really ashamed, because any woman . . . if she asks around about me, they [the neighbors] are going to talk badly about me and scare her away . . .
> Author: Has that ever happened to you? Has a woman ever found out?
> E: Yeah, I'm telling you because it's happened to me, and later they were making fun of me.
> A: What happened?
> E: Well, I never knew who said it, but she [a potential girlfriend] was interested in me and she started to ask people about who I was, who I hang out with, and they told her I'm a *bugarrón*, that I'm always in

Tropicalia, that I'm always taking *maricones* around to eat in strange places—they told her a bunch of stuff.

A: "They" were the neighbors?

E: Yeah, and what hurts me [*me duele*] is that I'd like to have a son, and if I have a son, I'm not going to be able to raise him there, because if they tell him that, it's a huge shame [*vergüenza*] for him.

Indeed, the desire to have children was strong among sex workers, and nearly half of the 200 survey participants (47 percent) already had children. This fact is even more significant when we consider that the average age of participants was only 24. Indeed, having fathered children was often considered more important than doing so within a stable co-habitating relationship or marriage. Francisco, for example, explained that he had recently begun an extramarital relationship because his wife had not yet given him a child. When I asked him if this was his main reason for the affair, he exclaimed, "Of course! I'm 22 and I still don't have even one [child]!" The value these men placed on their fertility—independent, to some extent, of their participation in actual child rearing—is also suggested by the fact that nearly half of those who had fathered children were not living with any of their children at the time of the survey (44 percent). Nonetheless, 83 percent of fathers indicated that they help to support their children economically,[19] and the cost of raising children was often cited as a primary reason for participation in sex work. The latter is illustrated by Martín's response when I asked him whether his income from sex work covers all his expenses: "No, it doesn't cover all of my expenses, but it helps me to take care of my children, . . . which is the most important thing."

Paralleling observations made in the previous section, contributions to wives and children were often framed within a gender logic that invalidated a woman's right to criticize any objectionable activity. Thus, despite their expressed fears about being discovered or "burned," many sex workers reacted to questions about a hypothetical future indiscretion by emphasizing the supposed immunity to moral criticism that was afforded them by their role as household provider. Cesar made this point clear when I asked him what typically happens when he argues with his wife about his late nights.

No, she doesn't argue too much, because I stop the conversation right there if she comes to criticize me. I always—I say, "What you need, when you ask for it, don't I get it for you? When you want some new shoes, or something for me to buy you, don't I buy it without looking back? I mean, I always have money. So, what you need, you know that I get it for you [*me lo busco*], so don't come to talk to me about that!" And I stop the conversation right there, and I leave.

Similarly, while Rafael was expressly fearful about his wife's discovery of his exchanges with men, his assessment of her possible reaction to the truth was somewhat incongruously nonchalant: "She wouldn't do anything. . . . Or maybe she'd say,

'Shit, what a pig!' But it's for my money, and I'd tell her, 'Well, you enjoy this also,' and she'd keep quiet. She wouldn't say anything more, you understand?"

Thus, it is significant that despite their anxiety about being exposed by their significant others, many men appealed to their role as household provider to rhetorically justify their participation in stigmatizing behavior, and to deflect any real or potential criticism from their wives or girlfriends. Such strategies point to the tenuousness of their support for their female partners and children, since built into this logic is a veiled threat: if you object to my behavior, I may choose to withdraw my support. It is also quite evident that many sex workers overemphasize their role as provider partly as a means to compensate for their engagement in stigmatizing behavior that is potentially discrediting of their masculine reputation. This is a particularly useful psychosocial strategy since it counteracts what would otherwise be considered a masculine failing—participation in homosexual exchanges—with presumed success in another masculine role: household provider.

The narratives that sex workers tell of their stigma management techniques demonstrate the ways that their patriarchal gender privilege provides them with particular resources, both symbolic and material, which they use to minimize the social effects of their stigmatizing behavior. That is, male sex workers are not prevented from accessing normative masculinity—since they have not chosen to disclose or make public their "spoiled identity"—and therefore can make strategic appeals to masculine privilege in order to justify their behaviors, to 'cover' the nature of their exchanges with men, and to place limits on their wives' interrogation of their activities. Hegemonic constructions of Dominican masculinity are embedded in the strategies that these men employ to manage stigma in their daily lives, demonstrating the complex intersections between normative and non-normative gendered practices that pervade their lives. This calls for the development of intersectional cultural theories for understanding how "liminal" genders and sexualities—that is, individuals who fall in-between the salient categories that organize a particular sex-gender system[20]—draw on, reproduce, and resist contradictory gendered meanings and expectations.

One such approach emerges out of recent ethnographically-informed discussions of "sexual silence" in Latin America and among Latino populations in the U.S. (Carrillo 2002; Díaz 1998). Sexual silence has been described as a key feature of the strategies that are implemented by sexually marginalized individuals to avoid certain kinds of sexual disclosure in the context of their social identities as presumed "normal men." It is therefore similar to the stigma management techniques described above, but involves a more complex cultural nuance that has been discussed by Héctor Carrillo in his eloquent book on Mexican sexuality, *The Night Is Young* (Carrillo 2002). Beyond functioning as a way of avoiding sexual communication, the system of sexual silence allows for and even fosters other kinds of veiled communication that are implied or 'between the lines.' Because sexual silence permits a constant ambiguity and uncertainty, it provides a highly productive system for indirect communication in a cultural context that does not permit (or at least encourage) more frank or serious expressions of the sexual.[21] It also allows for what Carrillo describes as "tacit agreements": "The unspoken message is sent by 'those who know' [that] 'I tolerate you and your behavior so long as we never talk about it.' The message in return is: 'I know you know, and I also know that you don't want me to talk about it'" (2002:140). Beyond these tacit agreements, the ambiguity of sexual silence allows for veiled modes of discourse that can be strategically deployed by sexually marginalized individuals in their relationships with a wide range of social peers—from "accomplices" (those who know the real truth and tolerate the behavior), to the "deceived" (those who have no idea about the truth), to the "suspicious" (those who are somewhere in the middle). The ambiguity of sexual silence provides social flexibility, since it permits the necessary communicative "fuzziness" to correct or disavow undesired interpretations if they should occur, while also, in some cases, allowing a great deal of communication about one's "other life" without ever explicitly broaching the topic.

Sexual silence is evident in the relationships between the participants in this study and their female partners, although it expresses itself differently in the Dominican Republic. First, sexual silence results in different kinds of communication because of the ways that sex workers make claims to normative masculinity as a result of their disavowal of homosexual identity, attraction, and the receptive sexual role. The majority of sex workers in this study denied being physically attracted to men or possessing a homosexual identity, and often sought to demonstrate this by "always being the man," that is, never becoming a symbolically penetrable (and therefore disparaged) *maricón* (fag). During moments of potential breaches of discretion with their family members and partners, some of these men therefore drew on these notions of Dominican masculinity to avoid further sexual communication or to communicate that they were, in fact, *hombres normales*. One useful example is provided by 21-year-old Gerardo, who explained what had happened when his girlfriend heard rumors that he was living with a *maricón*:

> One of my friends is a big charlatan, and he started to joke around and stuff [with my girlfriend], "This guy's running around with some guy." And she said, "And who is he?" Because it seemed like she knew him, because he was one from the *barrio*. And my friend said, "Go over there, he wants to talk to you," and I was telling him to shut up. But she saw the guy, and—on top of everything the guy was a real *maricón*[22]—and I told her, "No! *He's a maricón! I'm* not a *maricón*, I'm a *bugarrón!*" . . . And she said "What do you mean you're not a *maricón*, if you live with a man?" And I said they weren't the same thing. "What do you mean?" And I said, "No, because he's the one who receives, and I'm the one who gives." And she went two or three days really mad and then I went back and convinced her [I wasn't a *maricón*], and we went back to her house.

Gerardo's narrative provides a dramatic example of how the particular positionality of *bugarrones*—socially and sexually—produces a uniquely Dominican brand of "sexual silence." On one level, Gerardo's story of relational conflict does not seem to reflect sexual silence at all, since it involved very explicit communication about sexuality and sexual roles. However, arguments like Gerardo's may contribute to sexual silence in the Dominican Republic because they may deflect suspicion and dispel concerns about being a "true" *maricón*. By appealing to active-passive models of sexuality that are pervasive in Dominican gender socialization, some sex workers seek to normalize their stigmatizing behaviors by reinstantiating the symbolic and bodily boundaries between themselves and the *maricón*. Further, in the context of the tourism industry and the common instrumental uses of sexuality by both men and women, asserting one's identity as a *bugarrón*—as Gerardo did when backed into a corner—also suggests that these behaviors are compensated monetarily, a fact that further justifies them as a means of making a living. Thus, while not entirely eliminating the stigma associated with a sex work identity, traditional notions of masculinity can be strategically drawn on within a system of sexual silence to allay concerns about sexual deviance and avoid other kinds of sexual communication.

Indeed, this strategic assertion of a *bugarrón* identity is related to another important reason that sexual silence takes on a particularly Dominican expression among sex workers: *tigueraje*. As described at the beginning of this chapter, *tigueraje* is a specific Dominican expression of masculinity that valorizes ambiguity, trickery, and opportunism among men. In this sense, *tigueraje* is the great Dominican complement to sexual silence among sex workers, allowing these men to maintain a degree of masculine esteem through their opportunistic behaviors, while contributing to the gender inequalities and communicative breakdowns that tend to characterize their intimate and spousal relationships. The ways that male sex workers manage their intimate spousal relationships—avoiding conflict and detection through the skillful use of elaborate stories and "little lies"—reflect many of the distinguishing features of masculine *tigueraje*. Indeed, from one perspective, the identity of the *tíguere* would seem to predispose men to succeed at the social exigencies of sex work, since the continual management of information, described in the previous section, necessitates expertise in using ambiguity and paradox as "cover." Conversely, engagement in sex work might be seen to reinforce one's reputation as a *tíguere*, since it epitomizes in many ways the types of masculine behavior expected of the *tíguere*. Further, it bears mentioning in this context that many sex workers refer to themselves and their social peers as quintessential *tígueres*, demonstrating a certain internalization of the meanings of *tigueraje* in their gender identity and sense of self. Thus, the cultural notion of *tigueraje* provides a symbolic resource on which sex workers can draw in mitigating the social consequences of their engagement in stigmatized behavior and is quite effective in preparing many young men in the skills necessary to engage in, and simultaneously conceal, sexual-economic exchanges with tourists.

A fundamental point here is the fact that the tourism industry structures the economic parameters within which these complex interactions unfold, permitting us to examine the intersections between global economic shifts—most important the exponential growth of the tourism industry throughout the Caribbean—and the ways that relations of kinship and gender are organized and practiced. Indeed, such connections have been generally neglected by the vast number of studies of sex work in the Caribbean and globally, which have tended to artificially extract sex workers from the full context of their intimate lives beyond the brothel, bar, or beach. Among the male sex workers in this study, this tendency has marginalized a nuanced analysis of how the local effects of "queer tourism" may have reverberations beyond the strictly "queer." That is, the organization of normative heterosexual relations and kinship relations may be shifting as an emerging global gay market has begun to provide new opportunities for young, heterosexually identified men to make a living in the informal tourism economy, at the same time that such opportunities are dwindling in other sectors.[23] By examining the full context of sex workers' lives, this study makes it quite apparent that participation in sexual-economic exchanges with gay tourists has influenced these men's gendered practices of intimacy in both their natal and their conjugal households.

First, many of these men described a tension between the surveillance imposed by their co-residence with natal family members and the exigencies of the work in which they engaged. For some, this tension was related to the motivation to leave home and the desire to seek an independent residence. For others, complete independence from family members was precluded by men's dependence on household support, a situation that resulted in a greater need to employ a wide range of stigma management techniques to avoid damage to one's masculine reputation. Veiled or ambiguous forms of sexual communication characterized these men's relationships with family members, reflecting what has been described elsewhere as "sexual silence" in Latin American sex-gender systems (Carrillo 2002; Díaz 1998).

Second, intimate relationships with wives and girlfriends have clearly been influenced by sex workers' involvement in exchanges with tourists. Often, conflicts occurred with spouses and partners when frequent absences from home or interactions with tourists raised suspicions about a man's potential involvement in same-sex activities or sex work, or when rumors implied social involvement with *maricones*. Sex workers, almost universally self-described as "heterosexual,"[24] often feared a breach of discretion with female partners, whom they saw as both ideal intimate partners and necessary resources in upholding a solidly masculine reputation. To avoid a breach, men drew on a combination of culturally salient meanings and practices, including the shared system of sexual silence and the gender expectations embodied in the masculine *tíguere*. Indeed, sex workers' access to certain patriarchal gender ideologies, such as the notion that masculine men should be adequate household providers, offered a means to discontinue, avoid, or invalidate communication with female partners about involvement in non-normative sexual behaviors. In this way, the economic contributions to the household that were enabled by sex work—in combination with the symbolic confirmation of masculinity that these contributions bring—allowed some men to disavow any moral obligation to engage in more direct forms of sexual communication with their partners. From this perspective, men expressed the idea that a woman who gains economically from her husband's involvement in sex work—even if she presumably does so unknowingly—relinquishes her right to inquire about his outside sexual behavior.

In general, this chapter argues that the structures of the global tourism industry in the Dominican Republic have created new structural affordances for the social reproduction and transformation of local sex-gender systems. The growth of the tourism industry globally has brought with it new constraints on labor and on the values placed on sexuality. This study strives to demonstrate the analytical importance of tracing the linkages between such political-economic factors and their local reverberations in gender and sexuality. Future anthropological studies of tourism should seek to extend our knowledge of these linkages by examining the practices of love and intimacy within a self-consciously global framework in which tourism workers—including those who engage regularly or intermittently in sexual commerce with tourists—may bear quite high social costs for their participation in stigmatized labor and sexual practices. A crucial first step in this effort is to avoid theoretical frameworks that posit an essentialized notion of "sex workers" as a distinct category that can be presumably extracted from the social, familial, and spousal ties that shape and reproduce cultural systems of gender and sexuality.

Notes

1. *Merengue* and *bachata* are quintessentially Dominican musical forms, heard constantly in streets, businesses, and public areas. Although their evolution and social history are distinct (see Austerlitz 1997 on the social history of Dominican *merengue*, and Hernandez 1995 on *bachata*), many of the musical features of *merengue* and *bachata* are becoming increasingly blended in contemporary Dominican music, as each genre borrows from the other.
2. It is also important to remember that these musical styles tend to reproduce markedly male representations of gender, since the vast majority of writers, performers, and producers of popular music are men. As Austerlitz (1997) has also pointed out, even the recent emergence of women as *merengueras* or back-up singers has been co-opted by the machismo of the Dominican music industry, as female performers have been incorporated principally for their sensual presence and the provocative visuals of gyrating young women in bikinis.
3. For published examples, see the life history interviews of Dominican female sex workers collected in Murray (2002), as well as Brennan's (2004) discussion of female sex workers in her excellent ethnography *What's Love Got to Do With It?*.
4. The study involved the author's residence and continuous participant observation with sex workers in each of the two sites in the Dominican Republic between 1999 and 2002. The research involved collaboration with a local AIDS-related NGO with extensive experience among Men Who Have Sex with Men (MSM), which provided the institutional and human resources to conduct this large mixed-methods study. The methodology for the study is described in detail in Padilla (2007).
5. This ethnographic study was conducted with two local identity categories of male sex workers, *bugarrones* and *sanky pankies*. These terms are glossed here as "male sex workers" but also have other local meanings that are not addressed in this chapter. For a more thorough description, see Padilla (2007).
6. Hirschman (1984:13) estimates there are 5,000 *tricicleros* (tricycle riders) in Santo Domingo who make a meager living by distributing fruits, vegetables, coal, and a variety of other items. Driving *triciclos* is a common source of employment among poor urban males.
7. Ramah et al. (1992), in their survey study of a diverse group of 188 Dominican men who have sex with men, similarly report that two-thirds of their sample still lived with parents.

They comment that "given the large proportion of the sample living with their families, it is not surprising that over half of all sexual encounters take place in hotels or motels (59%)."

8. In their study of 76 *palomos* (street children who engage in sexual exchanges with men) and *bugarrones* in Santo Domingo, Ruiz and Vásquez (1993) found that 43 percent of them were helped economically by their families.

9. The reference to Goffman's (1963) definition of "covering" as an information management technique is self-conscious and is discussed further toward the end of this chapter.

10. Campbell et al. (1999:143) describe how Jamaican female sex workers employed in sex work establishments will cooperate with a fellow sex worker if the latter's family should suddenly appear, "pretending that their main occupation is nonsex work" (for example, waitressing). The authors do not, however, mention cases in which these alibis were compensated with cash in the ways I observed among Dominican male sex workers.

11. Campbell et al., in their discussion of female sex workers in Jamaica, report that sex workers' greatest fear is that their children will discover the true nature of their work, as illustrated by one informant who "consistently fabricates stories of what she does for a living in order to protect the child and hopes that she will never find out before she gets a chance to leave the sex trade, which she intends to do in the very near future" (1999:143).

12. In their work with female sex workers in the mining camps of Guyana, the Red Thread Women's Development Programme has recently noted that "for some of the women, family members, including current partners, knew how they were earning an income and there appeared to be no negative consequences, especially where financial support was forthcoming" (1999:274).

13. This quotation is paraphrased.

14. Such an interpretation parallels observations by some tourism researchers (Harrison 1992; Kinnaird et al. 1994) who suggest that interaction with tourists creates a "demonstration effect" that promotes certain forms of commodification and consumer practices.

15. Paralleling these findings, Ruíz and Vásquez (1993) report that most of the *bugarrones* above the age of 24 in their study of "homotropic" male sex workers functioned as informal pimps or role models for younger initiates, teaching them how to make contacts with clients and negotiate prices.

16. A subgroup of sex workers in this study were involved with women who work in brothels or bars as sex workers. These relationships typically have the benefit of greater openness about sexual exchanges but can also lead to abuses if the male controls his partner's income or brokers her sex work contacts.

17. Ethnographers have found a similar distinction in other Latin American contexts. Parker (1991) suggests, for example, that public norms of Brazilian sexuality do not necessarily reflect the realities of men's sexual behavior "between four walls" (i.e., in private). This argument is related to more recent ethnographic discussion of "sexual silence" in Latin America, a point to which I return later (Carrillo 2002; Díaz 1998).

18. Indeed, in his PhD dissertation on Dominican homosexuality and transnational identities in New York City, Carlos Decena argues that the use of the *sujeto tacito* (tacit subject) in Dominican language problematizes the very notion of the open "disclosure" of sexual identity, since "these men assume that most people in their lives either know they are homosexual or can infer it from the way these men live" (2004:viii).

19. This figure may be slightly skewed by the participants' overestimation of their actual contributions, since ethnographic observations suggest that sex workers' wives and girlfriends are frequently unsatisfied with their economic support. It is likely that the desire to portray themselves as good providers for their children within the context of the interview moved some participants to answer positively to the question regarding their economic support for children, when actually there was no such support or support was negligible.

20. Victor Turner's (1970, 1975) analysis of the ritual state of "liminality" in human societies is relevant here. While Turner's classic theory uses the notion of liminality to describe

a transient state of "anti-structure" during rites of passage in small-scale societies, he also acknowledges in his book *Dramas, Fields, and Metaphors* that modern societies may create permanent "marginals" who are not reincorporated into the social structure and "have no cultural assurance of a final stable resolution of their ambiguity" (Turner 1975:233).

21. As Carrillo (2002) points out, however, Mexican culture does encourage frank expressions of sexuality in the form of *albures*, an elaborate form of mostly lower-class joking or jabbing that also derives its cultural salience from humorous ambiguities in sexual communication.

22. Gerardo's use of *maricón* here implies more than sexual preference, since it suggests that the man was highly effeminate and "obviously" *maricón*.

23. For a thorough discussion of how recent changes in gender and work in the Dominican Republic are related to the sex tourism industry, see Padilla (2007).

24. Three percent of survey participants in the study self-identified as either "homosexual" or "gay."

References

Alexander, Jack
   1984   Love, Race, Slavery, and Sexuality in Jamaican Images of the Family. *In* Kinship and Ideology in Latin America. Raymond T. Smith, ed. Pp. 147–180. Chapel Hill: University of North Carolina Press.

Austerlitz, Paul
   1997   Merengue: Dominican Music and Dominican Identity. Philadelphia: Temple University Press.

Barrow, Christine
   1996   Ideology and Culture. *In* Family in the Caribbean: Themes and Perspectives. Christine Barrow, ed. Pp. 160–181. Kingston: Ian Randle.

Besson, Jean
   1993   Reputation and Respectability Reconsidered: A New Perspective on Afro-Caribbean Peasant Women. *In* Women and Change in the Caribbean. Janet Momsen, ed. Pp. 15–37. Bloomington: University of Indiana Press.

Brennan, Denise
   2004   What's Love Got to Do With It? Transnational Desires and Sex Tourism in the Dominican Republic. Durham: Duke University Press.

Cabezas, Amalia Lucía
   1998   Pleasure and Its Pain: Sex Tourism in Sosúa, the Dominican Republic. PhD dissertation, Department of Anthropology, University of California, Berkeley.

Campbell, Shirley, Althea Perkins, and Patricia Mohammed
   1999   "Come to Jamaica and Feel Alright": Tourism and the Sex Trade. *In* Sun, Sex, and Gold: Tourism and Sex Work in the Caribbean. Kamala Kempadoo, ed. Pp. 125–156. Lanham, MD: Rowman & Littlefield.

Carrillo, Hector
   2002   The Night is Young: Sexuality in Mexico in the time of AIDS. Chicago: University of Chicago Press.

Castaneda, Xochitl, Victor Ortiz, Betania Allen, Cecilia Garcia, and Mauricio Hernandez-Avila
   1996   Sex Masks: The Double Life of Female Commercial Sex Workers in Mexico City. Culture, Medicine and Psychiatry 20:229–247.

Decena, Carlos
   2004   Queering the Heights: Dominican Transnational Identities and Male Homosexuality in New York City. PhD dissertation, Program in American Studies, New York University.

De Moya, E. Antonio
  2003 Power Games and Totalitarian Masculinity in the Dominican Republic. *In*
        Interrogating Caribbean Masculinities: Theoretical and Empirical Analyses. Rhoda E.
        Reddock, ed. Pp. 68–102. Kingston: University of the West Indies Press.
Díaz, Rafael M.
  1998 Latino Gay Men and HIV. New York: Routledge.
Goffman, Erving
  1963 Stigma: Notes on the Management of Spoiled Identity. New York: Simon & Schuster.
Harrison, D., ed.
  1992 Tourism and the Less Developed Countries. London: Belhaven.
Hernandez, Deborah Pacini
  1995 Bachata: A Social History of a Dominican Popular Music. Philadelphia: Temple
        University Press.
Hirschman, Albert O.
  1984 Getting Ahead Collectively. New York: Pergamon.
Kane, Stephanie C.
  1993 Prostitution and the Military: Planning AIDS Intervention in Belize. Social Science
        and Medicine 36(7):965–979.
Kempadoo, Kamala
  1999a Continuities and Change: Five Centuries of Prostitution in the Caribbean. *In* Sun, Sex,
        and Gold: Tourism and Sex Work in the Caribbean. Kamala Kempadoo, ed. Pp. 3–33.
        Lanham, MD: Rowman & Littlefield.
Kempadoo, Kamala, ed.
  1999b Sun, Sex, and Gold: Tourism and Sex Work in the Caribbean. Lanham, MD: Rowman
        & Littlefield.
Kinnaird, Vivian, Uma Kothari, and Derek Hall
  1994 Tourism: Gender Perspectives. *In* Tourism: A Gender Analysis. Vivian Kinnaird and
        Derek Hall, eds. Pp. 1–34. New York: John Wiley & Sons.
Krohn-Hansen, Christian
  1996 Masculinity and the Political among Dominicans: "The Dominican Tiger." *In* Machos,
        Mistresses, Madonnas: Contesting the Power of Latin American Gender Imagery. Marit
        Melhuus and Kristi Anne Stølen, eds. Pp. 108–133. New York: Verso.
Momsen, Janet Henshall
  1994 Tourism, Gender, and Development in the Caribbean. *In* Tourism: A Gender Analysis.
        V. Kinnaird and D. Hall, eds. Pp. 106–120. London: John Wiley & Sons.
Murray, Laura, ed.
  2002 Laughing on the Outside, Crying on the Inside. Santo Domingo: AcciónSIDA/AED.
Olwig, Karen F.
  1990 The Struggle for Respectability: Methodism and Afro-Caribbean Culture on 19th-
        Century Nevis. New West Indian Guide 64(3/4):93–114.
Padilla, Mark
  2007 Caribbean Pleasure Industry: Tourism, Sexuality, and AIDS in the Dominican
        Republic. Chicago: University of Chicago Press.
Parker, Richard
  1991 Bodies, Pleasures, and Passions: Sexual Culture in Contemporary Brazil. Boston:
        Beacon Press.
Phillips, Joan L.
  1999 Tourist-Oriented Prostitution in Barbados: The Case of the Beach Boy and the White
        Female Tourist. *In* Sun, Sex, and Gold: Tourism and Sex Work in the Caribbean.
        Kamala Kempadoo, ed. Pp. 183–200. Lanham, MD: Rowman & Littlefield.

Press, C. M.
  1978   Reputation and Respectability Reconsidered: Hustling in a Tourist Setting. Caribbean
         Issues 4(1):109–119.
Pruitt, Deborah, and Suzanne LaFont
  1995   For Love and Money: Romance Tourism in Jamaica. Annals of Tourism Research
         22(2):422–444.
Puar, Jasbir
  2002   Introduction. Special issue, "Queer Tourism: Geographies of Globalization.". GLQ
         8(1–2):1–6.
Ramah, M., R. Pareja, and J. Hasbun
  1992   Lifestyles and Sexual Practices. Results of KABP Conducted among Homosexual and
         Bisexual Men. Santo Domingo.
Red Thread Women's Development Programme
  1999   "Givin' Lil' Bit fuh Lil' Bit": Women and Sex Work in Guyana. *In* Sun, Sex, and
         Gold: Tourism and Sex Work in the Caribbean. Kamala Kempadoo, ed. Pp. 263–290.
         Lanham, MD: Rowman & Littlefield.
Ruiz, Carlos, and R. Eduardo Vásquez
  1993   Características psicosociales y motivación para la prevención del SIDA en trabajadores
         sexuales homotrópicos. Master's thesis, Department of Psychology, Universidad
         Autónoma de Santo Domingo.
Turner, Victor
  1970   The Forest of Symbols: Aspects of Ndembu Ritual. Ithaca: Cornell University Press.
  1975   Dramas, Fields, and Metaphors: Symbolic Action in Human Society. Ithaca: Cornell
         University Press.
Vásquez, R. Eduardo, Carlos Ruíz, and E. Antonio De Moya
  1990   Motivación y uso de condones en la prevención del SIDA entre muchachos de la calle
         trabajadores sexuales. Santo Domingo: UASD/PROCETS.
Wilson, Peter J.
  1969   Reputation and Respectability: A Suggestion for Caribbean Ethnology. Man 4:70–84.
  1973   Crab Antics: The Social Anthropology of English-Speaking Negro Societies of the
         Caribbean. New Haven: Yale University Press.

3

"If there is no feeling . . ."
The Dilemma between Silence and Coming Out in a Working-Class Butch/Femme Community in Jakarta

Saskia E. Wieringa

With a firm wish to find this treasure of love,
I tied up [my boat] at the landing-place of the heavenly Ganges.
A cross-current from the river of desire tore loose [my boat] from
    its moorings.

What shall I say about love?
Desire is a branch, a creeper of love;
Without desire there is no awakening of love
    —Songs of Lalon

Jakarta is a fast-growing metropolis of over 12 million people from all over Indonesia. The business center of the city boasts impressive glass towers of the hotels and banks from which the national and international corporate elite steers the economy of this vast archipelago of some 220 million inhabitants into the vortex of the global financial markets. The wealth, procured out of unbridled profits and unchecked graft and corruption, of the fast-growing middle-class areas of Southern Jakarta is demonstrated by the Mercedes and BMW cars that cause interminable traffic jams and consumed in the myriad shopping malls that dot the sprawling suburbs. The majority of the population, however, live in simple, crowded one- or two-story houses. The business high-rises and multistory luxury apartment blocks rise like towering coconut trees up out of a sea of red-tiled roofs. Despite the close proximity of capitalist opulence there is a deep economic and cultural gap with the inhabitants of the sprawling deprived urban poor neighborhoods. The modern world comes to the inhabitants of these *kampung* (neighborhoods) through the detours of national television and the windows of the shopping malls they are not allowed to enter. Yet though the poor are socially and economically marginal, they are engaged with various competing global discourses.

This chapter discusses the dynamics of a group of lower- and lower middle-class female-bodied persons engaged in same-sex relations. Most of them live in the outskirts of Jakarta; socially and economically they live marginal lives as well. Socially, emotionally, and erotically they ascribe to a butch-femme pattern[1] modeled on the traditional Indonesian heterosexual gender regime. Yet globalization does not pass them by completely. Urbanization, democratization with its discourse of human and women's rights, the competing discourses of growing fundamentalism on one hand and economic liberalism on the other hand are variously impacting on them. This discussion focuses on the dilemma between the relative safety that the culture of silence surrounding their identities and sexual preferences affords them and the dangers and attractions of the new rights discourse. The discourse of silence allows them a social space, provided they fulfill the expectations of their neighbors and family members with respect to established gender norms and accept the discrimination and marginalization that this position entails.

The democratic opening of Indonesia after 1998, however, in the wake of an economic crisis that started in 1997, which was spurred on by groups advocating human and women's rights, has led to a discourse of equality and individual rights and a delegitimization of various forms of discrimination. This discourse presupposes a self-ascribed gay or lesbian identity that means a visibility of the sexual aspects of their relationship, the recognition of which they so far have tried to prevent. This "coming out" may have severe social and economic repercussions for the individuals who are brave enough to risk it. At the national political level, the growing uneasiness with individual sexual rights that do not conform to conservative patterns of heteronormativity is felt in the drafting of laws that circumscribe same-sex relations (and penalize other forms of nonmonogamous heterosexual sex) by the self-proclaimed custodians of an invented "traditional" morality, in this case fundamentalist Muslims.

These are not the only discourses the members of the Jakarta butch/femme (b/f) community are confronted with. The breakdown of the state has led to a wave of decentralization with new forms of disciplining and identity formation, in many instances based on religious affiliation. Global discourses on gay and lesbian rights are gaining some currency among middle-class persons with same-sex preferences. Groups of younger, better-educated middle-class lesbians are emerging who are making wide use of the Internet and other forms of information technology. They have more international contacts and are aware of lesbian communities in other parts of the world. Also, they espouse a feminist ideology of androgyny and sexual equality that is alien to the b/f community discussed here (though in practice b/f patterns are common in this group as well).

In this chapter I discuss the fast-changing "imagined world" of this b/f community as they negotiate their lives between the stringent political-economic constraints they are faced with and the multiple and contradictory discourses that confront them, caught as they are between traditional[2] notions of gender and the modern human/women/lesbian discourses. In this process the partners of the b/f couples I met negotiated sexuality, desire, and love.

The Scene: A Lower-Class Butch/Femme Community

Just as I am about to relax, as the discussion we have had so far seems to repeat itself, Diny,[3] who is sitting on a wooden stool beside me, whispers into my ear: "But when there is no feeling . . ." she shakes her head, her voice trails away. I look at her questioningly, and she repeats softly what she has just said, putting her hand on my wrist to emphasize her point. "When there is no feeling. . . . " I smile encouragingly at her and urge her to finish her sentence. She looks at me apologetically. Am I really so dumb that I don't understand her? Why do Westerners always have to hear the specific words, when the implication of what she is conveying to me is so obvious? Diny looks at the group, consisting of her own partner, two more butches and the femme partner of one of them, as well as two members of the lesbian group with who I am doing this research. Then she makes a vague movement of her head pointing to the other room, which has just been vacated by a distant relative of hers. This relative does not know or prefers not to know she is in a same-sex relation and we have had to talk in a very low voice the whole evening, so our conversation will not be overheard. Her two children have been popping in and out of the room. They are sympathetic to the relationship their mother has with her butch partner but have faced embarrassing confrontations with their schoolmates.

"All this," she finally says, "is it worth all of it when there is no love?"

She gets up to pour me another glass of tea. The other guests and our host/ess have not interrupted their conversation. We had just come to the conclusion that one of the major attractions that butches hold for femmes is the sexual competence of the butches. In contrast to heterosexual men, who just fall asleep after their own orgasm, butches really know how to sexually please their women, all femmes present, including Diny, agreed. The butches beamed proudly.

Diny's remark obviously put this butch bragging into context. For all butches' erotic skills, an enduring relationship with a femme depends on the love between the partners. The conversation had started with a discussion of the obstacles to a b/f relationship, the constant fears of social ostracism, the need to be always vigilant so that people such as Diny's distant relative will not find out, the economic difficulties the butches face, and the internal tensions caused by the constant social pressure under which they live. Though the irrational fire of desire obviously awakened their love—in this instance a desire initiated by Diny, who was enthralled by the shy masculinity of her younger partner—the "treasure of love" (Brother James 1987), as the Bangladeshi poet Lalon writes in the poem that opens this chapter, maintained their relationship. Before exploring some indigenous notions of love and attraction, I offer this sketch of the social context in which this b/f couple lives.

Jakarta's lower-class b/f community comprises several hundred women, as far as I am aware, living all over the city. I first came into contact with a core group of them when I did fieldwork on the history of the Indonesian women's movement in the early 1980s. Soon after that period of fieldwork I was blacklisted, and I could return to Indonesia only after the fall of the dictator Suharto, in 1998. During my first return visit I could no longer find the women. They had moved out of the city center where I had first met them and had gone even more underground than in 1983, when a few of them had made a valiant but short-lived attempt to set up the first lesbian organization in Indonesia, called Perlesin (Persatuan Lesbian Indonesia) (Wieringa 1987, 1999).

The women's movement was one of the engines driving the democratization movement that brought Suharto down, and in 1998 the Koalisi Perempuan Indonesia (Indonesian Women's Coalition, KPI) was set up. This was the first women's mass movement, after the Suharto regime had banned the Communist-oriented mass women's organization Gerwani (Gerakan Wanita Indonesia Indonesian Women's Movement) in the wake of the mass murders that followed an army putsch in 1965 (Wieringa 2002). At its first congress in December 1998, the KPI drew up its work plan. Fifteen sectors were established; sexual minorities was sector 15. Two years later, sector 15 had come into operation, and some members of the b/f community had joined. When I returned to Indonesia in 2001 I was invited to a party they organized for me. There they asked me formally to write down their history, because they wanted to take part in the new democracy that Indonesia was struggling to establish. "We have also suffered under the military dictatorship," they told me, "and this must be known. How else can we become full citizens? You have written down the history of Gerwani, so they are rehabilitated now. We also want to regain our pride. We have known you for almost 20 years now, we trust you, so we ask you to write down the truth about our lives."

I accepted their request (though with postmodern hesitations about the "truth" I would be able to dig up). The request came at a sensitive moment for them. Although their lives were no longer under direct attack from the military, a new challenge had presented itself, this time from within the feminist movement to which they had hesitantly but courageously allied themselves. Some members of the KPI leadership felt that b/f behavior was old-fashioned, patriarchal, and oppressive, particularly to the femmes. They let it be known that if members of this community wanted to join the women's movement they had to conform to the new feminist ideology of gender equality. I had already confronted this attitude of those members of the feminist leadership of the KPI, arguing that a b/f lifestyle is one of the manifestations of women's same-sex life and that it is not up to other lesbians or feminists to simply denounce it (see also Wieringa 1999). If there is violence between the partners it should be addressed, but, I argued, b/f erotics is a powerful sexual style and perfectly legitimate when it is what both partners want. The coordinator of sector 15, a self-identified lesbian woman, agreed with this view. We organized a seminar at the office of the KPI with the members of the b/f community to discuss b/f dynamics and the research objectives. The participants agreed to share their life stories with me in the interest of a collective process of consciousness raising and coming out. It took two more years before I could start the research.

With the help of the dynamic coordinator of sector 15, 20 female-bodied persons were asked to participate in the research, 10 femmes, and 10 butches, all between the ages of 40 and 60, all of them lower or lower middle class. I selected this age range because I wanted to trace their histories from the first lesbian organization ever set up, Perlesin, through the New Order period. Most of them were couples, since one of the goals of the research was to investigate the dynamics between the partners. The methodology consisted of oral history interviews, which were all transcribed, focus-group discussions on specific themes that emerged out of the interviews, participant observation of various events in their lives, such as parties, dinners, and informal meetings, as well as seminars on specific topics, with outside participation. I also interviewed some middle-class key informants who had been active in setting up lesbian organizations in the 1990s.

Most interviews were conducted in the homes of the participants; some of the interviews, particularly with the butches, were conducted on the veranda of the KPI office. The femmes would not come there easily on their own because it was a "public" space. One or two members of the KPI always accompanied me. Their presence was particularly useful when the femmes were interviewed because the butches tended to be suspicious. They classified me as a butch and therefore a possible predator of their wives. This perception was magnified because I insisted on a private interview with each of my narrators. The members of the KPI who accompanied me would chat with the butch partner so the interview could be conducted without disturbance.

Several participants were members of the KPI, particularly the butches. Their femme partners would join if there were particular activities. But not all butches were comfortable with the fact that the KPI is a feminist and a woman's organization. Diny's partner, for instance, considers herself to be a man, or at least someone whose female body is less important than hir male soul, and therefore feels that it is not proper for hir to join a women's organization. All butches said they had male souls, but Diny's partner is the only one who decided that as a man in a female body s/he could not join a women's organization.

One of the characteristics of the modern Western world is the democratization of relationships in which the partners share sexual and emotional equality (Featherstone 1999). Giddens 1992 speaks of "plastic sexuality," a sexuality freed from the needs of reproduction, which has become possible since the wide availability of contraceptives. Indonesia under Suharto had one of the most "efficient" population-control movements. However, the drive to curb population growth never reduced patriarchal control over women, since contraceptives were available only to married women with the consent of their husbands (Katjasungkana 1998). So in Indonesia the availability of contraceptives as such is not what leads to an incipient movement toward greater equality between heterosexual partners. The idea of gender equality is spread through the human and women's rights movement and the processes of democratization. Because feminists hesitantly explore the potentialities of what Giddens (1992) calls the "pure relationship," a sexuality freed from the dominant role of the phallus, the b/f community in Jakarta is watching this development warily, for their first experiences with these feminists was that their lifestyles were denounced. For the moment they prefer to conform to the dominant gender regime in society, with its ethos of romantic love, in which possessiveness and jealousy are valued elements and women's oppression and male superiority are assumed. Such romantic, sexual possessiveness is expressed in a popular song, sung by a female singer, with the following refrain: "When I will have become your wife don't ever give up wanting to possess me."

The Jakarta b/f women I worked with claim a sexual citizenship, in which there is space for the gender transgression of the butches, while their partners claim "sexual normalcy" as "wives" of their butch husbands. The detraditionalization and egalitarianism that dominate the discourses within a Western gay/lesbian movement (see also Weeks 1999) seem to hold little attraction for the b/f community in Jakarta. Instead they choose to extend the boundaries of the niche they occupy. They are proud and out, though not as lesbians. The couples I interviewed live together, and their neighbors and families accept, sometimes after a lot of resistance, the particular arrangement they have forged. The butches are proud to be called "Om" (uncle) by their neighbors, while their femme partners take care to share all the normal activities expected of married women, such as participating in the women's neighborhood associations. In one case a couple even adopted a child so they could be a "normal" family. Several of the couples I interviewed looked after children, usually from earlier marriages of the femme partners. In this liminal way, they have more space for maneuvering than most self-identified lesbians of the more educated middle classes, some of whom I also interviewed. These women, who engage in a much more direct way with the global gay/lesbian discourse, set up Internet websites and chat-rooms. But most of them are not publicly out and it is hard for them to live together. Paradoxically, therefore, it seems that the secrecy and silence surrounding the sexual practices in which the b/f couples live, and which I discuss later in more detail, affords them a more public life as a couple than "out" lesbians are able to carve out for themselves.

The most happy couples I interviewed were all in long relationships. Although they all cited the erotic same-sex impulse as the motivating factor determining their choice of partner, they sought the more enduring bonding of souls and bodies that a love relationship entails. The butches are the most obvious gender transgressors, with their masculine haircuts, clothing, and body language, but the same-sex erotic energy and impulse of the femmes, the ostensibly more "'normal," supposedly "passive" partners, was often the motor that drove the relationship, as I illustrate later in the interview with Mira.

Urbanization affected them in different ways. Most of them had traveled great distances, as first-generation immigrants from other islands. After the isolation and loneliness of their youth, particularly for the butches, the metropolis offered them a sense of community, a community without roots, however. For although Indonesia has a history of gender transgression, particularly but not exclusively of male-bodied persons, this history was unknown to them.[4]

Members of the Jakarta b/f community, then, are negotiating their identities and subjectivities within a tight web of multiple and contradictory discourses, respecting some boundaries, rupturing others. They bargain for acceptance in their communities by adhering to established patterns of heteronormativity. But in doing so they subvert these norms at the same time (see also Butler 1993). Socially they are subversive because they disrupt the sex-gender order as the butch partners destabilize the established boundaries between bodies and gender behavior while their femme partners publicly uphold them. Sexually they are subversive because femme pleasure rather than the satisfaction of the male partner drives the relationship. This rupture of the established order, however, is not always recognized by their major political allies, the feminist lesbians. They point to the ways the b/f partners perform particular established patterns of heteronormative behavior and point to instances of violence and excessive jealousy on the part of the butches.

Passionate Aesthetics and B/F Dynamics

Indigenous ideas of romantic passion were fiercely embraced by the b/f couples who narrated me their life stories. Their passion followed the "ethic, aesthetic and etiquette" (Paz 1996) of heteronormative romance, though with their own adaptations of this model. This culture of love is very much inspired by the Javanese Hinduized court culture. The most popular masculine models are the virile, ascetic Arjuna, his robust warrior-brother, Bhima, and the romantic, invincible Raden Pandji. The first two are characters of the immensely popular Mahabharata; the exploits of Prince Pandji are a genre in itself.

The Panji stories probably originated in the 12th century. Because they belong to an oral tradition, there are many versions. The plot summary that follows is of one of the more well-known adaptations in East Java, after Meyboom-Italiaander 1924.

Prince Pandji, the younger son of the ruler of Djengallah was betrothed to his niece, Dewi Sekar Tadji, a daughter of the ruler of Kediri. They had never met. Once, while the prince was hunting, he passed the house of the regent, who invited him in for a drink. He was served by the beautiful youngest daughter of the regent, Dewi Angreni. The young prince fell hopelessly in love with her and decided to marry her. Upon seeing the beauty of Dewi Angreni, his father agreed to the marriage.

When the lord of Kediri learned that his future son-in-law had married another wife, he became enraged and declared war on his brother, the ruler of Djengallah. Their elder sister, a hermit, intervened, however, and persuaded the brothers not to wage war, since Raden Pandji could still marry Dewi Sekar Tadji. Dewi Angreni, being of lower birth, would be the secondary wife, while Dewi Sekar Tadji would be his official consort. But Prince Pandji refused to marry another wife than his beloved Dewi Angreni, violating the orders of his father. Enraged, the sovereign of Djengallah sent Prince Pandji on an errand and ordered his eldest son to murder Dewi Angreni. The dutiful prince obeyed the order of his father and killed Dewi Angreni in the forest.

When Raden Pandji returned to the court, he went straight to the rooms of his wife. When he learned she had been killed on the order of his father, the young prince went mad. In his madness he looked for his wife everywhere, in the rice fields and among the flower beds. When he and his followers came in the forest, they encountered the tree under which Dewi Angreni was buried. She had turned into a stone. He took her in his arms and went to the beach. He boarded a ship with his loyal retainer and some slaves, all the time holding his dead wife in his arms.

They were surprised by a hurricane that after seven nights threw them on the coast of Bali. The loyal courtier convinced the prince that he should finally put Dewi Angreni to rest, suggesting that they might be reunited by the gods if he had conquered many realms of his enemies. Prince Pandji ordered his slaves to dig a grave. As they prepared to lower the body of Dewi Angreni into the deep hole, she suddenly flew up to heaven. This was surely a sign the gods loved her, so Prince Pandji took heart and started waging war on the king of Bali. He changed his name and soon gained the reputation of being an invincible warrior. All the time the prince thought only of his beloved wife and refused to marry the other princesses who were offered to him.

The loyal courtier advised the prince, who had become tired of fighting, to rest in the forests of the realm of Kediri. The prince did not know where he was. It so happened that the ruler of Kediri was being attacked by the mighty lord of Metaoen. A hermit advised the sovereign of Kediri to ask for the help of an invincible hero who rested in one of his forests, promising him the hand of his daughter, Dewi Sekar Tadji. The lord of Kediri had been informed that her former betrothed, Prince Pandji, had been killed in a hurricane, so that she was free to marry another man. Prince Pandji, under his new name, accepted the request of the ruler of Kediri and went to his court.

When the big battle between Prince Pandji and the ruler of Metaoen was to begin, Dewi Sekar Tadji, who was also called "the fearless princess" because of her prowess in spear fighting, demanded that she join her future husband in the struggle. She mounted her invincible white elephant. The lord of Metaoen rode his largest elephant and bombarded Prince Pandji with spears, which the prince fended off with his hands. Enraged, the ruler of Metaoen demanded that they alight and continue the fight on the ground. Prince Pandji killed him with his sword, a gift of the gods.

Prince Pandji was delighted when he found that Dewi Sekar Tadji resembled Dewi Angreni and married the princess of Kediri. But this news made the lord of Djengallah explode in anger. Hadn't Dewi Sekar Tadji been promised to his son, Prince Pandji? Even though the prince had been swallowed up by the waves, his body had not been found, so their bond could not be broken and he ordered his elder son to attack the lord of Kediri. When the two brothers met, they were reunited. For forty days the gamelan orchestra played tunes of love and happiness to celebrate the lawful marriage of Prince Pandji, who now reassumed his old name, and Dewi Sekar Tadji.

On the fortieth day the happy couple went to an island, where they met a girl who so strongly resembled Dewi Angreni that the prince was shattered. At that moment a messenger from the gods descended from heaven and informed him that the Upper God, Batara Goeroe, had decided that no two human beings should be the same. And since Dewi Angreni resembled so strongly Dewi Sekar Tadji, as twin stars in the sky, the gods had turned Dewi Angreni into a ray of the moon. "To demonstrate to you the resemblance of these two women you love so much," the messenger told him, "Dewi Angreni returned momentarily to earth. From now on they will be one person, called Tjandra Kirana, Ray of the Moon, and her beauty will be as radiant as her name." And so it happened.[5]

   This story illustrates several elements that are echoed in the many popular present-day dangdut songs: the irrational attraction of the two lovers, mysterious yet involuntary, the bonding of souls that cannot be broken, even in death, the prowess, loyalty, and steadfastness of the lover who must win many battles to find his beloved. Sexual attraction turned into love is a bond forged by the gods (the popular Islamized expression is *anugerah Allah*, "a gift of Allah"). This etiquette of love still pervades society, appearing, for instance, in the popular dangdut song "Renungkanlah" (Just muse about it).

Rasa cinta pasti ada
Pada makluk yang bernyawa
Takan hilang selamanya
Sampai datang akhir masa
Takkan hilang salamanya
Sampai datang akhirmasa
Renunkanlah

Perasaan cinta insan sama ingin cinta dan dicinta
Bukan ciptaan manusia tapi takdir yang kuasa
Janganlah engkau pungkiri segala yang Tuhan beri
Rasa cinta[6]

Two more themes can be discerned in the exploits of Pandji and his two wives. The first is the strong bond, fusion even, of the co-wives. Far from being rivals they support each other and either they become one in the moon or one worships the other. This bonding of the two women is presented as something beautiful, "shining," and as an unfolding on which Pandji himself, though the husband of both of them, has little influence. This theme is paralleled in another couple of co-wives, Srikandhi and Sumbadra. Srikandhi is the warrior-wife of Prince Arjuna, who often rescues her meek co-wife, Sumbadra. Srikandhi also teaches her friend the art of archery, in which Srikandhi excels. Like Prince Pandji, Prince Arjuna is a valiant, virile, and attractive husband, but the strong bond between his two consorts exceeds the conjugal bond.

   The second theme, remarkable from a postcolonial perspective when the recorded histories of warrior women have been driven out of social consciousness, is the prowess of the two valiant princesses, Srikandhi and Dewi Sekar Tadji.[7] Although the 1924 version on which I drew does not contain an account of her actually fighting, Dewi Sekar Tadji must have excelled in that, considering her nickname "the fearless princess."

Contemporary middle-class lesbian women have been quick to grasp the potential of this strong female bonding and the association with bravery that two of the princesses have. In the early 1990s a group called Chandra Kirana existed, a few years later another group of young lesbian women was established, Swara Srikandhi (the voice of Srikandhi).

Thus, two of the most popular mythical stories provide the background on which a heteronormative pattern of love etiquette is built, as well as the possibility of lesbian transgression of that model: the bonding of body and souls of two female protagonists, with one of the partners excelling in the masculine ways of fighting and chivalry. Many butch women told me proudly they were called Little Srikandhi in their youth.

Another interesting theme is the gendered division of *akal* (sense, rational intelligence) and *nafsu* (passion, associated with both irrationality and passivity). Men are supposed to possess more *akal* (and pride themselves on that), while women are seen to be prone to *nafsu*. Yet on closer scrutiny there is much overlap between the genders, and those who possess the most *akal* among the five Pandawa brothers (central characters in the Mahabharata) can also behave in most foolish ways. The elder Pandawa brother, Yudistira, is presented as an eminently ascetic and wise king. Yet he is so consumed by his passion for gambling that he destroys his wife's honor, loses his kingdom, and sends the whole family into exile. The great spiritual warrior Arjuna is also an incorrigible womanizer. Draupadi, on one hand, the wife of the five Pandawa brothers, manages to get the brothers their freedom after Yudistira's bout of gambling and proves to be a much better negotiator than any of them. In the Panji epos, on the other hand, it is the hermit sister of the rulers of Djengallah and Kediri who scolds her hot-headed brothers when they want to wage war and resorts to diplomacy instead. Panji himself is seen to be so consumed by passion that he loses his mind when the object of his love dies.

In contrast to orientalist and postcolonial stereotypes of feminine passivity and meekness, modeled after Sumbadra, women's agency and erotic passion are recognized cultural patterns.[8] Likewise, the b/f couples I interviewed did not conform to the heteronormative pattern of masculine sexual aggression and feminine dependence, unless in an eroticized, consensual way. Often the femme's erotic energy fueled the relationship. The butches, who were quick to announce that they were the men in the relationship, immediately agreed that usually they were seduced by their wives and that it was their honor to satisfy the desires of their partners. To give an impression of the b/f dynamic I encountered, I present some fragments of what Mira, one of the most erotically outspoken femmes in my research, told me about her sexual history:

My first sexual experience was when I was 16 years old and renting rooms with three other girls in Central Jakarta. Since then I am usually the one who seduces. I am often a bit confused and wonder how come I am so attracted to women. . . .

"I was the active partner, I was aggressive, I took the initiative in touching, kissing, licking, massaging, pressing her body. I started it. And I know she enjoyed very much what I did to her, [because] she always reciprocated every movement of my body. She also touched mine and licked my whole body until we both got an orgasm. . . . Since then I knew that I enjoy sex with women very much. But though we had sex very often we didn't have the kind of commitment to each other that we would say we have a relationship. When I was 18 years old I met Rita, who worked in the same night club as I did. She was a drug user and always needed money. Although our lovemaking was very sweet, Rita would sometimes let herself be made love to by men, in exchange for money. I loved her very much and knew from then on that I was 100 percent a lesbian, for I really wanted to possess her. I started to feel truly jealous.

"When I split with Rita I started seducing so many women that if I had been a man they would have called me a playboy. Finally in Jakarta I met a true butch and I seduced her. My mother became furious and forced me to marry a man. I stayed with him for two weeks and then ran away with a woman lover. Because I was pregnant I went back to my husband, though I never enjoyed having sex with him. After the birth of my second child I finally met and seduced the butch with whom I have stayed for 18 years since then. She already had a lover but separated from her to live with me. S/he looked so masculine, my children at first didn't know she was a woman. I also called hir "papa." In this relationship with my butch lover I really played the housewife. I did the domestic work, for actually I like that very much. I always made up our bed in as romantic a fashion as possible, so my butch partner would be very much aroused. I always wore sexy underwear, combed my hair, and applied perfume before we went to bed. In our lovemaking I always took the initiative. I am very aggressive. I always tried to find a position that would make me satisfied. I was usually on top and wanted to get an orgasm by whatever means possible. I have always thoroughly enjoyed sex, I could make love from 8 o'clock at night till 5 in the morning, and get up to seven orgasms."

Possessive romantic love and femme erotic energy are two themes that immediately emerge from the interview with Mira. Butch gender transgression is a common theme in the stories the butches told me. All butches said they had experienced gender nonconformity at a very young age. As they phrased it during the research, their subjectivity was built on the realization that they had a masculine soul. Later they became aware of their sexual attraction to women. For most femmes, however, sexual attraction to a butch was their first experience of gender nonconformity. Because they felt they were primarily attracted to the masculinity of their partners, they continued to identify themselves as "women." All femmes cited sexual satisfaction as an important reason they stayed with their partners. This admission made their butch partners proud, as the fragment about Diny and her butch partner shows, but also insecure. For what else could they offer their wives? Most of them experienced great economic problems. They were rarely accepted in the kind of masculine jobs they wanted. Diny and her partner are exceptions; they are moderately well off largely because of the business acumen of Diny, who initially employed and later spurred on her partner.

Both butches and femmes agreed that a "good" butch husband must primarily demonstrate responsibility not only erotically but financially. Husbands in general are supposed to give gifts to their wives. Wives don't have to reciprocate financially; instead they are supposed to feed the husband and prove their commitment by ensuring that the husband is provided with a constant supply of her favorite foods and snacks. At the moment, the primary area in which husbands have to demonstrate their financial responsibility is in their contribution to the education of their children. Their failure to do so is a cause of great bitterness, even if the wife is much richer. Good husbands should also accompany their wives to, or at least pick them up from, social events. Finally, husbands should not gamble and go womanizing; they should be loyal.

These expectations constitute the gender ideology, *kodrat*, advocated by the New Order regime Women are supposed to follow the Sumbadra model and be meek, sexually shy, obedient, self-sacrificing wives and devoted mothers. They are the ones responsible for the social harmony among neighbors and within the family. Women are also supposed to provide loving care (*momong*) to their husbands. Men are supposed to be the economic providers. They control public space and are supposed to be the spiritual and political guides of "their" women (Wieringa 2003).

This gender regime, as indicated earlier, is a one-sided interpretation of the traditional behavior of the Javanese nobility. Since the Javanese have always been politically dominant in the republic, this model became the hegemonic model for other ethnic groups and social classes as well. It is the model the f/b community attempts to emulate in their quest to be assimilated. As elsewhere, this pattern is clothed in the trappings of heterosexual romance, in which women's passivity and obedience is eroticized. The Indonesian model of romantic love, as endlessly portrayed in novels, television soaps, and the popular dangdut songs, emphasizes the extent to which the two partners possess each other. A common saying is "Cemburu tanda cinta" (Jealousy is a sign of love). It is even written on the back of trucks. Possessive jealousy is not seen as pathological; it is explained away as the inevitable sign of a great love.

Thus this *kodrat* has a strong influence on the intimacy of the f/b couples I interviewed. In many ways they try to conform to its ideals. The butches display various forms of chivalrous behavior, opening car doors, carrying parcels, making themselves useful to the household in the ways men would (though these ways are rather limited, since cooking and cleaning are not considered to fall within their domain).

Butches try to live up to those ideals, but since their gender-transgressive ways are not always accepted by employers, they find it hard to acquire the financial means to do so. This problem is compounded by lack of education: many butches left school at an early age, refusing to wear a school uniform with a skirt. Many b/f couples therefore have money troubles, which affect their relation deeply. During my research I watched the break-up of a relationship between Retno and Yusup. When I first met them, they were very much in love, and Retno was sitting on Yusup's lap, spoon feeding hir hir favorite food. However, Yusup, who had been a minor trader, lost her business in the wake of the 2002 bombings in Bali. After that their relationship deteriorated. Yusup became insecure, realizing s/he no longer commanded the respect s/h earlier enjoyed and became intensely jealous of Retno, who worked as a singer in a karaoke bar. Although Yusup tried valiantly to become more of a houseman, her frustration took over and when s/he became violent, exploding in a jealous fit of rage, Retno ended the relationship.

When butches do have regular work, however, they, like their wives, feel they are entitled to the complete loyalty of their partners. Ahmad, for instance, the trusted driver of a wealthy expat, was in a longstanding relationship with Indrawati. Indrawati preferred to keep their relationship secret, because she had children from her previous, male, partner and did not want them to know about her love for a woman. She therefore hesitated to come and live with Ahmad in the house s/he had acquired. Ahmad felt, however, that since s/he was a good provider and worked hard, s/he was entitled to the same perks of marriage hir male colleagues enjoyed, a wife at home, cooking and washing clothes for hir. Frustrated by Indrawati's hesitations, s/he had taken a younger lover who was prepared to live up to Ahmad's expectations. Indrawati desperately tried to prove her loyalty to Ahmad. Once, when we were all watching television in the house of another b/f couple, Indrawati, who had just entered the house, gave her mobile phone to Ahmad, who went quickly through the messages and deleted them all before handing it back to Indrawati, explaining to me, "You know, she doesn't know how to do that herself."

"Yes," Indrawati joined in, "Ahmad gave me this phone, so s/he can always reach me. When I receive messages Ahmad must know who they are from, so I ask hir to delete them."

Ahmad to me: "She doesn't want to learn."

Indrawati: "No, I don't need to know that, for now Ahmad can always see that I am loyal to hir and that I don't have contact with anyone s/he wouldn't know about.

Ahmad to me: "I don't show her my messages!"

Sex in the City

Jakarta's b/f couples live in one of the largest cities in the world, where increasing consumerism and a decadent capitalist lifestyle occur side by side with rising Muslim fundamentalism and adherence to traditional values of indigenous ethnic groups. The growth of religious fundamentalisms reflects global tendencies as well. Not only do the different fundamentalist groups relate to foreign religious organizations (though the "foreignness" of Saudi Arabia is felt to be less alien than the foreignness of the United States), but Muslim fundamentalism is fueled partly by the aggressive politics of the West, particularly the U.S. invasion of Iraq. This picture is complicated by the simmering resentment that is the legacy of the atrocities and racism of Dutch colonialism.

In moral questions, then, such as those related to sexuality, these global influences are variously invoked. The governor of Jakarta, for instance, in an effort to boost his image among Jakarta's pious Muslim groups following the first gay/lesbian film festival in 2003, allowed local thugs free rein to ransack bars and nightclubs during the Muslim fasting month of Ramadan and to utter death threats to gay/lesbian groups on television.

Jakarta is a melting pot in which the many ethnic groups of the Indonesian archipelago live side by side. For some, such as Diny, their old-Jakartan Betawi (the Dutch name for Jakarta) identity is the only ethnic identity they have, but most inhabitants maintain their original ethnic identities as well, whether they are first-generation immigrants or they were born in the city. Despite this diversity, there is a great emphasis on national unity and social harmony (*rukun*) and consensus. *Rukun*, however, is more apparent than real. What is important is that the surface is not disturbed by knowledge of facts that might rupture the tenuous and unstable religious or social consensus. This concern partly explains why the b/f couples I met are able to live in relative peace among their neighbors. My respondents often replied, "Nggak usah tahu" (They don't need to know) when I asked whether their b/f relation was accepted by their neighbours. *Tahu* refers to a rational way of knowing and is different from *merasa*, a much more implicit way of understanding issues. *Tahu* is associated with speaking, *merasa* with silence. A third level of knowing is *mengerti*, which is a thorough understanding of issues, including the social consequences these issues might entail. These variations in levels of understanding mean that as long as the couple does not force the neighbors to openly acknowledge their relationship as a sexual union, and as long as the nature of their love is not brought to the public surface of *tahu*, let alone of *mengerti*, their relationship need not be condemned. The Western, Protestant insistence on a rational "truth" that speaks its name has little value here. *Merasa* is seen as much more valuable because it does not disrupt social harmony. Insisting on rational "truths" is at times considered rude, for it may force issues to the surface that people would rather not be confronted with (see also Berman 1998). Diny, in the conversation recorded earlier, was loath to speak about the tensions she faced. I was supposed to know all about them without her mentioning them explicitly. Speaking about them would only add to the pain that they had already caused. And who would want to aggravate anyone else's troubles?

While there are considerable ethnic variations in this pattern (Javanese, for instance, are considered to be more secretive, while Batak are more outspoken) it is widespread. While facilitating a range of socially accepted norms, as long as the divergence is not too great, this culture of silence also hides underlying power relations and masks violence and discrimination. Gay and lesbian activists (Oetomo 2001; Ratri 2000) and women's rights advocates (Katjasungkana 2002; Komnas 2002; Syahrir 2000) try to break that silence. The b/f couples I worked with, however, negotiated their identities within the margins of *rukun*, outwardly accepting some established gender patterns (butches occupy the "public" space; their "wives" are responsible for the household) while, internalizing certain characteristics (jealousy, possessiveness, romantic passion, butch economic responsibility) and rupturing others (feminine sexual passivity, women's emotional dependence).

Yet this *kampungan* lifestyle incorporating public silence on sexual matters takes place in a city where the diversity of sexual practices is much like that found in any other global metropolis. In the bestselling collection *Jakarta Undercover: Sex 'n the City*, the former Islamic scholar Emka (2002) documents a wide variety of sexual possibilities the metropolitan society can participate in, using such labels as "sex sandwich sashimi girls," to "blue nite cowboy strippers" and the "sex-change party of the year" (Emka 2002). Jakarta also has a vibrant gay scene (Priaga 2003) and numerous venues for paid sex (see, e.g.. Gunawan 1997, 2002). Whereas most of these activities take place under the cover of silence, this public silence was violently ruptured in 2003 by the sensational appearance on the national scene of the dangdut dancer and singer Inul. The question whether her phenomenal "drilling" dance should be considered pornography and banned or should be merely enjoyed as an attractive dance style held the nation in its grip for months (Gunawan 2003), drowning the debates on the rampant and seemingly endless political and legal corruption, graft, and growing fundamentalism. Interestingly, defendants of her style of performing invoked such "modern" issues as her right to work and earn a living (Inul is from a poor rural Eastern Java background) and freedom of expression. Her adversaries called upon "traditional" moral values, invoking an invented past of Islamic sexual purity, quite at odds with established traditions of professional female entertainers such as the Western Javanese *ronggeng* associated with sex work. The hype around Inul brought to the fore that just below this surface of public silence on sexuality, it is one of the most popular topics of discussion in private conversations. In offices, among friends, in all kinds of informal situations, people continually make sexual jokes or innuendo.

The controversy sparked by the perceived erotic dancing of Inul served another purpose as well. It played into the growing anxiety of what it means to be a Muslim. The spate of Muslim terrorism and particularly the 2002 bombing of two nightclubs in Bali had shattered the complacent denial of the existence of an indigenous Islamic terrorist threat. Foreign intelligence services had long since alerted Indonesia to the dangerous radicalism of such groups as the Jema'ah Islamiyah. But staunch Muslims, led by then vice-president Hamzah Haz, had put these warnings down to Western hatred of Islam. The media hype around Inul brought the public debate on Muslim identity to safer ground, sexual morality. Apparently it was easier to build a Muslim identity on control over women's sexuality than on control over a radical terrorist group.

Indonesia has the largest Muslim population of the world. It is commonly assumed that some 90 percent of its 220 million inhabitants adhere to this faith. The majority of Indonesian Muslims follow a moderate interpretation (Boland 1982).

Yet there have always been tensions between radical Muslim groups who are prepared to fight for the introduction of Muslim law (syariah) and the secular state (Van Dijk 1981). During the reign of General Suharto, Jakarta came to be seen in the eyes of many as the symbol of a decadent and corrupt nationalism (Forrester and James 1998). The sudden process of decentralization initiated by Suharto's successor, President Habibie, led to a search for new local identities (Aspinall and Fealy 2003). Ethnicity and customary law gained more legitimacy (and were re-invented in the process); a renewed emphasis on Islamic values became another source of inspiration. As in other parts of the Muslim world (see, for instance, Yuval-Davis 1997), control over women's lives and sexuality is a crucial aspect in this process of Islamization. In certain regions women can no longer go out after a certain time of night without a male relative accompanying them. There have been incidents in Aceh, where women who have not covered their heads with the obligatory head scarf have had their hair cut off. Aceh, which is the throes of a violent military conflict between the national army and independence fighters, is the only province in Indonesia so far where syariah law is in force. In this climate of growing Islamic radicalization, homosexuality in general is seen as un-Islamic and imported from the West.

The development of democracy is a fairly new process in Indonesia. After a protracted war of independence against the authoritarian Dutch colonial state, Indonesia became fully independent only in 1949. The legacy of this struggle was the entrenchment of the military in the heart of Indonesia's politics (Jenkins 1984) and a state philosophy consisting of five principles (Pancasila) in which human rights were not recognized. The focus was on stability and social harmony, rather than on the recognition of individual entitlements to justice and equality. Among the dominant ethnic Javanese and other communities, feudal ideas about state power and hierarchies remained strong. President Sukarno, frustrated by the infighting and inefficiency of the parliamentarians, decided to sidetrack Parliament. In 1959 he set up a system euphemistically called "Guided Democracy" (Lev 1966). His successor, General Suharto, perfected the art of control of the people, stifling any opposition to his rule (Vatikiotis 1993). His regime was built in the aftermath of a genocide of between 1 and 3 million people, which was orchestrated by the military who created the myth of the castration of the nations' most senior generals (not including General Suharto). Through a combination of physical terror and economic capitalist development, the people were maneuvered into obedience. Any discussion of democracy, liberal thought, and human rights was linked with the emergence of a "new communist movement" that opened a Pandora's box of sexual orgies and mass murders, and the sexualization and demonization of women's quest for (political) autonomy (Wieringa 2003).

While democracy grew, beginning in 1998, Islamic fundamentalism also spread. The new ultra-right Islamic party, the PKS (Partai Keadilan Sejahtera, Party for Justice and Prosperity) gained around 6 percent of the vote in the 2004 national elections. The party is very strong in Jakarta, where they came out as the strongest faction, with 18 of the 75 seats of the Regional Council. They are utterly conservative in issues of women's and gay/lesbian rights. So far there are few signs that the Enlightenment values of rationalism, liberalism, humanism and personal autonomy, in which the global gay/lesbian movement developed, are accepted beyond a small educated urban elite of society, particularly in the NGO sector.

Conclusion

To what extent does the b/f community in Jakarta that I researched relate to globalizing tendencies? Adams et al. (1999) discuss the factors that led to the emergence of gay/lesbian visibility worldwide. They link this development to the growth of a modern capitalist world system, in which greater personal autonomy in the choice of one's partner, the ascendance of romantic love ideologies, and the expansion of subjective feelings as a "ground for bonding" combine with urbanization and the growth of a public space outside of the control of the traditional community. If these conditions exist, they suggest, a modern rights-based gay/lesbian movement can emerge that will then develop a two-part strategy, fighting discrimination and establishing a public space of its own. The picture in Indonesia, however, is more complex than this perspective suggests. The members of the Jakarta f/b community who shared their lives with me have carved out a public space for themselves by assimilating with their surroundings and at the same time pursuing a politics of separatism, as their most intimate relations are exclusively with the members of their own b/f community. They did this all through the repressive Suharto's New Order regime without much contact if any with an outside, global movement. They subscribe to an indigenous model of romantic love and a local gender ideology, both adapting themselves to and subverting them.

Altman, speaking particularly about Southeast Asia, suggests that "the gay world—less obviously the lesbian, largely due to marked differences in women's social and economic status—is a key example of emerging global subcultures, where members of particular groups have more in common across national or continental boundaries than they do with others in their own geographically defined societies" (2001:86–87). Adams et al. note the significant national differences in the communities described in their anthology; yet they maintain that although one may not very well speak of a blanket global gay movement, "national imprints of a global movement" are clearly discernible (1999:368). I feel these authors put too much stress on the determining influence "from above" (i.e., from globalizing or structural processes) on the existence of indigenous same-sex communities, such as those I researched. I do not see them as a "national imprint" or as a "global subculture" but rather as an autonomous national community that is firmly rooted in Indonesia's various traditions of transgender cultures and in Indonesia's gender regimes, such as that related to women's *kodrat* (nature). Recently, ideas of androgyny and politically informed practices of gender bending have become more common, partly spurred on by the budding feminist movement. But (so far) these practices have gained little currency in the b/f culture with which I worked. Jakarta's younger, middle-class lesbian groups have been more receptive to these ideas. The egalitarian ideology associated with these concepts is embraced to a certain extent by the members of sector 15. This has led to some confrontations a postmodern lifestyle. Yet Bauman does point to an significant element that most scholars who confidently discuss the proliferation of a global queer movement seem to ignore: the importance of desire and love. Those who focus on the constructed identities of gays and lesbians across the world downplay the power of the sexual agency of most people. If, as Giddens (1992) maintains, the self can be seen as a reflexive project, then identity formation is not a one-way phenomenon, fueled only by the discursive power of the knowledges inherent in the social formation in which one lives.

Without desire, there is no awakening as love, as Lalon sings. Paz (1996) maintains that "amatory feelings" are the basis of the aesthetics of love. The b/f desire as experienced by the participants in this research led them to a search for love within the confines of the complex Indonesian gender regime. While outwardly assimilating to their social surroundings, they disrupt the *kodrat* that circumscribes masculinity and femininity in the Indonesian context. Rather than identifying with a global queer culture, they reach out to modern, global discourses of human, women's, and gay/lesbian rights, carefully picking what suits them in their quest for sexual citizenship. Firmly rooted in an indigenous ideology of romantic love and a traditional culture of public silence about sexuality, and besieged by new discourses of sexual oppression by the rising fundamentalist movement in Indonesia (itself a global phenomenon), they weigh the risks and opportunities that a political process of coming out means.

Notes

1. The words *butch* and *femme* were not used by most of the respondents in this research, though they were aware of them. Younger butch women would sometimes use the term *butchie* for themselves and their male-identified friends. The male-identified participants in this research would usually refer to themselves as *laki laki* (men), while their feminine partners all said they were just "women" and "wives" of their partners. For the sake of convenience I refer to this group as a "butch-femme" community, although it has to be understood that the way they perform their butchness and femmeness is specifically Indonesian. When I refer to the butches I use *s/he* and *hir* to denote their subjectivity as possessing a male soul in a female body. I have attempted to approximate local grammatical usage in my incorporation of these terms throughout the chapter.
2. The notion of "traditional" is problematic in this regard. It refers to what is seen by the present-day society as "traditional," a reinvention by colonial, postcolonial, and conservative religious forces, in which earlier notions of gender transgression and female prowess were ignored. See Kumar 2000 and Stoler 1995 for accounts of how colonialism introduced certain sexist notions, and Boelstorff 2005 and Blackwood 2005 for several accounts of indigenous practices of gender transgression.
3. I use pseudonyms and otherwise hide the identities of the participants in the research.
4. I took pictures of a scene in the Balinese version of the *wayang* story of Bhima Swarga, in which the hero sets out to the underworld to rescue his parents. He comes upon two crossdressing *banci*, a female-bodied and a male-bodied person, and asks the guardian of the underworld what their sins are that they have to remain here. The answer is, "It is all right, they will soon go to heaven. Their situation is just something out of the ordinary" (Pucci

1992). I enlarged one of the pictures and hung it up in the KPI office to stimulate discussion. Members of sector 15 soon after started referring to their cultural roots.

5.   A later version (Rosjidi 1983) has it that Dewi Angraini was not killed but instead fell ill while Prince Pandji and she were on their way to meet Dewi Sekar Tadji. When everybody was finally together, Dewi Angraini died. Dewi Sekar Tadji and Prince Pandji then saw a light flying from the body of Dewi Anggraini to the moon. Because Dewi Sekar Tadji's face shone like the full moon, Prince Pandji loved both women as one. Dewi Sekar Tadji from then on worshipped the full moon, called Tjandra Kirana.

6.   The feeling of love surely will be / for creatures with a soul / it will not disappear / until the end of the times / it will never disappear / until the end of times, just muse on that. / The feelings of human beings who want to love and be loved / is not created by human beings but it is a strong [sign of] predestination. / Don't you ever deny all that God gives / this feeling of love. (Thanks to Rini of KPI, who loves singing dangdut songs and provided me the texts of some of the most popular ones.)

7.   See Wieringa 2002 for a description of the way the women guerilla fighters who joined the national liberation war against the Dutch are ignored in present-day historiography. Gerwani, the communist-oriented women's organization, consciously drew on the model of valiant womanhood and frequently invoked Srikandhi's name.

8.   For the way the New Order government of President Suharto imposed a model of feminine obedience and passivity on the nation, see Wieringa 2002, 2003.

References

Adams, Barry D., Jan Willem Duyvendak, and André Krouwel, eds.
    1999   The Global Emergence of Gay and Lesbian Politics: National Imprints of a Worldwide Movement. Philadelphia: Temple University Press.
Altman, Dennis
    2001   Global Sex. Chicago: University of Chicago Press.
Aspinall, Edward, and Greg Fealy, eds.
    2003   Local Power and Politics in Indonesia: Decentralization and Democratization. Singapore: ISEAS.
Baumen, Zygmunt
    1999   On Postmodern Uses of Sex. In Love and Eroticism. Mike Featherstone, ed. Pp. 19–35. London: Sage.
Berman, Laine
    1998   Speaking through the Silence: Narratives, Social Conventions, and Power in Java. Oxford: Oxford University Press.
Blackwood, Evelyn
    2005   Gender Transgression in Colonial and Post-Colonial Indonesia. Journal of Asian Studies 64(4):849–879.
Boellstorff, Thomas Davis
    2005   The Gay Archipelago: Sexuality and Nation in Indonesia. Princeton: Princeton University of Press.
Boland, Bernard Johan
    1982   The Struggle of Islam in Modern Indonesia. The Hague: Martinus Nijhoff.
Brother James, trans.
    1987   The Songs of Lalon, Translations. Dhaka: University Press.
Butler, Judith
    1993   Bodies That Matter: On the Discursive Limits of "Sex." New York: Routledge.
Emka, Moammar
    2002   Jakarta Undercover: Sex 'n the City. Yogyakarta: Galang Press.

Featherstone, Mike, ed.
 1999   Love and Eroticism. London: Sage.
Forrester, Geoff, and Ronald James, eds.
 1998   The Fall of Soeharto. Bathurst: Crawford.
Giddens, Anthony
 1992   The Transformation of Intimacy: Sexuality, Love, and Eroticism in Modern Societies.
        Stanford: Stanford University Press.
Gunawan, Rudy FX
 1997   Pelacur and Politikus. Jakarta: Pustaka Utama Grafiti.
 2002   Krisis Orgasme Nasional. Yogyakarta: Galang.
 2003   Mengebor Kemunafikan: Inul, Seks dan Kekuasaan. Yogyakarta: Galang.
Jenkins, David
 1984   Suharto and His Generals: Indonesian Military Politics, 1975–1983. Ithaca: Cornell
        Modern Indonesian Project.
Katjasungkana, Nursyahbani
 1998   Hak Kesehatan Reproduksi dan Seksual Remaja Dalam Perspektif Hukum. Mimeo.
        Jakarta: APIK.
 2002   Kasus-Kasus Hukum Kekerasan Terhadap Perempuan.Yogyakarta: Galang.
Komnas Perempuan
 2002   Peta Kekerasan: Pengalaman Perempuan Indonesia. Jakarta: Amepro.
Kumar, Ann
 2002   Imagining Women in Javanese Religion: Goddesses, Ascetes, Queens, Consorts, Wives.
        In Other Pasts: Women, Gender and History in Early Modern Southeast Asia. Barbara
        Watson Andaya, ed. Pp. 87–104. Honolulu: Center for Southeast Asian Studies:
        University of Hawaii.
Lev, Daniel S.
 1966   The Transition to Guided Democracy: Indonesian Politics, 1957–1959. Ithaca: Cornell
        University Press.
Meyboom-Italiaander, Jos
 1924   Javaansche Sagen, Mythen en Legenden. Zutphen: Thieme.
Oetomo, Dede
 2001   Memberi Suara pada yang Bisu. Yogyakarta: Galang.
Paz, Ottavio
 1996   The Double Flame: Essay on Love and Eroticism. London: Haverill.
Priaga, Lanang
 2003   Menembus Kaum Gay Jakarta. Jakarta: Abdi Tandur.
Pucci, Idanna
 1992   Bhima Swarga: The Balinese Journey of the Soul. Boston: Bullfinch.
Ratri, M.
 2000   Lines, Kumpulan Cerita Perempuan di Garis Pinggir. Jakarta: Millennium Publisher.
Rosjidi, A.
 1983   Chandra Kirana. 3rd edition. Jakarta: Pustaka Raya.
Syahrir, Kartini
 2000   Negara dan Kekerasan Terhadap Perempuan. Jakarta: Yayasan Jurnal Perempuan.
Stoler, Ann
 1995   Race and the Education of Desire: Foucault's History of Sexuality and the Colonial
        Order of Things. Durham: Duke University Press.
Van Dijk, Cornelis
 1981   Rebellion under the Banner of Islam: The Darul Isam in Indonesia. The Hague:
        Martinus Nijhoff.
Vatikiotis, Michael R. J.
 1993   Indonesian Politics under Suharto. New York: Routledge.

Weeks, Jeffrey
  1999 Sexuality and Its Discontents: Meanings, Myths, and Modern Sexualities. New York: Routledge and Kegan Paul.
Wieringa, Saskia
  1987 Uw Toegenegen Dora D., Reisbrieven. Amsterdam: Furie.
  1999 Desiring Bodies or Defiant Cultures: Butch-Femme Lesbians in Jakarta and Lima. *In* Female Desires, Same-Sex Relations and Transgender Practices across Cultures. Evelyn Blackwood and Saskia E. Wieringa, eds. Pp. 206–230. New York: Columbia University Press.
  2002 Sexual Politics in Indonesia. Houndmills: Palgrave.
  2003 The Birth of the New Order State in Indonesia: Sexual Politics and Nationalism. Journal of Women's History 15(1):70–92.
Yuval-Davis, Nira
  1997 Gender and Nation. London: Sage.

Part II
Love, Sex, and the
Social Organization of Intimacy

4

"Love Makes a Family"
Globalization, Companionate Marriage, and the Modernization of Gender Inequality

Jennifer S. Hirsch

At a recent meeting of the Movimiento Familiar Cristiano (Christian Family Movement) in Degollado, Jalisco, Mexico, we celebrated the six couples who had just returned from a three-day marriage retreat. They spoke about how they felt closer to each other and to God, about the importance of being reminded not to take their spouse for granted. Afterward, there were *tacos de papas* (potato tacos) and cake; as they cut the cake, couples stood up to feed each other a piece as they had done, perhaps, the night they were first married. Between the testimonials and the tacos, one of the town's four Roman Catholic priests rose to praise these couples and the Christian Family Movement for serving as a counterweight to globalization's bad influence on marriage. He mentioned Britney Spear's recent same-day marriage and divorce, the work of animal rights advocates who are, according to him, trying to legalize marriages between people and animals, and the international gay marriage movement, which, he said, is clearly working against what the Bible tells us, which is that a man should marry a woman to love and to procreate with.

In small-town church halls, big city newspapers, and national TV channels, debates rage in Mexico about globalization, love, and marriage. The hotly contested Ley de Convivencia, for example, a law that would grant domestic partner benefits to homosexual or heterosexual unmarried couples, was roundly condemned by the conservative press in Guadalajara as a part of the international gay rights conspiracy.[1] On the other side of the spectrum, progressive social activists complained vociferously about how the Third World Congress on the Family, entitled La familia natural y el futuro de las naciones: Crecimiento, desarrollo y libertad (The natural family and the future of nations: growth, development, and liberty) reflected the George W. Bush administration's moral colonialism and its efforts to impose neoconservative family policies on their southern neighbors (Sánchez 2004). All this speechifying, however, is essentially screaming to close the barn door after the horse is gone. Love already makes a family in Mexico; over the past generation, intimacy and pleasure have come to be seen as the building blocks of modern kinship. In this chapter, I describe these changing Mexican marital ideals, explore their relationship to globalization, relate this change in Mexico to broader historical and current global shifts in ideas about love and marriage, and close with some questions we might explore about love and globalization.

Degollado, Jalisco, is a small town in rural western Mexico. The 2000 census counted nearly fifteen thousand people, but the actual population depends greatly—as it has for nearly a century—on the season: in the late autumn the returning *norteños* bring dollars, Chicago Bulls and Atlanta Braves baseball hats, DVD players, pickup trucks, and—perhaps most important—a chance for all the girls promenading around the plaza to get married. The economy of love is intricately interwoven with the political economy of migration: young men return in November and December to court, marry, or march in the procession of returning migrants during the fiesta of the Virgin of Guadalupe, but they also come in the winter because it is the slow season in the U.S. agriculture and construction businesses. Today's migrants are the sons and grandsons—and, increasingly, daughters and granddaughters—of those who built the railroads, followed the harvests in California, and worked in the meat-packing industry in Chicago.

Los norteños say that there is no work in Degollado, but this is not entirely true: in this thriving county seat, which supports five money-changing places and two Internet cafes, there is serious money to be made in residential construction, in the workshops that carve the local pink sandstone for regional use and for export, in agave for tequila production, and in the commercial aspects of social life: the two discos, the cantinas, the billiards, and the table-dance halls that ring the town. Others eke out a living in the local pork-production industry, in its death throes since the early 1990s, in beauty salons, grocery stores, and ice-cream parlors, or as doctors, teachers, and accountants.

Couples who married in the 1950s and 1960s talked about marriage as a bond of obligation, held together by an ideal of respect and the mutual fulfillment of gendered responsibilities.[2] The man's job was to *arrimar* (to bring money into the house), and the woman's was to produce meals, wash and iron the clothes, raise well-mannered children, and keep a clean house. Love, if it existed, was the result of living well together, but it was not necessarily the goal. Women married knowing that if their husband turned out to be a drunk or violent or a womanizer or—worst of all, *desobligado* (not taking care of his family)—it would be up to them to *aguantar* (to put up with it). Some lived well; Doña Luz, for example, after 50 years of marriage, still puts on lipstick and earrings to go to Sunday Mass with her husband, after which they sit together contentedly on a bench in the plaza as couples promenade by. Doña Catarina, in contrast, suffered through her husband's violent drunken binges, and then a 20-year absence while he lived in the next town over with his lover while she raised their seven children—and yet she still took him back when he showed up, old and wrinkled and sick, asking her to care for him while he died. Both of these women crafted their marriages in relation to this older marital ideal, in which women earn respect through complying with the gendered ideals for public and private behavior, through following the steps in a dance led by their husbands. Marriage was a system for organizing social reproduction, not a project for personal satisfaction.

For men and women who married after about the mid 1980s, the measure of a good marriage is *confianza* (intimacy or trust). These younger men and women described several key features of this new style of marriage. First, they frequently emphasized to me that they made decisions together, that they share *el mando de la casa* (the decision-making power at home). Second, they talked about—and sometimes followed through with—the importance of spending time together as a family. A *buen padre* (good father) now means not just a man who provides for his wife and children but also one who enjoys spending time with them. Third, the younger men and women talked about the softening of a strictly gendered division of labor: men do not wash clothes or change diapers, but they might at least get up to get themselves a glass of water during a meal, and women are increasingly economically active outside the home. These actions, however, are seen as "helping"—it is still men's job to support the family, and women's to wash, cook, and clean.

Masculine performances of power, however, are interwoven with this apparently more egalitarian gendered division of labor. For example, after a leisurely Sunday lunch at the home of Gabriela and Mauricio (the sort of Mexican lunch that begins at 2:00 p.m. and winds down after dark with yet another trip to the candy store for the children and the last drops of a full bottle of tequila for the adults), my Mexican colleague, Sergio Meneses (who assisted with the data collection) sat in the backyard with Mauricio, enjoying a cigarette as the sun waned. Gabriela and I were in the kitchen, washing up, with the children underfoot. We heard Mauricio's sharp whistle—and Gabriela flew out the door to see what he wanted. After she brought him his water with ice in it, he lifted an eyebrow proudly at Sergio, as if to say "all this"—the pool, the house, the lawn, the perfectly seasoned meat and delicious salsas—"and she waits on me too."

The most prominent generational difference in marital ideals, however, is the importance younger couples give to *confianza*, to intimacy, and the way that mutually pleasurable sex demonstrates and enhances this *confianza*. Couples court to develop intimacy through shared secrets and kisses, and after marriage the development and maintenance of emotional and sexual intimacy is a central task of relationship building. Discursively (though not always actually), pleasure is the key force holding relationships together.

Veronica and Gustavo, for example, have been married for just over two years. He is a stone carver and she takes care of their two-year-old daughter. She told me, laughing, that they first kissed after only two weeks of dating and that he wrote her love letters while they dated. Once they married, she recounted, they had sex several times a day, keeping things spicy with the lingerie he bought her and the porn videos they occasionally watch. Gustavo, in his conversations with Sergio about their marriage, spoke as well about their intimacy, emphasizing not just its physical aspects but the fact that he wanted to marry her, rather than any of his previous girlfriends, because of the quality of their communication and the strength of their emotional connection. There are ways, though, in which Veronica's early married life differs little from her mother's experience. She and Gustavo live in a two-room shack, adjoining his father's house, which Veronica does not leave without his permission.

She has no access to the money he earns—and is not even really sure how much it is. On Saturdays when the workday ends early, he will usually bring a kilo of *carnitas* (deep fried pork) or rotisserie chicken for lunch—but sometimes he does not show up until the next morning, having left her lunch to get cold in the car while he drinks or plays pool with his friends. If she asks him where he was, he gets angry. Even if he wanted to leave her a message, though, he could not do so; his sisters hate Veronica—saying, among other things, that she is a whore because she worked as a waitress in a restaurant before they were married—and so they do not pass her telephone messages.

Across town, Veronica and Roberto both come from prominent local families. They became *novios* (boyfriend and girlfriend), when she was 12 and he was 16, but they did not marry until Roberto had finished his studies. He is trying to save his family business in the pork industry from going under, but it is hard to compete with meat from American agribusinesses, fed by government-subsidized grain. He is gentle and generous with his wife and his two young children, but Veronica wishes he were more available, less caught up in his work. At night though, he is the one who wishes she were more available; only recently (after eight years of marriage) has she begun to have orgasms. Though she frequently feigns sleep when he gets in bed at night, she said she also knows that for their marriage to last, they must work to keep their sex life interesting. To that end, they occasionally sneak off to a sex motel in a nearby town, renting a room with a Jacuzzi and round the clock porn on TV. When they cannot make it to the motel, he has downloaded the kama sutra onto his palmpilot—they call it the *palma sutra*—to help them be, as she calls it with a laugh, "creative." There are limits, though, to this creativity; she said that no, they had never actually fought over anything related to sex but that she refuses his requests for oral sex—I was surprised by her use of the graphic phrase *chupar su pene* (to suck his penis)—because it disgusts her. She asked me, though, if I thought she should see a psychologist to work through this disgust.

The lay—and, I would argue, lazy—answer to why the Sunday market does such a brisk business in thong underwear, why younger couples place such emphasis on marital *confianza*, is to blame the United States. Mexicans blame the United States (both the global reach of gringo culture and the personal influence of those who migrate) for children's increasing lack of respect for their parents and teachers, as well as for the growing percentage of female-headed households, the new visibility of sexual minorities, increases in teen pregnancy, increasing numbers of girls who get tattoos and drive motorcycles, rising rates of childhood obesity and sexually transmitted diseases, declining church attendance—and even for the time the devil was reportedly seen in the disco when it opened one year on Good Friday. But to explain the transformation in marital ideals and the shifting sands of the social construction of gender only through reference to *el norte* misses the importance of Mexican processes of social and economic transformation, oversimplifies how the United States' relationship to Mexico has actually promoted these changes, ignores the lived experience of migration, and omits altogether the way in which individual yearnings for moder-

Que se despierte
no quiere decir que
saldrá de la cama...

...darle un cálido despertar

Oblígalo a levantarse (en más de una forma) ofreciéndole este amoroso cariñito matutino. Llévale a la cama una taza de café acabadito de colar y entibia tus manos con ella. Coloca ahora la taza en su mesita de noche, cerca de su nariz, para que perciba el delicioso olor del café mientras tú deslizas tus cálidos deditos bajo las sábanas y lo excitas con un delicado trabajo manual. Usa tus dedos para trazar circulos en el interior de sus muslos, frota tus palmas sobre su estómago... haz lo que prefieras. Lo oirás gemir más alto que la alarma del reloj. ¿El único inconveniente? Se sentirá tan a gusto, que no querrá salir de la cama.

Figure 4.1. "Give him a warm wake-up." Example of a feature in a popular Mexican women's magazine.

nity, coupled with the economic and political powerlessness of rural Mexicans, has moved love front and center as a marital and life goal.

Over the past 50 years, everyday life in rural Mexico has been transformed. Age at first marriage has increased, as has neolocal residence; fertility and mortality have declined, and the census reveals ever-greater imbalances in sex ratios in the 15- to 24-year-old-age group, as more and more men head north to try their fortune. Rapid increases in literacy have provided people with access both to government-mandated formal sex education and to a wide range of informal sources of sex education, including magazines, newspapers, and comic books. A recent issue of one women's magazine, for example, includes a feature on masturbation, describing it as a normal and indeed important feature of women's sexual repertoire, while another in the same issue provides step-by-step instructions for how give a man "a warm wakeup" (see Figure 4.1).[3]

Help him get up (in more than one sense of the word) giving him this loving morning caress. Take him a freshly made cup of coffee and heat up your hands on it. Place the cup on his night table, near his nose, so that he smells the delicious coffee smell, while you slip your warm little fingers under the sheets and excite him with some delicate handiwork. Use your fingers to trace circles around his thighs, rub your palms on his stomach, . . . do what you like. You will hear him moan louder than the alarm clock. The only inconvenience? He will be so happy, he won't want to get out of bed.

As the illustration of this sexy morning scene makes clear, this is not necessarily a married couple: the woman lacks a ring. Magazines such as the one in which these instructions appeared are sold at the newsstand in Degollado's plaza and eagerly consumed and discussed by the town's younger generation.

Electricity, nearly universally available, makes it easier to see what you are doing in the dark, but also makes it possible to watch television and movies, an importance source of images about gender and sexuality. In the mid-1980s, satellite TV become accessible in Degollado, showing Mexican-produced *telenovelas* as well as U.S.-made films dubbed in Spanish. More recently, cable has even further widened the range of media available locally; in addition to the PG- and R-rated sex and violence featured on satellite TV, at least two cable stations run actual pornography every night starting around 10:00 p.m. Furthermore, the running water that has gone in less than 50 years from a luxury to a commonplace of domestic life makes it that much more palatable to try out the oral sex that is depicted so tirelessly in porn magazines and films. All of these social changes have taken place in an economic climate in which fewer and fewer families earn their living from the land.

Mexico may make its own history, but it does not make it as it pleases. Media influence provides a good example of the way that everyday life in rural Mexico is inextricably interwoven with the political economy of U.S.–Mexico relations. The *telenovelas* that tell Mexicans that machismo is dead, that the heroine's heart will be won not by a gun-toting mustachioed man on horseback but by a BMW-driving, cell-phone-toting blonde doctor (Hirsch 2003:151), reach viewers in rural Mexico via televisions and satellite dishes—the vast majority of which were purchased with migrant remittances, a vital part of the Mexican economy. Similarly, the shift from patrilocal to neolocal residence—which makes for more privacy and companionship and, at least potentially, better sex—is a product not just of changing family ideals but also of the wealth generated by migrant labor. Political pressure from the United States has also indirectly promoted neolocality in rural Mexico: in the 1990s the Mexican ruling party under Carlos Salinas, in the face of pressure from the north for democratization without instability, worked hard to shore up their hold on power through a series of populist policies that, around Degollado, took the form of distributing small lots to local families and providing limited municipal services (electricity, sewer lines) to these new *colonias* springing up on the outskirts of town. These were the same lots on which many of Degollado's migrant families subsequently built two-story houses with their earnings from trips north.

The lived experience of migration has also supported the development of a companionate ideal. First, the sons and daughters of the Bracero migrants of the 1950s and 1960s, who saw their mothers manage alone for 10 or 11 months a year, and who shyly welcomed home the stranger whom they were expected to call *papa*, now negotiate joint migration during courtship. Young women say, "No me voy a casar para estar sola" [I am not going to marry just to be alone]. Second, the returning migrants are an important source of cultural change. People in both Mexico and Atlanta told me again and again that *en el norte la mujer manda* (in the United States women give the orders), and in my work in these transnational migrant communities in Atlanta I saw how the privacy of big city life, the legal protections against family violence, and the possibilities for women to survive economically without a man—combined with the comparative loss of masculine privilege experienced by Mexican men (especially those who migrate without papers)—give Mexican women in the United States more bargaining power than their sisters at home. These migrants come back every year at Christmas or during the summer holidays, bringing new fashions and new status symbols, as migrants have done in this part of the world for nearly a century, and so these cell-phone-carrying, minivan driving, beach-vacationing, companionately married couples become the ideal against which young Mexican couples measure themselves. They do this in the context of global dialogues about masculinity—and especially about the problematization of machismo—such as those discussed by Gutmann (1996, 2003) and many others.

New consumptions practices play a critical role in people's experience of these emerging forms of affect. During the weeks leading up to Valentine's Day, red hearts dominated public space in Degollado, with stands featuring stuffed animals and mylar balloons that said "I love you" (in English), heart-shaped balloons assembled into even larger hearts hung in many local stores, red streamers everywhere, and the actual day itself a frenzy of getting and sending—in all price ranges, from single wilted roses to large 100,000 peso ($100) arrangements. Year round the Sunday market brims with thongs and push-up bras, as well as t-shirts for girls with provocative messages (again, in English) such as "Looking for a new boyfriend. My old one turned out to be a loser." Most nonmigrant men and women in rural Mexico cannot afford SUVs or trips to Disneyland, but buying a thong, whispering endearments by cell phone, celebrating Valentine's Day, or looking together through the palma sutra are other ways to perform modern identities. The political and economic context also reinforces people's choice to become modern lovers and modern consumers, since other less private forms of feeling part of progress are out of reach in this politically corrupt and economically disadvantaged corner of the world.

Curiously, apparently similar transformations took place in late 19th- and early 20th- century America and Europe. According to D'Emilio and Freedman (Shumway 2003), in a "companionate marriage," as these new marriages were increasingly called, "a successful relationship rested on the emotional compatibility of husband and wife, rather than the fulfillment of gender-prescribed duties and roles. Men and women sought happiness and personal satisfaction in their mates; an important component of their happiness was mutual sexual enjoyment" (D'Emilio and Freedman 1988:265–266, cited in Shumway 2003). Shumway 2003 credits the shift to the way capitalist industrialization weakened the role of the extended family and promoted individualism, transforming the family from a productive unit and thus a necessary means for survival into (supposedly or at least ideally) a sphere for the creation and enjoyment of pleasurable affective relations.[4] Romance films and novels, advice manuals to help couples succeed at the new work of intimacy, and urban pleasures such as dance halls and movie theaters reinforced the changes in kinship wrought by these economic shifts. Increases in age at first marriage, declining fertility, declines in infant mortality, and consequent gains in life expectancy transformed the demographic shape of the family. Giddens (1992) describes this new model of modern kinship in which love makes—and unmakes—a family, using the phrase "pure relationship" to denote relationships held together through mutual preference and satisfaction rather than obligation and locating the new marital ideal within a broader shift to families of choice. His argument, noteworthy for the inclusion of homosexual and heterosexual relationships under the same analytic lens, suggests that capitalism, by creating the modern individual, laid the groundwork for modern sexualities and modern loves.

Caldwell (1976) was an early observer of similar ideologies of marital love in the developing world, writing in the 1970s about the "emotional nucleation" of the Nigerian family, which he attributed to the combined influences of Christian missionaries, increasing literacy, the media, and the commodification of sexuality. Chan (2006) has described more recently how young women in Singapore melt down the wedding jewelry they receive from their in-laws, refashioning the gold into rings and necklaces in more modern styles—or else simply selling it for cash to buy something really useful, like a computer—unlike their mothers who treasured these gifts from their in-laws as a marker of their place in the family. Among the Huli of Papua New Guinea, Wardlow (2006) writes that newly married couples often live together, rather than in the separate men's and women's houses of the past, claiming that "family houses," as they are called, are the "modern" and "Christian" way for loving couples to live. In Nigeria, Smith (2000) tells us that although marriage is still very much regarded as a relationship that creates obligations between kin groups as well as between individuals, courtship at least has been transformed into a moment for young men and women to demonstrate their modern individuality. Yan (2003) writes about how in China girls look for boyfriends with whom they can talk intimately, and Inhorn (1996) describes how in Egypt those couples who have developed the strongest affective bonds are best able to weather the personal and social tragedy of infertility. Rebhun's (1999) and Gregg's (2003) work on love in Brazil is also relevant here, as is Ahearn's (2001) work on love letters in Nepal and Parikh's (2000) on love letters in Uganda, Collier's (1997) work on capitalism and desire in rural Spain, Cole's (1991) work on marriage in Portugal, Pashigian's (2002) research on marital ideals among infertile couples in Vietnam, and Kanaaneh's (2002) research on ideologies of reproductive modernity among Palestinians in Israel. Around the world, young people talk increasingly about how affective bonds create marital ties, deliberately contrasting their loves to those of their parents and grandparents.

As Appadurai (1996) warns us, however, we should not make the mistake of assuming that our past is their present. In the United States and Europe, these changing marital ideologies were accompanied by industrialization, urbanization, and other social, economic, and demographic transformations. The causal paths promoting the companionate ideal more recently differ in key ways: in some places companionate ideologies seem to be a product of economic transformation but not exactly industrialization (see Collier 1997; Yan 2003) and in other places they seem to have taken hold despite a striking lack of economic transformation (Wardlow 2006; Smith 2000; Kanaaneh 2002). Other research on modern love turns our attention to its intertwining with ethnicity—a factor apparently entirely absent from the American and European shifts—as a force for change (Maggi 2001, 2006). In all of the examples provided, however, literacy, fertility decline, the media, and the intertwining of sexuality, modernity, desire, and commodification do seem to play important roles (Hirsch and Wardlow 2006). The similar images of marital companionship around the world does not mean that the historical forces at work in late 19th- and early 20th-century European cultures are currently at work around the world; these stories hint at modernities but not necessarily modernization.[5]

Furthermore, it would be naïve to assume that the spread of the white wedding (and its evil companion, the boring wedding video) is proof of global cultural homogenization. The comparative ethnography of companionate marriage highlights the diversity in local interpretations of these global ideologies of love, companionship, and pleasure. These ideologies and practices intersect in diverse ways with sexualities, with gender, with economic transformation, individualism, and projects of the state. To conclude, I point to some of the particular axes of difference we might usefully explore in our discussions of love and globalization, focusing on three broad issues: love and inequality, love and cultural change, and love and public policy.

In thinking about love and gender inequality, it is useful to recall Connell's (1987) three aspects of gender regimes: labor, power, and affectivity. Approaching marriage as an institution within which gender is negotiated and reproduced, this reminder of the distinct—and sometimes distinctly orthogonal—dimensions of gender is critical. When we look both at the discursive focus on pleasure and emotion and at the organization of labor and power in these relationships, we see that the story is one of the modernization of gender inequality rather than the modernist fantasy of becoming unbound by gender. In Mexico, the actual day-to-day question of who earns the money and who gives the orders has just been papered over with a veneer of sweet words and passionate kisses. At the same time we must acknowledge the voices from the field, the chorus that claims these more pleasurable relationships as an improvement over their parents' marriages. We should look critically at how these companionate ideals are used and at the strategic implications of these ideologies for gendered interactions, to see both what they obscure and how they work as resources in various situations.

Economic inequalities between countries, classes, and couples also intersect with the problems of modern love. In terms of inequalities between rich and poor countries, we might consider the lived experience of love in rich countries, the ideals and consumption practices on the other end of those economic forces that pull migrants out of rural Mexico and elsewhere. In terms of the precarious domestic bargains middle-class women and American women strike, our fragile progress toward do-mestic "equality," our own companionate marriages, are largely predicated on off-loading work we consider unpleasant on women from the developing world. Con-sidering how love intersects with social-class differences within countries, at least in Mexico the poor seem to use discourses of love to resist their permanent disad-vantage as consumers; cell phones and SUVs are beyond reach, but a walk through the plaza holding hands is free. Another issue here is what Schneider and Schneider (1995) call "ideologies of reproductive stigma" or what Kanaaneh (2002) calls "the reproductive measure"; around the world, fertility declines that have begun among the upper classes have contributed to ideologies depicting the poor as overly sexual and uncontrollably fertile. The public health parallel is research that depicts all sex among the poor as the product of violence, lust, or need—and so we might ask how classist ideologies obscure the actual experiences of affect among the poor around the world.

There is also the issue of economic inequality between partners; Giddens's (1992) phrase, "the pure relationship," seems to suggest that relationships unpol-luted by the nasty stink of economic dependence are morally superior. Not only does the phrase obscure the nagging truth that many women do in fact depend economically on marriage in a way their husbands do not, but it also implies that all sexual relationships fall along a moral spectrum between, say, the pure relationship and the ultimate transactional relationship, commercial sex. Here we might ask how love operates as a practice, a resource, and an ideology in conditions of economic dependence or independence.

Ethnicities and nationalisms also intersect in complicated ways with gender and sexuality, and so too they must with love: We might then ask what are the impli-cations for practices and ideologies of love when gendered forms of nationalism become intertwined with resistance to perceived forces of globalization? Returning Mexican migrant men, for example, shine in the sartorial glory of Mexican mascu-linity—ostrich and alligator boots, leather belts with custom-made, cod-piece-like buckles the size of a saucer, and, of course, cowboy hats—but Mexican migrant women rarely show parallel folkloric touches, preferring a tailored suit and heels to even the finest of silk *rebozos*. More generally, how do love and sexuality get interwo-ven with the global struggle between the burqah and the bikini? Women in Mexico complain about how their husbands are *enfadosos* (always asking for sex)—but they also ask me, with a glimmer of pride, if it isn't true that Mexican men are more lively in the sack than their pale American counterparts.

As we talk about globalization and cultural transformation, the Mexico example is useful because it directs us to how the ideologies of love as a cultural aspect of globalization exists in tension with the structured inequalities of class and gender that have been in some ways undermined, and in other ways reinforced, by eco-nomic aspects of globalization. This speaks to the need to tease apart the various flows of globalization—perhaps using Appadurai's (1996) taxonomy of ethnoscapes, technoscapes, financescapes, mediascapes, and ideoscapes, but perhaps modifying it strategically to our needs to focus more on gender, sexuality, and kinship—to be a bit more specific when we talk about how, exactly, globalization is remaking how we make love.

We need also look at how local social structures co-opt and transform ideas about love for their own agendas—such as the example of the Christian Family Movement in Mexico. Individual agency and strategy also come into play here, reminding us to attend to how people use these ideologies on the ground and combine them syncretically with other pre-existing discourses about affect and kinship. The consistency with which the ethnography of companionate marriage suggests that people think it is better because it is more modern makes me wonder why people persistently choose gender and sexuality as the idioms through which to express their modernity. In the Mexican case, I suggest that these private revolutions appeal because they feel within reach while other more public forms of change are not, but it is also true at least since the Enlightenment that people have measured the modernity of other societies by—as George Bush might say it—how they treat their women. The idea that some forms of gendered practice are more modern than others is so much a part of our intellectual landscape as to be invisible, but it seems hard to talk about changing ideas of love without also addressing more directly these questions about gender and modernity.

Finally, there are vital policy issues to be considered—disease and divorce. For most women around the world, the greatest risk of HIV infection comes from marital sex. In Mexico, companionate marital ideals coexist with a social organization of masculinity that actively promotes extramarital sex, with the result that the only change in men's sexual behavior seems to be that men make marginally more effort to hide their infidelities, in order not to interrupt the flow of oral sex and cozy chat at home. We need to consider how our own attachment to marriage as a good thing may have slowed the recognition of the deadliness of marital sex and to explore how spreading ideologies of marital love around the world may actually increase women's risk of marital infection (Hirsch et al. 2007; Parikh 2007; Smith 2007; UNAIDS 2000; Wardlow 2007).

The rise of love has coincided with the outsourcing of caring, at least in the developed world, so that now the changing of diapers of both the very young and the very old—as well as the cleaning of the toilets of those who are, however temporarily, between Huggies and Depends—is done largely by darker-skinned hands. The idea that love is about pleasure rather than commitment is a social problem insofar as it relates to the persistent devaluation of the work of caring. The left and the right have different responses to the crisis in social reproduction—but my point here is merely that we should connect our discussions here about love and globalization to broader shifts in kinship and the organization of social reproduction. As part of the same broader issue of kinship in the era of the supposedly pure relationship, the rise of love has also coincided with the rise in divorce. Again, the issue here is not to come up with some ridiculous neo-conservative program to preserve marriage but rather to recognize the futility of legal or policy efforts to make marriage back into what it was in the 19th century. There is no going back, no remaking kinship, and so we might rather look ahead, honestly, at what love has wrought, and where we might go from here.

Notes

1.   See, for example, the speech "El respeto al amor ajeno es la paz," given by Arturo Vázquez Barrón on February 14, 2002, in Mexico City and circulated via *Agencianotiese@mailman. laneta.org* listserve on February 17, 2002; the Ley de Convivencia was finally approved by the Mexico City Legislative Assembly on November 10, 2006, after six years of heated debate.
2.   The ethnographic data on this chapter were collected as part of two projects. As described in Hirsch 2003, the first consisted of 15 months of participant observation in Degollado and in Atlanta, Georgia, with people from Degollado. I also worked in a small agricultural community outside of Degollado, El Fuerte, and with women from El Fuerte who were living in the Atlanta area. The primary method of data collection was life history interviews, concentrating on 13 pairs of women (sisters or sisters-in-law), in which one woman of each pair was living in the Atlanta area and other one had remained in or returned to the Mexican field sites. I also interviewed eight of the life-history informants' mothers and eight of their husbands. (For more information on the study methods, see Hirsch 2003:28–56.) The second study, part of a larger multi-site project exploring married women's risk of HIV infection (supported by NIH, R01HD041724), involved six months of fieldwork in Degollado, during which time Sergio Meneses and I conducted participant observation and collected data using a variety of other methods, as described in Hirsch et al 2007.
3.   *Cosmopolitan* (Mexico version), June 2004, 132, 100.
4.   Shumway 2003 also notes that the extent to which marriages frequently failed to fulfill these demands for pleasure is suggested by increases in rates of marital dissolution early in the century.
5.   Local possibilities for "coming out" provide some ethnographic evidence, for example, for my argument that the way industrialization and economic change intersected with kinship, individuality, and sexuality in early 20th-century America is not the same as how they intersect with kinship in early 21st-century Mexico. In his work on the history of homosexuality, D'Emilio (1999) argues for the importance of macrolevel structural changes in promoting the growth of urban gay communities. Carrillo (2002), working in urban Mexico in the 1990s, talks about the lengths that even people who identify as "gay" (as opposed to other MSM sexual identities) go to hide themselves from their families. In my analysis, the nonemergence in Mexico of the sort of urban gay communities that exist in the developed world is due in large part to the way that people of all sexualities in Mexico continue to depend on their extended families for social and economic support. In other words, despite the rise of a cultural affective individualism in Mexico, there has not been the same parallel economic changes as were seen earlier in Europe and North America. This is what I mean by modernity without modernization.

References

Ahearn, Laura
   2001   Invitations to Love: Literacy, Love Letters, and Social Change in Nepal. Ann Arbor: University of Michigan Press.
Appadurai, Arjun
   1996   Modernity at Large: Cultural Dimensions of Globalization. Minneapolis: University of Minnesota Press.

Caldwell, John C.
  1976   Toward a Restatement of Demographic Transition Theory. Population and
         Development Review, September/December:321–366.
Carrillo, Hector
  2002   The Night Is Young: Sexuality in Mexico in the Time of AIDS. Chicago: University of
         Chicago Press.
Chan, Selina Ching
  2006   Love and Jewelry: Patriarchal Control, Conjugal Ties, and Changing Identities.
         In Modern Loves: The Anthropology of Romantic Courtship and Companionate
         Marriage. Jennifer S. Hirsch and Holly Wardlow, eds. Pp. 35–50. Ann Arbor:
         University of Michigan Press.
Cole, Sally
  1991   Women of the Praia: Work and Lives in a Portuguese Fishing Community. Princeton:
         Princeton University Press.
Collier, Jane Fishburne
  1997   From Duty to Desire: Remaking Families in a Spanish Village. Princeton: Princeton
         University Press.
Connell, R.W.
  1987   Gender and Power: Society, the Person and Sexual Politics. Stanford: Stanford
         University Press.
D'Emilio, John
  1999   Capitalism and Gay Identity. *In* Culture, Society, and Sexuality: A Reader. Richard
         Parker and Peter Aggleton, eds. Pp. 239–248. London: UCL Press/Taylor and Francis.
D'Emilio, John, and Estelle Freedman
  1988   Intimate Matters: A History of Sexuality in America. New York: Harper.
Giddens, Anthony
  1992   The Transformation of Intimacy. Stanford: Stanford University Press.
Gregg, Jessica
  2003   Virtually Virgins: Sexual Strategies and Cervical Cancer in Recife, Brazil. Stanford:
         Stanford University Press.
Gutmann, Matthew, ed.
  1996   The Meanings of Macho: Being a Man in Mexico City. Berkeley: University of
         California Press.
  2003   Changing Men and Masculinities in Latin America. Durham: Duke University Press.
Hirsch, Jennifer S.
  2003   A Courtship after Marriage: Sexuality and Love in a Mexican Transnational Families.
         Berkeley: University of California Press.
Hirsch, Jennifer S., and Holly Wardlow, eds.
  2006   Modern Loves: The Anthropology of Romantic Love and Companionate Marriage.
         Ann Arbor: University of Michigan Press.
Hirsch, Jennifer S., Sergio Meneses, Brenda Thompson, Mirka Negroni, Blanca Pelcastre, and
         Carlos del Rio
  2007   The Inevitability of Infidelity: Sexual Reputation, Social Geographies, and Marital HIV
         Risk in Rural Mexico. American Journal of Public Health 97(6):986–996.
Inhorn, Marcia
  1996   Infertility and Patriarchy: The Cultural Politics of Gender and Family Life in Egypt.
         Philadelphia: University of Pennsylvania Press.
Kanaaneh, Rhoda Ann
  2002   Birthing the Nation: Strategies of Palestinian Women in Israel. Berkeley: University of
         California Press.

Maggi, Wynne R.
  2001   Our Women Are Free: Gender and Agency in the Hindu Kush. Ann Arbor: University
         of Michigan Press.
  2006   "Heart-Stuck": Love Marriage as a Marker of Ethnic Identity among the Kalasha of
         Northwest Pakistan. *In* Modern Loves: The Anthropology of Romantic Courtship and
         Companionate Marriage. Jennifer S. Hirsch and Holly Wardlow, eds. Pp. 78–94. Ann
         Arbor: University of Michigan Press.
Parikh, Shanti
  2000   Desire, Romance, and Regulation: Adolescent Sexuality in Uganda's Time of AIDS.
         PhD dissertation, Department of Anthropology, Yale University.
  2007   The Political Economy of Marriage and HIV: The ABC Approach, Safe Infidelity,
         and Managing Moral Risk in Uganda. American Journal of Public Health
         97(7):1198–1208.
Pashigian, Melissa
  2002   Conceiving the Happy Family: Infertility and Marital Politics in Northern Vietnam.
         In Infertility around the Globe: New Thinking on Childlessness, Gender, and
         Reproductive Technologies. Marcia C. Inhorn and Frank Van Balen, eds. Pp. 134–151.
         Berkeley: University of California Press.
Rebhun, L. A.
  1999   The Heart Is Unknown Country: Love in the Changing Economy of Northeast Brazil.
         Stanford: Stanford University Press.
Sánchez, Rocío
  2004   Fox y su apuesta por la defensa de la "familia natural." Electronic document at Agencia
         NotieSe, http://mailman.laneta.org/mailman/listinfo/agencianotiese, accessed March
         22, 2004.
Schneider, Jane, and Peter Schneider
  1995   Festival of the Poor: Fertility Decline and the Ideology of Class in Sicily, 1860–1980.
         Tucson: University of Arizona Press.
Shumway, David R.
  2003   Modern Love: Romance, Intimacy, and the Marriage Crisis. New York: New York
         University Press.
Smith, Daniel Jordan
  2000   "These Girls Today Na War-O": Premarital Sexuality and Modern Identity in
         Southeastern Nigeria. Africa Today 47(3):141–170.
  2001   Romance, Parenthood and Gender in a Modern African Society. Ethnology
         40(2):129–151.
  2007   Modern Marriage, Extramarital Sex, and HIV Risk in Southeastern Nigeria. American
         Journal of Public Health 97(6):997–1005.
UNAIDS
  2000   Men and AIDS: A Gender Approach; 2000 World AIDS Campaign. Geneva: Joint UN
         Programme on HIV/AIDS.
Wardlow, Holly
  2006   All's Fair When Love Is War: Attempts at Companionate Marriage among the Huli of
         Papua New Guinea. *In* Modern Loves: The Anthropology of Romantic Courtship and
         Companionate Marriage. Jennifer S. Hirsch and Holly Wardlow, eds. Pp. 51–77. Ann
         Arbor: University of Michigan Press.
  2007   Men's Extramarital Sexuality in Rural Papua New Guinea. American Journal of Public
         Health 97(6):1006–1014.
Yan, Yunxiang
  2003   Private Life under Socialism: Love, Intimacy and Family Change in a Chinese Village,
         1949–1999. Stanford: Stanford University Press.

5

The Strange Marriage of Love and Interest
Economic Change and Emotional Intimacy in Northeast Brazil, Private and Public

L. A. Rebhun

"If the mayor had love, my son would walk!" The woman spoke with deep indignation in response to my question: Que significa "amor"? (What does "love" mean?). I had heard many different answers to my question during fieldwork in Northeast Brazil. Some people answered with concerns about the emotional ties that bind families together, especially those between mothers and children, citing a familiar aphorism: "Amor só de mãe" [Mother love only]. Others answered with discussions of romance, and the major changes in courtship that had swept the region in the past 50 years. And a third group, like the woman quoted above, gave me unexpected answers. "What do you mean?" I asked. Walking up to her adolescent son, seated at a nearby table making baseball caps on a sewing machine, she pulled out his crutches from behind the sewing table. "In your country, do they have polio?" she asked, and then answered herself: "No, because there the mayors have love for the little children and give them vaccines!" In 1990 the country was in the midst of an ultimately successful polio vaccination campaign, but her son had been crippled long before, and as she later detailed, she had fought long and hard for the medical care promised all citizens in the national health plan but too often not delivered to the poor. The sewing machine itself gave eloquent testimony to her maternal devotion: her son could work it with hand controls instead of the usual foot pedal. She detailed a long battle with city officials to find someone willing to consider ways for a boy with paralyzed legs to make a living, someone who had the imagination and skills to create the hand-controlled machine. "I could not rest," she told me, "until I knew he would be able to take care of himself once I am gone." But, she repeated, "if the mayor had love," she would not have had to undertake this battle; he would have been vaccinated, or he would have received better medical care, physical therapy, and occupational support and training without her having to work so hard for it.

On the surface, it would seem that this woman's phrasing of her political complaints within the idiom of love has little to do with the shifts in couple formation accompanying urbanization and the increased integration of this backwater area into the national economy. However, I think it reflects the same changes in the morality of human connections as changes in romance and family form. The woman's criticisms point directly at the issues of who owes what to whom, the moral-emotional ties that bind together communities. The shift from semi-arranged cousin marriage to romantic courtship that I was documenting speaks to the same issues of obligation, consideration, love, and loyalty as the woman's criticisms of government neglect. In the pages that follow, I trace the lines of this argument, beginning with a description of my fieldwork and field site, followed by a consideration of theories on emotion and on romance, and concluding with a discussion of the "politics of affection" (Fernandez 2000) that shape both public and private life in Northeast Brazil.

Social Change in a Rural City

From December 1988 through December 1990, I lived in Caruaru (population 300,000), a city in the interior of Brazil's Northeast. Caruaru, second largest city in Pernambuco state, located two hours by bus inland from state capital, Recife, boasts the largest regional agricultural market, where tourists shop for ceramic figurines and block prints depicting rural life, and locals stock up on food, clay dishes, and clothing, among other necessities. Much of the agricultural produce of the interior first goes to market in Caruaru, retailed to locals while truckers pick up their loads wholesale to bring to Recife and beyond. Although the tourist art garners more national and international attention, the clothing industry constitutes a larger sector of the economy, especially the production of blue jeans, baseball hats, and plastic sandals, mostly by pieceworkers at home or in small factories. Many inhabitants of Caruaru migrated there from rural homesteads to the east of the city in the agricultural Agreste region, or from the Sertão, the famously arid cowboy country to the west. Despite its relatively large population, Caruaru remains a conservative city with a strong agrarian sensibility. Even those born in the city tend to retain strong ties with rural relatives, and there is a constant traffic between rural and urban zones for family visits as well as for commercial purposes.

Northeast Brazil, markedly more rural, poorer, more recently and less thoroughly engaged than the south of the country with such markers of economic development as paved roads, involvement in the national monetary economy, access to modern medical care, has long been celebrated in song and story as a backward backwoods area where bandits and cowboys alike suffer through the periodic droughts that wreak such havoc on local agriculture. Historically an area of plantation slavery, the Brazilian Northeast remains sharply divided by class. The region has undergone massive rural-to-urban migration since the 1950s and has become more closely involved with the unstable national economy so that wage labor and transactions in cash have become more prominent, and local people are more likely than their parents were to have a worldview that encompasses worldwide trends and international markets. Caruaru has also seen marked labor migration to the cities of the south, especially of young men, leaving a skewed gender balance. Women are much more likely than in the past to work full time not only outside the home but also away from family surveillance, often in domestic service, than in the rural area, where families often labor together on their own land or for wages.

Modernization has been complicated by economic instability. During my two years of fieldwork, the inflation rate varied from 1 to 4,000 percent a year. In addition, the past 30 years have seen the largest rural-to-urban migration in Brazil's history: One in five Brazilians migrated to cities between 1960 and 1970 (Perlman 1976:5), and by 1980 the Northeast had shifted from majority rural to majority urban (de Araujo 1987:167). Today's Caruaru struggles with an ambiguous economy in which personal ties have remained central even as first cash and then credit increasingly spread throughout the economy. The moral underpinnings of emotional relationships are different under capitalism and reciprocal exchange: In modern Caruaru principles of exchange and standards of personal relationship intertwine, and people consider questions about whether, how much, and how truly their associates love them as matters not only of personal importance but also of economic survival.

I draw my data from a combination of direct and participant observation and 120 tape-recorded interviews. These interviews used several types of questions, including questions on demographic issues, such as birthplace and marital status, and questions about types of emotional experiences, and finally open-ended questions designed to elicit stories of life events and opinions about social relationships. I also interviewed religious healers and their patients about folk medical complaints, as well as about the involvement of healers in attempts to manipulate romantic relationships through magic and to treat the various emotional sequelae of love gone wrong.

History, Anthropology, and Love

Most of the theorizing on love has focused on sexual passion through examination of couple formation. Historians of northwestern Europe theorize that urbanization, monetized economies, and the expansion of wage labor develop in sync with the idea that discourses of romance properly form part of legitimate courtship leading to marriage (Gillis 1988; MacFarlane 1987; de Rougemont 1972; Stone 1977). Wage labor allows people to function as individuals in the market, young people no longer depend as much on land inheritance as the basis of their economic lives, and couples begin to believe that marriage partners should choose one another rather than rely on their parents to make matches, according to this model. These changes in turn lead to a system in which people see marriage as an emotional partnership in addition to an economic and social one, and choose mates, or at least claim to choose mates, on the basis of personal attraction rather than family alliance. The exact details and dates of this transformation remain in dispute (MacFarlane 1987).

Anthropologists, working in a variety of urbanizing, globalizing world areas have found similar relationships among economic change, conversions of family form, agrarian transformation, and romantic discourse in contemporary societies (Adrian 2003; Collier 1997; Hirsch 2003; Hoodfar 1998; Jankowiak 1995; Kendall 1996;

Rebhun 1999; Yan 2003). Emerging models of romance and globalization have also been influenced by changes in theory on the nature of culture and especially of emotion. Contemporary anthropologists reject older models of cultures as bounded entities, preferring a more dynamic conception emphasizing how social reality emerges from interpersonal interactions. This insight transformed anthropological work on emotion in the 1980s, leading theorists to examine emotion as part of social process. Here, emotion emerges in what social actors experience and communicate, forming part of moral discourse, and figuring in the micropolitics of interpersonal interactions (Lutz 1988:10). Rather than seeing emotions as individual experiences, ethnopsychologists describe them as fundamentally interpersonal and culturally various.

Inspired by anthropological studies of emotion in the 1970s and 1980s, I went to Brazil in December 1988, intending to study how people describe emotion in the local language (cf. Lutz 1982; Rosaldo 1984). My interests focused on emotion glosses as moral concepts within local folk medicine. Believing that emotional expression encompasses more than spoken language, I intended to expand theoretical concepts of emotion vocabulary by examining the many folk ailments of the region as a kind of metaphorical gloss in which illness writes emotion on the body of the sufferer. In particular, I focused on how women understand and express love (*amor*) and anger (*raiva*), through the folk ailments of *mau olhado* (evil eye), *peito aberto* (open chest), *nervos* (nerves), and *susto* (shock sickness).

My investigation revealed unanticipated complexities not only in the folk ailments themselves but in the definitions people applied to the words that describe their underlying sentiments. I found the region I worked in embroiled in major social change, including, especially, mass migration into cities, and the increasing integration of the remaining agrarian sector into the emerging market economy of the area. The people I spoke with were much more interested in talking about love than anything else, often phrased in terms of "What's wrong with men?" "What's wrong with women?" "young people nowadays," or "old people as they used to be," and hillbillies and city slickers; and most of all, sexual passion. Romance, courtship, heartbreak, and how things had changed seemed topics of endless fascination.

Love life, one's own and that of others, is always a fascinating topic everywhere and you do not need complex anthropological theory to figure out why people like to talk about it. But I think that love and romance became even more perplexingly fascinating topics in the late 20th century in Caruaru for reasons that can be explained by social science. Talking with locals on topics such as *amor* and *paixão* (passion, infatuation) inevitably brought up such issues as the complex difficulties of human connection and the relation of physical passion to emotional intimacy, as well as family form and couple formation, and how they had changed during the massive urbanization of the second half of the 20th century, when Brazil also underwent military coup, transition back to democracy, and the opening of its markets to international capital while inflation in Brazilian currency experienced heights for which whole new vocabularies had to be invented.

Discussions of love expanded past considerations of romance to what Damián Fernández (2000) calls "the politics of affection," the ties of loyalty that bind extended families and the political aggregations of patronage that take on all the symbolic emotionalism of family bonds in Latin America. This is the form of love to which the mother of the disabled son referred when she condemned the mayor for his lack of love for the little children.

Reciprocal versus Contractual Relationships; or, Love and Interests

I now relate some general impressions about what people said about love, with the caveat that no two answers were identical. But there were some generalities. One concerned the relationship between purity of sentiment and economic involvement in family relationships. That is, in general, people I spoke with in Caruaru distinguished between true love (*amor verdadeira*) and what they called "interests" (*intereses*) or economic stakes in the beloved, saying that to mix love with pecuniary interest was to sully the purity of the sentiment, properly a selfless generosity. This tendency was as marked for familial as for conjugal relationships and courtship of couples, as well as for descriptions of the relationships of "friends," a category now overtaking that of cousin in the urban area as a major form of relationship. The idea, which can also be seen in Christian biblical precepts as exemplified in First Corinthians 13:4–7, enjoys widespread secular currency as well and is hardly unique to this area. Many scholars interested in the sentiments that bind and separate members of social groups have unselfconsciously adopted this religiously based folk model, in which emotion and economic interest constitute conflicting, morally opposed forces (Medick and Sabean 1984:10). In practice however, love and economic interest cannot easily be distinguished.

I saw a contradiction local people did not see in their description of true love. People claimed a total separation of sentiment and economics, while in practice, when asked how you know someone loves you, people described showing love by sharing food, money, clothing, access to credit, employment opportunities, labor, and child care—which I saw as economic transactions—while they were reluctant to so label them. They also described these acts as gifts, without explicit need for remuneration, but they could, when pressed, reluctantly, make an accurate accounting of such gifts, and judge people's character on the basis of whether they gave as good as they got.

Among older women and women living in rural areas, when I asked for definitions of love, I heard most frequently about mother love, presented as the epitome of true love.

> We have lots of acquaintances [*colegas*], but [as a] true friend we only have our mother. You can trust your mother in everything. You can confide in her. She will help you, you can depend on her. Without my mother I would not have

survived until now, not only when I was a baby and she raised me, but now, advising me on how to manage my husband, helping me raise my children, nursing me when I am sick, lending me money when I am broke.

What locals called *consideração* was the second major theme to emerge in definitions: love formed in the practices of cohabitation, and defined by labor. In marriage, this kind of love includes respect and friendship within the performance of traditional gender roles, in which the physical labor the partners perform not only reflects but constitutes their love. People spoke of having obligations (*obrigações*) that could be ignored or carried out resentfully or indifferently or with *consideração* (consideration) as a marker of love. Consideration was, for example, the difference between preparing a meal of indifferent quality and preparing one's husband's favorite meal well.

> Because I love my husband, because I cook his food, because I wash his clothes, because I clean his house, because I do his service [have sex with him], because I bear his children, the people say, love and faith in actions you see, in these actions that I do, in my work is my love. And my husband, he works in a factory in the city, and he brings his pay check home, and he pays the costs of the household and he shows his love for me.

This view of love-as-labor reflects, I believe, historical change and also life-cycle issues. That is, some older women may have given a definition of love differing from that of younger women because the older woman had lived through long years with their husbands, while the younger ones were still in the early stages of courtship or a honeymoon phase of their cohabitation. The change in definition, however, also reflects a historical change in how people talk about their relationships, what they expect from their partners, and what they consider fundamental to their bond. The old-fashioned views of older women may also reflect the conservative mores of the countryside when compared to the city.

Couples described marked changes in the practices of formal courtship over the last thirty years. Older people described how men used to have to woo their young cousins under the watchful eyes of their uncles, as fathers tried to supervise formal visits by a recognized suitor to a young woman and her family (with varying success). Girls as young as 12 or 14 were often paired with men in their thirties, as fathers sought well-established sons-in-law, and tried to marry off young women before they were physically capable of embarrassing the family with a pregnancy.

> I saw her, and then I went and spoke marriage to her father. He told me that marriage is a serious commitment, and asked me if I had a house. . . . She was very young, so we arrived at an accord about her age and how the courtship [*namoro*] would be. So it was once a week, on Saturday or Sunday that we met [with] . . . every one conversing in the living room, her there, me here talking

to her father, trying to sneak a glance at her sometimes, having very serious conversations, about the future, like the old-time people used to talk, different from today. So then her father would start to tell ghost stories, which was the signal for me to leave. So I got on my bicycle and left "raining" [very fast].

In practice, many of these older couples had eloped after some waiting years for permission to marry, and the number of women who gave birth fewer than nine months after marrying suggests that couples who were officially engaged had more physical approximation in the past than they were willing to admit. They may have used an elopement or a pregnancy to force the issue of marriage. These older couples reported an attraction expressed in glances and smiles, often strong, passionate attractions that went largely wordless, except when notes or messages were carried by intermediaries under the noses of suspicious fathers and brothers. For many couples, the first time they were alone together was the night they eloped or married. Older couples tended to say that true love develops after marriage or cohabitation, as the couple learn each other's preferences, raise children together, and form a partnership. They described a social world in which women socialized mainly with their mothers, sisters, aunts, and female cousins, while men hung out with their brothers, male cousins, and uncles. They regarded the emotional content of the conjugal bond as a private matter; in public spouses treated each other with formality and avoided displays of affection.

Young, urban people, in contrast, described going out to various entertainments in small groups, with the conservative mores of this inland city permitting an unaccompanied dating relationship only for couples who had announced themselves engaged for marriage. They described dancing, gazing into each other's eyes for hours, and holding long, intense personal conversations, as well as lots of gifts and compliments from young male suitors. From their reports, slipping away from the group for a physical encounter in a motel was not enormously difficult, as long as the couple defined themselves, however temporarily, as engaged to be married.

Even more commonly, young couples engaged in "street-corner love" (*amor na esquina*) in which they carried out their carrying on in semipublic, using passersby as temporary chaperones. These couples describe falling in love before marriage (or cohabitation) and basing their conjugal arrangements on that romantically defined sentiment, and many young women complained that after they set up household with a man, the romance disappeared, and they were left tied to a man they no longer believed loved them.

Urban people older than about 40, and people living in little villages and farms complained that young people nowadays marry strangers (*desconhecidos*), by which they meant noncousins unknown to their parents, while young, urban people exclaimed over how their parents used to marry strangers, by which they meant cousins with whom they had little personal approximation, given the social mores of chaperonage at the time. The difference in the definition of who constitutes a stranger reflects the shift from the village's family-based social world to the urban arena where identities have become more individualized, and relationships contracted on the basis of personal initiative rather than family position.

I need to add a caveat here: when historians discuss courtship, they refer to courtship-leading-to-marriage, with marriage formally recognized by church and/or state. Although some of the people I worked with had contracted formal civil unions, and others had performed religious ceremonies (which have no legal standing in Brazil), most were not legally married or had left some earlier marriage and now cohabited with a new paramour. In the rural area, a lack of both civil registrars and priests meant that couples recognized as married by the community were not legally bound, since the gaze of the state did not penetrate the hinterlands much. In the city, many people live out a series of courtships that include cohabitation for often brief periods. Most people used the terminology of marriage to refer to their partners: *marido* (husband) and *mulher* (woman) or *esposa* (wife) in the absence of formal rites. Thus, unlike many comparable scholars, I am not discussing courtship leading to romantic marriage. People speak of couplehood in the idiom of marriage, but they are not, for the most part, actually contracting marriages: Like their parents and grandparents, they keep their conjugal relationships out of the view of both state and church, while paying lip service to the greater respectability of civil and religious blessing on unions.

Another thing that has changed in the modern city is that the place of sexuality within the lives of officially respectable women has changed. In the villages, people strongly defended the fiction of universal premarital virginity, and postmarital chastity for women, while recognizing that men often had both short-term and long-term sexual liaisons outside of marriage. Indeed, in the older system, infidelity often was the location of romance, at least for men of higher status, who could have a respectable wife with legitimate children while pursuing women they found attractive. In some of these extramarital affairs, both man and woman experienced romantic attractions, in others, a man exploited a woman of lower status through coerced union, and in still others, a woman might encourage a liaison with a married man for the economic and social benefits it brought her (Trigo 1989).

The reasons certain women become classed as respectable and others do not are too complex to review here; suffice it to say that color, class, and family reputation all figure into it, as well as personal reputation. In the lower classes, most women do not have the ascribed characteristics necessary for respectability; nonetheless, some women strive for it. One of the utopian promises of modern ideas and sexual liberation is the possibility of respectability for most women. In Caruaru, I found a complex mix of mores in which people contradicted themselves in their answers to my questions: Virginity both was and was not essential to women's reputation, women both could not and could recoup damaged sexual reputations. Perhaps it is most accurate to say that people spoke in terms of an ideal in which virgin women married chastely but could be forgiving of imperfections in reaching that ideal—but not in every instances.

The idea of couplehood has relevance for marital practices and family formation and also reflects a shift away from corporate families based on brotherhood and cousinship to social groupings based on sexual attractions and personal companionship. The individualism of modern societies privileges associations of choice over kinship obligations; but the moral ideal of a corporate group within which emotional warmth and moral standards of interaction prevail continues to inspire. The development of a variety of identities based on homosexual practices publicly proclaimed (Parker 1999) also reflects ideals of individual choice in identity and association.

My findings on couple formation are similar to those of other scholars studying other parts of the world (e.g., Argyrou 1996; Collier 1997; Hirsch 2003; Kendall 1996) and reflect, I believe, the effect of a shift from the kind of social relations common in small, kinship-based villages to those in wage-labor-based cities, in which the definition and expression of conjugal attachment becomes more verbal, less instrumental, more romantic. The individual begins to emerge as a major social category, and so too does the couple, and concepts of love reflect this shift. Even people who engaged in short-term sexual relationships in the city tended to speak of them (sometimes sarcastically) in terms of love and marriage, a gloss reflecting their desire for respectability, despite the officially scandalous, if common, nature of their behavior.

So far, I have reviewed some of the answers that people gave to my questions about how to define love. But what I have not yet discussed is the frequency with which people answered my questions by saying, "I don't know"; "I can't figure it out"; "I have never been able to work it out in my own life, no matter how many times I try"; or "I simply don't believe in it any more."

Today, young urban couples also face not only a sharper distinction between domestic and public spheres than did their parents, and more confusing, shifting sexual mores, but a world in which men's and women's economic activities take place separately, rather than forming the interdependent whole their rural parents and grandparents created. In cities, men's and women's economic activities diverge more. Many men can no longer show their love through economic support because so much economic opportunity has dried up for them. The economic situation in modern Caruaru increasingly isolates men socially from women and children, to the economic detriment of families. At the same time that social and economic forces pull women and men apart, urban society expects an unprecedented degree of emotional intimacy between them, creating much sorrowful confusion. Also, despite romantic discourse, men tend to socialize mainly with all-male *turmas*,[1] still, and women with female relatives and neighbors, so that the expectation of emotional intimacy in the conjugal sphere receives little structural support.

Even when social and economic issues do not intrude, creating and maintaining a stable pair bond presents significant difficulties: Unrequited love, immaturity, or lack of sufficient bonding to survive the fading of passion complicates many love stories, as does the failure to make love exclusive. The people I interviewed found love confusing; they did not always know what they felt, they changed their minds, fooled themselves, and made mistakes.

Politics of Affection versus Politics of Law

What does all this have to do with mayors' love and polio vaccines? Fernández, in an analysis of contemporary Cuban politics, argues that theorists must understand both affection and passion to comprehend why people behave as they do: He rejects "rational man" models of human behavior. Fernández defines the politics of affection as "an instrumental and affective logic that justifies breaking the norms of the state to fulfill personal needs (material and otherwise) as well as those of loved ones" (2000:1). The politics of affection, he argues, are morally opposed to the utopian promises of modern society, in which citizens contract with each other and the state as individuals. Given the marked bifurcation of economic and political power in modern Latin American states and the failure of state institutions to deliver on promises of prosperity, access, and opportunity to citizens, people create social networks that attempt to make good on empty political promises by sharing within the network and excluding outsiders. In this moral system, members owe loyalty and affection to other members but not to outsiders. Fernández defines affectionate social relations as "network capital" (2000:106–107), a resource as important as, if not more important than, money. The politics of affection permeate society and form the basis of the informal economic sector and also of the personal informality that characterizes Latin American self-images as warmly outgoing, friendly, and compassionate.

The informal sector that makes up most of the economic activity of the poor in Latin American countries such as Cuba and Brazil and the network capital that sustains poor people both exist extralegally, often in opposition to the state as well as in attempts to compensate for the failures of states. When the mother of the disabled son lamented the mayor's lack of love for the little children, she compared the idealized warm emotional relations within networks with the comparatively cold attitudes of state officials. I also think that she criticized the mayor for being a poor patron, using a model of politics derived from small-town life, where whole communities often constitute a single lineage, and the leader takes a role as symbolically benevolent father to the whole group.

Historians of Brazil have described a rural family formation called the *parentela* as an extended patriarchal family of the past, in which cousin marriage sustains property within the family, and hired workers, servants, and clients take positions as *aggregado* or attached to the main property-holding group. Some *aggregados* may be biologically related to the main family because of nonlegitimized sexual relations between propertied men and their servants, but position within the *parentela* is determined by one's relationship to the often mythic glorious founder of the family.

The *parentela* as corporate patrilineage no longer exists in cities, but individuals older than 40 described growing up in *parentelas*, and many of the small towns outside of Caruaru today still consist of single extended families, whose patriarchal forms contrast strongly with urban matrifocal families, with their extended networks linking clusters of children and mothers abandoned by men, or living with nondomesticated men who float among households, drink to excess, and in general fail to fulfill the ideals of honorable manhood found in rural areas. People like the mother of the disabled son continue to relate to mayors as their parents related to family patriarchs, and to expect paternal care-taking, discussed under the gloss of *amor* from those in positions of power. Her criticism attempts to merge the politics of affection with the state apparatus, in a way that reflects the utopian ideals of modern states while condemning their failures.

This love is the old-fashioned *amor* of familial affiliation, not the meeting of soul mates promised by the romantic ideal. Of course, in reality, network relations may be highly exploitative. The old-fashioned *parentela* was rife with injustice, exploitation of labor, extortion of sexual favors, and deeply felt inequities between members of the legitimate line, and *aggregados*. I have already called love a story, a frame, an attitude; here I add the definition of love as an ideal, rarely achieved, but powerfully compelling as a moral archetype.

The rise of romantic couplehood derives from the shift from familial to contractual relationships in the broader society, whose impersonality strikes many Northeast Brazilians as immoral, in much the same way as familism strikes U.S. social scientists as amoral or corrupt. Many relate to the state and its representatives as their parents did to the patriarch and his subordinates and expect family values, such as mutual care-taking, glossed as love, from their political leaders.

Conclusion

Love takes on very complicated and disparate meanings in the answers people gave to my questions about what it means. But threading through the variations from familial affiliation to romantic passion, from patronage to couplehood was the idea that people who love each other support each other socially, emotionally, and economically. Love is the content of social connection for the people I interviewed in Caruaru, the glue that holds society together. Its nature and substance changes as demographic, economic, and social circumstances shift. Their definitions of love show the complexity of human social bonds, the confusion and uncertainty that characterize much emotional experience, and the moral vicissitudes of a shift from small-scale family-based villages to impersonal cities within the legal entity of the state. Love and interest always find themselves in strange marriage whether in village or city because both govern affiliation. Although the impersonal contractual relations of modern states differ markedly from the politics of affection in kin- and patronage-based villages, both attempt to order moral issues about who owes what to whom and under which circumstances: in other words, love and interests.

Note

1.   Northeast Brazilians use the word *turma* to refer to a group of young men who socialize together. Usually made up of brothers and cousins, the turma goes out drinking, skinny-dipping, picnicking, playing games, and sometimes visiting prostitutes together. It comprises a young man's closest social group; unlike social groupings in more modernized areas, it includes relatives rather than workmates or neighbors.

References

Adrian, Bonnie
   2003   Framing the Bride: Globalizing Beauty and Romance in Taiwan's Bridal Industry. Berkeley: University of California Press.
de Araujo, Tânia Bacelar
   1987   Nordeste: Diferenciais Demográficas Regionais e Seus Determinantes. Cadernos de Estudos Sociais Recife 3(3):167–192.
Argyrou, Vassos
   1996   Tradition and Modernity in the Mediterranean: The Wedding as Symbolic Struggle. Cambridge: Cambridge University Press.
Collier, Jane Fishburne
   1997   From Duty to Desire: Remaking Families in a Spanish Village. Princeton: Princeton University Press.
Fernández, Damián
   2000   Cuba and the Politics of Passion. Austin: University of Texas Press.
Gillis, John R.
   1988   From Ritual to Romance: Toward an Alternative History of Love. *In* Emotion and Social Change: Toward a New Psychohistory. Carol Z. Stearns and Peter N. Stearns, eds. Pp. 87–122. New York: Holms and Meier.
Hirsch, Jennifer S.
   2003   A Courtship after Marriage: Sexuality and Love in Mexican Transnational Families. Berkeley: University of California Press.
Hoodfar, Homa
   1998   Between Marriage and the Market: Intimate Politics and Survival in Cairo. Berkeley: University of California Press.
Jankowiak, William, ed.
   1995   Romantic Passion: A Universal Experience? New York: Columbia University Press.
Kendall, Laurel
   1996   Getting Married in Korea: Of Gender, Morality, and Modernity. Berkeley: University of California Press.
Lutz, Catherine
   1982   The Domain of Emotion Words on Ifaluk. American Ethnology 9:113–128.
   1988   Unnatural Emotions: Everyday Sentiments on a Micronesian Atoll and Their Challenge to Western Theory. Chicago: University of Chicago Press.
MacFarlane, Alan
   1987   The Culture of Capitalism. Cambridge: Basil Blackwell.
Medick, Hans, and David Warren Sabean, eds.
   1984   Interest and Emotion: Essays on the Study of Family and Kinship. Cambridge: Cambridge University Press.
Parker, Richard
   1999   Beneath the Equator: Cultures of Desire, Male Homosexuality, and Emerging Gay Communities in Brazil. New York: Routledge.

Perlman, Janice
   1976   The Myth of Marginality. Berkeley: University of California Press.
Rebhun, L. A.
   1999   The Heart Is Unknown Country: Love in the Changing Economy of Northeast Brazil. Palo Alto: Stanford University Press.
Rosaldo, Michelle Z.
   1984   Toward an Anthropology of Self and Feeling. *In* Culture Theory: Essays on Mind, Self and Emotion. Richard A. Schweder and Robert A. LeVine, eds. Pp. 137–157. Cambridge: Cambridge University Press.
de Rougemont, Denis
   1972   O Amor e o Ocidente. Translated by Paulo Brandi and Ethel Brandi Cachapuz. Rio de Janeiro: Editora Guanabara.
Stone, Lawrence
   1977   The Family Sex and Marriage in England, 1500–1800. New York: Harper Colophon.
Trigo, Maria Helena Bueno
   1989   Amor e Casamento No Seculo XX. *In* Amor e Família No Brasil. Maria Angela D'Incão, ed. Pp. 88–94. São Paulo: Editora Contexto.
Yan, Yunxiang.
   2003   Private Life Under Socialism: Love, Intimacy, and Family Change in a Chinese Village, 1949–1999. Stanford: Stanford University Press.

6

A Fluid Mechanics of Erotas and Aghape
Family Planning and Maternal Consumption in Contemporary Greece

Heather Paxson

A decade ago when I was living in Athens, I was having dinner with a Greek friend when conversation turned to the topic of romantic relationships: "From my perspective," Moira said, alluding to her divorcée status and contrasting her 40 years to my 25, "it's more difficult for women today. Now that we [Athenian women] have the freedom to live on our own, more educational and occupational opportunities— now we don't know what we want. No one knows how to live in today's society." The question of how to live and love amid social and economic "Europeanization" was at the center of ethnographic fieldwork I conducted in Athens between 1993 and 1995, exploring the impact of global forces on middle-class women's reproductive subjectivity (Paxson 2004). Such forces materialize in family planning rhetoric that touts personal choice and rational action as a vehicle for properly modern subjectivity. They crystallize too as new opportunities and demands for consumerism. This chapter traces how two quite different sorts of transnational trends—public health campaigns developed in Britain and the United States to promote safe sex worldwide, and the decentralized, market-driven consumerization of motherhood—have generated friction within local Athenian "structures of feeling" concerning sexual relations and parental responsibilities. Stories of romantic and maternal love, I argue, are telling of how local communities selectively realize and rechannel globalizing influences. The ways people talk about their experiences of and hopes for love scale the individual to household and family, and to community and nation. Tensions between ideologies and experiences of love lie at the heart of women's visions of a modern, gendered subjectivity that remains recognizably Greek.

To comprehend how Athenians perceive social change and, through the language of love, reflect critically on it, we must disaggregate *love* into the Greek notions of *erotas* and *aghape*. Erotas and aghape are not merely Greek words for "love," nor do they point us to fixed ideologies of affective relationships. Rather, I take the terms to constitute what Raymond Williams calls "structures of feeling"—erotas and aghape are cultural hypotheses that both Athenians and I use to understand "meanings and values as they are actively lived and felt," as well as the relationship between these "feelings"—"elements of impulse, restraint, and tone"—and more formally held systematic beliefs about, say, marriage, romance, sexual agency, and motherhood (1977:132). Erotas—passionate, physical love that Athenians described to me as "crazy" and "fleeting"—is distinct from aghape, an enduring love epitomized by a mother's care for her child, and also increasingly present in cultural scripts for romance. Erotas eclipses or transcends the self; when you're "in erotas, you can think of nothing," one unmarried 40-year-old woman said to me. In time, though, erotas may mature into aghape. Aghape makes porous the boundaries between self and other and is characterized as a sort of mutual dependency. Adult siblings may say, "We are in love with one another" (*aghapiómaste*), to indicate how involved they are in each other's daily affairs. But these local meanings of love, of erotas and aghape, are unsettled.

In the first half of this chapter, I address how in the sphere of heterosexual relations citations of romantic love—of the erotas that can transform into aghape—are challenged by imported family-planning and safe-sex campaigns. By the 1980s, the abortion rate had climbed to as high as three times the live birth rate and, by the end of the century, the national total fertility rate was among the lowest in the world, at 1.28 children per woman of reproductive age. Amid national anxiety over demographic decline, nongovernmental and state-sponsored family planning initiatives have largely aimed at reducing the abortion rate by encouraging the use of condoms and medical contraceptives, primarily the pill and intrauterine devices. To do so, family planners' rhetoric has redefined the role of "love" in sexual relations—to change the meaning of erotas. This strategy has not worked out as planned. To show how family planners operate on erroneous assumptions about Greek culture, I juxtapose local visions of erotas and their implications for premarital and marital sexual expectations with public health assumptions about a "culture" of intimacy that family planners believe impedes people's rational use of medical contraceptives. Nevertheless, in forwarding imported models of love and responsibility, family planning rhetoric does contribute to a new turbulence in how Athenians speak of heterosexual relations.

In the second half of this chapter, I turn to how the aghape of maternal practice is both central to and newly problematic for women's subjectivity in a consumer age. Compared with family planning attempts to encourage the adoption of prophylactic mentalities through new meanings of love and responsibility, consumerism, at least among the middle-class women I met, enjoys a smoother path of incorporation into longstanding values and virtues of maternal sacrifice. In both cases, erotas and aghape offer Athenians a distinctly Greek vocabulary with which to call into question some of the cultural and social transformations implicit, if not fully realized, in biomedical visions of the sexual subject and in the consumerization of maternal care. Using the metaphorics of fluid mechanics, I conclude with some thoughts about what attention to love might teach us about global flows.

Erotas in the Time of Prophylaxis

Greek romantic ideology suggests that erotas "happens to" men and women and is to be valued precisely because it defies human will. As 40-year-old Phoebe, an office administrator, spoke to me of romance:

> What's the difference between aghape and erotas? Erotas, with the meaning of sex, or of passion that you can feel first for an individual, is passing. Aghape is something that stays forever. I believe that as you set out in your relationship with an individual, you start out first with erotas, this attraction that exists between two persons, and then either it will fade, it will never become anything else, or it will be followed by aghape and this lasts, certainly, for all the years of your life.

While erotas may lead to marriage, by its very nature it fades. Greeks have not always expected erotas to endure in marriage. Prostitution and a gendered double standard concerning extramarital affairs—including sexual encounters between men—have been built into the architecture of the "classic Greek family." In the recollected agrarian past, when marriages were often arranged by a young couple's parents through a marriage broker, expectations for marital relationships were oriented toward economic collaboration, including the reproduction of heirs, rather than erotic or emotional fulfillment. The Greek word for spouse, *sizygos*, means "under the same yoke." While husband and wife shared common burdens, "the father was the chief," as one woman in her seventies put it to me. His patriarchal authority was never openly questioned, although, as Ernestine Friedl (1967) has pointed out, that never precluded women from manipulating events behind men's backs. Nonetheless, only a "fortunate" couple enjoyed a relationship of aghape.

As elsewhere, urbanization, industrialization, and the commercial consolidation of agriculture, alongside women's increased educational opportunities and imported models of "love marriages," have led to social criticism, championed by the Europeanizing Greek state, of traditional dowry arrangements and arranged marriages (see Hirsch 2003 for a comparative discussion). More and more since the 1980s, with couples dating and marrying "for love" rather than because their families have arranged their marriage, Athenian women and men have come to expect the erotas of attraction to mellow into a marriage of aghape and *filia* (the love of friendship). According to 25-year-old Eva (two years before becoming engaged to a man from her natal village in northern Greece), "After erotas comes aghape. When I'm in erotas[*erotevmeni*] I have a passion for this man. I like him. I want him [sexually]. Then after a while I believe that the passion and my erotas will continue to exist, but aghape will prevail." If it does not, no-fault divorce—introduced in the 1980s when Greece joined the European Economic Community—is increasingly considered appropriate. My friend Moira divorced because her husband expected her to find pleasure in his pleasures. Phoebe divorced after eight years of marriage because she and her husband "couldn't communicate." Erotas for these women failed to flower into marital aghape. That Greeks view physical attraction and sexual experience as preceding and potentially leading to the enduring love of aghape remains a point of pride for Athenians. Several explained this point to me, contrasting it to a more puritanical way of doing things in America or Britain—Greeks are often amused that Anglo-Americans might wish to "save" sex for their "soul mates," as though a soul mate could be discovered without erotic experience. In a modern Greek ideology of romantic love, erotas, simply put, is a gamble on aghape.

This notion is conceptually consistent with the most widespread method of pregnancy prevention in Greece, what is called "being careful," which includes withdrawal and the rhythm method (abstinence during the fertile days of a woman's menstrual cycle) (Symeonidou 1990; Apostolopoulou 1994; Emke-Poulopoulou 1994). Unlike the pill or intrauterine device, women do not control these methods. Their success depends on the regularity of a woman's menstrual cycle and the co-operation of her male partner. Withdrawal and the rhythm method can work rather successfully (Greer 1984; Schneider and Schneider 1995), but success requires communication and understanding—precisely those qualities that women I interviewed most frequently cited as elements of a successful marriage; they are qualities of aghape. If women with "not nice" husbands had to resort to repeat abortion, women with "good" husbands who cooperated in "being careful" were spared the "necessary evil" (anangeo kako) of abortion.

Middle-aged women explained to me that their mothers and grandmothers "discovered" abortion to limit their families to a responsible size. The upheaval, famine, and urban relocation of World War II and the subsequent Greek Civil War triggered a dramatic fertility decline. Following a decade of war, state industry and an urban civil service grew with seed money from the Marshall Plan. As production moved out of the agrarian household, children were transformed, as one grandmother put it to me, from "hands" useful in increasing family wealth to "mouths" needing to be fed (Shorter 1975; Katz 1990; Greenhalgh 1995). Greece did not see a postwar "baby boom." In the 1950s, just as abortion was criminalized, doctors quietly took over its practice from midwives, effectively medicalizing abortion as a routine gynecological procedure often described as "bringing on" a woman's period. For women who already had the number of children they could raise appropriately, abortion offered a behind-the-scenes back-up to the contraceptive methods they knew, including natural sponges doused in lemon juice, but primarily "being careful" (condoms have been associated with prostitution and extramarital affairs). For physicians, abortion became a reliable source of income, tax free because it was an under-the-table exchange of service for cash. A common perception among women today is that for decades, callous doctors withheld from them information about medical contraception to protect this source of income (and the contraceptive pill continues to be associated with cancer, a notion many women say they learned from their doctors). In subsequent generations, younger women who grew up watching their mothers have abortions to limit family size began turning to abortion earlier in their lives, to delay childbearing.

In interviews, while women explained to me that abortion became common practice within patriarchal marriages that have lacked "communication" and aghape—and because doctors "would pounce on you" to perform them—family planners tended to emphasize a different element of "traditional Greek culture," a conceptual fusing of sex and reproduction. Family planning advocates, including physicians and health educators, argue that abortion is more culturally acceptable to Greeks than modern contraception because abortion, unlike barrier or hormonal contraceptives, does not disrupt a "traditional" procreative equation between "making love" (*kani erota*) and "making children" (*kani pedhi*). As I see it, family planners, most having trained in the United States or Britain, have adopted a biomedical understanding of "sex" as a discrete act, whereas erotas is fundamentally relational and, moreover, unfolds within a power dynamic that, in heterosexual relations, is deeply gendered (Paxson 2002, 2004). That family planners have mistaken erotas as "Greek" for a biomedical definition of "sex" (that act which leads to conception) has generated static in their prophylactic message.

Believing, anachronistically, that an agrarian-based procreative ethic of sex held sway in Greece well into the 1990s, and that this (rather than, say, patriarchal power dynamics) accounted for why it was taboo for women to talk about sex with their husbands, family planners seek to reframe appropriate sex as prophylactic sex by conceptually separating sex and reproduction. They promote a pleasure ethic of sex—but one that overlooks the cultural logics that transform erotas into aghape. Greek family planning brochures and condom advertisements enjoin women and men to "enjoy life and erotic love" (see Paxson 2002, 2005). The message is to have as much sex as you want, with whomever you want—as long as you make the correct "choice" to use prophylactics. Adults are coached that they will be best able to choose to act appropriately—that is, prophylactically—"in the heat of the moment" if they adopt a modern "philosophy of life": the conscious exercise of calculated reason to maximize personal interest. As a family planning advocate editorialized in a Greek women's magazine, to establish prophylactic practice among adolescents, "the meaning of erotas" must include a "profound respect for the body—our own and others" (Doxiadi-Trip 1993:321). But this revises the ideology of erotas. Local understanding has figured the body as the subject of erotas; when one is "in erotas," one's body, not mind, exercises agency. In contrast, safe sex and family planning rhetoric works to reframe the body as the proper object of erotic love, serviced by the will guided by one's mind. An implicit message of safe sex campaigns is "have" sex and love thyself.

On the view of safe sex, erotic pleasure can and should be a matter of mental attitude. A similar configuration of pleasure and subjectivity appeared in the April 1997 American issue of *Glamour* magazine. An editorial column entitled, "How to Make Condom Use a Habit" advised readers, besides carrying a condom with you:

> It might also help to think about what kind of person you want to be. Insisting on condom use makes you an advocate on your own behalf and shows that you expect your partner to treat you with respect. Protecting yourself brings

the pleasure of behaving as a responsible adult; it may even move you to a new level of self-respect.

Asked to bring erotas under the umbrella of rational action, women and men are promised they will derive a new sexual pleasure from the knowledge that, by looking out for themselves in protecting against disease and inopportune pregnancy, they are, indirectly, looking out for their loved ones. In this sense, aghape is upheld as a precondition of erotas. No longer the ideal telos of erotas, aghape itself becomes a resource for erotic pleasure.

As I see it, the public health attempt to reformulate erotas suffers from a misguided reading of the cultural role of erotas. Family planners overemphasize the productive, procreative value of sex in so-called traditional Greece. Yes, making love has led to making babies—but not every time. Nadia instructed me about natural uncertainties that, in her view, undermine the scientific rationale for oral contraceptives.

> There are women who can conceive only two to three times in all their life, and not because of [secondary sterility following] abortion. It's clearly this fertility of theirs, you understand. Now some scientists admit it and some don't admit it. Whatever the scientific research says, I believe that the woman does not conceive every month during her dangerous days. I know this both from personal experience and from friends, that when you make love one day it doesn't [necessarily] mean you conceive a child. When conceptions are dangerous [i.e., during the fertile days of the menstrual cycle], it happens more easily, this has happened, and it has also happened that you can't conceive a child. I had a friend who birthed a child—she wasn't able to conceive a child for a long time, and she [conceived] the child during her [menstrual] period.

If sex does not necessarily lead to conception, physiologically or conceptually, neither is the cultural or even spiritual value of erotas reducible to procreation; if it were, prostitution and abortion might be less widespread than they are. Viewing sex as a discrete, physical act, rather than an instantiation of a social, even metaphysical, relationship, family planners fail to comprehend that local concepts of erotas, of physical love, encompass meanings far beyond the material consequences of procreation or disease transmission that remain at the center of biomedical public health portraits of what erotas has been and what modern sex should be. In pressing people to see sex as a harmful risk to one's self, family planners neglect to consider how women and men might view sex as a hopeful gamble on aghape.

Steeped in this discourse, young women are responding to new models of romantic love and "proper" sex in ways that family planners never anticipated. For example, desiring both erotas and aghape in marriage, young women beginning a "sex life" prior to marriage may appreciate condoms, withdrawal, and the rhythm method precisely because they are male methods. These women grew up hearing their mothers and grandmothers evaluate "good" and "not nice" husbands on the basis of whether wives had to resort to repeat abortion to cover over men's lack of sexual control. For them, "succumbing" to erotas without prophylaxis may not only seem appropriately feminine, it may provide a means of testing out their boyfriends: Is this a responsible man, a man who cares, a man whom I could love and who could love me? Contraceptive cooperation can signal the seeds of an aghape desired in a marriage. As Jennifer Hirsch writes of modern-minded Mexican women who also prefer withdrawal and rhythm, "When a woman's husband 'takes care of her' [the Mexican equivalent of the Greek 'being careful'], she experiences in an intensely physical way her husband's commitment to developing a shared, non-reproductive sexuality. . . . These methods make fertility regulation a shared project, the embodiment of a joint commitment to building a certain kind of family and a certain kind of marriage" (2003:261). Here, sex and reproduction are separated, but without the adoption of medical methods of fertility control themselves. Athenian and Mexican women are using "traditional" contraceptives in "modern" ways.

Family planners seem not to recognize how Greek notions of erotas have already been transformed by "modern" ways of feeling and behaving, and thus they naïvely pitch their safe sex message as the one modern way of thinking and doing, contrasting it to what they suppose to be a "traditionally Greek" fusing of sex and procreation. Athenians in the nineties expressed confusion over the mixed messages they were receiving. A safe-sex backlash emerged in the popular media. To illustrate the structure of feeling that the biomedical gaze fails to recognize, let me offer a popular cultural critique to the globalizing imperative of family planning, the 1999 Greek film comedy with the English title *Safe Sex*.

With 1.5 million domestic ticket sales, *Safe Sex* (directed by Mihalis Reppas and Thanasis Papathanasiou) was a Greek blockbuster. I saw the U.S. premiere in 2000 at a Greek film festival in New York.[1] The movie's centerpiece is a dinner party where guests, connected through a sticky web of hetero- and homosexual encounters, debate the philosophical merits of erotas. A man comments, "Erotas overflows marriage" (his wife quips that he was late for his own wedding because he was at his girlfriend's place). A younger man agrees that erotas is "inexplicable," not rational. While "marriage is a social contract" with set rules, he argues, erotas is exempt from this contract: "Only in the bedroom do we not follow rules" of civilization, culture, social norms. To think otherwise is to "be afraid of passion [*pathos*]." Erotas, he insists, resists sexologists' efforts to biologize it as mere libido; erotas is something else, something "spiritual." Pathos, erotas is the stuff of worldly transcendence.

Like all successful satire, the film's dialogue rings true to Greek popular culture. After all, erotic engagement and devotional worship can lead to *ek stasis* (ecstasy)— meaning to be thrown out of one's position, to be driven out of one's wits. Even the Greek Orthodox Church recognizes that erotas is fundamental to human nature, a condition of original, not mortal sin. "A man of God may win an individual and inward control over the condition of sensuality, but ordinary men need the help of kinsmen and the support of institutions in the unequal fight" (Campbell 1964:326). Greeks both embrace and struggle with sensuality as an important feature of humanity. Erotic self-restraint—being at war with one's emotional impulses much like

Plato's charioteer—is not only a sexy game but a moral test. The ecstatic potential of erotas is undermined, however, by the rational philosophy of prophylaxis. From a local or "traditional" perspective, under certain circumstances, prophylaxis, far from indicating moral responsibility, may be a moral crutch.

Admittedly, an ecstatic view of erotas is an idealized romantic one and it, like the rationalized view of family planners, fails to recognize how erotas, at least the everyday variety that does not lead to *ek stasis*, is produced by and produces double standards for properly gendered behavior. The psychologist Aliki Andoniou (a pseudonym), active in family planning circles, said to me in an interview:

> It's still taboo, the issue of sex and having a sex life [sex *ke erotiki zoë*]. It's still exclusively linked to reproduction, not to people's satisfaction. This doesn't mean that it happens in practice [that sex only leads to reproduction] . . . but in their minds . . . the young boys believe that the girls who, let's say, go to bed with them easily, they are worth nothing.

I heard men brag about sexual conquests one moment and label their transitory partners shameless prostitutes the next. In a 1980s survey of 1,200 Athenians, 24.3 percent of men admitted to extramarital sex in past three years while only 5.8 percent of women did (Agrafiotis et al. 1990). (In a final scene of *Safe Sex*, the philanderer from the dinner party is arrested for murdering his wife in a rage of sexual jealousy.) While several professional women told me this particular gender gap was closing—that more women were stepping outside marriage for erotic pleasure or emotional fulfillment—the relative transition in male-dominated societies from a procreative to a pleasure ethic of sex might well be understood in terms suggested by Caroline Whitbeck, that "individualism or what I call 'the rule of the sons,' has largely replaced patriarchy or 'rule of the fathers' as the structure of the dominant culture" (1990:221). In practice, the ethic of heterosexual egalitarianism, like liberal individualism, remains grounded in a fraternal model of masculinist ideals (Hirsch 2003). But gender still matters. While family planners exhort men and women alike to look out for others by looking out for oneself, Athenian women continue to speak of looking out for oneself by looking out for others (Paxson 2005).

Aghape in an Age of Maternal Consumerism

Nowhere is this feminine ideological imperative—look out for yourself by looking out for others—stronger than in the maternal relationship. Iconographic Christian imagery of sacrificial maternal femininity, viewed by many as the backbone of the "classic Greek family," offers women an idiom in which to appeal for filial devotion. But here, global forces of market capitalism are clearly transforming women's demonstrations of maternal love. In today's consumer society, maternal suffering is increasingly translated into a consumerist idiom and takes the guise of economic sacrifice. I found that some middle-class Athenian women are finding demands for the material expression of maternal love—the quintessential manifestation of aghape—

potentially compromising of a "modern" self-actualizing female subjectivity, also founded on achieved status claims. Here, the language of aghape offers women a vocabulary to criticize the gendered obligations of new forms of social reproduction, those activities and relationships involved in the reproduction and daily maintenance of individuals, and that also reproduce the intergenerational social status of families. Increasingly burdened by new consumer demands, some women are seeking alternative models of family love that do not reproduce patterns of ongoing parental sacrifice for which women as mothers are often accountable.

Aghape, at the center of Greek maternal practice, makes suffering a virtue. Distinguishing between erotas and aghape, 35-year-old Niki explained that aghape obtains "mostly with the mother and the child who is a part of her self, from her body; she had it nine months inside her. [The mother-child relationship] is something different." Greeks describe the fetus as part of the woman's body: the "same blood runs through both." What exists between a pregnant woman and her fetus is an ontology of being-in-relation that exemplifies aghape. In this sense aghape is an ongoing, transformative relationship that connotes a Christian sense of selflessness and that, in Whitbeck's (1990) words, designates a "non-oppositional" ontology in which the self is defined not against "the other" but in mutually enabling relation with others.

Childbirth is the dramatic, painful moment marking the beginning of the social, maternal relationship. Women told me they want to feel the pain of birth. Two felt cheated by Caesarean deliveries. Ariadne, who conceived using in vitro fertilization, told me in an interview: "I wanted to grow a child inside my belly. I wanted my belly to swell up. . . . I wanted to feel the child get bigger, kick. As I told you, I birthed naturally, it hurt—I wanted to feel the pain to get the pleasure out of it." Far from acquiescing to the pain of childbirth as God's Edenic punishment, Greek women deploy the pain and blood of birth to justify the active social role they will play in their children's lives. Nadia Seremetakis writes, "Women labor, suffer, and endure pain for others. Pain is the concept that determines the social character of women's labor, whether this takes place in the mortuary ceremony or the agricultural and domestic economies. Through pain, Maniat women [in southern Greece] link kinship, the division of labor, agricultural and domestic economies—all male-dominated institutions—into an experiential continuum" (1991:115).

Through suffering, Jill Dubisch suggests, Greek women "demonstrate to and remind others of the difficulties inherent in the performance of their roles" (1995:217). Mothers demand children's respect and gratitude by reminding them, "Look what I suffered for you! My child!" (Dubisch 1995:225–226). I argue elsewhere that Athenian women have made sense of the routinization of abortion in Greece with reference to the praxis of maternal love and self-sacrifice (Paxson 2004). Abortion, they say, is a "necessary evil" that a woman endures to enable her to care properly for children she already has, and to avoid bringing a child into a stigmatized or economically disadvantageous existence (the extramarital birth rate in Greece is around 2 percent of all births).

When women's employment is regarded as prerequisite to raising children, "good" mothering is described as providing "the best" material goods and educational opportunities for one's children. As Maila Stivens writes of middle-class urban Malaysia, speaking equally to Athens: "To be a modern mother is to be an active consumer under great pressure to acquire all the commodities necessary for the satisfactory performance of motherhood" (1998:63). Today, a mother's success is dependent not merely on producing children who will inherit the family's name and assets but on raising successful children—children with advanced degrees, who speak two or three languages and can succeed in a competitive job market. Athenian parents routinely send teenage children to *frontistiria*, private institutes open after public school hours, to prepare them for the competitive entrance examinations to the state university system. "High-quality" children are produced through the acquisition of academic and cultural capital attained through considered parental consumption. Anna, a 31-year-old administrative assistant and mother of an eight-month-old who is looked after during the day by her mother, told me, "I would *like* to have another child. At least one more. But it's difficult because I'm working, and because now we want to have everything for our children. You don't decide easily to have more children because you want to provide them *everything*." In research conducted in Athens in 1989, a social psychologist I interviewed found that children's private schooling, clothing, extracurricular activities are paid for by women's financial contributions to household economies.

In a consumer society, where choice and personal achievement signal social status, reputation is assessed on the basis of one's consumer "style." A woman demonstrates her moral worth as a mother by receiving recognition from others that she "chooses" to spend her hard-earned money on her children. Consumerism materializes and exteriorizes the self-sacrifice of motherhood. And maternal love is as calculating as it is passionate and moral. Through this sort of love, through the structure of feeling of maternal love, Greek women look out for themselves by looking out for others.

A good mother has always been a giving mother, but in recent years the material measure of maternal devotion has been subject to inflation. Litsa, the working mother of a seven- year-old, offered this analysis:

> Earlier, when we went to school we wore uniform pinafores; one would last the year with its tears mended. But now, there's this consumerism. Tomorrow my child will see someone wearing such-and-such shoes and he'll tell me, "Me too!" You'll tell me I should fix it so my kid is not interested in name brands. You'll say I don't *have* to send him to extra classes to do a foreign language—I was the last child of five. What my sister wore one year I would take the next, it didn't matter to us. We weren't bombarded by television. Of course, we have done this to our lives. We are the consumers. Tomorrow at the Supermarket we see something new, we try it, we like it—and there's the good discount—so, it's difficult.

It's difficult because, in a consumer society, desire is tricky to disentangle from need. An advertisement for a Greek bank credit card appearing in a women's magazine featured a young girl gazing longingly into a bassinet holding a shiny plastic doll and is captioned, "We grew up . . . and our desires became needs." The ad trades on women's naturalized desire for motherhood in order to naturalize need for financial flexibility in an age when consumption is the most direct means in which a woman provisions her family. Such magazines are filled with advertisements for "baby gear" from fashionable maternity clothes to high-end strollers.

But does the child really need the expensive Italian stroller? No. The mother does, or thinks that she does, to demonstrate that the money she earns as a working woman is appropriately spent on her children. The personal, even erotic pleasure of consumerism is legitimated, moralized when women can incorporate it into narratives of maternal self-sacrifice. Moreover, in reconceptualizing consumption as maternal gift giving, the mother displaces the market thinking that went into the purchase of the stroller (easily equal to the price of her monthly salary as, say, a civil servant). In presenting consumption as maternal sacrifice, the mother incorporates new economic practices into "traditional" social relations such that the child (and witnessing adults) believes it is the recipient of sacrificial love, not a modern woman's consumer pleasure.

Some middle-class women, shouldering the burdens of a "double day" and learning the subjective stance of self-determination, are beginning to raise questions, not the moral ideal of maternal love, but about the economic and emotional costs of being a good, "giving" mother in today's society. I heard middle-class women, as they encounter motherhood in a consumer society, voice cultural criticism of the implications of maternal aghape for female subjectivity.

Lela, who works in civil service and whose 15-month-old son is being brought up largely by her own mother and father, who live in an apartment downstairs, said to me:

> I do not think that motherhood has changed from the past. That is, the relationship between mother and child hasn't changed. What *has* changed is the position of the woman in society. . . . The woman who works doesn't sit at home and raise the kid, as happened before.

Forty-year-old Nadia, whom I met when she appeared at my doorstep peddling foreign-language tapes, elaborated:

> Today's women work. From that moment she also has her personal vigor [*nevro*], her own ambitions, she has many problems, and of course this creates a situation in the home. For example, she would want her husband to help. The Greek man is phallocratic [*fallokratis*]. This means to have been raised to a way of life in which work is made to be either men's or women's. Somehow they don't agree. This creates innumerable problems in a relationship. To put it simply, the woman today is not the woman of the past who stayed under

[*kathotane ipo*] the man. [This] means without voicing her opinion, without voicing her problems, without a lot.

Such statements hint at the friction of modern motherhood in urban Greece: As mothers, women should be self-sacrificing but as modern women, they should be self-actualizing. Athenians, wanting to reconcile being good mothers and good women, struggle to draw a line between virtuous selflessness (aghape) and destructive self-compromise akin to what Sara Ruddick (1980) has called "inauthenticity" in maternal thought. The relational ontology of motherhood makes it difficult for women, as Vasso, a social psychologist who teaches women's assertiveness training workshops, complained to me, to separate their own "needs" from those of their children. To be a good mother means to be a giving person. But should a mother really give up her self for her family? Two conflicting demands supported by modern pressures—for maternal self-sacrifice and for women's self-realization—generate a friction.

Searching for a self outside a relational ontology, I heard a few middle-class women—with and without children—voice a counter-hegemonic claim not only that motherhood is insufficient to realize proper womanhood but that motherhood can compromise women's autonomy. Ariadne, a new mother in her early thirties, voiced skepticism of "modern" women's so-called liberation in comparison with her mother's generation: "My mother used to tell me, 'Look, when you become married, then you can do what you want.' And I used to tell her that when I become married I would not be able to do what I want. From then on you 'do' a family. You do what you want when you are single." Now that women's moral worth is evaluated more in terms of maternal behavior than sexual comportment, motherhood may not signal a woman's freedom so much as the loss of it. Narrating shifts in the material conditions of motherhood, Athenian women see their very selves as changing, historically as well as over the life course.

Whereas mothers in their thirties bring a critical reflexivity to their mothering, women in their twenties whose kin-based gender identity remains as daughter rather than mother can recognize the emotional and subjective toll that today's parenting ethic is taking on their own mothers and fathers. Aliki, an unmarried graduate student in her late twenties, articulated a pervasive generation gap circa the early 1990s. Speaking of her generation, she explained:

We grew up in a period of economic growth [1970s–1980s]. We learned [what it was like] to have relatively nice houses, to have nice clothes, a car. Unfortunately, however, we reached a point where we got stuck. When the basic wage is around 100,000 [drachmes] and you want a home in a nice area the rent will be 70,000 a month.[2] This is normal, it's not some absurd amount. You think that you can't live. It's very hard. And if you want everything this is what you do: the parents of a friend of mine used to eat bread and cheese while their kids ate [regular] food [including meat] so they could gather the money to buy a flat.

Aliki's parents are making sacrifices to help finance her advanced degree from a British university. While most of Aliki's college friends continue to live with their parents (in villages or in Athens), her friend Sophia, a record store clerk who also tutors English, explained to me how her own parents feel badly that they cannot offer her more economic support since they had to "abandon" her in Athens:

> I live alone. My parents had to go back to the village in Crete. I pay rent, and every month they try to send me what they can, and I see every time I go down to Crete that they worry they can't give me 40,000 a month. If there's a month when they can't send me money they waste 10,000 calling me on the phone to tell me they're sorry.[3] If my family were in Athens I wouldn't try to live on my own.

With Greece's productive infrastructure lagging behind its consumption rate, even middle-class Athenians are able to accumulate only what are perceived as the basics—an apartment, a limited wardrobe of decent clothes, a regular diet of meat—with the aid of others, usually their parents or in-laws. A professional woman I know, in her late thirties and single, lives alone in a Halandri (suburban) flat purchased for her by her father, a flat she could not have afforded on her salary alone. As L. A. Rebhun writes (this volume), love is simultaneously expressed through social, emotional, and economic support. Love and interest continuously implicate one another because, Rebhun notes, "both govern affiliation." In these cases, young people recognize the moral system in which their parents operate—based in an era when status flowed from parents to children by way of inherited character and property—while at the same time planning for themselves a life that their parents can barely imagine.

Soula, a 39-year-old clerk who works for a foreign embassy who had her first child just over a year before we spoke, voiced ambivalence in articulating the tensions of socioeconomic change in Greece that are absorbed by family and household relations:

> The institution of the family in Greece is still strong. There is still the meaning that "This is my child and I have some obligations." Of course in certain cases I think it gets dragged out a bit, overdone—the kids get married and the parents think that they still have obligations. But there is also the other extreme [which she sees elsewhere in Europe and in the United States] that as soon as the kids turn 18 or 20 that's it, finished. The parents don't have any responsibility, nothing on their plate. I agree with this because at some point the [Greek] parents begin to interfere in their children's life when they grow up, when they get married and have their own families and they have the reins. There are the two sides: the parents who say "We brought you into life and we are obliged to serve you all our lives," and the others who say "We brought you up now you have to take care of us." What I'm trying to say is that there's something that I like and something that I don't like in the Greek family. While it's very tight,

in certain ways it pulls you apart a little; they want to be continuously together but you can't.

Many of the young adults, my contemporaries, whom I knew in Athens consciously worked to protect their parents' sense of themselves as "good," giving parents. Despina worked a part-time job in the British city where she attended graduate school to supplement her modest scholarship that her parents already supplemented every few months. She told me she "can't" divulge her job to her parents; they would feel that she "had" to take a job because they had "failed" to provide adequately for her, when Despina herself has no such criticism of her parents. These middle-class women in their twenties recognize and respect their parents' need to feel they are providing adequately for their children, revealing a new generation-based (rather than gender-based) rift between the appearance of prestige and the reality of power (cf. Friedl 1967). They negotiate a measure of independence without hurting their parents' feelings because they have not rejected the principle of family solidarity, even as they cultivate a more independent, achievement-based subjectivity. This is love. But it's not self-sacrificing. It is, perhaps, as much a matter of erotas as it is aghape.

Thinking with Love about Subjectivity and Globalization

To speak of familial love in terms of erotas is not the same as speaking of maternal aghape. I heard women—mothers, daughters, single women (often divorcées)—who live alone, whose subjective relations do not conform to the model of maternal self-sacrifice, speak of familial love using the language of erotas. I interpret this as a nuanced criticism of the self-sacrifice implied in feminine aghape, exemplified by maternalism.

Over a bottle of wine at dinner one night, Moira, who teaches modern Greek to foreigners, expressed her distress that the word *erotas* is abused in other languages, reduced to an erotics linked to pornography. This is an injustice to erotas, she declared, quoting Plato's *Symposium*, which she had recently reread (ancient Greek language as well as classical texts are part of the national school curriculum; Moira has a degree in philology). As Diotima schooled Socrates, in Moira's interpretation of Plato's text, erotas is itself a beautiful thing, a relationship that brings one out of one's self with an awareness of one's engagement with the world. Moreover, the transcendental potential of erotas—*ek stasis*—is not limited to physical, sexual eroticism. Moira explained that she could be *erotevmeni*, in erotas, with one of her classes, with a flower, with her cats (one is named Socrates!).

This conversation reminded me of one I had earlier with Phoebe, who, like Moira, was once married but divorced after deciding not to have children. Both women intimated to me that their decision to divorce was prompted in part by a realization that their husbands turned out not to be men with whom they wanted to have children. At the time of our interview, Phoebe, then 40 years old, told me she still hopes to become a mother. "But," she said, "I believe that within a woman exists feelings of motherhood. And you will see this even in women who haven't had a child, it comes out in their behavior towards an animal, let's say, a dog, or a cat. A special behavior, which seems somewhat like the feeling of motherhood." Phoebe, like Moira, works with students and, I suggest, narrates her subjective experience of this work as akin to mothering, in terms of love.

Phoebe, Moira, and others I encountered speak in terms of a love that embraces erotas as well as aghape. If aghape can award both virtue and power through the calculated care of others, the power of erotas is self-transformative (and see Lorde 1984). One falls in love with one's child, one's class, one's cat—and realizes something about oneself. When one is *erotevmeni*, one thinks and feels differently about one's place in the world. The trick—"risk" discourse in Greece takes the language of gaming (Malaby 2003)—is that erotas may lead one astray, away from one's true self (or a self one is happy with), or—one thinks! one believes! one hopes!—erotas may lead one to a place of security and self-affirmation. This sort of erotic can speak to the hopes, expectations, and risks of both romantic and maternal love.

Spinning away from my ethnographic data but still holding to the threads of my conversations with Moira, Phoebe, Sophia, Despina, and others, I have toyed with the notion of a maternal love that embraces the ideology of erotas, a desire of or for an other that is not viewed as opposite of or oppositional to the self. Caroline Whitbeck has named this a "feminist erotics," based on a feminist sense that "the distinctness of others does not require that they be counted as opposite in character to the self" (1990:211). Maternal love can embrace such feminist erotics. The notion of "falling in love" with one's child, with all the ambivalence and tension and fear and joy this entails, certainly rings true to the experience of many Western mothers.

Erotas and aghape are good to think with about subjectivity because they speak, in ways that force attention to the mutual constitution of gender, sexuality, and kinship (Yanagisako and Collier 1987), alternately and at once of relationality and self-perception, reputation and virtue—qualities that gain meaning within historically specific configurations of civil society. If love is good to think with about subjectivity, this volume suggests it should also be useful to think with about the impact of global forces on local socialities and structures of feeling. To what extent is this true? We should not assume that "global flows"—of media, of biomedical bodies, of consumption opportunities—inevitably transform in uniform, predictable ways local understandings of love and intimacy. This, indeed, is the fallacy under which many family planning programs operate, in Greece as elsewhere (see Adams and Pigg 2005).

Instead, I find useful Anna Tsing's (2005) recent discussion of global "frictions"—not unidirectional, unimpeded "flows" or "impacts." "Speaking of friction is a reminder of the importance of interaction in defining movement, cultural form, and agency" (Tsing 2005:6). If any social activity routinely generates friction, it's sex. If any discourse is made routinely to articulate people's subjective experience of social friction, it's love. Love, I am suggesting, is not so much itself a potent site of social change as it provides a powerful vocabulary in which ordinary people try to speak to their subjective experiences, hopes, and fears of social change. Love is "thought as felt and feeling as thought"—but thought that tries to define, articulate "a social experience with is still in process, often indeed not yet recognized as social but taken to be private, idiosyncratic"; it is a frictional "structure of feeling" (Williams 1977:132).

My argument is inspired, too, by Lila Abu-Lughod's essay "The Romance of Resistance," in which she uses "resistance as a diagnostic of power" "to trace how power relations are historically transformed—especially with the introduction of forms and techniques of power characteristic of modern states and capitalist economies" (1990:48, 42). Writing of young Bedouin women who came of age under sedentarism and who "resist" traditional patriarchal codes of feminine modesty by buying lingerie and cosmetics, Abu-Lughod comments, "As the veils they wear get sheerer and these young women become more involved in the kind of sexualized femininity associated with the world of consumerism . . . they are becoming increasingly enmeshed in new sets of power relations of which they are scarcely aware" (50). Such power relations are familiar to Western feminists: women's status and well-being is to some extent reliant on their ability to persuade men to buy them things. But the young Bedouin women do not see this. What feels to them like resistance in relation to the Bedouin camp constitutes, for Abu-Lughod, new forms of subjection in the encroaching world of Egyptian market relations, "a world in which kinship ties are attenuated while companionate marriage, marital love based on choice, and romantic love are idealized, making central women's attractiveness and individuality as enhanced and perhaps necessarily marked by differences in adornment" (50).

Abu-Lughod raises a question for comparative study: "[D]o certain modern techniques or forms of power work in such indirect ways, or seem to offer such positive attractions, that people do not as readily resist them?" (1990:52). Rephrased with the present study in mind: Are Athenian women so seduced by new opportunities to experience and demonstrate romantic and maternal love that they overlook tradeoffs in their exercise of agency, what Kandiyoti (1988) would call the erosion of women's traditional "patriarchal bargains"? My ethnographic answer must be to equivocate. New forms of productive power rarely displace old forms but rather run in parallel, at some moments in mutual reinforcement, at others in cross-cutting tension. They produce friction. "As a metaphorical image, friction reminds us that heterogeneous and unequal encounters can lead to new arrangements of culture and power" (Tsing 2005:5). Tsing offers the imagery of a road to conceptualize "how friction works: Roads create pathways that make motion easier and more efficient, but in doing so they limit where we go. . . . Friction inflects historical trajectories, enabling, excluding, and particularizing" (6).

To return to family planning and consumerism in Athens, let me introduce a more watery set of metaphors from fluid dynamics to conceptualize how global flows may meet frictional resistance. New notions of love and responsibility introduced by family planning rhetoric do not flow unimpeded into the stream of Athenian social life but are tossed into turbulence with traditional notions of erotas and aghape. Family planners work unsuccessfully to change the meanings of *erotas* and *aghape* to align better with Anglophonic *sex* and *love*. Athenians respond with wary skepticism to the liberating promise of safe sex, achieved by "looking out for others by looking out for oneself." Women do not all seem eager to give up the patriarchal bargain of recourse in abortion for romantic promises of self-interested sexual love, even—or especially—when such promises are made by the authoritative voice of a medical system that has been known to be misogynistic, influenced by Western forces that have been known to be paternalistic toward Greek ways of living (Paxson 2004). Erotas and aghape, sex and love spin together in turbulent solution without precipitating out a newly modern, fully "globalized" ideology of sexual agency.

As a standard daily practice, consumerism, however, flows more freely into the slipstream of daily middle-class life, offering women new means of expressing enduring maternal values. Yet here, too, friction is met in the form of a hydraulic system calibrated to the self-other relationships described in terms of erotas and aghape. When poured into purchases for one's child, the self-realizing pleasures of erotic consumption can be balanced by the self-sacrifice of maternal aghape. But for some women, there is a point at which the pressure entailed in earning the economic capital and in gaining the shopping savvy of being a super(mom)-consumer may force out of reach what Audre Lorde (1984)—and my friend Moira—might call the self-realizing potential of the erotic. A mother can go too far. As a resource through which she looks out for herself by looking out for others, her love is not infallible.

The turbulence introduced into sexual relations by family planning is immediate and apparent and therefore easy to resist. The hydraulic cost-benefit dynamics generated by consumerism is—again, at least for the middle classes—delayed, contingent. What begins as a rewarding balance between the erotic pleasure of consumerism and the self-sacrifice of maternal giving can gradually build up enough pressure—on her time, her income—to force open a floodgate through which self-sacrifice becomes self-compromise.

Acknowledgments

I would like to thank the editors of this book for inviting me to contribute, and especially Jennifer Hirsch for her helpful comments on a draft of this chapter. I also thank Stefan Helmreich. My research in Athens was funded by the National Science Foundation and Stanford University.

Notes

1. I have been unable to view the movie a second time to verify quotations jotted down during my initial viewing. I apologize for any inaccuracies.
2. This price would fetch a one- or perhaps two-bedroom flat, depending on the size, the floor (ground versus higher with possible view), and the neighborhood.
3. Relative prices in US$ as at 1994 are $174 and $43. Compared with housing in U.S. cities, housing in Athens is inexpensive, while material goods are exorbitant.

References

Abu-Lughod, Lila
   1990   The Romance of Resistance. American Ethnologist 17(1):41–55.
Adams, Vincanne, and Stacy Leigh Pigg, eds.
   2005   The Moral Object of Sex: Science, Development, and Sexuality in Global Perspective. Durham: Duke University Press.
Agrafiotis, Dimosthenis, P. Pantzou, E. Ioannidis, A. Doumas, Ch. Tselepi, and A. Antonopoulou
   1990   Knowledge, Attitudes, Beliefs, and Practices in Relation to HIV Infection and AIDS: The Case of the City of Athens, Greece. Athens School of Public Health, Department of Sociology. Draft.
Apostolopoulou, Sophia
   1994   Population Policy and Low Birth Rate in Greece. Planned Parenthood in Europe 23(2):14.
Campbell, John K.
   1964   Honour, Family and Patronage: A Study of Institutions and Moral Values in a Greek Mountain Community. Oxford: Oxford University Press.
Doxiadi-Trip, Anthi
   1993   Pro-profilaktiká [Pro-prophylactics]. Yinéka, May:320–321.
Dubisch, Jill
   1995   In a Different Place: Pilgrimage, Gender, and Politics at a Greek Island Shrine. Princeton: Princeton University Press.
Emke-Poulopoulou, Ira
   1994   To dhimoghrafikó [Demographics]. Athens: Ellin.
Friedl, Ernestine
   1967   The Position of Women: Appearance and Reality. Anthropological Quarterly 40(3):97–108.
Georges, Eugenia
   1996   Abortion Policy and Practice in Greece. Social Science of Medicine 42(4):509–519.
Greenhalgh, Susan
   1995   Anthropology Theorizes Reproduction: Integrating Practice, Political Economic, and Feminist Perspectives. In Situating Fertility: Anthropology and Demographic Inquiry. Susan Greenhalgh, ed. Pp. 3–28. Cambridge: Cambridge University Press.
Greer, Germaine
   1984   Sex and Destiny: The Politics of Human Fertility. London: Secker & Warburg.
Hirsch, Jennifer S.
   2003   A Courtship after Marriage: Sexuality and Love in Mexican Transnational Families. Berkeley: University of California Press.
Katz, Jonathan Ned
   1990   The Invention of Heterosexuality. Socialist Review 20(1):7–33.
Kandiyoti, Deniz
   1988   Bargaining with Patriarchy. Gender and Society 2(3):274–290.
Lorde, Audre
   1984   Sister Outsider. Freedom, CA: Crossing Press.
Malaby, Thomas
   2003   Gambling Life: Dealing in Contingency in a Greek City. Urbana: University of Illinois Press.
Paxson, Heather
   2002   Rationalizing Sex: Family Planning and the Making of Modern Lovers in Urban Greece. American Ethnologist 29(2):1–28.

2004   Making Modern Mothers: Ethics and Family Planning in Urban Greece. Berkeley: University of California Press.

2005   Family Planning, Human Nature, and the Ethical Subject of Sex in Greece. *In* The Moral Object of Sex: Science, Development, and Sexuality in Global Perspective. Vincanne Adams and Stacy Leigh Pigg, eds. Pp. 95–124. Durham: Duke University Press.

Ruddick, Sara
1980   Maternal Thinking. Feminist Studies, 6 (2):342–364.

Schneider, Jane, and Peter Schneider
1995   Coitus Interruptus and Family Respectability in Catholic Europe. *In* Conceiving the New World Order: The Global Politics of Reproduction. Faye D. Ginsburg and Rayna Rapp, eds. Pp. 177–194. Berkeley: University of California Press.

Seremetakis, C. Nadia
1991   The Last Word: Women, Death, and Divination in Inner Mani. Chicago: University of Chicago Press.

Shorter, Edward
1975   The Making of the Modern Family. New York: Basic Books.

Stivens, Maila
1998   Modernizing the Malay Mother. *In* Maternities and Modernities: Colonial and Postcolonial Experiences in Asia and the Pacific. Kalpana Ram and Margaret Jolly, eds. Pp. 50–80. Cambridge: Cambridge University Press.

Symeonidou, Haris
1990   Apaschólisi ke ghonimótita ton yinekón stin periohí tis protévousas [Occupation and fertility of women in greater Athens]. Athens: Ethnikó Kéntro Kinonikón Erevnón.

Tsing, Anna Lowenhaupt
2005   Friction: An Ethnography of Global Connection. Princeton: Princeton University Press.

Whitbeck, Caroline
1990   Love, Knowledge and Transformation. *In* Hypatia Reborn: Essays in Feminist Philosophy. Azizah Y. al-Hibri and Margaret A. Simons, eds. Pp. 204–225. Bloomington: Indiana University Press.

Williams, Raymond
1977   Marxism and Literature. Oxford: Oxford University Press.

Yanagisako, Sylvia J., and Jane F. Collier
1987   Toward a Unified Analysis of Gender and Kinship. *In* Gender and Kinship: Essays toward a Unified Analysis. Jane F. Collier and Sylvia J. Yanagisako, eds. Pp. 14–50. Stanford: Stanford University Press.

7

Loving Your Infertile Muslim Spouse
Notes on the Globalization of IVF and Its Romantic Commitments in Sunni Egypt and Shia Lebanon

Marcia C. Inhorn

Since the birth in 1978 of Louise Brown, the world's first test-tube baby, in vitro fertilization (IVF) has spread around the globe, reaching countries far from the technology-producing nations of the West. Perhaps nowhere is this globalization process more evident than in the 22 nations of the Muslim Middle East, where a private IVF industry is flourishing. Today, IVF centers have opened in nations ranging from the small, petro-rich Arab Gulf countries such as Bahrain and Qatar, to larger but less prosperous North African nations such as Morocco and Egypt. As of 2005, Egypt boasted nearly 50 IVF centers, outstripping its high-tech neighbor Israel, with its 24 IVF centers (Kahn 2000). Yet, the tiny neighboring country of Lebanon has nearly 15 IVF centers for a population of less than 5 million, constituting one of the highest per capita concentrations of IVF centers in the world.

As I argue in this chapter, assisted reproductive technologies are not transferred into cultural voids when they reach places like Egypt and Lebanon. Rather, local considerations, be they cultural, social, economic, or political, shape and sometimes curtail the way these Western-generated reproductive technologies are offered to and received by non-Western subjects. Thus, the assumption by global producer nations that assisted reproductive technologies—as value-free, inherently beneficial medical technologies—are "immune" to culture and can thus be appropriately transferred and implemented anywhere and everywhere is subject to challenge once local formulations, perceptions, and actual consumption of these technologies are taken into consideration.

The global spread of assisted reproductive technologies provides a particularly salient but little discussed example of what Arjun Appadurai has termed a "technoscape," or the "global configuration, also ever fluid, of technology, and the fact that technology, both high and low, both mechanical and information, now moves at high speeds across various kinds of previously impervious boundaries" (1996:34). Appadurai reminds us that this movement of technologies around the globe is both a deeply historical and inherently localizing process. In other words, globalization is not enacted in a uniform manner around the world, nor is it simply culturally homogenizing—necessarily "Westernizing" or even "Americanizing" in its effects. The global is always imbued with local meaning, such that local actors, living their everyday lives at particular historical moments in particular places, mold the very form that global processes take. As Akbar Ahmed and Hastings Donnan note, "It is the cultural flows between nations which above all else seem to typify the contemporary globalization process (or its current phase)." Thus, "Even though the same cultural 'message' may be received in different places, it is domesticated by being interpreted and incorporated according to local values" (1994:3). Similarly, as Carla Freeman (2000) reminds us, it is important to ask how third world recipients of global technologies resist their application, or at least reconfigure the ways in which these technologies are to be adopted in local cultural contexts.

This acknowledgment of the importance of locality in the global dispersion of modern biotechnologies has been a theme of much recent work in medical anthropology, particularly in the anthropology of reproduction and global reproductive health policy. Faye Ginsburg and Rayna Rapp (1995) argue that the global technoscape through which new reproductive technologies spread is an uneven terrain, in that some nations and regions within nations have achieved greater access to these fruits of globalization than others. However, Ginsburg and Rapp are quick to point out that the power to define reproduction is not necessarily unidirectional—flowing from the West, with its money and technology, to the rest of the world. Rather, "people everywhere actively use their cultural logics and social relations to incorporate, revise, or resist the influence of seemingly distant political and economic forces" (1995:1).

In the anthropology of reproduction, much of this concern with locality has to do with local moral systems, or what Arthur Kleinman (1995) has called "local moral worlds." According to Kleinman, local moral worlds are "moral accounts, [which] are the commitments of social participants in a local world about what is at stake in everyday experience" (45) Through an "ethnography of experience," Kleinman urges medical anthropologists to pay close attention to moral issues of spiritual pain and social suffering, which may accompany the arrival of new biotechnologies, such as IVF, around the globe.

Although the focus of Kleinman and many other medical anthropologists has been on social suffering, it is also useful to turn our medical anthropological attention to the under-examined topic of this volume, love. The goal of this chapter is to highlight the love that commits infertile couples to use assisted reproductive technologies, and the love that keeps them together when these technologies fail, as they often do. As I argue here, rapidly globalizing assisted reproductive technologies such as IVF are accompanied by loving commitments, even in an area of the world that is rarely characterized, at least in the Western media, as a loving terrain. Indeed, in the aftermath of September 11 and in the midst of a current tragic U.S.–led war in Iraq (and Afghanistan), as well as the ongoing violence between Israel and Palestine, the lack of Western understanding of the Middle East and Muslim peoples has become abundantly apparent, as have the many stereotypes of the Muslim world as a hotbed of religiously driven politics, violence, and terrorism. In this chapter, my goal is to help unseat some of these pervasive "tropes of terrorism" by focusing in-stead on Muslim men and women's everyday lives and loves in Sunni Egypt and Shia Lebanon. There, Islam, as the dominant religion, encourages science, biotechnology, and therapeutic agency in the face of illness and adversity, such as infertility. As I show, Islam also profoundly shapes the moral experience of IVF for Muslim couples, in ways quite different from the West. The practice of IVF in Egypt, where the dominant Sunni version of Islam is practiced, differs significantly from its practice in Lebanon, which has a Shia Muslim majority, with implications for love, marriage, and gender relations that are profound.

Notes on Love in the Middle East

It is important to begin this chapter by attempting to describe what love is and means in the Muslim Middle East, in the light of the increasing theorization and empirical investigation of this concept within the discipline of anthropology. Since the 1980s, anthropologists have increasingly taken up the topic of love, focusing primarily on so-called romantic (or passionate) love and its biological, cognitive, and social parameters (De Munck 1996). One of the major goals of this growing body of literature has been to disprove an early scholarly notion—one found within the discipline of anthropology itself—that romantic (or passionate) love could not be found in non-Euro-American contexts. Most earlier studies maintained the very ethnocentric and Eurocentric bias that romantic love "is a European contribution to world culture" (Jankowiak and Fischer 1992:149). However, William Jankowiak and Edward Fischer, in their groundbreaking cross-cultural study of romantic love in 166 societies, discovered that romantic love is a "near-universal" feature of the societies they studied, with romantic love being defined by them for the purposes of their in-vestigation as "an intense attraction that involves the idealization of the other, within an erotic context, with the expectation of enduring for some time into the future" (1992:150). They contrasted this definition of romantic love with "the companion-ship phase of love (sometimes referred to as attachment) which is characterized by the growth of a more peaceful, comfortable, and fulfilling relationship; it is a strong and enduring affection built upon long term association" (150).

Such dualities are common in the scholarly literature on love. As noted by Vic-tor De Munck (1996) in his study of love and marriage in a Sri Lankan Muslim community, anthropological studies in South Asia have tended to divide marriage into two types: "arranged" and "love" marriages. The increasing frequency and ac-ceptability of love marriages in otherwise arranged-marriage societies throughout the region has generally been attributed to processes of social change, including indus-trialization, modernization, urbanization, and Westernization, all of which are seen as correlated with the decreasing importance of the joint or extended family as a cor-porate unit and the consequent growth of nuclear families and individual autonomy. As De Munck discovered in his own study of a Muslim community, however, "love can be accommodated to an arranged marriage model," with many arranged mar-riages being, in fact, "romantically motivated" (1996:698).

This division of conjugality into two oppositional types—romantic versus companionate, arranged versus love—is inherently problematic, since many marriages around the world may combine features of both simultaneously. In the Middle East, for example, the widely held expectation is that romantic love and sexual desire will develop in time within arranged marriages, such that arranged marriages become love marriages. Furthermore, as in De Munck's South Asian example, many so-called arranged marriages in the Middle Eastern region begin with desire, longing, and sexual attraction, or, to use De Munck's term, "romantic motivation." Similarly, the romantic/companionate marriage duality is inherently problematic, in that many long-term "companionate" marriages in the Middle East are characterized by on-going "romance" and satisfying sexual lives. The assumption that romantic love somehow fades in time into a friendly—but sexually stagnate—"companionship" needs to be questioned for marriages in the Middle East, as elsewhere.

Furthermore, what Jankowiak and Fischer call "the validity of an affectionless past"— that love is a fairly recent European invention with no historical tradition outside of the West—is patently untrue. As shown by anthropologists working in non-Western societies around the world, "long traditions of romantic love" (Smith 2001:130) may be found and even valorized in many societies through fables, songs, poetry, and other forms of popular culture (Larkin 1997). In her seminal study *Notes on Love in a Tamil Family*, Margaret Trawick (1990b) shows how love saturates Tamil society in South India. Speaking of her informants' lives, Trawick writes, "They had been exposed to many formal teachings expounding upon and extolling love, and they were surrounded, filled, and made into human beings by a culture that said in a thousand ways that love was the highest good" (1990a:91).

As these studies suggest, the challenge for anthropology is to interrogate the very real possibility that love exists in "unlikely places," including, from Western eyes, the supposedly violent and loveless Middle East. Like Trawick, I argue here that, love, or *hubb* as it is called in Arabic, is a highly extolled virtue, expounded on in many formal spiritual teachings and literally saturating everyday Middle Eastern life in the realms of popular culture and actual affective relations between spouses, families, and other close kith and kin.

In terms of popular culture, the Middle Eastern region is replete, both now and in the past, with love stories in music, literature, and poetry. The most popular Arabic songs and movies depict *hubb* as involving longing, attraction, desire—often unrequited—thus leading to even more pronounced longing, attraction, and desire, as well as heartbreak and suffering. Indeed, the world of popular culture in the Middle East is profoundly imbued with *hubb*, as is the world of actual affective relations. In the Middle East, spouses, parents and children, close kin, and close friends refer to each other by the derivative term *habibi* (male) or *habibti* (female), literally translated as "my love" or "my loved one" but also glossed semiotically as "my dear" or, when between friends, "my chum." That one of the most common terms of reference in the Arabic-speaking world is derived directly from the word *hubb*, or love, reflects the importance of this emotion and its salience for connecting one into a web of deeply emotionally enmeshed relations of affection and care.

Furthermore, *hubb* is a major part of the spiritual realm in the Muslim world. In his treatise on Islamic mysticism, Alexander Knysh (2000) explains that an ascetic and mystical tradition known as sufism has been implicitly present in Islam since its very inception, eventually becoming explicit during the first Islamic centuries (the seventh and eighth centuries C.E.). Instead of focusing on the Day of Judgment and the wrath of hell, sufi mystics focused on God's limitless grace, mercy, and divine majesty. This emphasis on the "love of God" found justification in the Qur'anic verse, "He [God] loves them, and they love Him" (5:54/57). As noted by Knysh, "Inspired by this and similar verses and traditions, the early mystics began to celebrate their longing for the Divine beloved in poems and utterances of exceptional beauty and verve. It was this exalted love and longing which, in their eyes, justified the austerities to which they subjected themselves in order to demonstrate their faithfulness to the heavenly Beloved" (2000:9)

Love of an inherently loving God continues to be extolled as one of the most important elements of Islam, not only in its mystical form. The Qur'an and other Islamic scriptures, which provide behavioral and spiritual guidelines for the world's 1.3 billion practicing Muslims, describe God as loving, compassionate, and merciful, particularly toward those Muslim believers who are faithful and loving to God in return. Yet, it is important to note that love per se—including conjugal love and affection—receives no particular ideological valorization in the Islamic scriptures, although expectations of sexual fulfillment and fidelity are mandated (Musallam 1983).

Indeed, an argument can be made—as it has been—that Islam actually militates against strong, loving marriages by way of Islamic personal status laws that lead to the "fragility of marital bonds" (Charrad 2001). As Mounira Charrad convincingly argues, "Far from fostering the development of long-lasting, strong emotional ties between husband and wife, the law underplays the formation and continuity of independent and stable conjugal units. This shows in particular in the procedure to terminate marriage, the legality of polygamy, and the absence of community property between husband and wife" (2001:35). With regard to infertility, Charrad notes that the legality of polygamy allows a man to marry a second wife in the hope of having heirs, particularly sons. However, she also notes that despite Western stereotypes of widespread marital polygamy and "images of harems [that] have captured the imagination of Western observers" (38), polygamy is statistically insignificant in most Middle Eastern countries, practiced by only a few, generally less than 2 percent.

Both demographically and culturally, marriage is a highly valued and normatively upheld institution throughout the Middle East. While allowing for divorce, Islam clearly extols the virtues of marriage, regarding it as *Sunna*, or the way of the Prophet Muhammad. Thus, Middle Easterners are among the "most married" people in the world (Omran and Roudi 1993), with well over 90 percent of adults marrying at least once in a lifetime. Divorce rates are also relatively low, half the 50 percent rates found in the United States.

Furthermore, many marriages in the Middle East are characterized by what I have termed "conjugal connectivity" (Inhorn 1996). In my own work,[1] I draw on Suad Joseph's (1993, 1994, 1999) provocative insights on "patriarchal connectivity" in the Middle East—or the ways in which patriarchy operates through both male domination and deeply enmeshed, loving commitments between Arab patriarchs and their female and junior family members. According to Joseph, socialization within Arab families places a premium on connectivity, or the intensive bonding of individuals through love, involvement, and commitment. Joseph also notes that connectivity exists independently of patriarchy and probably occurs in most cultures in which individuation, autonomy, and separation are not valued or supported. In such cultures, perhaps especially in the Arab world, family members are generally deeply involved with each other, expecting mutual love, exerting considerable influence over each others' lives, prioritizing family solidarity, and encouraging subordination of members' needs to collective interests. Persons are thus embedded in familial relational matrices that shape their deepest sense of self and offer security when the external social, economic, and political situation is uncertain, as it in much of the Arab world.

While Joseph's research focuses on the Arab family, my own work focuses on the couple, a social dyad for which there is no term in Arabic. Extending Joseph's analysis, I suggest that the loving commitments of patriarchal connectivity, which are socialized within the Arab family, also operate in the marital sphere. In my own work in Egypt and more recently Lebanon, I suggest that both men and women, including poor men and women, are negotiating new kinds of marital relationships— relationships based on the kind of loving connectivity experienced and expected in families of origin but that has heretofore been unexpected and unexamined within the conjugal unit. That conjugal connectivity is true even among infertile Middle Eastern Muslim couples attests to shifting marital praxis and the importance of love, mutual respect, and the sharing of life's problems even in the absence of desired children. Despite widespread expectations within the Middle East that infertile marriages are bound to fail—with men necessarily blaming women for the infertility and divorcing or replacing them if they do not produce children, especially sons—such expectations may represent indigenous stereotypes based on the aforementioned features of Islamic personal status law described by Charrad (2001). As I would argue instead, the success of so many infertile marriages in the Middle East bespeaks the strengthening of conjugal connectivity at the expense of patriarchy, which, according to my own work and that of other Middle Eastern feminist scholars, is being undermined (Inhorn 1996).

I argue that the tremendous growth of IVF clinics in this region of the world over the past two decades bespeaks the deep feelings of love, loyalty, and commitment experienced by many couples, including both husbands and wives in childless marriages. The potential of love and conjugal connectivity to shape the IVF experience, as well as the potential of IVF to transform notions of love, companionate marriage, and gender relations in the Middle East, should become abundantly apparent in this chapter on IVF in Egypt and Lebanon. Furthermore, for many poor and middle-class couples in these two Middle Eastern countries, IVF would not be possible if it were not for the financial and emotional support of family members, who can prove their loving commitments by facilitating couples' access to IVF. In IVF clinics in Cairo and Beirut, mothers, mothers-in-law, fathers, brothers, sisters, cousins, nieces, and nephews sometimes accompany their infertile family members during IVF trials—filling waiting rooms in expectant anticipation and paying the bills on the way out. In short, the "coming out" of IVF in the Middle East over two decades has drawn the family in. Whereas IVF was deeply stigmatized and kept private by most couples only a decade ago (Inhorn 2003a), today IVF is a well-known solution for infertility that has lost much of its tabooed status, at least in urban centers. The acknowledgment of IVF as a solution for infertility has softened families' patriarchal pressure on sons to divorce their infertile wives. Furthermore, it has made IVF a "family affair" in many cases, with kin demonstrating their love for sons, daughters, sisters, and brothers through tangible aid and deeply enmeshed participation in the quest for an IVF "take-home baby."

On Finding Love: Methods and Goals

The goal of this chapter, then, is to demonstrate the conjugal and familial love fueling the IVF industry in the Middle East, but with very different implications among Sunni and Shia Muslim couples in Egypt and Lebanon. In both countries, I have conducted qualitative, ethnographic interviews with Muslim IVF patients, both husbands and wives, now totaling nearly 400 patient couples since I began my research in Egypt in 1988. The findings presented here are based on ethnographic research carried out in 1996 and 2003 in four IVF clinics in two urban Middle Eastern locales: Cairo, Egypt, and Beirut, Lebanon. In Egypt, I spent the summer of 1996 studying 66 infertile couples attending IVF clinics in two elite suburbs of Cairo. Among 40 percent of the couples in the study, both husbands and wives participated in the interviews, agreeing to speak with me about a wide variety of issues pertaining to IVF in Egypt (Inhorn 2003a). Seventy percent of the 66 couples in my study suffered from male infertility, and in most of these cases, the husband's infertility was the sole cause of the couple's childlessness. Through this study, I obtained rich interview data on male infertility and its treatment, even though I had not originally been seeking it.

Indeed, before I began my Egyptian IVF study, I had been highly skeptical that I would be able to conduct research with infertile Middle Eastern men, given the sensitivity of the subject as well as general cultural barriers surrounding intergender communication between a female ethnographer and male informants. However, my position as a foreign female *duktura*—that is, as a knowledgeable, empathic listener, ethnically committed to confidentiality—seemed to put infertile Egyptian men at ease (Inhorn 2004b). Furthermore, Middle Eastern–born male colleagues subsequently convinced me that my gender status might, in fact, be advantageous. In their view, Middle Eastern men may be much less likely to reveal their reproductive vulnerabilities, as well as their feelings of love and compassion for their spouses, to another man, since virility and fertility are areas of intense masculine competition.

Thus, despite the impending U.S.–led war in Iraq, I decided to return to the Middle East for eight months in 2003, this time to Beirut, Lebanon. There, I conducted a study I titled "Middle Eastern Masculinities in the Age of New Reproductive Technologies," interviewing 220 Lebanese, Syrian, and Lebanese-Palestinian men. As in my Egyptian study, I was fortunate to gain ethnographic access to two of the busiest and most successful IVF clinics in central Beirut. One was located in a large, private university-based teaching hospital and catered to a religiously mixed patient population of both Sunni and Shia Muslims, Christians of a variety of sects, Druze (a minority Muslim subsect), and various immigrant and refugee populations. The other was a private, stand-alone IVF clinic catering primarily to southern Lebanese Shia patients but with occasional Christian and Sunni Muslim patients from both Lebanon and neighboring Syria.

As in my Egyptian study, about half of my interviews were conducted in Arabic and half in English, depending on the preference and ability of informants (many of whom spoke excellent English). Although I tape-recorded some interviews in Egypt, most of my interviews in both countries were not taped, because of considerable discomfort over confidentiality posed by the "permanency" of taping.[2] My assurances of confidentiality, however, put most of my informants at ease, and although not all informants were particularly forthcoming, I was able to record detailed and often animated reproductive and marital histories from many of the men in my study, including men who were themselves fertile but who were married to infertile wives. Examples of their stories, as they described them to me, appear later in this chapter to illustrate the meaning of conjugal love in these infertile couples' lives.

Thus, this chapter is based on nearly 20 years of multisited research on the globalization of IVF to the Middle East. In the first section, I highlight the differences between the Sunni and Shia variants of Islam regarding the permissibility of IVF and particularly third-party gamete donation. In the next section, I examine the implications of these differing versions of Islam on the love and marital expectations of infertile couples who are seeking IVF. In the final section I present several case studies of Sunni and Shia Muslim couples, drawn from my more recent research in Lebanon. In these stories of husbands, wives, and their family members, I hope to demonstrate the loving connectivity that shapes infertile marriages, familial involvements, and the use of assisted reproductive technologies in the Muslim world.

IVF in the Muslim World

In the Muslim Middle East, it is extremely important to explore the particular "local moral worlds" in which IVF is carried out. There, where religious rulings have profound effects on marriage and gender relations, religion plays a significant role in shaping the in vitro fertilization experience for infertile couples. Most infertile Muslim couples are extremely concerned about making their test-tube babies in the religiously correct fashion. To that end, they seek out the "official" Islamic opinion on the practice of IVF in the form of a *fatwa*, or a nonbinding but authoritative religious pronouncement made by an esteemed religious scholar. In recent years, many such *fatwa*s on a wide variety of reproductive health issues, including IVF, have been issued in Muslim countries.

Sunni Islam and IVF

With regard to IVF specifically, the first authoritative *fatwa* on medically assisted reproduction was issued by the Grand Sheikh of Egypt's famed religious university, Al Azhar, on March 23, 1980. This initial *fatwa*—issued only two years after the birth of the first IVF baby in England, but a full six years before the opening of Egypt's first IVF center—has proved to be truly authoritative and enduring in all its main points. In fact, the basic tenets of the original Al-Azhar *fatwa* on IVF have been upheld by other *fatwa*s issued since 1980 and have achieved wide acceptance throughout the Sunni Muslim world. Sunni Islam, I must emphasize, is the dominant form of Islam found in the Middle Eastern region and throughout the Muslim world. It is practiced by more than 90 percent of the world's 1.3 billion Muslims, including 90 percent of Egypt's citizens.

What is the Sunni Islamic position on IVF? To summarize the main points, in vitro fertilization of an egg from the wife with the sperm of her husband followed by the transfer of the fertilized embryo(s) back to the uterus of the same wife is allowed, provided that the procedure is indicated for a medical reason and is carried out by an expert physician. However, since marriage is a contract between the wife and husband during the span of their marriage, no third party should intrude into the marital functions of sex and procreation. This means that a third party donor is not allowed, whether he or she is providing sperm, eggs, embryos, or, in the case of surrogacy, a uterus. The use of a third party is tantamount to *zina*, or adultery, and a donor child is considered to be an *ibn haram* (literally, "son of sin"), or an illegitimate child.

But to what degree is this *fatwa* declaration—which allows IVF but explicitly prohibits any form of third-party donation or surrogacy—actually followed by physicians in the Sunni Muslim world? A global survey of sperm donation among assisted reproductive technology centers in 62 countries provides some indication of the degree of convergence between official discourse and actual practice. In all of the Sunni Muslim countries surveyed—including the Middle Eastern countries of Egypt, Kuwait, Jordan, Morocco, Qatar, and Turkey and the non–Middle Eastern Muslim countries of Indonesia, Malaysia, and Pakistan—sperm donation in IVF and all other forms of gamete donation were strictly prohibited. As the authors of this global survey, Meirow and Schenker, state, "In many Islamic countries, where the laws of Islam are the laws of the state, donation of sperm was not practiced. AID [artificial insemination by donor] is considered adultery and leads to confusion regarding the lines of genealogy, whose purity is of prime importance in Islam" (1997:134).

With regard to the issue of marriage and adultery, Islam is a religion that can be said to privilege—even mandate—heterosexual marital relations. As is made clear in the original Al-Azhar *fatwa*, reproduction outside of marriage is considered *zina*, or adultery, which is strictly forbidden in Islam. Although third-party donation does not involve the sexual "body contact" of adulterous relations, nor presumably the desire to engage in an extramarital affair, it is nonetheless considered by Islamic religious scholars to be a form of adultery, by virtue of the introduction of a third party into the sacred dyad of husband and wife. The very fact that another man's sperm or another woman's eggs enter a place where they do not belong makes donation of any kind inherently wrong and threatening to the marital bond.

Shia Islam and IVF

Having said this, it is very important to point out that things have changed for Shia Muslims since this global survey was published in 1997. Shia is the minority branch of Islam found in Iran, and parts of Iraq, Lebanon, Bahrain, Saudi Arabia, Afghanistan, Pakistan, and India. It has been much in the news lately because of the U.S.–led war in Iraq. Many of the Shia religious authorities support the majority Sunni view: they agree with Sunni clerics who say that third-party donation should be strictly prohibited.

In the late 1990s, however, the Supreme Jurisprudent of the Shia branch of Islam, Ayatollah Ali Hussein Khamanei, the chosen successor to Iran's Ayatollah Khomeini, issued a *fatwa* effectively permitting donor technologies to be used. Invoking the Shia practice of *mut'a*, or temporary marriage, which is forbidden in Sunni Islam, Ayatollah Khamanei stated in his *fatwa* that donation "is not in and of itself legally forbidden," as long as egg donors are taken as temporary wives. He stated, furthermore, that both donors and infertile parents must abide by the religious codes regarding parenting. Thus, the child of the donor has the right to inherit from him or her, because the infertile parents are considered to be like "adoptive" parents.

The situation for Shia Muslims, however, is actually much more complicated than this. Because Shia practice a form of individual religious reasoning known as *ijtihad*, various Shia clerics have come to their own conclusions regarding the rightness or wrongness of sperm and egg donation. Even among those who accept the idea of donation, there are major disagreements about (1) whether the child should follow the name of the infertile father or the sperm donor; (2) whether donation is permissible at all if the donors are anonymous; and (3) whether the husband of an infertile woman needs to do a temporary *mut'a* marriage with the egg donor, then release her from the marriage after the embryo transfer, in order to avoid *zina*, or adultery. However, because a married Shia Muslim woman cannot marry another man other than her husband (i.e., polyandry is not allowed in the Muslim world), she cannot do a *mut'a* marriage with a sperm donor. Technically, the child born of a sperm donor would be a *laqit*, or an out-of-wedlock child, without a family name and without a father. Thus, in theory, to avoid the implications of *zina*, or adultery, only widowed or otherwise single women should be able to accept donor sperm. In the Muslim countries, however, single motherhood of a donor child is unlikely to be socially acceptable.

Married infertile Shia couples who are truly concerned about carrying out third-party donation according to religious guidelines find it difficult to meet these various requirements. This difficulty is especially true of sperm donation, which was officially outlawed in Iran in 2003, despite Ayatollah Khamanei's permissive *fatwa* (Tremayne 2005). Nonetheless, in the Shia Muslim world, including in Iran and in Lebanon, at least some Shia couples are beginning to receive donor gametes, especially donor eggs and embryos, and are donating their gametes to other infertile couples. For infertile Shia couples who accept the idea of donation, the introduction of donor technologies has been described as a "marriage savior," helping to avoid the "marital and psychological disputes" that may arise if the couple's case is otherwise untreatable.

In Lebanon, the recent Shia *fatwa*s allowing egg donation have been a great boon to marital relations. There, infertile couples are signing up on waiting lists at IVF clinics to accept the eggs of donor women. Some of these donors are other Shia IVF patients, some are friends or relatives, and some are young American women, who are being recruited to Lebanon to anonymously donate their eggs to religiously conservative Shia couples—who, in fact, may belong to Lebanon's Hizbullah political party, which is officially described by the U.S. administration as a terrorist organization! In other words, the ironies of global reproductive technoscapes are becoming increasingly surreal in this politically charged new millennium.

Love, Marriage, and Gender Relations

But where does this leave infertile Sunni Muslim couples, as well as those Shia couples who do not accept the idea of third-party gamete donation? Their firm conviction that parenthood of a "donor child" is an impossibility is clearly linked to the legal and cultural prohibitions against adoption throughout the Muslim world. The Islamic scriptures, including the Qur'an, encourage the kind fostering of orphans but do not allow legal adoption as it is known in the West. As a result, few Muslim IVF patients, both Sunni and Shia, will contemplate adoption, stating with conviction that it is "against the religion" and that they could never feel appropriate parental sentiments for either an adopted or a donor child.

In the absence of adoption and gamete donation, infertile Muslim couples have no choice but to turn to IVF and other new reproductive technologies to solve their infertility problems using their own gametes. Because Middle Eastern societies are pronatalist—they highly value children for numerous reasons and expect all marriages to produce them—the notion of a married couple living happily without children is unthinkable. Children are desired from the beginning of marriage in most instances, and are usually loved and cherished once they are born (Inhorn 1996).

As a result, childless couples are often under tremendous social pressure to conceive. In the Muslim world, infertile women may live in fear that their marriages will "collapse," for, as noted earlier, Islamic personal status law considers a wife's barrenness to be a major ground for divorce. Although Islam also allows women to divorce if male infertility can be proven, a woman's initiation of court-ordered divorce continues to be so stigmatizing that women rarely choose this option unless their marriages are truly unbearable (Inhorn 1996, 2003a).

Ironically, however, the emergence of an otherwise revolutionary new IVF technology called intracytoplasmic sperm injection, or ICSI, has increased the potential for divorce in the Muslim Middle East (Inhorn 2003a). With ICSI, infertile men with very poor sperm profiles—even azoospermia, or lack of sperm in the ejaculate—are now able to produce biological children of their own. As long as a single viable spermatozoon can be retrieved from a man's body, including through painful testicular aspirations and biopsies, this spermatozoon can be injected directly into the ovum under a high-powered microscope. What ICSI requires, then, is high-quality ova, despite low-quality sperm. However, the wives of many of these men, who have "stood by" their infertile husbands for years, even decades in some cases, may have grown too old to produce viable ova for the ICSI procedure. In the absence of adoption or of any kind of egg donation, infertile Muslim couples with a reproductively elderly wife face four difficult options: (1) to remain together permanently without children; (2) to legally foster an orphan, which is rarely viewed as an acceptable option; (3) to remain together in a polygynous marriage, which is rarely viewed as an acceptable option by women themselves; or (4) to divorce so that the husband can have children with a younger wife.

Because of the Sunni Islamic restrictions on the use of donor eggs, at least some Muslim men are choosing to divorce or take a second wife, believing that their own reproductive destinies lie with younger, more fertile women. However, in my research in both Egypt and Lebanon, the first option has proven to be much more common: Infertile husbands and their 40-something wives often love each other deeply and remain together in long-term marriages without producing any children. Thus, divorce is not the immediate consequence of infertility that it is stereotypically portrayed to be, including in the new era of ICSI.

These technologies seem to be giving infertile couples, both Sunni and Shia Muslims, new hope that their infertility problems can be overcome, thereby increasing sentiments of conjugal love and loyalty. Indeed, I have always been struck by the tremendous amounts of love and commitment displayed by Muslim women to their long-term infertile husbands, and this has been a major theme of two of my books on Egypt (Inhorn 1996, 2003a). But I was equally impressed in 2003, when I interviewed men alone for the first time—including 100 healthy, fertile Lebanese, Syrian, and Palestinian men who were married to infertile women. Over and over, men told me that they loved their infertile wives and would never consider divorcing them, even if it meant living a life without children. When I asked men routinely, "Is this your first marriage?" the most common response was "the first *and* the last," with some men adding emphatically, "I love my wife. She is a good person." For some of these fertile Muslim men, loving one's infertile wife meant taking the plunge into the brave new world of donor technologies. Thus, I met several couples who were in the midst of receiving donor eggs, as well as several husbands who asked me whether I could help them find a donor for their wives.

Stories of Love in the Era of Middle Eastern IVF

To enliven this discussion of love and connectivity in the Muslim Middle East, I present several brief stories of infertile Muslim couples, all of them seeking IVF in Lebanon.[3] The stories were selected to demonstrate both marital and familial commitments, often in cases of long-term, intractable infertility. Furthermore, the stories were chosen to reflect differences in social class, regional backgrounds, and male versus female infertility. Most important, two of the couples described are Sunni Muslims and two are Shia Muslims. The differences between these two religious sects should stand out in the IVF experiences of these four couples. The solutions they pursue—often in the midst of considerable adversity and moral uncertainty—should demonstrate the degree of conjugal connectivity found among many infertile couples in the Muslim Middle East as they consider their difficult options. In short, these stories highlight the fact that love among infertile Muslim spouses is the norm among couples in the Middle East, who search for ways to overcome their infertility, including through recourse to globalizing reproductive technologies.

Ibrahim and Mayada

I interviewed Ibrahim on February 23, 2003, in a private Beirut IVF clinic serving a largely working-class, southern Lebanese Shia clientele. Ibrahim himself is Sunni, the eldest son of a Lebanese father and a Palestinian mother. He was pulled out of school in third grade to work in his father's carpentry shop and to help support the other eight children. Having come from a "huge" family, Ibrahim deeply desires his own children, explaining to me, "There is no family without children. I want children *a lot, a lot, a lot*! I'm the eldest, and I raised my brothers and sisters. And the eldest is supposed to have children. It is the traditional way." Thus, it grieves the handsome, olive-skinned, green-eyed Ibrahim that his beautiful wife of eight years, Mayada, has been unable to have children.

Over the course of their marriage, Ibrahim and Mayada have visited many doctors. "Some said the problem is hormones, and some said her ovaries are not so good," Ibrahim explained. Like many men married to infertile women, Ibrahim also accepts partial responsibility for the childlessness, insisting that he once suffered from a low sperm count for which he was given pharmaceutical treatments. However, his current spermogram is perfectly normal, and his physician is convinced that Ibrahim is healthy and fertile.

Like many infertile women in the Middle East, Mayada feels responsible for depriving Ibrahim of his rightful children, and she has encouraged him to divorce her. As Ibrahim explained, "She told me, 'If you want to get married [again], please go. But I said, 'No, never! And don't speak like this anymore. This is our fate [*nasib*] from God, and if God gives us a child, okay, and if not, okay, too. I want only you. I have both love and faith."

Mayada's friend delivered a beautiful IVF daughter after many years of childlessness and told Mayada that she and Ibrahim should come to the Beirut IVF clinic.

Mayada asked Ibrahim whether he wanted to do this and he agreed. According to Ibrahim, "We came directly." However, the $5,000 required for one cycle of IVF was an exorbitant amount for a poor Lebanese carpenter. During the interview, Ibrahim kissed the back of his hand and then placed it on his forehead to show his gratitude to God. He explained how his large Lebanese family rallied to raise the necessary money, and how Mayada's brothers helped them financially as well. "All of them know, on both sides," he explained. "If we didn't tell them, all the family will be upset, asking, 'Why didn't you tell us?' So we cut the road short. Like any operation, it's a little expensive, and we needed their help. But I will pay them back."

When I asked Ibrahim if he had any religious concerns about IVF, he answered immediately, "In the religion, it [IVF] is permitted [*hallal*]. God allowed us to do it, because it is from the husband and the wife. But I would refuse to take sperm from another man—*never!* Nor egg donation. Why take something from a strange body to put it inside my wife?"

Ibrahim is hoping for twins from their first IVF trial and claims that he ultimately wants "a football team!" However, he has not ruled out adoption, even though he knows it is "against the religion." As he explained, "If there is no way to get her pregnant, and she wants to have [an adopted child], I would do it for her. Only if *she* wants to have a child to raise it, then I will do it for her."

Fortunately for Ibrahim and Mayada, their first trial of IVF was more than they had ever hoped for. When I left Lebanon, a very pregnant Mayada was on bedrest in American University Hospital in Beirut, being carefully monitored with triplets.

Karim and Mona

At the same Beirut IVF clinic, I met Karim and Mona, a truly handsome, self-ascribed "career couple" who, like many Lebanese migrant-entrepreneurs, owned a successful graphics company in West Africa. Mona's family had migrated there during the Lebanese civil war, following an explosion that cost Mona the three middle fingers of her right hand. Karim's family, concerned for his safety in a country where most young men were being recruited into warring militias, sent Karim to the United Arab Emirates to wait out the war years. There, Karim was very sexually active and entered two brief and unsuccessful marriages with European women. As an educated, secular Shia Muslim, Karim says he feels no particular guilt about his early sexual exploits and heavy drinking, although he does worry that too much sex with several hundred women affected his sperm count. Karim has severe oligospermia, or a very low sperm count, which makes it quite unlikely that he can impregnate Mona, who has been proven fertile through a variety of diagnostic tests.

As Karim explained, "Actually, we have in our tradition, if we don't have kids, they always look to the woman. They blame the woman. So the first thing I did, when I got the news, was telling my mom. 'We may have kids, we may not. But it's *me*—*my* problem.' As always, she prayed to see my kids, but she died last August." Tearing up, he added, "For me, it's very sad, because we were *very* close."

On his part, Karim ardently desires children, saying he has wanted a family most of his life. "I adore kids," he stated. "I really love kids. Even when I was a young boy, I always took care of kids. I always liked to play with them."

As for Mona, she says that she is "not caring" whether she and Karim have children. "If it happens, it happens," she explained. "Really, we work, and we're very busy. *Maybe* if I'm sitting at home doing nothing, I'd feel differently. But to be frank, if it doesn't happen, it doesn't happen. Even when I have my period, I am never crying or getting depressed. I'm not going to kill myself. We've been married for six years, and we love each other, and we have a good life. That's enough for me."

At this point, Mona left the room to meet with their IVF physician, who had already seen them through two unsuccessful trials of ICSI. Altogether, Mona and Karim have undertaken four trials of ICSI, including two that succeeded but were followed by miscarriages. Karim continued the interview, stating, "Honestly, I told [the doctor] if this time it didn't happen, I wouldn't be capable of doing it again. It's not a matter of money. When we travel, we come [to Lebanon] on a holiday. But we spend the month here between doctors and injections. We became tired and exhausted, really. So, from my end, I would say, yes, I would stop with this one. But I don't know what Mona thinks. I know she wants kids, but she's not trying to let it even bother her. But deep inside, I'm sure she's thinking about having a baby."

When I asked Karim about adoption, he responded readily, "Adoption, that's one solution. We did actually think about it. We said if we don't succeed [with ICSI], we should go for adoption, here most probably [in Lebanon]. I mean, we know it is not really something they would advise or agree on in our religion. You should not give the kid your name, and at a certain age, you should inform the child [about the adoption]. But it's a possibility for us if this time [ICSI] fails."

Two weeks after the interview, I saw Karim and Mona at the IVF clinic, where a post-ICSI pregnancy test revealed a negative result. Calm and collected, they were about to return to Africa, where the future of their loving marriage seemed certain, despite their ongoing childlessness.

Abbass and Hanaa

On a busy May day at the same IVF clinic, I met Abbass and Hanaa, a young couple from the predominantly Shia city of Baalbek, which had been a Hizbullah stronghold during the Lebanese civil war. There, Abbass worked as a police officer, although he was studying at night to become a lawyer. Married to his first cousin Hanaa, Abbass has assumed the responsibility for the infertility, undergoing repeated sperm tests showing "borderline" results. Highly intelligent and self-taught in English, Abbass attributes his sperm problems to his psychological depression, about which he spoke freely. "I think that there is a main reason for the quantity and quality problems," he said. "It's mainly the quantity of sperm. And it is depression—it affects the number of sperm. I think this is the main reason." When I asked him about the source of his depression, he continued, "It's most kinds of depression—economic, my living situation, in general. It's stress. [The doctor] told me my [variable] sperm counts depend on my mood. And I think my bad mood is permanent!" he laughed. "After 1996 exactly, the economic situation [in Lebanon] has gotten bad, and also I have a problem in my family. My mother and father got divorced; they split in 1991, but the real divorce was in 1994. And because I'm the only man, the only son, I'm taking care of my mother and my sisters. I have three sisters, and my father doesn't support them. And now he's asking me to support him!"

In addition to these life stresses, Abbass and Hanaa have undergone a reproductive rollercoaster. Early in their marriage, Hanaa experienced two ectopic pregnancies, the second one of which almost killed her and required an emergency surgery. Since then, Hanaa has suffered from tubal infertility and requires IVF to become pregnant. Their first trial of IVF was covered by insurance from the Lebanese Order of Police but was unsuccessful. To finance their second IVF cycle, Abbass has had to take a loan against his future retirement benefits. Because the loan amount was not enough to cover the entire operation and medications, Hanaa was in the process of selling her bridal gold at the time I met them.

Fortunately for Hanaa and Abbass, Hanaa produced many eggs during her second IVF trial, and Abbass was clearly delighted when his sperm count was normal on the day of fertilization. Because Hanaa produced so many eggs, the IVF physicians asked the couple whether they were willing to donate excess eggs to other infertile couples on the donor-egg waiting list at the clinic. As Shia Muslims who follow the spiritual guidance of Ayatollah Khamenei in Iran, Abbass and Hanaa were willing to donate, once they received permission to do so from Ayatollah Khamenei's branch office in Beirut. Of the 30 eggs harvested from Hanaa's ovaries, 19 were kept by Abbass and Hanaa for their own use, and 11 were donated to other couples. Only seven of Hanaa's 19 eggs fertilized; five were implanted as embryos in her uterus, and two embryos were frozen for future use.

When I saw Abbass and Hanaa at the clinic on the day of embryo transfer, they were beaming. A broadly smiling Abbass had his arm around his small, plain wife, who was dressed in a black veil and a pretty blue-flowered jacket. When Hanaa left to begin preparations for the embryo transfer, Abbass told me about his feelings for his wife, whom he clearly loves and admires. "You know, here, most people don't have this kind of information about infertility. Especially in the older generation, when a man and woman get married and there are no children for five years, they always blame the woman, and they tell him to go get married to another. But my mother, she *never* asked or said one word. She said, 'Live your life. As long as you are happy with your wife, and everything is good, don't worry yourself about this.' And so I take her advice about this. I don't get stressed. And my wife, she is a real good one—a very strong person. She is a believer, and she has hope. She is optimistic, not pessimistic. She is optimistic that she will have children, and I think this attitude will help us to succeed."

Unfortunately for Abbass and Hanaa, none of their five embryos implanted. Furthermore, all of the eggs that Hanaa donated failed to lead to pregnancies in other couples. According to the IVF physicians, the issue of poor egg quality makes the likelihood of a future IVF pregnancy for this couple slim. Because Abbass and

Hanaa know that adoption is forbidden in Islam, they will not contemplate this as a route to parenthood. Thus, one can only hope that their strong marriage and religious faith will keep them together, since their dreams of biological parenthood may never become reality.

Hatem and Huda

I met Hatem and Huda at another hospital-based IVF clinic in Beirut, which catered to all of the religious sects found in multisectarian Lebanon. However, Hatem and Huda were not Lebanese; they had traveled from rural Syria to Beirut to undergo a trial of IVF. Like most of the Syrian medical migrants I met in my study, Hatem was convinced that Lebanese IVF clinics were superior to the fledgling clinics in neighboring Syria. Thus, he had been bringing his wife to Beirut for IVF over six years. Hatem had another reason for bringing Huda to Lebanon: There, they could access donor eggs, which were unavailable in the Sunni-dominant country of Syria, where third-party gamete donation is strictly prohibited.

Double first cousins married for 17 years, Hatem and Huda clearly love each other, despite the perplexing dilemma of her premature ovarian failure. Although Huda was only 36 at the time of our interview, she had entered menopause in her twenties and required hormonal stimulation followed by IVF in order to achieve a pregnancy. After five unsuccessful trials of IVF, the IVF physicians recommended egg donation as the most likely successful option. As Sunni Muslims, Hatem and Huda knew that egg donation was forbidden in the religion. Yet, they rationalized their use of donor eggs in a previous IVF cycle in the following way, "As long as the donor agrees," Hatem said, "then this would reduce the forbiddenness [*haram*] based on our religion. Because she, the donor, is in need of money, she gave nine to 10 eggs, and the doctor divided the eggs between that couple and us. We took five, and that couple, who were recently married, took five. And I personally entered into the lab to make sure that *my* sperm were being used. It's okay because it's *my* sperm."

Indeed, Huda became pregnant with donor twins, a male and a female, in 1999. At six months and 17 days of pregnancy, she began to miscarry, and Hatem rushed her to a hospital in Syria. As Hatem recounts, "They opened her stomach [by cesarean], and there were twins, who still lived for 48 hours. They had lung deficiency because they were little and not fully developed. The girl died twelve hours before the boy."

After this traumatic experience, Huda no longer accepts the idea of egg donation. According to Hatem, who spoke for Huda as she sat quietly in the room, "She was tortured [during the pregnancy]. She stayed four months vomiting whatever she ate, and she lost weight—from 194 pounds to 121 pounds. And she was under a lot of stress because of our social environment in Syria. In our [farming] community, they stare at babies and see if they resemble the mother and father. We are not living in a city of 4–5 million. We are in a closed community of 15,000 people. And so, the first time, when we had twins, they did a blood test and everyone was surprised. Their blood group was AB, and it didn't match ours. Now everyone will *really* examine the personal traits of this [donor] baby if we do it again. They will look at us suspiciously. Not the doctors; they keep everything confidential. But people in the community who might come to visit and look at us curiously."

For his part, Hatem is willing to accept donor eggs again and has already made inquiries about finding another donor in Syria. On the day of our interview, we also spoke about the possibility of finding a willing donor within the Beirut IVF clinic. Hatem sees no other way to achieve parenthood, because he loves his wife and refuses to divorce her. Although Hatem is an affluent farmer from a large family of 20 children (by one father and three co-wives), he continues to resist all forms of social pressure to divorce or marry polygynously. His commitment, he says, is based on his deep love for Huda. As he told me, "Had I not loved her, I wouldn't have waited for 17 years. I would have married another. By religious law, I can remarry, but I don't want to."

He continued, "She told me I should marry another woman, and she even offered or suggested that she would get me engaged, because we're already old. We've reached middle age without kids. We're living in a large family with six of my brothers, and they all have children. That's why she's feeling very depressed and very angry that she's alone without children, although she's always surrounded by children. But, of course, she keeps these feelings to herself."

He finished, "The love between us—I love her *a lot*. I was the one who considered going for IVF, for her sake. But we must keep it secret, because if my parents knew about us having an IVF child, the child would be marginalized and living a lonely life. So we keep everything secret, and we just mention to our families that she's receiving treatment."

As in so many IVF stories, Huda and Hatem were ultimately unsuccessful in their seventh attempted IVF trial. Huda's own eggs failed to mature under hormonal stimulation, and no egg donors were currently available at the clinic. Thus, Hatem and Huda returned home quietly to Syria, with little remaining hope of achieving parenthood, but with the love that had kept them together for nearly 20 years.

Conclusion

As these stories show, love and marital commitment generally characterize the IVF quests of infertile Muslim couples in the Middle East. Without this love, marriages might terminate under Islamic personal status laws, making IVF essentially unnecessary. Thus, the tremendous growth of the IVF industry in the Muslim Middle East is a testament to loving commitments not only among infertile couples but among their concerned family members.

Differences in Muslim couples' responses to IVF, however, emerge along religious lines, particularly according to sect. In the Sunni Muslim world, the use of IVF and ICSI—with the simultaneous prohibition on donor gametes—has clearly led to an entrenchment of deeply held religious beliefs about the importance of marriage, which no third party should tear asunder. Furthermore, the Sunni proscriptions against third-party donation represent, in some sense, the materialization of conjugal connectivity and the literal embodiment of emotion, in that love of one's partner—including his or her gametes—must prevail over the desire to have children "by any means." In this light, donor technologies represent a betrayal of sorts, a confession that having children is more important than loving one's infertile spouse. For this reason, donor gametes continue to be shunned in the Sunni Muslim world, with donation itself equated to *zina*, or adultery.

Yet, the globalization of these technologies to other parts of the Shia world has fundamentally altered understandings of what love means within a marriage and the ways that marriages might be saved through the uses of assisted reproductive technologies. Shia men and women—but Shia men in particular, who may be pressured by society at large to divorce infertile or otherwise reproductively "elderly" wives—are clearly reassessing their marital options in cases of childlessness. For Shia men, choosing donor egg technologies "out of love" for their wives has emerged as a new possibility. It is a possibility that bespeaks a new kind of marital love and commitment—of loving a wife "so much" that a man must make considerable financial and emotional sacrifices for her, even accepting the eggs of another woman for her to experience the joys of pregnancy and motherhood. Such loving sacrifices have been facilitated by the frankly "adventurous" attitude of otherwise conservative, male Shia religious leaders, who themselves view third-party donation as a "marriage savior."

In IVF clinics in Lebanon (as well as Iran), there is now a veritable clamoring for donor eggs among childless Shia couples. Furthermore, in multi-sectarian Lebanon, the recipients of these donor eggs are not necessarily only Shia Muslim couples. Indeed, some Sunni Muslim patients from Lebanon and other Middle Eastern Muslim countries (as well as Christians of all sects) are quietly "saving their marriages" through the use of donor gametes, thereby secretly "going against" the dictates of Sunni Muslim orthodoxy. The transformative possibilities of assisted reproductive technologies in the realms of Middle Eastern marriage and love were probably never imagined when these technologies first arrived in the Middle East 20 years ago. But conjugal love itself is changing as these technologies continue to evolve in the region.

As the assisted reproductive technologies become further entrenched in the Muslim world, and additional forms of global reproductive technology become available, it is important to interrogate new local moral dilemmas, as well as new manifestations of love and conjugal connectivity that are likely to arise in response to this variant of globalization. The pace of change evident in the production of new reproductive technologies themselves—as highlighted in the recent *Nova* special called "18 Ways to Make a Baby"—as well as the rapid spread of these technologies into far reaches of the non-Western world is, indeed, striking. Thus, as one science and technology studies scholar, David Hess rightly observes, "Anthropology brings to these discussions a reminder that the cultural construction of science is a global phenomenon, and that the ongoing dialogue of technoculture often takes its most interesting turns in areas of the world outside the developed West" (1994:16).

In conclusion, my own medical anthropological research carried out in Sunni-dominant Egypt and Shia-dominant Lebanon has explored the implications of IVF globalization for Muslim marriages in a part of the world that is still described by some Middle Eastern feminist theorists as "one of the seats of patriarchy" (Ghoussoub and Sinclair-Webb 2000:8). Although the Sunni Muslim ban on third-party donation may be particularly disadvantageous to women—as some infertile men begin to divorce their reproductively elderly wives to try the newest variant of ICSI with younger, more fertile women—the patriarchal consequences of divorce and social devastation are not the inevitable consequences of infertility for Muslim women that they are stereotypically portrayed to be. Rather, as my research has shown, patriarchy is being undermined by infertile couples themselves, who are choosing to remain in long-term, loving marriages, even in the absence of children. The new assisted reproductive technologies, particularly donor-egg technologies, are enhancing this love by providing hope of technological salvation. Furthermore, with the introduction of these new reproductive technologies, particularly ICSI for male infertility, families can prove their loving commitments by supporting the IVF and ICSI quests of their sons, daughters, siblings, and cousins. As shown in some of the stories above, IVF in Lebanon is truly a family affair, with parents in particular demonstrating their love and concern for infertile offspring through financial aid and emotional succor.

Ultimately, then, it should come as no surprise that the Middle Eastern IVF industry is flourishing. Indeed, when all is said and done, it is the love among committed infertile Muslim couples that has brought this industry to the Middle East. And it is this conjugal love—now aided and abetted by familial love and enmeshment—that will keep the IVF industry alive in this region as it faces a troubled new millennium.

Acknowledgments

I want to express my gratitude to the numerous men and women in Egypt and Lebanon who spoke to me about their infertility, IVF experiences, and marital lives. I also owe a debt of gratitude to numerous IVF physicians in both countries, who welcomed me into their clinics. In Lebanon, the American University of Beirut provided me and my family with a fine home and institutional affiliation, particularly during the unsettling initiation of a U.S.–led war in Iraq. This research was generously supported by the National Science Foundation and the U.S. Department of Education Fulbright-Hays Program. I want to thank Nina Kohli-Laven for bibliographic assistance. I thank Mark Padilla for inviting me to participate in this seminal volume.

Notes

1. Over the past 20 years, I have been writing about infertility and assisted reproductive technologies in the Middle East (Inhorn 1994, 1996, 2003a). In recent years, I have turned my attention to male infertility in the era of the new reproductive technology ICSI (see, for example Inhorn 2002, 2003b, 2004a).

2. The option to be tape-recorded was presented to each informant on the written informed consent form. Most informants asked about this, and when I told them it was not necessary to tape-record the interview, they uniformly declined, usually with visible relief. This "tape-recorder-less" strategy, which I have used in most of my interviews in both Egypt and Lebanon, requires me to take almost verbatim, shorthand notes, which I learned through a previous career as a journalist.
3. All names are pseudonyms.

References

Ahmed, Akbar S., and Hastings Donnan
  1994 Islam in the Age of Postmodernity. *In* Islam, Globalization and Postmodernity. Akbar S. Ahmed and Hastings Donnan, eds. Pp. 1–20. London: Routledge.
Appadurai, Arjun
  1996 Modernity at Large: Cultural Dimensions of Globalization. Minneapolis: University of Minnesota Press.
Charrad, Mounira M.
  2001 States and Women's Rights: The Making of Postcolonial Tunisia, Algeria, and Morocco. Berkeley: University of California Press.
De Munck, Victor C.
  1996 Love and Marriage in a Sri Lankan Muslim Community: Toward a Reevaluation of Dravidian Marriage Practices. American Ethnologist 23:698–716.
Freeman, Carla
  2000 High Tech and High Heels in the Global Economy: Women, Work, and Pink-Collar Identities in the Caribbean. Durham: Duke University Press.
Ghoussoub, Mai, and Emma Sinclair-Webb, eds.
  2000 Preface. *In* Imagined Masculinities: Male Identity and Culture in the Modern Middle East. Mai Ghoussoub and Emma Sinclair-Webb, eds. Pp. 7–16. London: Saqi Books.
Ginsburg, Faye D., and Rayna Rapp
  1995 Introduction: Conceiving the New World Order. *In* Conceiving the New World Order: The Global Politics of Reproduction. Faye D. Ginsburg and Rayna Rapp, eds. Pp. 1–18. Berkeley: University of California Press.
Hess, David
  1994 Parallel Universes: Anthropology in the World of Technoscience. Anthropology Today 10:16–18.
Inhorn, Marcia C.
  1994 Quest for Conception: Gender, Infertility, and Egyptian Medical Traditions. Philadelphia: University of Pennsylvania Press.
  1996 Infertility and Patriarchy: The Cultural Politics of Gender and Family Life in Egypt. Philadelphia: University of Pennsylvania Press.
  2002 Sexuality, Masculinity, and Infertility in Egypt: Potent Troubles in the Marital and Medical Encounters. Journal of Men's Studies 10:343–359.
  2003a Local Babies, Global Science: Gender, Religion, and In Vitro Fertilization in Egypt. New York: Routledge.
  2003b "The Worms Are Weak": Male Infertility and Patriarchal Paradoxes in Egypt. Men and Masculinities 5:236–256.
  2004a Middle Eastern Masculinities in the Age of New Reproductive Technologies: Male Infertility and Stigma in Egypt and Lebanon. Medical Anthropology Quarterly 18(2):162–182.

2004b Privacy, Privatization, and the Politics of Patronage: Ethnographic Challenges to Penetrating the Secret World of Middle Eastern, Hospital-Based In-Vitro Fertilization. Social Science and Medicine 59 (10):2095–2108.

Jankowiak, William R., and Edward F. Fischer
1992 A Cross-cultural Perspective on Romantic Love. Ethnology 31:149–155.

Joseph, Suad
1993 Connectivity and Patriarchy among Urban Working Class Arab Families in Lebanon. Ethos 21:465–484.

1994 Brother/sister Relationships: Connectivity, Love, and Power in the Reproduction of Arab Patriarchy. American Ethnologist 21:50–73.

Joseph, Suad, ed.
1999 Intimate Selving in Arab Families: Gender, Self, and Identity. Syracuse: Syracuse University Press.

Kahn, Susan Martha
2000 Reproducing Jews: A Cultural Account of Assisted Conception in Israel. Durham: Duke University Press.

Kleinman, Arthur
1995 Writing at the Margin: Discourse between Anthropology and Medicine. Berkeley: University of California Press.

Knysh, Alexander
2000 Islamic Mysticism: A Short History. Leiden: Brill.

Larkin, Brian
1997 Indian Films and Nigerian Lovers: Media and the Creation of Parallel Modernities. Africa 67:406–440.

Meirow, D., and J. G. Schenker
1997 The Current Status of Sperm Donation in Assisted Reproduction Technology: Ethical and Legal Considerations. Journal of Assisted Reproduction and Genetics 14:133–138.

Musallam, B. F.
1983 Sex and Society in Islam. Cambridge: Cambridge University Press.

Omran, Abdel Rahim, and Farzaneh Roudi
1993 The Middle East Population Puzzle. Population Bulletin 48:1–40.

Smith, Daniel Jordan
2001 Romance, Parenthood, and Gender in a Modern African Society. Ethnology 40:129–151.

Trawick, Margaret
1990a The Ideology of Love in a Tamil Family. In Divine Passions. Owen M. Lynch, ed. Pp. 137–163. Berkeley: University of California Press.

1990b Notes on Love in a Tamil Family. Berkeley: University of California Press.

Tremayne, Soraya
2005 The Moral, Ethical, and Legal Implications of Egg, Sperm, and Embryo Donation in Iran. Paper presented at the conference Reproductive Disruptions: Childlessness, Adoption, and Other Reproductive Complexities, University of Michigan, Ann Arbor, May 19.

Part III
Fantasy, Image, and the Commerce of Intimacy

8

Playcouples in Paradise
Touristic Sexuality and Lifestyle Travel

Katherine Frank

Sociological and anthropological analyses of tourism often focus on the problematic power relations involved, such as the complex and often exploitative relationships between tourists, their hosts, and the local sites. Tourism may seem to offer a panacea to economic ills facing modern communities and thus is often actively pursued on a number of developmental levels (Rothman 1998:17). Yet at the same time, tourism has been called a "devil's bargain," its growth leading to a transformation of the local landscape that comes with "unanticipated and irreversible consequences, social, cultural, economic, demographic, environmental, and political consequences that communities, their leaders, and their residents typically face unprepared" (10). In time, tourism may generate an increasing strain on the host countries and the local workers as the number of visitors grows (Smith 1989), a progressively unequal distribution of wealth or an exacerbation of existing cleavages in the communities affected (Greenwood 1989) and significant changes in the local landscape and the fabric of the existing community at the tourist destination (Nunez 1989). Understandably, such issues have taken priority in theorizations of globalization, tourism, and the commodification of experience.

Specifically in relation to sexuality, there is a great deal of focus in the literature on globalization and on tourism to the inequalities and exploitations associated with sex tourism (see Brennan 2004; Kempadoo and Doezema 1998; Bishop and Robinson 1998; Sanchez Taylor 2001). Dennis Altman forcefully argues that such tourism "has become the most significant and visible arena of global sexual inequality" (2001:106). Global economic forces have situated some locales as sexual playgrounds for wealthier nations, and deeply entrenched inequalities of race, ethnicity, social class, sexuality and gender often influence (without determining) which individuals become situated as laborers and which as leisure-seekers at any given destination.[1] As racial and cultural difference has long been a source of erotic fascination, it is especially important to highlight the power differentials and othering processes that can become magnified in such international travel in the search for paid sexual encounters.

With all of the intellectual attention understandably paid in anthropology and related disciplines to Western sex tourists visiting locales such as Thailand, the Dominican Republic, and other parts of the Caribbean and the political, cultural, and economic effects of their practices, as well as the attention paid to the movement of sex workers from developing nations to Japan, Germany, Amsterdam, Australia, and other places to ply their trade, there has been less academic exploration of the significance of "sex-focused" holidays for different groups of travelers. (For exceptions, see Hughes 1997 and Clift and Forrest 1999 on gay men's vacations and Josiam et al. 1998 on college students and spring break.) Also often overlooked in both the academic and the commercial tourism literature has been the connection between tourism and intimacy in existing interpersonal relationships (Trauer and Ryan 2005). Yet sex and travel have lengthy historical associations, and the search for sex, bodily pleasures, intimacy, or erotic excitement are also acknowledged motivations for many travelers more generally (some, but not all, of whom might be considered "sex tourists," depending on how the term is defined in contemporary discourse). While one must always critically interrogate the search for pleasure and satisfaction—such quests are rarely worthy of unilateral celebratory acclaim and are always implicated in existing power structures—it is worth distinguishing between and examining in more depth the motivations, goals, and experiences of different kinds of erotic travelers.

This chapter explores some of the fantasies and pleasures that inform couples' practices of touristic "sex play" through a look at the international leisure events developed and hosted for "swingers" (also called "lifestylers" or "playcouples").[2] The conventions, parties, or week-long get-aways are held in U.S. tourist hot spots such as Miami Beach, New Orleans, New York City, and Las Vegas, as well as in other well-known tourist locales such as coastal Mexico, the South Pacific, and the Caribbean. Although this kind of travel remains a niche market, industry insiders claim that this kind of tourism "more than tripled" between 1998 and 2002 (Guthrie 2002) and the offerings are still expanding. While many attending couples are from the United States, couples also travel from Canada, Eastern and Western Europe, South America, Asia, and the host countries. Though the sexual practices of attending couples may vary, playcouples generally engage in or support a variety of nonmonogamous sexual behaviors and encounters at the same time as they remain heterosexually "coupled" (a requirement for attendance at the events in many instances and a personal value for many lifestylers, although there are some singles who consider themselves lifestylers). Many playcouples are married, though marriage itself is not a requirement for membership or attendance at the events,[3] and lifestylers are often (though of course not always) committed to emotional monogamy even as they are nonexclusive in their sexual practice. The focus here is thus on tourism that is undertaken specifically to commune with other like-minded individuals, and usually to also procure novel sexual experiences not with the locals or the hosts but with other travelers. The sexual experiences are not necessarily framed by the eroticization of racial or cultural otherness—this may be a component of certain attractions but is not usually a primary motivation because couples are specifically seeking others "like themselves." Significantly, these particular sexual experiences are often explicitly conceptualized by the participants as "play" or as a form of personal exploration.

In his important work on the tourist gaze, John Urry expanded the idea of tourism by developing the concept of "touristic practice." A key feature of tourism, according to Urry, has become the search for "difference between one's normal place of residence/work and the object of the tourist gaze" (1990:11)[4] whether or not this search involves actual travel. Urry's idea of touristic practice is useful because it allows us to focus on the way that a particular ethos of consumption organizes people's motivations and experiences.[5] The term *touristic sexuality* is used in this chapter in a similar manner as a way to discuss sex-focused vacationing more generally, as well as to denote a wide-ranging ethos of sexuality and sexual behavior that can be considered emergent in contemporary U.S. intimate relationships. Jansson argues, "The logic of consumer society by definition works for the reproduction of touristic activities—that is, activities implying a temporary retreat from the environments of everyday life" (2002:441). Sex has long been one of these spaces of retreat, and this is part of the reason sex is so easily used to market commodities and so easily translated into a form of commodity itself. Postmodern and postindustrial capitalism arguably revolves around the consumption of services and experiences more than the consumption of tangible goods, with leisure becoming organized as spectacle and sensation (Rothman 1998; Rojek and Urry 1997). Sex and sexuality are intertwined with such contemporary forms of spectacle and sensation-seeking in a variety of interesting and compelling ways. To fully explore the various permutations of touristic sexuality more generally is beyond the purview of this chapter; however, in the United States, touristic sexuality can be seen in the continuing differentiation of the sex industry, the growth of sexual products and services, the plethora of sexually oriented sites on the Internet (including some like *www.marriedandflirting.com* that cater to individuals with an urge to explore or change the meaning of sex in marital relationships), an elaboration of the exploratory attitude toward dating and casual "hook-ups" espoused by younger generations, the popularity of romance and sexuality-oriented reality television programming and journalistic accounts of celebrity sexual exploits, and many other cultural practices, productions, and discourses.

Though it maybe tempting to construct a typology of sex-oriented touristic behaviors, motivations, and experiences—to elaborate the differences between "sex tourism," other types of "sex-focused" vacations, and more general touristic sexual practices in terms of power relations, erotic orientations, or global effects—it would be less useful than other approaches because a typology is static. Instead, it may be more productive to expand the idea of sexual leisure as involving much more than the sex industry as traditionally figured, and then to explore the nuances and particularities of various kinds of sexual leisure. An analysis of the practices and experiences of playcouples engaged in touristic sexual practices at leisure events and conventions can shed light on changing conceptualizations of love, sex, and commitment and the ways that these understandings intertwine with fantasies of consumption in an ever-changing global context. In these sites of transnational and transdyadic desire, sex is not necessarily or exclusively linked to love as part of the glue holding relationships together but can also figure as a leisure activity (often quite literally referred to as "play") with the potential to transform everyday life. As a leisure activity pursued away from "home," sex in these contexts is also linked quite explicitly to consumption (of bodies, identities, fantasies, commodities), in opposition to the everyday implicit links between sex and the market made through various forms of media. The activities engaged in, then, revolve around relations of spectatorship and consumption as much as on sexual relations, as couples play at sex with others but also play with fantasies of fame, wealth, and leisure.

Recently, there has been an increased interest in the selves and meanings constructed out of tourist interactions and touristic practice (Wearing and Wearing 2001; Frank 2003) and the connections between play, learning, and pleasure travel (see Mitchell 1998) in order to explore the more productive aspects of leisure behavior. The tourism scholar Richard Mitchell notes that for infants, exploratory play may be the most important way of learning and suggests that the same may be true of exploratory play for adults, of which tourism may be one form (1998:184). This is not to deny that adult play, like any other facet of social life, unfolds within a social context that may involve inequalities, prejudices, and even exploitations. It suggests, however, that we should not focus only on those negative aspects of and the deleterious effects that are generated by tourism but should also explore the ways that touristic practice may foster feelings of belonging, connection, intimacy, self-expression, and self re-creation for those individuals who partake of its temptations.

The continued exploration of touristic practice as a form of adult play may lend balance and texture to existing theorizing about tourism, as well as to social theory more generally. As Graeber (2001) notes, critical theory may eventually have a paralyzing effect on politics and the imagination. Critical theories, he argues, were originally "seen above all as ways to probe beneath the surface of reality," as a means by which to "unmask the hidden structures of power, dominance, and exploitation that lay below even the most mundane and ordinary aspects of daily life." And, he argues, certainly such things are there to be found. However,

> if this is all one is looking for, one soon ends up with a rather jaundiced picture of social reality. The overall effect of reading through this literature is remarkably bleak; one is left with the almost Gnostic feeling of a fallen world, in which every aspect of human life is threatened with violence and domination. Critical theory thus ended up sabotaging his own best intentions, making power and domination so fundamental to the very nature of social reality that it became impossible to imagine a world without it. Because if one can't, then criticism rather loses its point. Before long, one had figures like Foucault or Baudrillard arguing that resistance is futile (or at least, that organized political resistance is futile), that power is simply the basic constituent of everything, and often enough, that there is no way out of a totalizing system, and that we should just learn to accept it . . . And if everything is equally corrupt, then pretty much anything could be open for redemption. (2001:30)

I would like to suggest that we can, and should, attempt to distinguish between more or less exploitative practices, despite the inherent difficulties in and limitations of such a project. Further, I would also like to suggest that we explore the potential positive transformations created by new or growing possibilities for touristic practice, recognizing, that benefits or pleasures are not yet reaped equally across social classes or national boundaries.[6] Understanding those pleasures, and the promise that seeps into everyday life as they are anticipated or relived, will shed light on tourist motivation and the almost ubiquitous appeal of particular consumptive opportunities, sexual or otherwise.

While lifestyle events often do involve either national or international travel for playcouples, the ethos of sexuality from which they derive some of their appeal, especially as it is linked to forms of consumption, is a result of broader changes in and experiments with the conceptualization of love, sex, and commitment. Now certainly there have always been individuals for whom sexual activity has had a recreational component, and the behaviors lifestyle couples engage in have gained popularity among married couples in other periods and places as well, perhaps most recently and well publicized during the 1970s in the United States. Yet while these behaviors have often in the past been linked to discourses of social rebellion and utopian change, such overtly revolutionary ideas are more muted in the contexts discussed here. Rather, swinging and group sex at these events are usually conceptualized as ways of both "escaping" and legitimating the everyday, as leisure activities. But, as a form of dynamic play, and through the quest for a "couple's paradise," I argue that the touristic sexuality playcouples engage in can be seen as also potentially transformative of the everyday and of normative ideas of relationships.

Methods and Ethnographic Context

The research this chapter is based on is just part of a much larger project on the understandings and experiences of sexual exclusivity of American married couples.[7] A colleague and I officially began studying the different ways that couples negotiate the boundaries of monogamy in 2002 and have collected both quantitative survey data and qualitative interview data from couples and individuals in different kinds of marital relationships. The concerns of this study provide a backdrop for some of the issues I take up here. More central to my analysis in this chapter, however, has been ongoing participant observation in the lifestyle "community" at a variety of events and venues.[8] I have been attending organized lifestyle events, parties, and conventions since the mid 1990s, both as a single woman and as part of a married couple, and both as part of the entertainment when I worked as an exotic dancer[9] and as part of the convention crowd. I have also attended numerous private parties and clubs for lifestylers in these same capacities in the United States, Canada, and Europe. During this time and at the events, I have had the opportunity to speak informally with dozens more people about the issues taken up in my research. I also regularly read on-line discussion forums and web blogs for lifestylers, as well as publications focusing on the practice and ethics of swinging or on erotic tourism. There is a growing literature on the lifestyle in the form of "self-help" or "how to" guides for swingers (Bellemeade 2003), memoirs (Moore 2005; Marks and Marks 1994), and in a somewhat salacious, but journalistic style for a popular audience (Gould 1999; Lister 2006).

Organizations

There are numerous events for playcouples throughout the year, sponsored by a variety of organizations. The Lifestyles Organization (LSO), one of the largest and oldest, was founded by Robert and Geri McGinley in 1969 in Southern California. The LSO has created its own travel agency, Lifestyles Tours and Travel, and through this agency and its specialized division, Lifestyles International, the organization sponsors conventions and events at tourist destinations in several countries. At first, it was a rather small group associated with their on-premise[10] swing club, Club Wide-World, in Anaheim (Gould 1999). Since then, however, the organization has grown to encompass around 35,000 association members worldwide and a variety of leisure offerings: local parties in Southern California, houseboat getaways on Lake Mead, group trips to various tourist spots around the globe, cruises, organized regional conventions and parties every few months in the United States, and an extremely large annual convention in Las Vegas (sometimes with thousands of couples attending). The conventions are usually held in large hotels and may include an erotic art show, a marketplace where venders sell sex toys and costumes, workshops and seminars, daytime pool parties, and evening dances. Unofficially, attendees also hold parties in private rooms at the chosen hotel for swapping, group sex, and other kinds of erotic play. Further, LSO is partnered with several prominent resorts catering to lifestylers. They sponsor a resort take-over for a month every year at Hedonism II in Jamaica, as well as shorter weeklong takeovers at Hedonism II and III and at Grand Lido Braca, and they also sponsor lifestyle weeks at the Desire Resort and Spa in Cancun and at the Qualton Club in Ixtapa, Mexico. They organize and promote international trips and cruises (in 2004 to Greece, for example) and tend to return to venues that are hospitable to the sexual proclivities of the guests.

During the day at the conventions, seminars and workshops are offered on such topics as massage, jealousy, polyamory, safety and STDs, swinging etiquette, managing relationships, sexual practices and techniques, how to use the Internet to meet other couples, legal issues for nontraditional couples, and the business aspects of running swing clubs or groups. While only a fraction of the couples attend these events, the fraternity-like games and mingling at the pool parties are much better attended. Nonetheless, these seminars and workshops are important to the LSO because they help legitimize and justify the conventions through the "testimony" of experts. They also offer information for newcomers to the scene and provide a distraction for those "newbies" who may be too nervous to participate in the more overtly sexualized events. This is not to say that seasoned lifestylers do not also use the seminars to learn techniques or discuss relevant issues, but what is important here is that these conventions combine erotic and "educational" events.

Over the years, the LSO has helped facilitate relationships between lifestyle couples who otherwise might not meet, and recently those efforts have been aided, in large part, by the growth of the Internet. In addition to being linked with many swingers' websites,[11] the LSO sponsors message boards and chat rooms which singles can use to find dates for the events and couples can use to contact each other before an event to set up encounters or to find each other afterward. One couple I spoke with who had been in the lifestyle for over 20 years, for example, said that before the Internet they had "hung out in bookstores," looking at sexuality books and hoping to run into like-minded individuals. The LSO is also linked to swing clubs around the world through the North American Swing Club Association (NASCA), a trade organization founded in 1980 that McGinley was influential in forming (Gould 1999:33). On its website, NASCA now lists swing clubs in 26 countries.

While other tourist agencies also exist to serve the needs of couples interested in swinging, few have such a large membership or long history as LSO, and the term *lifestylers* has frequently been used to describe contemporary swinging couples in related publications. Some couples identify as lifestylers regardless of their relationship to the LSO, while others vehemently resist the term because they want to downplay the influence of the LSO in their own practices. Still others may use the term to describe their sexual practices but have never even heard of the LSO.

In recent years, new players have been getting into the organized couples' tourism game, setting up interactive websites and arranging their own hotel takeovers and weekend get-aways. Local groups have begun to capitalize on its popularity by providing travel opportunities for their members—co-sponsoring events with groups in other locales or arranging for trips to Hedonism or similar resorts. Other couples have begun hosting their own (sometimes for-profit) private parties and events around the country.

Demographics and Identities

Increasingly in my research on sexual exclusivity in marriage, I have found it more constructive to focus on practices and beliefs than on identities, despite the current wealth of literature and interest in identity in the social sciences. As an identity marker, the term *swingers* has an outdated, 1970s stigma attached to it, and one hears questions such as "How long have you been in the lifestyle?"; "How long have you been playing?"; or "Do you party?" more frequently than "Are you a swinger?" or "Do you swing?" In this chapter, then, the term *swinging* is used as a verb that denotes a practice, and I use the terms *lifestylers* or *playcouples* to discuss identities (although the use of both words is sometimes contested). Although the lifestylers discussed here may be united in their desire for leisure and their belief in the pleasures or benefits of recreational, consensual, and conjoint extradyadic sex, for example, they do not always organize neatly around any particular terms or identities, sexual or otherwise. Some couples attending lifestyle gatherings and conventions may identify as polyamorous (though, in my experience, polyamorists are often critical of both the focus on emotional monogamy observed by lifestylers and the casual sex or conspicuous consumption engaged in at the conventions). As with all definitions, these distinctions are easily deconstructed. For other couples, no designation seems necessary or desirable to describe their practices and beliefs around sexual exclusivity.

Demographic information on lifestylers is difficult to obtain, and therefore most existing research relies on community or convenience samples. The size of the U.S. population involved in such activities has been estimated at 1 to 2 percent, although these figures are dated and problematic. Studies have consistently found, however, that couples involved in co-marital sex generally fall into the middle and upper middle classes, are above average in education and income, and tend to be white and to hold professional and managerial positions (Jenks1998:509). Convention and event fees can be costly. Some couples save for quite some time to afford convention attendance—the price of plane tickets, hotel reservations, and registration fees (alone over $500 per couple at some conventions, for example), in addition to meals, costumes, alcohol, and other expenses—while others travel widely and frequently for sex play. In my experience, the occupations represented at lifestyle events cover a wide range, and while occupation may influence an individual or a couple's ability to be "out" about their involvement in the lifestyle, it does not necessarily determine with whom one "parties." One may not even collect any explicit background information on one's sexual partners at such an event, since some participants desire anonymity back in the "real world."

Although age has been analyzed in the literature, with many lifestylers reported to be somewhere between their mid-twenties and their late forties (Jenks 1998), the limited scope of the samples (often based on just one community or organization) makes it difficult to generalize. Despite the stereotype of swingers as desperate middle-aged suburbanites, in the past decade I have witnessed more and more younger couples, either married or dating, attending the conventions and initiating their own local social groups dedicated to nonmonogamous sexual practices. While there is probably more intergenerational interaction at LSO events than you would find in a regular sexualized social venue such as a nightclub—you may see grandparents on the dance floor at a convention, for example, dressed in skimpy attire and laughing with the younger couples—there is still a great deal of segregation at the circuit parties and private play parties based on age and appearance. What some participants term "pretty parties" are often invitation-only gatherings that attract a younger, flashier crowd; such events may even have a guard stationed at the door to deny entry to couples who are not deemed attractive enough or who are not on the prescreened guest list. In fact, age and appearance seem to govern the unofficial groupings far more than race, nationality, occupation, education, and other related social categories.

Early social science literature on swinging in the United States shows many participants to have been fairly conservative politically, with "general white suburban attitudes" (Bartell 1971:45). More recent research on self-identified swingers, however, indicates that they placed a high importance on marriage and on satisfaction from marriage and valued companionship more highly than personal freedom in forced-choice questions, the same as the general population (Bergstrand and Williams 2000:5). They also espoused more liberal stands than the general public on marriage and sexuality, such as being more likely to favor gay marriage, less likely to condemn premarital sex or sex among teens (14–16 years), and more likely to reject traditional sex roles in their relationships (Bergstrand and Williams 2000:4). The researchers also argued that swingers "were less racist, less sexist, and less heterosexist than the general population" (5). Still, lifestyle participants are not known for being politically active around issues affecting those with alternative sexualities (although this may change in the future).

Notes on Sexual Practices

Though couples necessarily consist of a man and a woman at most organized events, the sexual identities and proclivities of participants may vary. Bisexual activity among women is accepted and widely practiced, and women often classify themselves in extremely fluid terms, for example, as bisexual, bi-sensual, bi-curious, bi-comfortable, or bi-playful. Some women identify as straight even though they play with other women. A minority of women refuse sexual play with other women, as do the majority of men with other men. Same-sex contact among men is still stigmatized in most settings and parties where men engage in overt same-sex contact are generally underground at the larger conventions.

There are some long-standing assumptions to challenge with regard to what actually happens in the sexual situations sought by playcouples. First, in general, lifestylers are not practicing what has been referred to in the past as "open marriage," that is, each partner is not necessarily pursuing outside relationships on his or her own. Lifestylers usually court and carry out their sexual encounters as a couple, and the conventions provide them an opportunity to do so. Second, some writers have assumed that swing clubs or parties present a sexual free-for-all for the participants, especially the men (see, for example, Pittman 1989:83); others analyze nonmonogamous marital sexuality as an act of shameless exhibitionism, pathological desire, and even coercion on the part of one or both spouses. Yet these analyses miss the way that many couples actually cultivate certain kinds of erotic experiences together, selecting partners and scenarios based on fantasies they co-create (but that may or may not be supported by the convention themes, as I explain later). Third, swinging encounters, though "sexual" and infused with eroticism for the participants, do not always involve intercourse or even intimate contact with outside partners. Open voyeurism and exhibitionism is common, and at larger parties may be quite acceptable, though smaller, private gatherings may eventually require some element of participation (with a bit of leeway for newcomers to the scene). Some couples may attend events just to mingle, flirt, and dance with like-minded people in a sexualized environment. There are also a variety of options for sexual engagement, should that occur. Some couples prefer what is sometimes referred to as "closed" swinging, which means that once two couples have agreed to switch partners they form two new hetero couples and retire to separate rooms. Far more common among the younger crowd, however, in my experience, is "open" swinging, where participants in an encounter remain in the same room. These encounters may be "hard," or "full swap," involving couples in intercourse with another partner (or partners), or "soft swap," where nonmonogamous touching, oral sex, or other activities short of intercourse may occur. In these soft situations, intercourse may be reserved for preexisting couples only, either publicly or privately. Sometimes other activities may also be reserved for the primary partners, such as kissing or orgasm, depending on the idiosyncrasies or concerns of the couples involved.[12] While play gatherings may involve couplings or groupings of various sizes, just because couples are naked together in a sexualized situation, and may be intimate with a given individual in that scene, does not mean that they will engage with everyone intimately or equally. These situations are highly negotiated, rarely developing into the free-for-alls portrayed by popular representations and fantasies. Further, there are differences in how couples maneuver through such scenarios: Some couples may remain together throughout the evening; some may split up and work the room separately, getting together only at the end of the evening to share stories (and, often, intense sex). Though I do not have space to detail them here, most couples also have some system of rules and an understanding of the sexual and emotional boundaries that ideally should govern their interactions with others (even if the rule is to "not restrain each other with rules").

Love, Sex, Play, and Profit in Late Capitalism

The Playcouple™ Philosophy

Adult men and women are sexual beings and they have relationships. Many in our society, such as the religious and political right wing, proselytize that open sexual expression is sinful and worthy of condemnation, while the political left wing seeks to inhibit and restrict sincere and honest expression. Others seem to resent or are threatened that somewhere there are men and women who are fully enjoying their life and sexuality. By contrast, the *Playcouple* supports both freedom of expression and tolerance towards the private lives of others. They encourage the potential for full and lasting enjoyment in each and every way. They are comfortable with their sexuality and willingly explore new ways to heighten their sensuality. They believe that romance is one of life's greatest adventures just as love is one of life's greatest joys. From sharing erotic fantasies to traveling exotic paths, the *Playcouple* places the highest value on the intimacy they share with each other and those around them.(Lifestyles Organization materials)

Love, as has been suggested, is not necessarily linked to sexual exclusivity in the LSO philosophy or in the beliefs and practices of lifestyle couples, or at least not in the ways that might be expected. While overt social and sexual monogamy remains a dominant standard for married couples in the United States, for example, there are several competing and emergent discourses of intimacy circulating in the contemporary global sphere, in part because of the spread of tourist practice, the growth of the Internet and its use to foster alternative sexual "communities," and the influx of young couples into "alternative relationships" (many of whom are dissatisfied with the thought of a traditional monogamous marriage). Nonetheless, at least for most of the U.S. couples, while certain kinds of sex are seen as recreational,[13] love is still often conceptualized as the glue that binds and sustains the relationship. In the beliefs of many playcouples, then, emotional monogamy is thus institutionalized and celebrated (in contrast to the beliefs and practices of polyamorists, for whom emotional nonmonogamy is allowed and venerated).[14] Further, sex explicitly has multiple meanings—it may be an expression of love and commitment in the marriage (or reconnection after a play party), as well as a form of recreation with other partners and in other contexts.

Lifestylers are not necessarily interested in overt resistance to dominant discourses of love and marriage, and many are "closeted" about their sexual adventures even to close friends and relatives.[15] The primary motivation for their travels, and for their participation in the lifestyle, is the search for pleasure. While one may find a few booths set up by groups promoting and politicizing other sexual minorities, it is possible to attend a convention and never even talk about world events or political or sexual orientations. (At a party during a Miami convention just after the U.S. invasion of Iraq, however, I did overhear a British couple jokingly exclaim, "We're fucking our allies!" Several American couples also joked about their presence at the convention as a form of "spending for our country," alluding to the exhortation to continue consuming and traveling after the events of September 11, 2001.)

The sexual practices engaged in at events are an example of touristic sexuality in that they are often recreational (drawing on the particular understandings of love and sex that can be developed and deployed in these settings), commodified, organized, and infused with meanings that are derived from the contrasts between "home," "away," "work," and "play." As a form of "special interest tourism," rather than identity tourism (Howe 2001), lifestyle events may also provide for a more enduring involvement and intimacy with others and between each couple than other leisure activities. Trauer and Ryan suggest that such involvement can be twofold: first, the interest in the activity, and second, "a sharing with like-minded people in a social world that extends from home to tourist destination and return" (2005:481). Swinging is not just sexual; it is also highly social.

Several authors have noted the shift in the worldwide economic system from a continual expansion of production as the primary means of growth to the expansion of consumption, the continual development of new commodity forms (Wonders and Michalowski 2001; Lury 1996). The commodification and provision of personal services, sexual and emotional, have also been part of this means of expansion, as has the commodification of experience in tourism and touristic practice more generally (see Urry 1990). Lifestylers travel for many of the same reasons that other tourists do. Their travels and participation in organized events, in part, must be seen as a desire to have a particular kind of experience rooted in the complex network of relationships between "home," "work," and "away." Touristic practices, according to John Urry, "involve the notion of 'departure,' of a limited breaking with established routines and practices of everyday life and allowing one's senses to engage with a set of stimuli that contrasts with the everyday and the mundane" (1990:2). The sights that are gazed upon, or the experiences that are sought, are chosen because they offer "distinctive contrasts" to work and home and also because "there is an anticipation, especially through daydreaming and fantasy, of intense pleasures, either on a different scale or involving different senses from those customarily encountered" (Urry 1990:3). Things can happen at conventions that would certainly not happen at home, especially because couples are meeting others who desire to engage in the same sexual practices. Further, the anticipation and preparation for events may infuse the everyday with an element of eroticism for participants before and after the events.

Like other tourists (and especially like sex tourists, although there are significant differences as well),[16] lifestylers may be seeking anonymity and privacy, and a cover story to give to friends and relatives. They may also be escaping their own prohibitions and inhibitions by traveling away from everyday realms to a space where "out-of-town rules" about sexual activity apply and where they are less fearful of recognition. Often they are also attempting to find more hospitable venues in which to engage in certain legally or culturally proscribed practices or to get around laws prohibiting certain kinds of behavior, such as public nudity/alcohol regulations or lewd behavior statutes, which are quite variable in the United States.

One aspect of the lifestyle that the LSO and other growing organizations have understood quite well, and that has contributed to their financial success, is the importance of providing couples with on-premise opportunities for sexual activity, even if they are unofficial: hotels or cruise ships, for example, may prohibit any sexual activity in the ballrooms or public spaces, but private guest rooms are readily available for parties after the day's events have concluded. Another important ingredient of the events is privacy and discretion, and thus the organizations often strive for complete "take-overs" of the chosen spaces so that "straights" or "vanillas" cannot easily gawk or spy on the couples (booking every room in a hotel or every space at an all-inclusive resort, for example).

The LSO has capitalized on the special needs that playcouples have—for discretion and privacy, for finding other couples with similar beliefs and interests (and for continually meeting new couples and potential sexual partners), and for venues in which to engage in recreational sex and nonmonogamous sexual practices. Despite the different opinions and different ideas about political strategy public figures in the community express,[17] and despite the different aims of the convention goers (ranging from the desire to create new modes of intimate relating to the simple desire to add notches to the marital bedposts), playcouples often have difficulty finding venues in which to engage in sexual play. As a result, a nascent community has formed around the organized events. Hughes (1997) argues that for gay men, holidays are a significant and necessary agent of identity construction, because their practices may be scrutinized, restricted, and censured at home. As lifestylers find themselves similarly at odds with normative ideas about sexuality and relationships, and often similarly "closeted" at home about their sexual preferences and practices, such events may provide similar opportunities in the future.

Place and Space

The eroticization of particular destinations is also important as a motivating factor for travel and for the selection of particular sites as destinations: Las Vegas has a reputation as an "adult playground" in the United States, for example, and Jamaica, where the all-inclusive resort Hedonism is located, is portrayed as a place "for uninhibited sex, drink, food, and recreation" (Mullings 1999:74). Researchers have noted that there has been a conscious decision at a national level "to promote tourism as the answer to Jamaica's economic woes" and that "the marketing of Jamaica's tourism may be said to be concentrated around the four S's—sun, sand, sea, and sex" (Campbell, Perkins, and Mohammed 1999:127). It makes sense, then, that there are numerous organized excursions every year to Jamaica for lifestylers and that the Hedonism resorts are well represented at the larger conventions, where they host party suites and dances.[18] The largest LSO convention of the year takes place in Las Vegas, a highly symbolic city worldwide. In 1999, Hal Rothman notes, "Las Vegas surpassed Mecca as the most visited place on earth" (2002:xvii). Las Vegas also has a place in the cultural imaginary as a place of glitz, glitter, and reinvention, and it is a destination for characters in many Hollywood films. According to Rothman, Las Vegas "fulfills the desires of the baby boomers, reflects the abundance that they take for granted and the selfish indulgence, the hedonistic libertarianism, that is the legacy of the American cultural revolution of the 1960s"; it is the "therapeutic ethos of our time run amok, our sociopsychological promise to ourselves to be eternally young writ large on the landscape of aging self-indulgence," "the promise of a luxury experience for a middle-class price" (xiii).

"To generations of Americans," Rothman writes, "Las Vegas is a code for self-indulgence and sanctioned deviance" (2002:xvi). The sexual side of this self-indulgence and sanctioned deviance is alluded to in the recent tourist slogan: "What happens in Vegas stays in Vegas." While cities like San Francisco and Amsterdam are also linked with sexuality in the popular imagination (see Howe 2001), Las Vegas is significant because the sexualities associated with it are quite heteronormative—bachelor and bachelorette parties, guys' weekends, strip clubs and brothels, a perfect place for cheating on the wife or husband back home. It is also, according to Rothman, "a frontier town, maybe the last in the United States" (2002:xxv). Sexual activity has long been linked to discourses of freedom, rebellion, and revolution.

An in-depth historical and economic analysis of either place is beyond the purview of this chapter. Perhaps more important here, however, is the idea of space. As others have noted, place is not always important in the same way for travelers. For example, Trauer and Ryan argue that there is a "romance of tourism wherein the place has importance for attributes that contribute to otherness, but where such otherness is directed to a loved one and rests largely independent of place characteristics as conventionally assessed through itemizing physical attractions and facilities" (2005:483). "The place of escape," they write, "possesses importance as a place of self-recovery and re-creation, and thus obtains a sense of being an intimate place by reason of the visitor attributing to it a sense of self and 'other caring' that are the underpinnings characteristic of intimacy" (484). In couples' tourism, what matters most are the experiences the couple has together and with other individuals, whether the party is held in a local Holiday Inn or at the Mandalay Bay in Las Vegas. Certainly, an exotic locale can be conducive to erotic fantasy, yet locale is not necessarily always as important as the functional and symbolic space that is created by an event.

Lifestylers too often find themselves reviled, whether they are at home or among other tourists at a given location. Events provide an opportunity for sexual expression that is often inappropriate in other spheres, and participants have a general understanding of the rules of conduct and engagement that are involved (which do not always apply when couples attempt to generate encounters in other settings). In a discussion of "queer pilgrimages" to San Francisco by gay and lesbian tourists, Howe writes: "Tourism, as a 'privileged practice' (Towner 1985) of the economically endowed, is inverted when considering a distinctly marginalized group such as gays and lesbians because tourism is . . . linked to older forms of pilgrimage to the world religious centers" (Howe 2001:37). Like the gays and lesbians (and other individuals marginalized on the basis of their sexuality) who can afford to travel to San Francisco, lifestylers who can afford to attend the conventions are noticeably privileged. Yet although lifestylers can also be criticized for being heteronormative in certain ways—often apolitical, ambivalent to uneasy about male/male sexual contact (though not about female/female sexual contact), and committed to straight institutions such as marriage and the couple form—they are simultaneously also stigmatized and legally repressed for their desires and practices just as other sexual minorities are. The "escape" the conventions and other events offer is thus very real; they provide one of the primary ways to commune with other individuals who are at least open to their beliefs and practices.

It is easy to homogenize heterosexuals, and to unproblematically equate heterosexuality with privilege, but it is important to realize that some heterosexuals are actually still "in the closet" because of their sexual practices. Heteronormative ideals sanction only certain kinds of sexual practices, and those individuals involved in alternative lifestyles are not always given the legal protections of supposedly monogamous heterosexual marriage (or risk having those protections taken away upon exposure). Many heterosexuals, including those in the communities discussed here, also share the belief that a "stereotypical" heteronormative life is oppressive (to themselves as well as others) but may not always challenge it publicly for fear of losing their jobs, children, or social networks. (As one researcher pointed out, swingers may be the "new gays" in terms of how violently they are hated and feared by society.) These fears are real. There are highly publicized "busts" of swing clubs around the United States and internationally, and photos of "outed" couples have appeared in local newspapers. Four of seven people featured in a documentary on swinging, entitled *Sex with Strangers*, lost their jobs when employers learned of their practices (Guthrie 2002:2).

For women, the importance of space cannot be underestimated when it comes to sexual expression. Fear of male violence has long inhibited how women use public space (Skeggs 1999). Lifestyle events, no matter where they are located, provide a significant degree of safety for female participants. There are written and unwritten rules of conduct that are enforced by participants at the official events and at the private parties I have attended. Women often initiate and negotiate sexual contact, and male harassment is reprimanded explicitly or by ostracization from ongoing activity. There are, of course, occasionally unfortunate violations of these rules, although women that I have spoken with have tended to associate such violations much more with open settings or public suite parties (where potential participants can enter and leave the space at will) than during smaller or more selective parties and groupings. Women who wish to engage in sex play with other women find it to be accepted and encouraged not just as voyeuristic material for male observers but as activity they can control and display as they wish. The focus on explicit consent and female initiation and choice, along with the fact that sexual activity at events can be "soft," or remain focused on foreplay (flirting, kissing, oral sex) and not necessarily on penetrative sex (although it can quickly be if a woman so desires), may also make this environment attractive to many women.

Fantasies: Freedom, Celebrity, Paradise

While the daytime events at the conventions are geared to legitimizing certain kinds of sexual and intimate lifestyle choices, the evening events (such as dances and parties) are often themed to encapsulate fantasies of wealth, glamour, and power. The commodification of experience, according to Wonders and Michalowski, includes "the desire to experiment with different identities," the opportunity to buy "products, services and experiences that create the illusion of becoming someone else" (2001:552). In this context, I would resist using the term *illusion*, because what is purchased at conventions is a series of fantasies that infiltrate the everyday, possibly for months ahead of time and afterward, especially because these fantasies intersect with one's erotic life and marriage. Themes for the evening dances at the larger events are posted on the website months in advance, and many couples spend as much time preparing for the events.[19] Past themes have been Arabian Nights, Sexy Lingerie, Jungle Party, Mardi Gras, and Red, White & Blue night (held during the 2002 Miami convention after the U.S. invasion of Iraq). The themes also sometimes borrow from popular movies with an erotic bent, such as *Eyes Wide Shut* or *9½ Weeks*. The annual convention in Las Vegas in July 2004 featured a *Moulin Rouge* Lingerie Nite, as well as the Saturday night grand finale event with the theme Hollywood Glitz and Glamour. In promotional materials, participants were invited to "take a stroll down Saturday night's Red Carpet into a lust filled night of Hollywood Glamour & Glitz dressed like one of your favorite movie stars or characters." Although I did not recognize many celebrity impersonations at this event, I did see an abundance of long velvet gowns, boas, pearls, and gloves on the women, along with hats and suits on the men.

Not every individual participates in the evening's theme at a party or convention—it is certainly not a requirement and costumes are often quickly discarded at the private parties anyway—yet couples do indeed think about how they present themselves and sometimes wear extremely revealing erotic attire or ostentatious garb that would be inappropriate in almost any other social setting. Often the themes provide an excuse to shop for, and wear, such items (and to do so requires quite a bit of preparation). At some larger events, awards are given out for the best erotic costumes for men, women, or couples. Photos of the couple in costume may be used later when seeking partners on-line. Some of the outfits border on the outrageous or comical, others may be more subdued but still usually filtered through ideas of "sexiness" and glamour (even if the actual effect on any given observer is "cheesy" or "trashy"). Women may dress as prostitutes, strippers, lingerie models or as if they are going to attend a cocktail party; the men may present themselves as gladiators, wrestlers, cowboys, "sheiks," and pirates. Interestingly, although these are stereotypical masculine figures associated with violence and aggression, the conventions are an extremely safe space for women to dress or behave provocatively (the only "gang-bangs" that are likely to occur are those arranged by the women themselves).

For some couples, the sex is the most important part of the convention—the organized events are attended, if at all, only in order to meet potential partners. But couples can engage in other leisure activities during the conventions: dancing, flirting, sunbathing, drinking alcohol,[20] informally mingling and meeting new people, and attending pool parties, happy hours, and private parties, for example. For some couples, however, a large draw of the convention seems to be the opportunity for self-expression in this grandiose manner, the opportunity to live out fantasies of identity, coded through popular notions of wealth, glamour, and sexiness, and, especially, the opportunity to feel desired. Elsewhere I have written about how individuals use swinging to combat feelings of "deadness" in long-term relationships and public events like the conventions to experience themselves and their partner as other. The themes and dances, like the play parties, provide an opportunity to see oneself and one's partner in a new and different light, as both desiring and desired by others.

In a time when a significant segment of the media seems focused on glitz and glamour—think of the popularity of the Entertainment channel, the widespread fascination with the lives of celebrities (especially around love and sex) in tabloid publications, the overwhelming sexualization of fame and consumption, the increase in "reality TV" programming where average Joes find their 15 minutes of fame (and sometimes, as with ABC's *The Bachelor*, live out a harem fantasy; see Frank 2007)—it makes sense that individuals with the means to do so would find ways to "play" at fame, to capture the excitement of the lives of television and movie stars, and to experience their partners and themselves as objects of desire (the red-carpet attention).

Any kind of engagement in leisure activities should be examined with a critical eye, for leisure and tourism are often used to legitimate the everyday lives of the participants and by implication, the global power structures that maintain everyday inequalities and social positionings. Further, the idea of sex as recreation expressed in swinging fits well with a consumer-oriented society (Butler 1979), and one's take on the commodification of sexual experience will thus undoubtedly be shaped by one's view of the spread of capitalism more generally. Other issues to be taken into consideration as well include the focus in the lifestyle on youth and attractiveness. Preparations may include diet and exercise, even plastic surgery (and some surgeons advertise on site, even poolside, at the conventions). The idea of sex as recreation needs to be explored also for the interpersonal power differentials as well as structural power differentials that shape its expression: What is recreation for one individual may be a matter of survival or emotional acquiescence for another. I do not have space here to discuss the nuances of the negotiations engaged in by playcouples or the ways that dominant discourses of gender, sexuality, and intimacy affect these negotiations, nor can I elaborate on the complexities of any single couple's decisions in this realm, although I do so elsewhere. With all of this in mind, however, the practices of playcouples can be seen as part of an impetus toward a more egalitarian and fulfilling sexuality for certain privileged groups of heterosexual couples, whether or not such an aim is always achieved. The practices of lifestylers are also, at least in part, a way of negotiating social changes that impact couple formation and marital experience for these same groups: longer periods of singlehood and an increased incidence of premarital sex that makes lifelong monogamy more problematic for some individuals, changing gender roles in heterosexual relationships, greater opportunities for meeting extramarital partners (especially for women), and greater expectations for the role of sexuality and sexual pleasure in one's life and marriage.

Conclusion

Individuals (especially men, historically) have long traveled in search of sexual otherness (whether to other locales, other bodies, or both), and the erotics involved in the journey away from "home" or spouse are intertwined with systems of gendered, classed, and racial privilege as well as with patterns of economic and social conquest at a global level (Curtis and Pajaczkowska 1994). Is there a search for otherness that can escape some of the negatives associated with many such border crossings (literal or figurative)? Certainly, lifestyle conventions and organized events are not and will never be a form of utopian revolt, and for some couples, swinging practice might pose an utter personal disaster. Depending on one's personal political concerns, problems might be found in the conspicuous consumption involved in this kind of touristic sexuality (environmental degradation, the exploitation involved in the service economy, etc.), in the idea of tourism itself (inequality in international relations that make it easier for couples from some countries and social strata to travel in the first place) or in the multiple meanings of love being employed by the playcouples.

Adult play, like any other facet of social life, cannot be somehow removed from the greater social, cultural, political, and economic contexts that shape its meanings and position the individuals involved.

Clearly, we must proceed with caution, because discourses of love and sex also vary around the world and for different social groupings. Many of the American lifestylers I have spoken with, for example, have emphasized the values of honesty in their relationships, freedom of sexual expression, the benefits of sexual pleasure, and equality for the sexes in terms of sexual appetite and opportunity. Yet when I asked an Argentinean woman about the appeal of the lifestyle for her, she argued that "because all men cheat in South America, all of them do," the lifestyle offered an opportunity for her to participate in this behavior, to possibly "hold onto her man" in a situation where she was already disadvantaged. In situations where women may be extremely dependent on men for financial support or social acceptance, a woman's acquiescence to the lifestyle, and even her enjoyment of it, may derive from quite different discourses and understandings of sex, love, and commitment. (It is worth noting that in this comparison there are also different understandings of marriage at work as well that would need to be explored.)

Yet on another level, for some privileged groups, the practices lifestylers engage in are emblematic of a gender democratization of touristic sexuality and may be seen as an example of the impetus to a less exploitive sexuality in general. Although impossible to predict with any certainty, there is also the potential for both the formation of a more overtly political community consciousness and for a diffusion of the alternative ideas about sex, love, and marriage expressed by lifestylers to impact normative understandings of heterosexuality.

Altman argues that "in the rich world" "sex is increasingly seen as a form of recreation." Still, however, he notes that we cannot "dismiss the search for pleasure as purely the luxury of the rich" because sexual pleasure does become significant, especially to women, as they become more able to express their desires (2001:162). He points out that while questions of sexual freedom are deeply connected to other social struggles, they are "meaningless in the absence of other forms of freedom and equality" (163). Sexuality thus remains "both a battlefield and a legitimate area for political action" (164). Pleasure, sexual or otherwise, is not in and of itself political, as I have argued in other work (see Frank 2002b); rather, what matters most is the interpretations that are made of pleasurable experiences. Again, this is not to say that a less exploitative sexuality has been actualized in some utopian form at the conventions or elsewhere but simply to point out that the spread of ideals of consumption and leisure to the most intimate aspects of sexual engagement and the development of new forms of adult play in the global marketplace in the form of touristic sexuality can create new outlets for developing intimacy, rethinking normative ideas about gender and relationships, and engaging in fantasy that can infuse the everyday with hope and eroticism.

Acknowledgments

I would like to thank the attendees at the "Love and Globalization" conference, Mailman School of Public Health, Center for Gender, Sexuality, and Health, Columbia University, April 30–May 1, 2004, as well as Mark Padilla and Laura Agustín for helpful comments on drafts of this chapter.

Notes

1. Such a distinction is not absolute. Sex workers may travel for business or pleasure (or both) and at times may find themselves occupying positions other than laborer or engaging in different kinds of labor along the way (see Agustín 2006).
2. I use these terms interchangeably throughout this text.
3. Because there are far more men than women with an interest in "the lifestyle," until 2005, women were allowed to attend the official Lifestyles events without a partner. Some clubs catering to lifestylers allow single men on particular nights or limit their numbers; most allow as many single women as wish to attend. Though some men may hire an escort to accompany them to an event, this practice is frowned upon by other couples.
4. Urry argues that the tourist gaze can take two forms, the romantic and the collective. The romantic form of the tourist gaze has an emphasis on solitude, privacy and a personal or semi-spiritual relationship with the object of the gaze (1990:45). The collective form, in contrast, relies on the presence of other tourists to create atmosphere and to add excitement and glamour to the experience (46). The lack of authenticity, he writes, is more of a problem under the romantic gaze than for those engaged in the collective gaze, "where congregation is paramount" (34).
5. In previous work, I have discussed the idea of touristic practice in the context of men's visits to strip clubs and their interactions with the dancers (see Frank 2002a, 2002b, 2003). My work on sexuality in committed relationships has continued this line of thinking, as I have tracked the ways that individuals and couples often search for excitement and "difference" outside their relationships (in the form of infidelity or various forms of open sexual nonexclusivity) or within their relationships through certain forms of intimate work (increasing communication and intimate "sharing," dressing up for partners, learning new sexual techniques, using sexual services and products, sharing fantasies, etc.).
6. I am not suggesting that capitalism itself has brought such openings into view or that there is an "emancipatory potential in the rhetoric of globalization itself" (see Miyazaki 2006:163). Rather, I am here interested in the creativity invoked as individuals work to make their lives meaningful within social, cultural, political, economic, and psychological constraints.
7. My research affiliate for this project is John DeLamater at the University of Wisconsin, Madison. Our research was assisted by a fellowship from the Sexuality Research Fellowship Program of the Social Science Research Council with funds provided by the Ford Foundation.
8. The term *community* can be used only loosely, because there is little indication that lifestylers consider themselves part of any coherent community. However, the term is used here to denote structures of communication (websites, national and local publications) and groups of leisure events dedicated to individuals participating in particular kinds of non–sexually exclusive practices.
9. I worked as an exotic dancer off and on for six years, in part while I was collecting data for a project on the meanings and experiences of strip club visits for American men (Frank 2002a).

10. Clubs and other venues are designated "on-premise" if sexual activity is allowed in the space. On-premise venues often have beds or specific rooms set aside for sexual activity. Off-premise events allow couples to socialize but they must go elsewhere to engage in explicit sexual activity; these events may be seen as involving "less pressure" for newcomers to the scene. Hotel parties may offer a mix of both options—the public spaces often have restrictions on nudity and "lewd" behavior, especially if alcohol is being served, but the private rooms allow for more freedom.

11. One of the larger adult websites, *www.adultfriendfinder.com*, posts listings from 178 countries.

12. Couples may be cautious because of worries about venereal disease or pregnancy, or limitations in sexual activity may be a way to manage jealousy or maintain emotional monogamy with their spouse or partner.

13. One reviewer asked whether lifestylers were perhaps simply transferring restrictions on nonmonogamy to a smaller subset of sexual practices. My research on sexual exclusivity and relationships in general has found that dyads almost always set boundaries, explicitly or implicitly, about what would constitute a breach of the relationship. Even some polyamorous couples who claimed to have "no rules," for example, also discussed potentially transgressive behaviors that their partner might engage in (such as suddenly trying to institute a specific boundary or rule). As traditional monogamy is quite clearly breached by extradyadic sexual contact, reserving specific acts such as kissing or orgasm for primary partners is still quite a departure from such restrictions.

14. Polyamorists also often object to and differentiate themselves from "swingers" (I heard this outmoded term used more often in a negative sense in these kinds of discussions, in on-line forums and elsewhere), although the groups also tend to overlap in practices. The conspicuous consumption, the heterosexual and class privileges experienced by the couples, the focus on appearance, and the sanctity of the marital (or dyadic) bond are some of the things polyamorists objected to.

15. Many of the terms and phrases used are similar to those used in reference to gay and lesbian relationships and identities: lifestyle, coming out of the closet, passing, etc.

16. Lifestylers are not necessarily trying to procure sex with "the locals," and they put a strong emphasis on the empowerment of women and on sex that is recreational for both parties.

17. The term *community* is used loosely in this context; whether or not lifestylers would constitute an identity community is debatable. Certainly, however, many of the couples involved in such practices of recreational sex will have similar needs and concerns in the current political and social environment.

18. Although all-inclusive resorts may have the effect of meaning that profits circulate back to the country of tourist origin, instead of the host community, this is not the reason that they are chosen by guests. Wong and Kwong (2004) found that such package tours were chosen for "tour arrangement and service quality, attractions, hotels and airlines, TV promotions and customer care, routing, personal interests, word-of-mouth, and time."

19. Private parties may also be themed, but they are of a much smaller scale and may be based on practices instead of appearances (since attendees will most likely be shedding their costumes): for example, Oral and Oil, All Anal, or Jack and Jill (masturbation only).

20. Drinking plays some role in social lubrication at events but couples are usually reluctant to drink too much because alcohol affects sexual performance and relationship dynamics. Drugs are also used carefully, if at all, for the same reasons (unless, of course, the drugs are designed to enhance sexual performance, such as Viagra).

References

Altman, Dennis
  2001   Global Sex. Chicago: University of Chicago Press.
Agustín, Laura
  2006   The Disappearing of a Migration Category: Migrants Who Sell Sex. Journal of Ethnic
         and Migration Studies 32 (1):29–47.
Bartell, Gilbert
  1971   Group Sex: A Scientist's Eyewitness Report on the American Way of Swinging. New
         York: Peter H. Wyden.
Bellemeade, Kaye
  2003   Swinging for Beginners: An Introduction to the Lifestyle. N.p.: New Tradition Books.
Bishop, Ryan, and Lillian S. Robinson
  1998   Night Market: Sexual Cultures and the Thai Economic Miracle. New York: Routledge.
Bergstrand, C., and J. B. Williams
  2000   Today's Alternative Marriage Styles: The Case of Swingers. Journal of Human Sexuality,
         vol. 3, October 10.
Brennan, Denise
  2004   What's Love Got to Do with It? Transnational Desires and Sex Tourism in the
         Dominican Republic. Durham: Duke University Press.
Butler, Edgar
  1979   Social Origins of Swinging. In Traditional Marriages and Emerging Alternatives. E.
         Butler, ed. New York: Harper & Row.
Campbell, Shirley, Althea Perkins, and Patricia Mohammed
  1999   Come to Jamaica and Feel All Right: Tourism and the Sex Trade. In Sun, Sex, and
         Gold: Tourism and Sex Work in the Caribbean. Kamala Kempadoo, ed. Pp. 125–156.
         Lanham, MD: Rowman & Littlefield.
Clift, S., and S. Forrest
  1999   Gay Men and Tourism: Destinations and Holiday Motivations. Tourism Management
         20(5):615–625.
Curtis, Barry, and Claire Pajaczkowska
  1994   "Getting There": Travel, Time, and Narrative. In Traveller's Tales: Narratives of Home
         and Displacement. G. Robertson, M. Mash, L. Tickner, J. Bird, B. Curtis, and T.
         Putnam, eds. Pp. 199–215. London: Routledge.
Frank, Katherine
  2002a G-Strings and Sympathy: Strip Club Regulars and Male Desire. Durham: Duke
         University Press.
  2002b Stripping, Starving, and Other Ambiguous Pleasures. In Jane Sexes It Up: True
         Confessions of Feminist Desire. M. L. Johnson, ed. Pp 171–206. New York: Four
         Walls, Eight Windows.
  2003   Just Trying to Relax: Masculinity, Masculinizing Practices, and Strip Club Regulars.
         Journal of Sex Research 40(1):61–75.
  2007   Primetime Harem Fantasies: Marriage, Monogamy, and a Bit of Feminist Fanfiction
         on ABC's The Bachelor. In Third Wave Feminism and Television: Jane Puts It in a Box.
         Merri Lisa Johnson, ed. Pp. 91–118. New York: I. B. Tauris.
Gould, Terry
  1999   The Lifestyle: A Look at the Erotic Rites of Swingers. N.p.: Random House Canada.
Graeber, David
  2001   Toward an Anthropological Theory of Value: The False Coin of Our Own Dreams.
         New York: Palgrave.

Greenwood, Davydd J.
   1989   Culture by the Pound: An Anthropological Perspective on Tourism as Cultural
          Commoditization. *In* Hosts and Guests: The Anthropology of Tourism. V. Smith, ed.
          Pp. 171–185. Philadelphia: University of Pennsylvania Press.
Guthrie, Julian
   2002   Partner Swapping Comes Out of Closet. San Francisco Chronicle, July 9. Electronic
          document, *www.sfgate.com/cgibin/article.cgi?f=/c/a/2002/07/09/MN242428.DTL*,
          accessed February 14, 2007.
Howe, Alyssa Cymene
   2001   Queer Pilgrimage: The San Francisco Homeland and Identity Tourism. Cultural
          Anthropology 16(1):35–61.
Hughes, H.
   1997   Holidays and Homosexual Identity. Tourism Management 18(1):3–7.
Jansson, Andre
   2002   Spatial Phantasmagoria: The Mediatization of Tourism Experience. European Journal
          of Communication 17(4):429–443.
Jenks, Richard J.
   1998   Swinging: A Review of the Literature. Archives of Sexual Behavior 27(5):507–521.
Josiam, B. M., J. S. P Hobson, U. C. Dietrich, and G. Smeaton
   1998   An Analysis of the Sexual, Alcohol, and Drug-Related Behavioural Patterns of Students
          on Spring Break. Tourism Management 19(6):501–513.
Kempadoo, Kamala, and Jo Doezema, eds.
   1998   Global Sex Workers: Rights, Resistance, and Redefinition. New York: Routledge.
Lister, Ashley
   2006   Swingers: True Confessions from Today's Swinging Scene. London: Virgin Books.
Lury, Celia
   1996   Consumer Culture. New Brunswick, NJ: Rutgers University Press.
Marks, Steve, and Cathy Marks
   1994   Swing: Dawn of a New Era. Ocala, FL: MSW Publishing.
Mitchell, Richard D.
   1998   Learning through Play and Pleasure Travel: Using Play Literature to Enhance Research
          into Touristic Learning. Current Issues in Tourism 1(2):176–188.
Miyazaki, Hirokazu
   2006   Economy of Dreams: Hope in Global Capitalism and Its Critiques. Cultural
          Anthropology 21(2):147–172.
Moore, Jerry L.
   2005   Private Diary: Our First Year in Swinging. West Conshohocken, PA: Infinity.
Mullings, Beverly
   1999   Globalization, Tourism, and the International Sex Trade. *In* Sun, Sex and Gold:
          Tourism and Sex Work in the Caribbean. Kamala Kempadoo, ed. Pp 55–80. Lanham,
          MD: Rowman & Littlefield.
Nunez, Theron
   1989   Touristic Studies in Anthropological Perspective. *In* Hosts and Guests: The
          Anthropology of Tourism. V. Smith, ed. Pp. 265–279. Philadelphia: University of
          Pennsylvania Press.
Pittman, Frank S.
   1989   Private Lies: Infidelity and the Betrayal of Intimacy. New York: W. W. Norton.
Rojek, Chris, and John Urry, eds.
   1997   Touring Cultures: Transformations of Travel and Theory. London: Routledge.
Rothman, Hal
   2002   Neon Metropolis: How Las Vegas Started the Twenty-First Century. New York:
          Routledge.

Rothman, Hal K., ed.
 1998　Reopening the American West. Tucson: University of Arizona Press.
Sanchez Taylor, Jacqueline
 2001　Dollars Are a Girl's Best Friend? Female Tourists' Sexual Behavior in the Caribbean. Sociology 35(3):749–764.
Skeggs, Beverly
 1999　Sexualities in Leisure Spaces. Leisure Studies 18:213–232.
Smith, Valene L., ed.
 1989　Hosts and Guests: The Anthropology of Tourism. Philadelphia: University of Pennsylvania Press.
Towner, John
 1985　The Grand Tour: A Key Phase in the History of Tourism. Annals of Tourism Research 12:297–333.
Trauer, Birgit, and Chris Ryan
 2005　Destination Image, Romance, and Place Experience: An Application of Intimacy Theory in Tourism. Tourism Management 26(2005):481–491.
Urry, John
 1990　The Tourist Gaze: Leisure and Travel in Contemporary Societies. London: Sage.
Wearing, Stephen, and Betsy Wearing
 2001　Conceptualizing the Selves of Tourism. Leisure Studies 20:143–159.
Wonders, Nancy A., and Raymond Michalowski
 2001　Bodies, Borders, and Sex Tourism in a Globalized World: A Tale of Two Cities—Amsterdam and Havana. Social Problems 48(4):545–571.
Wong, Chak-keung Simon, and Wai-Yan Yan Kwong
 2004　Outbound Tourists' Selection Criteria for Choosing All-Inclusive Package Tours. Tourism Management 25:581–592.

9

Buying and Selling the "Girlfriend Experience"
The Social and Subjective Contours of Market Intimacy

Elizabeth Bernstein

In the back room of a discreetly furnished apartment in a quiet San Francisco neighborhood, I am sitting on a brown leather sofa talking with Amanda, who
has just said good-bye to the day's first customer. We drink tea as the early afternoon
sunshine streams into the room, illuminating many overstuffed bookcases, an exercise bicycle, and Amanda herself—a slender woman in her late thirties with dark
hair and serious eyes. Smiling slightly, she shrugs when I ask her how the session
with her client went.

> Actually, I spent most of the time giving him a backrub, and we also spent a
> lot of time talking before we had sex. In the end, we went over [time] by about
> seven minutes. . . . You know it's really funny to me when people say that I'm
> selling my body. Of all the work I've done, this isn't abusive to my body. Most
> of my clients are computer industry workers—about half. Sometimes I ask
> myself: what about their bodies? These men spend 40 hours a week hunched
> over a desk. They live alone, eat alone, drive to work alone. Other than seeing
> me, they don't seem to even have time for a social life.

Amanda goes on to explain that today's client was a marketing executive for a
prominent Silicon Valley software company. This client is a "regular," someone she
has seen before, who has often complained to her that he is overworked and too busy
to meet women. I wonder aloud how it is that he nonetheless has the time to drive
two and a half hours on his lunch break to come and see her. Amanda observes with
bemusement that for the majority of her client pool—educated, professional men
who have contacted her through an on-line ad—such paradoxes are the norm.

This chapter is about the ways in which recent transformations in economic and
cultural life have played themselves out at the most intimate of levels: the individual

---

*Adapted from *Temporarily Yours: Intimacy, Authenticity, and the Commerce of Sex* (Chicago:
University of Chicago Press, 2007)

experience of bodily attributes and integrity, and the meanings afforded to sexual expression. The lens through which I examine these transitions is sexual commerce, the exchange of sex for money in the globalized, late-capitalist marketplace. My contention is that experiences such as those of Amanda and her clients reflect and thus offer insight into broader trends at work within intimate life in the contemporary West.[1]

Once largely restricted to face-to-face interactions and the small-scale circulation of pornographic images, sexual commerce has grown to include a vast and ever-expanding range of commercially available products and experiences— fetish clubs; live sex shows; erotic massage; escort agencies; telephone and cyber-sex contacts; "drive-through" striptease venues; sexual "emporiums" featuring lap and wall dancing; sex tourism to developing countries and within global cities; and all variety of sexually explicit texts, videos, and pictures, in print and on-line—what is purportedly a more than $20-billion-a-year industry, and a mainstay of both first and third world economies (Weitzer 2000; Kempadoo and Doezema 1998; Lopez 2000). By examining this growth and diversification of sexual commerce from the perspectives of the purveyors of sexual services and their consumers, my aim has been to articulate a political economy of sexual practices and desires. By detailing the relationship between money and sex at the "micro" level of bodies and subjectivities, I seek to reveal the relationship between economy and desire more broadly.

My argument is that the global restructuring of capitalist production and investment that has taken place since the 1970s has had consequences that are more profound and more intimate than most economic sociologists ever choose to consider.[2] The desires that drive the rapidly expanding and diversifying international sex trade have emanated from corporate-fueled consumption, an increase in tourism and business travel, and the symbiotic relationship between information technologies and the privatization of commercial consumption.[3] At the same time, the rise in service occupations and temporary work, as well as an increase in labor migrations from developing to developed countries, have fueled the growth and diversification of sexual labor. For many sectors of the population, these shifts have resulted in new configurations of familial life as well as in new erotic dispositions, ones that the market is well poised to satisfy.

Old and New Markets in Sexual Labor

To historically situate my claims about the "newness" of late capitalist configurations of eroticism and desire, I begin with a brief review of some of the scholarship that documents the shifts in the social organization and meaning of prostitution that have taken place in the United States and Western Europe over the past few centuries. As social historians such as Judith Walkowitz (1980), Ruth Rosen (1982), and Barbara Hobson (1987) have pointed out, despite the frequent equation of "prostitution" with the "oldest profession," what many of us typically think of as prostitution has not existed for very long at all. The rise of large-scale, commercialized prostitution in the West emerged only with modern-industrial capitalism and its attendant features in the late 19th century: urbanization, the expansion of wage labor, and the decline of the extended-kin based "traditional family." These structural transformations brought with them new cultural ideologies of gender and sexuality, and new symbolic boundaries between public and private life. Accentuated gender differences produced a "double standard" in sexual relations, dichotomizing women along class lines. While white, bourgeois, married women practiced sexual restraint in the private sphere of the home, many working-class women and women of color joined men in the public sphere as wage laborers and sexually available prostitutes.[4] By the early 20th century, numerous "vice commissions" had been created to study—and thereby constitute—the social problem of modern prostitution.

By contrast, what historians typically refer to as "premodern" forms of sexual commerce were self-organized, occasional exchanges in which women traded sexual favors during limited periods of hardship. Premodern prostitution was small in scale, frequently premised on barter, and generally took place within the participants' own homes and communities. Only with the onset of modern-industrial capitalism did large numbers of women find themselves sequestered in a space that was physically and socially separate, thereby affixing them with the permanently stigmatizing identity of "prostitute." During the Progressive Era in the United States, red-light districts were officially shut down and the sex trade was criminalized, but this did not fundamentally alter the meaning of modern prostitution, which marked the female prostitute (but not her male customer) as a criminal outsider. Instead, associations with the image of a dangerous and gritty underworld were dramatically exacerbated, and prostitutes now had to cope with the added stigma of criminality.

The terms *modern* and *premodern* facilitate the comprehension of social realities that are in fact much messier than this simple categorization permits. Prototypically premodern forms of sexual barter never disappeared entirely but exist to this day as the dominant mode of commercial sexual exchange in many impoverished communities throughout the world, and in the sex-for-drugs barter economy of the inner city. The terms, nevertheless, capture something important in terms of large-scale social change. They highlight the ways in which new forms and meanings of sexual exchange emerge at particular historical junctures, coexisting with, and at times eclipsing, the forms that preceded them.

The globalized, late capitalist era of the late 20th and early 21st centuries has witnessed a similar transitional moment in paradigms of commercial sexual exchange. In postindustrial cities such as San Francisco, Amsterdam, and Stockholm, the boundaries of vice have been remapped in such a way so as to curtail the "deviant underworld" of modern prostitution, while the commercialization of sexual services overall has expanded.[5]

For example, in San Francisco, by the late 1990s the nine-square-block area of the City that had housed the city's primary street prostitution strolls for over 75 years was on its way to being incorporated into Union Square, the principal tourist district, as fashionable restaurants and high-priced apartment complexes continued to widen their spread. At the same time, advertisements for prostitution in the newspapers and through the new on-line services exploded, as did prostitution in 11 of the City's 17 legal strip clubs. Many of the very same women and men who had been working on the streets now began to get cell phones and to take out ads, or to look for work in indoor venues. Unlike streetwalking, the new markets in sexual commerce were not concentrated in a de facto urban red-light district but were dispersed throughout the city, housed in inconspicuous Victorians in quiet residential neighborhoods, or relocated to indoor businesses in the city's suburban periphery.[6] In similar fashion, the number of licensed massage parlors in the city overall was actually increasing, despite the police crackdown on Asian-run massage parlors in the Tenderloin. The explosion of commercial sexual services was met by an almost complete lack of concern by the police, despite their intense focus upon the prostitution of illegal migrants and on visible streetwalking.

The transformation that was under way in San Francisco did not merely concern the fate of a few hundred street prostitutes and their customers but was about a more wide-sweeping reallocation of urban space, in which the inner city was reclaimed by the white middle classes, while those at the social margins were pushed to the city's literal periphery (Smith 1996; Pred 2000; Solnit and Schwartzenberg 2000). Although the neighborhood residents actively opposed flagrant and visible prostitution on their streets, it is important to note that, in contrast to moral reform movements of eras past, they did not issue a denunciation of the intermingling of sexuality and the market.[7] To the contrary, the young, white professionals who flooded the city during the 1990s to work in high-tech, multimedia, and other industries were at the forefront of a new economy in sexual services, by creating a demand for them and facilitating new conditions of production. The sex trade did not disappear but instead changed its predominant form: the subterranean world of street prostitution, along with its classic paraphernalia—the pimp, the police officer, the prostitute as "public" and therefore disreputable woman—had begun to recede into the distance, while an array of spatially dispersed sexual services emerged to take its place. In table 9.1, I summarize the key spatial and political transformations of postindustrial sexual commerce, as well as the subjective components of these changes that I elaborate upon in the following discussion.

The Subjective Contours of Market Intimacy

The economic transformations of recent decades have restructured the social geography of sex work and the subjective meanings that guide the experience from within. While a fair amount has been written about the ways in which the new globalized economy has spawned a lucrative traffic in women and children from Asia, Africa, Latin America, and more recently, Eastern Europe (Demleitner 2001; Ehrenreich and Hochschild 2002; Bales 1999), I would like to point to a different level at which new global economic realities have been significant to the development of the sex trade in the West. They have contributed to a transformation in practices and meanings (what we might think of as the subjective contours of market intimacy) for participants on both sides of the commercial sex-work encounter.

In modern prostitution, what was typically sold and bought was an expedient and emotionally contained exchange of cash for sexual release.[8] To survive in the trade, prostitutes learned to develop strategies to distance themselves from their la-

Table 9.1. Paradigmatic distinctions between modern-industrial prostitution and post-industrial sexual commerce

	Modern-industrial prostitution	Postindustrial sexual commerce
What is being sold	Heterosexual intercourse or receptive oral sex	Diversified and specialized array of sexual products and services (images, performances, acts)
Where the exchange takes place	Red-light districts in urban tenderloins (brothels or streets) (Sequestration maintains social divide between "public" and "private.")	Dispersed throughout the city and surrounding suburbs (in private homes, hotels, and commercial venues; over the telephone and on-line; no clear division between the sexual ideologies of "public" and "private" space
State interventions	Criminalized or regulated by state agents; where criminalized, gendered specification of "prostitution" as a crime	Interventions focus on street-based exchanges or illegal migrants
What is being bought	Quick sexual release (the emotionally void counterpart of private-sphere romance and love)	Bounded authenticity (relational meaning resides in the market transaction)

bor, to treat their commercial sexual activity as "work." In my interviews with street-walkers, many strived to emphasize the difference between "career prostitutes" and "crack prostitutes," not only because crack prostitution involved sex-for-drugs rather than sex-for-money, but because most career prostitutes felt that crack prostitutes did not maintain a clear division between public and private selves.

For self-identified "career prostitutes" one important way the public/private boundary is maintained is through a particular remapping of erotic bodily geography, in which one keeps certain sexual practices, aspects of the self, and segments of the body off-limits. As Susan Edwards has observed:

> The belief that, for women who supply the service, "anything goes," is widespread, as women who sell sex forfeit the right to say "No." . . . While sections of the public world may hold this view, the selling of sex by prostitute women is carefully circumscribed. . . . Prostitute women care less about the genitals and breasts, and much more about the mouth, the lips, the kiss, and tenderness, for them the truest meaning and expression of intimacy. (1993:98)

In addition to extreme vigilance about the use of condoms (as a physical and a psychological barrier) and working "straight" (rather than drunk or high), most of the street-based sex workers that I interviewed strenuously insisted that they would not engage their clients in a mouth-to-mouth kiss. In Oslo, one woman explained to me that her work had "nothing to do" with her sexuality, because "the most intimate thing that I have is not what I am selling. I am simply selling the man his orgasm." Karolyn, a Swedish street prostitute, explained similarly:

> If you work like this, you need to have unseen borders you don't let people trespass. If you do, then you start to drink or use drugs, because you can't bear to see yourself in the mirror afterwards. There are things that you allow, and there are things that you don't allow, things that you won't do for money. There has to be a private place inside of you. You can't be the same person when you go out to work.

And Ulla, who has worked on the streets of Stockholm and Helsinki, described the necessity of "leaving my private me at home so that I can go to work."

By contrast, within an emergent postindustrial paradigm of sexual commerce, what is being bought and sold frequently incorporates a great deal more emotional, as well as physical labor within the commercial context.[9] The term *sex work* has come into increasingly widespread use since the 1980s, when it was first coined by prostitutes' rights activists to signal that the sale of sex for money need not imply a unique degradation of self (Leigh 1997). Yet, ironically, it has been precisely during this period that the sexual labor that is exchanged within the transaction is less defined by the sexual acts themselves and more likely to implicate one's "private" erotic and emotional life.

With the relocation of sexual labor from the street to indoor venues such as private homes, rented apartments, and "gentlemen's clubs," the quality of sexual labor that is entailed is also transformed.[10] Sex workers increasingly emphasize the central-ity of emotionally engaged conversation to their work, as well as a willingness to participate in a diversity of sexual activities (e.g., bodily caresses, full-body touching, receiving "pleasure," all of which can require a tremendous amount of emotional labor on the part of the sex worker), and bestowing mouth-to-mouth kisses. Com-pared to the labor of streetwalkers, the labor of indoor, self-employed sex workers is likely to require a larger investment of time with each client (typically an hour, as opposed to 15 minutes for streetwalkers), to take place within the confines of one's own home, and to remain outside the purview of the criminal justice system. Contemporary "intimacy providers" (as some in the industry have taken to calling themselves) charge by the hour rather than for specified acts, so their sexual labor is diffuse and expansive, rather than delimited and expedient.[11]

In contrast to the quick, impersonal sexual release associated with the street-level sex trade, much of the new variety of sexual labor resides in the provision of what I call "bounded authenticity"—the sale and purchase of authentic emotional and physical connection. Katharine Frank (2002) has similarly observed the pre-mium placed on authenticity in contemporary strip clubs, arguing that clients' desire for the real and the authentic is palpable even amid the postmodern simulations of make-up, costumes, breast implants, and stage names (not to mention cash ex-change). Based on ethnographic observations and interviews, Frank documents the numerous ways that clients seek to signal the authenticity of their commercial sexual transactions with strippers, including payments through gifts or cocktails (more per-sonal than cash transactions), and the persistent interest in dancers' real lives and identities.[12] As both Frank's research and my own make clear, what is being bought and sold is something quite other than an ephemeral consumer indulgence, yet also distinct from premodern forms of sexual exchange that naturalize the provision of nonsexual forms of intimacy. In postindustrial sexual commerce, emotional authen-ticity is incorporated explicitly into the economic contract.

For many sex workers, the provision of bounded authenticity resides in ful-filling clients' fantasies of sensuous reciprocity through the self-conscious simulation of desire, pleasure, and erotic interest. For others, it may involve the emotional and physical labor of manufacturing genuine (if fleeting) libidinal and emotional ties, endowing their clients with a feeling of desirability, esteem, or even love.

> When I first started out, I enjoyed the sex. I'd go to work and "have sex." Now, I don't have that association that much. But my clients seem to think that being a nice guy means being a good lover. They do things to me that they should do with a girlfriend. Like they ask me what I'm into, and apologize for coming too soon. So I need to play along. They have no idea that for sex workers, the best client is the one that comes immediately.
> —Amanda, 39, independent escort

> I have been told by certain clients that what I do is better than what the psychiatrists and psychologists do. I had one client who was very fat, kind of unkempt, and really, really ugly. Apparently, the week before he saw me, he

had gone to see two escorts that had turned him down. They told him that not even for money would they fuck him. But I did, plus I made him feel really, really good. So he thanked me. And he said to me, "Don't ever let anyone try to tell you that what you're doing isn't important work. I was lonely, tired, and I needed someone to make me feel good, and that's what you did. What you provide is the most valuable service."

    —Michael, 37, independent escort

What I've noticed is that a lot of people really want to be witnessed when they come. They really want to feel that. You know, I totally get their desire and I want to be able to offer that. And so what I've learned how to do is to look at them deeply and very, very lovingly. . . . For them, it feels great, like it's so personal, like girlfriend stuff. But I feel that I'm just offering them . . . love from the earth, coming up my feet and coming out to them. So they get love. I'm just channeling love.

    —Zoey, 30, erotic masseuse

In apparent contrast to indoor sex workers' accounts of the premium their clients place on erotic authenticity were comments from the clients themselves. During our interviews, they repeatedly stressed to me that one of the chief virtues of commercial sexual exchange is that the encounter is clear and bounded. In prior historical epochs, this "bounded" quality may have provided men with an unproblematic and readily available sexual outlet to supplement a relationship with a pure and asexual wife in the domestic sphere. What is unique to contemporary client narratives, however, is the explicitly stated preference for this type of bounded intimate engagement over other relational forms. Paid sex is neither a sad substitute for something that one would ideally choose to obtain in a nonmarket romantic relationship nor the inevitable outcome of a traditionalist Madonna/whore double standard.

Many of the clients I interviewed described a preference for a life constructed around living alone, intimacy through close friendships, and time-efficient, safely contained commercial sexual encounters. As such, they provide us with a concrete example of the profound reorganization of personal life that has occurred in postindustrial urban centers and nationwide during the past 30 or so years. Demographic transformations such as a decline in marriage rates, a doubling in the divorce rate, and a 60 percent increase in the number of single-person households have had subjective and erotic consequences that few sociologists have paused to consider.[13]

Harold Holzman and Sharon Pines (1982) have argued that it is the fantasy of a mutually desired, special, or even romantic sexual encounter that clients are purchasing in the prostitution transaction—something notably distinct from a purely mechanical sex act and from an unbounded, private-sphere romantic entanglement. They observed that the clients in their study emphasized that the warmth and friendliness of the sex-workers as characteristics that were at least as important to them as the particulars of physical appearance (Holzman and Pines 1982).

The clients that I interviewed were also likely to express variants of the statement, "If her treatment is cold or perfunctory, I'm not interested." They were consistently critical of sex workers who are "clock watchers," "too rushed and pushy," who "don't want to hug and kiss," or who "ask for a tip mid sex act." For clients, successful commercial transactions are those in which the market basis of the exchange serves a crucial delimiting function that facilitates—rather than inhibits—the fantasy of authentic interpersonal connection.

One of the most sought-after features in the prostitution encounter has thus become the "girlfriend experience," or GFE. Among both clients and providers, the GFE has often been described in the following way (and here I quote from the explanation of one sex worker who specializes in this service):

> A typical non-GFE session with an escort includes one or more of the basic acts required for the customer to reach a climax at least one time, and little else. A GFE-type session, on the other hand, might proceed much more like a nonpaid encounter between two lovers. This may include a lengthy period of foreplay in which the customer and the escort touch, rub, fondle, massage, and perhaps even kiss passionately. A GFE session might also include activities where the customer works as hard to stimulate the escort as she works to stimulate him. Finally, a GFE session usually has a period of cuddling and closeness at the end of the session, rather than each partner jumping up and hurrying out as soon as the customer is finished.

Ads for escorts in print media and on-line now feature the GFE experience in their advertisements, and there are entire web pages where people who specialize in this service can advertise.

Note, however, that the GFE is not, from the client's perspective, a sad substitute for a real girlfriend. The attachment of a monetary fee to the transaction provides a crucial boundary for both client and sex worker, the significance of which is illustrated by the consequences that ensue when boundaries are violated. Amanda, one of the few sex workers I have spoken with who admitted to occasionally looking for dating partners among her client pool, said that she had given up offering her preferred clients "freebies" or "bargain rates," because the offer inevitably met with negative results.

> They pretend to be flattered, but they never come back! If you offer them anything but sex for money they flee. There was one client I had who was so sexy, a yoga teacher, really fun. . . . Since good sex is a rare thing, I told him I'd see him for $20 (my normal rate is $250). Another guy, he was so sexy, I told him, "Come for free." Both of them freaked out and never returned. The men want an emotional connection, but they don't want any obligations. They don't believe they can have no-strings-attached sex, which is why they pay. They'd rather pay than get it for free.

Christopher, a male sex worker who had also once tried to redefine his relationship with a client, recounted something similar: "I called a trick once because I wanted to have sex with him again. . . . We agreed in advance that it was just going to be sex for sex's sake, not for pay, and that was the last time I ever heard from him!"

The notion of bounded authenticity I am offering here has been misinterpreted by some critics of prostitution who continue to regard the commercial sexual encounter from within a paradigm of romantic love that is premised upon monogamous domesticity and intertwined life trajectories. Thus, Carole Pateman (1988:199) asks why, if not for the sake of pure domination would "15 to 25 percent of the customers of Birmingham prostitutes demand what is known in the trade as 'hand relief,'" something that could presumably be self-administered. Yet as one client insisted, after explaining to me that he studied and worked all the time, and consequently did not have time to pursue a traditional relationship, "It's more real and human than would be satisfying oneself alone." This client reveals an underlying erotic paradigm that is premised on the discrete sexual encounter and thus compatible with the rhythms of his individually oriented daily life. Increasingly, what is true for him is also true for other men like him, with similar white, middle-class, sociodemographic profiles.

Transformations in Economy, Kinship, and Sexuality

Finally, I would like to consider some of the broader social implications of the shift in commercial sexual markets I have been describing. Table 9.2 summarizes the theoretical model I developed to understand these transitions, but I do not intend to suggest an absolutist, teleological model of history. What is crucial to recognize about the aspects of social life summarized under the heading "Late Capitalism" in the final column is that they do not supplant the features of the prior historical epochs but take their place (however comfortably or uncomfortably) alongside. As with the series of economic, familial, and sexual transformations ushered in by modernity, the shift to a postmodern sexual ethic has been gradual and highly uneven. Nearly a quarter of Americans still live in nuclear families, and more than half continue to work in "non-flexible" jobs.[14] In the most recent national survey of sexual attitudes and behaviors in the United States, nearly 15 percent of those surveyed stated that they believe sex should be for procreation only.[15] Despite the evident frailty of marriage and long-term relationships in late-capitalist society, romantic love of the modernist variety remains a crucial repository of meaning for significant numbers of individuals. At present, there is a fierce political struggle being waged in the United States between the "old" and "new" regimes of intimacy, which has crystallized most visibly around the issues of gay marriage and abortion (both of which signal a distance from the "procreative" normative orientation toward sex).

Nor do I intend to suggest that the defining features of what I have termed the "postindustrial" paradigm of sexual commerce have emerged without important historical precedents. The tradition of the European courtesan (prized as much for conversation and culture as for her erotic capacities) and the "patronage prostitution" of Japanese geishas and Indian *devadasis* are but two well-known instances of emotionally expansive yet explicitly transactional erotic arrangements (Griffin 2001; Dalby 1983; Downer 2001; Ramberg 2006).[16] Although I contend that contempo-

Table 9.2: Paradigms of economy, kinship, and sexual ethics in three historical periods

	Early modern capitalism	Modern-industrial capitalism	Late capitalism
Economy	Domestic production	Wage labor	Services, finance, and information; flexible accumulation
Kinship	Extended kin networks	Nuclear families	Recombinant families, isolable individuals
Sexual ethic	Procreative	Amative–companionate	Bounded authenticity

rary commercial sexual transactions incorporate some decidedly new features—in terms of their formal organization and in terms of the explicitly bounded and commoditized (as opposed to naturalized) quality of the intimacy that is transacted—sex workers have clearly traded in capacities other than sex throughout much of history. The wide range of such cases suggests that the "Taylorized sex" (a term coined by the historian Alain Corbin to describe the concentration, rationalization, and standardization of prostitution in France during the interwar years) featured within the paradigm of modern-industrial prostitution may itself constitute an exception, rather than the rule (Corbin 1990:338).

Although sociologists and historians of sexuality have amply described the "modernization" of sex, they have barely begun to theorize its "postmodernization" in the contemporary period. Theorists such as Manuel Castells (1996), Steven Seidman (1992), and Zygmunt Bauman (1998) do begin to point us in this direction. When Castells speaks of the "normalization" of sex, when Seidman refers to "unbounded eros," and when Bauman describes "the postmodern erotic revolution," they are most certainly evoking something similar. As Bauman writes, "Sex free of reproductive consequences and stubborn, lingering love attachments can be securely enclosed in the frame of an episode, as it will engrave no deep grooves on the constantly re-groomed face being thus insured against limiting the freedom of further experimentation" (1998:27). In a sweeping journey through global sexual politics, emergent sexual subcultures, and different varieties of globalized sex commerce, Dennis Altman has perhaps gone furthest, declaring it his aim to "connect two of the dominant preoccupations of current social science and popular debate": globalization and the preoccupation with sex (2001:1). Altman excepted, most of the existing efforts to link sexuality and globalization are premised on a naturalism I seek to avoid. In these analyses, "sex" is something that exists beneath the social layers of human existence, by which it can either be constrained or freed. Although I diverge from Foucault (1978) in granting primacy to material conditions, with him I suggest that there is no "true" form of sex that lurks beneath its socially paradigmatic expressions.

Meanwhile, social historians such as Kristin Luker (1984) and John D'Emilio

(1983) have linked the "relational" model of sexuality (also referred to as "amative" or "companionate") to the rise of modern romance and the nuclear family under capitalism, contrasting it with the prototypically procreative orientation of preindustrial society. Thus, Luker (1984) has deciphered contemporary abortion debates in the United States in terms of a contest between procreative and relational worldviews, linking women's ideological positions on the question of abortion to disparate sets of material interests. In similar fashion, D'Emilio (1983) has explained the ways in which the peculiarly modern notion of gay identity could emerge only within a sexual ethic premised upon intimate relationship, since both were products of the individualizing freedom from domestic production and extended kin networks that was provided by a system of wage labor.

Following D'Emilio's analysis of the emergence of a relational sexual ethic during the rise of industrial capitalism, I propose that the proliferation of forms of service work, the globalized information economy, and postmodern families peopled by isolable individuals have produced another profound transformation in the erotic sphere. Both the traditional "procreative" and the modern "companionate" models of sexuality are increasingly being supplemented by a sexual ethic that is premised on bounded authenticity. Instead of being predicated on marital or even durable relationships, this sexual ethic derives its primary meaning from the depth of physical sensation and from emotionally bounded erotic exchange. Whereas domestic-sphere, relational sexuality derived its meaning from its ideological opposition to the marketplace, bounded authenticity bears no antagonism to the sphere of public commerce. It is available for sale and purchase just as readily as any other form of commercially packaged leisure activity. When sex workers advertise themselves as "girlfriends for hire" and describe the ways in which they offer not merely eroticism but authentic intimate connection for sale in the marketplace, when overworked high-tech professionals discuss their pursuit of emotional authenticity within the context of paid sexual transactions, and when municipal politicians strategize about the best means to eliminate the eyesore of street prostitution while encouraging the development of corporate "gentleman's clubs," we can witness the unfolding of precisely this transformation.

Conclusion

What is the significance of the transformations that I describe for sex workers and clients, as well as for other inhabitants of postindustrial cities? In this chapter I have sought to complicate the view that the commodification of sexuality is transparently equitable with emotionally diminished erotic experience. Such an argument does not do justice to the ways in which the spheres of public and private, intimacy and commerce, have interpenetrated one another and thereby been mutually transformed, making the late-capitalist consumer marketplace one potential arena for securing authentic yet bounded forms of interpersonal connection.

Venturing into modernity, and postmodernity, may be seen as the ambivalent privilege of individuals from specific classes, racial-ethnic backgrounds, regions, and nations. It should thus come as no surprise to find that more men than women, more middle-class professionals than working-class people, more of the young than the old, and more whites than blacks have been among the first social groups to fully partake in the sexual ethos that I have termed "bounded authenticity."[17] A thorough assessment of the meanings of the incursion of the market into intimate life can therefore be a difficult and contradictory task—particularly for women. What Arlie Hochschild has termed "women's uneasy love affair with capitalism" (1997:229) is made all the more acute when we consider that many of the flourishing sectors of the late-capitalist service economy—such as child care, domestic labor, and sex work—are commercialized refinements of services that women have historically provided for free. As service industry workers, women now conduct this labor within the context of market-generated (as opposed to status-based) social hierarchies. As consumers, women as well as men are gradually gaining access to the particular conveniences and pleasures--and emotional confinement--of commercially mediated interpersonal relations.[18] The emergence and success of new sexual markets provides evidence that female, as well as male sexuality, is currently being reconstructed as a series of isolable techniques for the provision of personal meaning and pleasure, as opposed to an expression of enduring connection with a particular individual. For increasing numbers of women as well as men, passion, emotional authenticity, and connection have not disappeared but have been packed ever more tightly into market commodities.

Notes

1. Ethnographic fieldwork and face-to-face interviews were conducted with a diverse array of sex workers (both female and male), clients, police officers, and municipal officials in San Francisco, Stockholm, and Amsterdam between 1994 and 2001. The names and identifying features of all individuals that I quote here have been changed to protect their anonymity.
2. Of the multitude of recent works on "global economic transformations," two massive edited collections (see Held and McGraw 2000; Lechner and Boli 2000) are indicative of this omission. While they include sections on the implications for politics, culture, and identity, only one essay, notably titled "The Gender Dimension" (Steans 2000) makes any mention of the body or sexuality. Harvey's (1990) landmark treatment of the transition from Fordism to flexible accumulation and Sassen's (1998) analysis of the emergence of significance of global cities also lack sustained discussions of the sexual domain.
3. By the "international sex trade," I am not referring to a coordinated social or economic network but to a highly diversified set of dispersed transactions and actors.
4. Male prostitution was also prevalent in urban centers during this period, but male prostitutes were typically subsumed under the new and more socially salient banner of "homosexuals" in sociological, medico-psychological, and political discourses (Weeks 1981).
5. By "postindustrial cities" I am referring to cities with local economies weighted heavily toward tourism, business and personal services, and high technology (Smith 1996; Milkman and Dwyer 2002; Swedish Institute 2001).
6. My colleague Elizabeth Wood, who similarly observed the suburbanization of sexual commerce in one mid-sized New England city, has referred to this pattern as the "strip-mall" phenomenon (personal communication).
7. For an analysis of evangelical women's moral reform movements in the 19th century, see Hobson (1987). Although contemporary Christian Right and radical feminist groups (as exemplified by as the Coalition Against Trafficking in Women) object to the intermingling of sexuality and the market in private as well as in public, articulating a condemnation of

prostitution that is strikingly similar to those of earlier moral reform movements, the neighborhood residents in San Francisco did not espouse this view.

8. Laura Agustín has described a transition from "pre-industrial" to "industrial" forms of sex work for migrants from Latin America who come to Europe to work in brothels: "Displaying [her]self nude in a window in Amsterdam for fourteen hours a day, or standing next to a road in the Casa de Campo in Madrid . . . are forms of prostitution which might be described as 'industrial,' compared with types at home that perhaps involve dancing and drinking with clients in a more leisurely manner and having sex with two or three in one night" (2000:156).

9. The phrase *emotional labor* derives from the work of Arlie Hochschild (1983:7). She defines the term as that which is required "to induce or suppress feeling in order to sustain the outward countenance that produces the proper state of mind in others. . . . This kind of labor calls for a coordination of mind and feeling, and it sometimes draws on a source of self that we honor as deep and integral to our individuality."

10. As Katherine Liepe-Levinson (2002) observes, the number of strip clubs (or "gentleman's clubs") in major U.S. cities roughly doubled between 1987 and 1992.

11. For similar observations, see Lever and Dolnick (2000).

12. See also Bernstein 2001 for a fuller discussion of the significance of authenticity to prostitutes' clients.

13. By 1988, nearly a third of American households consisted of a single individual. In Western European countries, single-person households have been the most rapidly growing household type since the 1960s, with from 25 percent (in the United Kingdom) to 36 percent (in Sweden) of the population living alone (Sorrentino 1990; Kellogg and Mintz 1993). In the United States the percentage of unmarried adults rose from 28 percent to 37 percent between 1970 and 1988. And according to the most recent census data in the United States, by 2000, less than a quarter of Americans were living in nuclear families (U.S. Bureau of the Census 1989, 1992, 2001).

14. Castells (2001) defines "non-flexible" employment as full-time, year-round, salaried work with over three or more years in the same company.

15. On the distribution of "procreational," "relational," and "recreational" normative orientations toward sexuality in the United States, see Laumann et al. (1994).

16. Historians have also noted that commodities other than sex were offered in the luxury bordellos of 18th-century Paris as well as in 19th-century China, where clients would come to dine, to socialize, or to share confidences with the madam (Norberg 1998; Hershatter 1997).

17. See Laumann et al. 1994, 518–529, for a detailed statistical breakdown of the correlation between normative sexual orientation and membership in master status groups in the United States.

18. Although the bounded authenticity that women seek in their erotic lives is not necessarily provided by the direct purchase of commercial sexual services, there is nonetheless a growing market in sexually evocative romance novels, sex toys, "women friendly" pornographic texts and performances, and sex classes and sexual advice manuals for female consumers (Snitow 1983; Loe 1998; Juffer 1998, Hardy 2001).

References

Agustín, Laura
   2000   Working in the European Sex Industry: Migrant Possibilities. OFRIM/Suplementos, June:155–172.
Altman, Dennis
   2001   Global Sex. Chicago: University of Chicago Press.

Bales, Kevin
  1999   Disposable people: New Slavery in the Global Economy. Berkeley: University of
         California Press.
Bauman, Zygmunt
  1998   On Postmodern Uses of Sex. Theory, Culture, and Society 15(3–4):19–35.
Bernstein, Elizabeth
  2001   The Meaning of the Purchase: Desire, Demand, and the Commerce of Sex.
         Ethnography 2(3):375–406.
  2007   Temporarily Yours: Intimacy, Authenticity, and the Commerce of Sex. Chicago:
         University of Chicago Press.
Castells, Manuel
  1996   The Net and the Self: Working Notes for a Critical Theory of the Informational
         Society. Critique of Anthropology 16 (1):9–38.
  2001   The Network Society. Paper presented at the Center for Working Families, University
         of California, Berkeley, April.
Corbin, Alain
  1990   Women for Hire: Prostitution and Sexuality in France after 1860. Cambridge: Harvard
         University Press.
Dalby, Liza
  1983   Geisha. New York: Vintage Books.
D'Emilio, John
  1993   Capitalism and Gay Identity. In The Lesbian and Gay Studies Reader. Henry Abelove,
         Michele Aina Barale, and David Halperin, eds. Pp. 467–479. New York: Routledge.
Demleitner, Nora
  2001   The Law at a Crossroads: The Construction of Migrant Women Trafficked into
         Prostitution. In Global Human Smuggling: Comparative Perspectives. David Kyle and
         Rey Koslowski, eds. Pp. 257–294. Baltimore: John Hopkins University Press.
Downer, Lesley
  2001   Women of the Pleasure Quarters. New York: Broadway Books.
Edwards, Susan
  1993   Selling the Body, Keeping the Soul: Sexuality, Power, and the Theories and Realities
         of Prostitution. In Body Matters: Essays on the Sociology of the Body. Sue Scott and
         David Morgan, eds. Pp. 89–104. London: Falmer Press.
Ehrenreich, Barbara, and Arlie Russell Hochschild, eds.
  2002   Global Woman: Nannies, Maids, and Sex Workers in the New Economy. New York:
         Metropolitan Books.
Foucault, Michel
  1978   The History of Sexuality: An Introduction. New York: Random House.
Frank, Katherine
  2002   G-Strings and Sympathy: Strip Club Regulars and Male Desire. Durham: Duke
         University Press.
Griffin, Susan
  2001   The Book of the Courtesans: A Catalogue of their Virtues. New York: Broadway Books.
Hardy, Lisa Allyn
  2001   Sex in the City: Where to Learn about the Birds, the Bees, and Sexual Bliss. San
         Francisco Bay Guardian, May 23:31.
Harvey, David
  1990   The Condition of Postmodernity: An Enquiry into the Origins of Cultural Change.
         Cambridge: Blackwell.
Held, David, and Anthony McGraw, eds.
  2000   The Global Transformations Reader: An Introduction to the Globalization Debate.
         Cambridge: Polity.

Hershatter, Gail
  1997 Dangerous Pleasures: Prostitution and Modernity in 20th-Century Shanghai. Berkeley: University of California Press.
Hobson, Barbara Meil
  1987 Uneasy Virtue: The Politics of Prostitution and the American Reform Tradition. Chicago: University of Chicago Press.
Hochschild, Arlie
  1997 The Time Bind: When Work Becomes Home and Home Becomes Work. New York: Metropolitan Books.
  1983 The Managed Heart: Commodification of Human Feeling. Berkeley: University of California Press.
Holzman, Harold, and Sharon Pines
  1982 Buying Sex: The Phenomenology of Being a John. Deviant Behavior 4:89–116.
Juffer, Jane
  1998 At Home with Pornography: Women, Sex, and Everyday Life. New York: New York University Press
Kellogg, Susan, and Steven Mintz
  1993 Family Structures. In Encyclopedia of American Social History, Vol. 3. Mary Kupiec Cayton, Elliot J. Gorn, and Peter Williams, eds. Pp. 1925–1941. New York: Scribner.
Kempadoo, Kamala, and Jo Doezema
  1998 Global Sex Workers: Rights, Resistance, and Redefinition. New York: Routledge.
Laumann, Edward O., John H. Gagnon, Robert T. Michael, and Stuart Michaels
  1994 The Social Organization of Sexuality: Sexual Practices in the United States. Chicago: University of Chicago Press.
Lechner, Frank J., and John Boli, eds.
  2000 The Globalization Reader. Oxford: Blackwell.
Leigh, Carol
  1997 Inventing Sex Work. In Whores and Other Feminists. Jill Nagle, ed. Pp. 223–232. New York: Routledge.
Lever, Janet, and Deanne Dolnick
  2000 Clients and Call Girls: Seeking Sex and Intimacy. In Sex for Sale: Prostitution, Pornography, and the Sex Industry. Ronald Weitzer, ed. Pp. 85–103. New York: Routledge.
Liepe-Levinson, Katherine
  2002 Strip Show: Performances of Gender and Desire. London: Routledge.
Loe, Meika
  1998 Dildos in Our Toolboxes: The Production of Sexuality at a Pro-Feminist Sex Toy Store. Berkeley Journal of Sociology 43:97–137.
Lopez, Steve
  2000 Hold the Pickles, Please: This Drive-Through Has a New Menu Item. Time, October 2:6.
Luker, Kristin
  1984 Abortion and the Politics of Motherhood. Berkeley: University of California Press.
Milkman, Ruth, and Rachel E. Dwyer
  2002 Growing Apart: The "New Economy" and Job Polarization in California, 1992–2000; The State of California Labor 2002. Berkeley and Los Angeles: University of California Institute for Labor and Employment.
Norberg, Kathryn
  1998 Prostitution in Eighteenth Century Paris: Pages from a Madam's Notebook. In Prostitution: On Whores, Hustlers, and Johns. James E. Elias, Vern L. Bullough, Veronica Elias, and Gwen Brewer, eds. Pp. 61–79. Amherst, MA: Prometheus Books.

202 Part III: Fantasy, Image, and the Commerce of Intimacy

Pateman, Carole
1988 The Sexual Contract. Stanford: Stanford University Press.
Pred, Allan
2000 Even in Sweden: Racisms, Racialized Spaces, and the Geographical Imagination. Berkeley: University of California Press.
Ramberg, Lucinda
2006 Given to the Goddess: Devadasis, Kinship, Ethics. PhD dissertation, Department of Anthropology, University of California at Berkeley.
Rosen, Ruth
1982 The Lost Sisterhood: Prostitution in America, 1900–1918. Baltimore: Johns Hopkins University Press.
Sassen, Saskia
1998 Globalization and Its Discontents: Essays on the New Mobility of people and Money. New York: New Press.
Seidman, Steven
1991 Romantic Longings. New York: Routledge.
Smith, Neil
1996 The New Urban Frontier: Gentrification and the Revanchist City. New York: Routledge.
Snitow, Ann
1983 Mass Market Romance: Pornography for Women Is Different. *In* Powers of Desire: The Politics of Sexuality. Ann Snitow, Christine Stansell, and Sharon Thompson, eds. Pp. 245–264. New York: Monthly Review Press.
Solnit, Rebecca, and Susan Schwartzenberg
2000 Hollow City: The Siege of San Francisco and the Crisis of American Urbanism. London: Verso.
Sorrentino, Constance
1990 The Changing Family in International Perspective. Monthly Labor Review 113(3):41–58.
Steans, Jill
2000 The Gender Dimension. *In* The Global Transformations Reader: An Introduction to the Globalization Debate. David Held and Anthony McGrew, eds. Pp. 366–374. Cambridge: Polity Press.
Swedish Institute
2001 Telecommunications and Information Technology in Sweden. Swedish Industry 125.
U.S. Bureau of the Census
1989 Studies in Marriage and the Family. *In* U.S. Government Printing Office Current Population Reports. Pp. 23–162. Washington, D.C.: Department of Commerce.
1992 Marriage, Divorce, and Remarriage in the 1990's. *In* U.S. Government Printing Office Current Population Reports. Pp. 23–180. Washington, D.C.: Department of Commerce.
2001 Household and Family Characteristics: Summary Tables. Electronic document, *www.census.gov/population/www/socdemo/hh-fam-sum98tab.html*, accessed June 13.
Walkowitz, Judith R.
1980 Prostitution and Victorian Society: Women, Class, and the State. Cambridge: Cambridge University Press.
Weeks, Jeffrey
1981 Inverts, Perverts, and Mary-Annes. *In* The Subcultures Reader. Ken Gelder and Sarah Thornton, eds. Pp. 268–281. London: Routledge.
Weitzer, Ronald, ed.
2000 Sex for Sale: Prostitution, Pornography, and the Sex Industry. New York: Routledge.

10

Love Work in a Tourist Town
Dominican Sex Workers
and Resort Workers Perform at Love

Denise Brennan

"A Double Wedding" and "Love in the Caribbean," the news headlines read.[1] The local event in Sosúa—a tourist town on the north coast of the Dominican Republic—had become national news. Two white English female tourists met—and soon married—two Afro-Dominican male resort workers in a shared ceremony. They married two months after they had first met at the all-inclusive hotel in Sosúa where the men worked and the women had been guests. The marriage ceremony took place after the men had been refused entry into England. Even though the men had tourist visas and all the necessary paperwork, when they landed at Heathrow, British immigration officials detained them, questioned them separately, and decided that they were so young, at 18 years old, that they might have the intention of overstaying their tourist visas and looking for work. But it was also on the issue of love—and its implausibility—that the officials denied the Dominican men entrance. "The authorities concluded that it was not reasonable that two young English women, with less than 15 days to get to know the men, would have sent two tickets to visit England, with no other additional motives," a leading Dominican news magazine reported (Victoria 1994:45). If officials reasoned that they were not really in love, they must have seen the men as pretending or performing being in love.[2]

President Joaquín Balaguer issued a statement on the wedding, the media led with the story, and neighborhood gossip in Sosúa picked up on this event. The wedding became symbolic of how the Dominican Republic sells itself through tourism. Dominicans and foreign residents of Sosúa alike declared, "There is no way the men love these women." "These guys are sankies, they want visas; that's it." By characterizing the men as sankies—essentially male sex workers—Sosúans assumed the men were in the relationships solely for material gain. This assumption is clear in a cartoon from a now-defunct Dominican satirical magazine that lampoons the overnight weddings. The cartoon plays up the "predatory" side of the Dominican men in featuring in the second frame the mother of one of the English women crying, "Cuidado con los Sand Key Pants Kids!" (Be careful with the sanky-pankies!). It is just as illustrative of the presumed naïveté of the English tourists, who are portrayed as initially rejecting the advances of the predatory sanky-pankies. This cartoon, and the media frenzy in general that surrounded the tourists' relationship with the Dominican men, inspires myriad questions: Why did these weddings grab national attention? Why were so many Dominicans embarrassed by it? Why are relationships in Sosúa between Dominicans and foreigners, particularly tourists, questioned, doubted, and sometimes even laughed at? Why were the men portrayed as sanky-pankies? And most strikingly, why were these relationships dismissed as mere performances of love and not seen as the "real thing"?

The "real thing," marriage *por amor*, is understood by Sosúans in the context of Sosúa as "sexscape"—which I explain later—as driven by romance and emotional needs rather than strategy and financial needs (marriage *por residencia* or for a visa).[3] Unlike L. A. Rebhun's research on love in Caruaru, Brazil, where the people she interviewed "expressed confusion over the nature of love and about the changes they had seen during their lifetimes in the definitions of love" (1999:11), in my interviews with Sosúans they regularly echoed one another's descriptions of relationships based on "real love." Rebhun aptly expresses just how difficult it is to do research on love because of the "slippery nature" of emotions: "now conscious, now unconscious, now openly expressed, now indirectly expressed, and always manipulated" (1999:11).[4]

In this chapter I am not attempting to determine which relationships were rooted in emotion and which grew out of strategy; rather, I am interested in analyzing why Sosúans drew the conclusions they did about other people's relationships. I cannot possibly measure "real love" in one relationship or another or guess precisely what motivates individuals. My aim is to make sense of why Sosúans described others' relationships as "real" or not. When sex workers and resort workers told me their own relationships were based on strategy and not on emotion, it took me out of the guessing game. Elena, a former sex worker who worked with foreign clients, for example, laughed when I asked whether she was in love with a German man whom she married in the spring of 2001: "You know how it is. It's not love. My children and I will have more opportunities in Germany." It is important, however, to keep in mind the various motivations that could shape self-reporting on love. Positing love could make Sosúan sex workers (and former sex workers) appear foolish. No matter what they feel for their foreign boyfriends, these women have an incentive to portray themselves as not naïve enough to actually fall in love.

Even though sex workers in Sosúa talk about the possibility of marriage *por amor*, I only rarely heard sex workers describe having experienced this kind of emotion-driven love as opposed to strategy-driven love. (Nanci's love story that I tell here is unusual.) Rather, sex workers' descriptions of what they want in relationships—in marriage or in consensual unions with either foreign or Dominican men—do not center on emotions but on the concern for better treatment in the household (greater gender equity), sexual fidelity, and financial security. For Sosúa's sex workers, choosing to "fall in love" with one man over another is a rational process with serious material consequences. Contrary to the notion of "falling in love" as a kind of elation that comes with losing control of one's senses or wits, for these women being in love—or pretending to be in love—requires alertness, savvy, and determination.

Rebhun comments on this idea that in the United States "we tend to believe that sentiment is genuine only if it is spontaneous; conventional, required, manipulated sentiment seems false . . . and its falseness morally reprehensible." But, Rebhun continues, "deliberation and requirement are as much a part of emotion as spontaneity" (1999:29–30).

This chapter examines the practices and meanings of "love" within the Dominican community in Sosúa that have emerged with the growth of the tourist and sex-tourist trades.[5] Specifically, I focus on how resort workers and sex workers try to parlay their access to foreign tourists into marriage proposals and visa sponsorships. At the discos, bars, and beaches, it is possible for any Dominican to meet—and perhaps to marry—a foreigner. Dominican resort workers, in particular, have many opportunities to spend time with tourists. Love takes on multiple meanings in this tourist setting, and marriage has specific uses. Marriage in a tourist economy—especially in an internationally known sex-tourist destination—often has nothing to do with emotion-driven love or romance. Later in the chapter, I recount several women's and men's marriage choices, and though they might describe having experienced emotion-driven love, they chose to marry individuals as a strategy to get ahead (*progresar*). They use the discourse and practices of romantic love to secure marriage proposals for a visa. Why waste a marriage certificate on romantic love when it can be transformed into a visa?

Sosúa as Sexscape

With its constant influx of Dominican and Haitian migrants for work in the sex and tourist trades and of European tourists for play, as well as a large foreign-resident community living there year-round, Sosúa has become a transnational sexual meeting ground. I am particularly interested in how the transnational process of sex tourism has quickly and flamboyantly changed daily life in Sosúa—especially for Dominican women—as well as informed Dominican and foreign perceptions of Sosúa and Sosúans in different ways than has tourism. Since Sosúa has become known as a place where tourists can buy sex, Sosúa and Sosúans have experienced monumental changes. Because sex tourism has played a critical role in the town's transformation, I see it as a space inextricably tied up with transactional sex—it has become a "sexscape" of sorts. I use the term *sexscape* to refer to both a new kind of global sexual landscape and the sites within it. The word *sexscape* builds on the five terms Arjun Appadurai has coined to describe landscapes that are the "building blocks" of "imagined worlds": "The multiple worlds which are constituted by the historically situated imaginations of persons and groups spread around the globe" (1990:4). He uses the suffix *-scape* to allow "us to point to the fluid, irregular shapes of these landscapes" (with such terms as *ethnoscape, mediascape, technoscape, finanscape,* and *ideoscape*) as he considers the relationship among these five dimensions of global cultural flows (6–7). Sex-for-sale is one more dimension of global cultural flows, and Sosúa is one site within a global economy of commercialized sexual transactions.

Sexscapes link the practices of sex work to the forces of a globalized economy.

Their defining characteristics are international travel from the developed to the developing world, consumption of paid sex, and inequality. In a sexscape such as Sosúa there are differences in power between the buyers (sex tourists) and the sellers (sex workers) that can be based on race, gender, class, and nationality. These differences become eroticized and commodified inequalities. The exotic is manufactured into the erotic—privately in consumers' imaginations and quite publicly by entire industries that make money off this desire for difference.[6] Let me be clear: these differences, between sex workers in the developing world and sex tourists traveling from the developed world, are essential to distinguish sexscapes in the developing world from red-light districts (or other sites where paid sex is available) in the developed world. So too are the radiating effects of consuming practices—of paid sex—which undergird social and economic life in sexscapes. Within sexscapes, the sex trade becomes a focal point of a place, and the social and economic relations of that place are filtered through the nightly (and daily) selling of sex to foreigners. In contrast, the sex trade in red-light districts in the developed world—such as in Frankfurt, Rome, Brussels, or New York—by no means defines social and economic life outside of these districts. Nor do the female citizens of these places necessarily become associated with sexual availability or proficiency. As Altman notes in his book *Global Sex*, although sex is "a central part of the political economy of all large cities" few cities can base their economies on sex (2001:11).[7]

When sexscapes emerge within a globalized economy, globalized hierarchies of race, class, gender,[8] citizenship, and mobility create undeniable power differentials between the actors in these geographic spaces, which, in turn, give them unequal opportunities.[9] In Sosúa, there are very different and often uneven opportunities for foreigners and locals, and men and women, while race and age also play a role. The asymmetries and inequalities that result from the mix of differences in Sosúa reveal the "unevenness" Appadurai describes in his discussion of modernity as "decisively at large, irregularly self-conscious, and unevenly experienced" (1996:3). In this sexscape, the buyers eroticize these differences—particularly gendered and racialized differences—as part of their paid-sex experiences. Meanwhile, the sellers often struggle to capitalize on these differences. One way is through their "performance of love."

Marriage in a Sexscape

Sosúan sex workers'—and resort workers'—transactional use of marriage is an ages-old story. What is new is how marriage-as-transaction operates in a globalized world where legal crossing of national borders requires passports and visas. In Sosúa's sexscape, marriage between Dominicans and Europeans and between Dominicans and Canadians emerges as an economic strategy as well as a legal route to securing the papers necessary to migrate off the island. Within what Constance Clark (2001) calls the "the politics of border crossing," research on so-called mail-order-brides vividly underscores how marriage to foreigners is often the only viable option for legal migration for citizens of certain countries. For example, young Chinese women are able to gain the exit visas and passports that most Chinese spend years waiting for—or never get—by marrying foreign men from Japan or Singapore through marriage introduction agencies (Clark 2001:105).[10] Research on marriage-as-transaction, such as Nicole Constable's work on marriage introduction agencies, throws into relief Western "culture-bound assumptions about what constitutes a 'good' marriage." It also demonstrates that the Western, white, and middle-class feminist critique of marriages based on traditional division of labor does not consider the calculus of women who have "worked in fields or a factory for subsistence since childhood" (2003:65). For them, marriage, even those that take the most traditional forms—and are not based on "love"—can be a vacation from back-breaking work and daily financial crises. With their own work loads lightened,[11] their material comfort improved, and the possibilities to remit money back to their families expanded, marriage for migration and economic security can be good enough. Love may not be missed. Indeed, although some Dominican sex workers ideally might hope for love and greater gender equity in the household (as an alternative to Dominican machismo) within marriage to foreign men, most regard these marriages as strictly business transactions.[12] Of course, migration through marriage is not a possibility for all. Gays and lesbians cannot legally marry; older women have a more difficult time finding foreign partners through the sex trade or marriage introduction agencies; and men do not have the same opportunities as women through marriage agencies. Despite these limitations, the prospect of marriage, at least for young sex workers (and resort workers) engaging in heterosexual relationships in Sosúa, dangles the possibility of a legal and expeditious exit from the Dominican Republic and its hardships.

Other scholars have documented poor women's use of the sex trade as a first step to marriage and greater financial security. Kamala Kempadoo (1998) writes about migrant Colombian and Dominican women who work in the sex trade in Curaçao's Campo Alegre/Mirage whose work with clients might develop into "close and intimate" relationships that lead to marriage. Migrant women also might pay to acquire Dutch citizenship by marrying, which would allow them to stay and work legally as sex workers in Curaçao or travel to Europe without restriction. Sylvia Chant and Cathy McIlwaine (1995:248) also write about the sex trade as a possible route to marriage—and sometimes to migration—between Europeans and Filipina women. Much like the perceptions Dominican sex workers maintain of life in Europe, Filipina sex workers also perceive a better life for themselves and their children in Europe. And like their Dominican counterparts, these Filipina women are locked out of opportunities for legal migration.

SOME RELATIONSHIPS, HOWEVER, are not easily described. Many relationships that start out as transactional (by one or both parties) can transform into something else entirely. In the sex trade, in particular, the line between love and money can become "very fuzzy," as Yos Santasombat (Hamilton 1997) has observed in relationships between Thai sex workers and farang men (white-skinned Westerners). In fact, many sex workers and resort workers in Sosúa hope for romantic love even while they doubt the "authenticity" of the relationships around them. No relationship between foreigners and Dominicans escapes scrutiny. In this context of transnational desires and economic ambitions, these relationships become fodder for the gossip mill. "So are they really in love?" is a common response by both Dominicans and foreign residents of Sosúa when they hear about a relationship between a Dominican and a foreigner. The possibility of love for migration is almost immediately mentioned, and then either waved away or confirmed. In fact, when stories of the double wedding hit the newsstands, Sosúans (both Dominicans and foreign residents) had a field day.[13] Comments flew about how plain and overweight the women were and how handsome and well-muscled the men were. Quite simply, I could find no one—in either the Dominican or the foreign-resident communities—who believed that for the Dominican men these were relationships of emotion-based love. Like the British immigration officials, Sosúans did not believe that, at least for the men, these relationships could be the "real thing." Rather, Sosúans understand—indeed expect—that many relationships beginning in their town are strategic performances on the part of Dominicans. Their love-skepticism emerges from Sosúans' knowledge that, in Arlie Hochschild's (1983: ix) language, "active emotional labor" is involved—indeed demanded—in jobs at hotels, bars, and nightclubs. Hochschild sharply observes that "simply having personality does not make one a diplomat, any more than having muscles makes one an athlete"; along these lines, if we focus simply on the exchange of sex for money (or goods) in Sosúa, we will miss "a sense of the active emotional labor involved in the selling" (1983: ix). Sosúans know that many sex workers and resort workers are hard at work selling romance along with the other goods and services they deliver.

With much of any tourist experience relying on fantasy, Edward Bruner's description of "touristic borderzones" as "performative space[s]" calls attention to the performative aspects of tourist encounters. He writes, "The touristic borderzone is like empty space, an empty stage waiting for performance time, for the audience of tourists and for the native performers" (1999:58). Tourists on vacation often engage in behavior and activities they would never engage in at home, such as paying for sex or, as Deborah Pruitt and Suzanne LaFont (1995) observed in Jamaica, having cross-racial relationships. When I interviewed male tourists in Sosúa, they often told me that they never had paid for sex at "home," but since they were on vacation they thought, "Why not?" Chant and McIlwaine also found that some foreign men—who had not intended at the outset to pay for sex—buy sex in Cebu's bars in the Philippines because of "peer pressure." One man boasted to his friends, for example, that he had bought five women in one night (1995:225). In encounters between locals and foreign tourists, locals often have more practical goals—such as laying the groundwork to receive money wires from tourists once they return to Europe—and might need to "perform" for tourists to achieve them, whereas foreign tourists primarily seek fun and pleasure.

SEX AND ROMANCE IN SOSÚA have thus become more than just sites for the production of intimacy, pleasure, and emotional comfort. They have become, in a way, sites of capitalist production and consumption (with Dominicans possibly supplying sex or "romantic love" for foreign consumers), which can result in inequalities, discomfort, and sometimes even violence. Sexual exchanges across interracial and international borders can reinforce existing racial hierarchies and inequalities. Karen Kelsky's research with "yellow cabs," for example, suggests that sexual exchanges not based on money can also reinforce racial hierarchies and inequalities. The term *yellow cabs* refers to young, single Japanese women who spend their savings on "erotic adventure with a variety of non-Japanese men" in places such as tourist resorts in Hawaii or U.S. military bases in Japan. Although these women might seek to have sex with these non-Japanese men, they will not marry these men, because of ideas of "racial purity."[14]

Relationships in Sosúa *por residencia* also can be a kind of stage for Dominicans to resist such racial hierarchies as well as inequalities based on gender, class, and citizenship. For example, the strategizing of Dominican women within Sosúa's sex trade sometimes has economically advantageous results. Some clients have paid for the education of their "girlfriend's" children, or have helped sex workers get a fledgling business off the ground (such as a clothing store or hair salon). In these cases, sex in a postcolonial context, much like in a colonial context, can be used as a "vehicle to master a practical world" (Stoler 1997:44). Because, as Frantz Fanon has observed, any use of sex between black local women and white foreign men in a postcolonial context is a "crucial transfer point of power, tangled with racial exclusions in complicated ways" (Fanon 1967:63, quoted in Stoler 1997:44), today's sex trade is inextricably linked with a violent colonial history for Hispaniola's women. In the relationships between sex tourists and sex workers, there are similarities to the relationships between the colonizer and the colonized. I do not mean to suggest, however, that Dominican sex workers (or resort workers) are "enslaved" but want to underscore that they stand to lose more—materially—than love gone awry.[15]

Not every Dominican worker in Sosúa's tourist economy, of course, tries to parlay access to foreign tourists into marriage proposals and visa sponsorships, yet many are perceived as doing so. Sosúans (Dominicans and foreign residents) and Dominicans outside of Sosúa brand as "sankies" a wide range of men who do not trade their bodies for money. For example, young, good-looking Dominican men who have migrated to work in Sosúa's hotels, bars, and beaches often are glibly referred to or derided as sankies.[16] Male resort workers, particularly "activity directors"—the resort position held by the two young men who married in the double wedding—often are talked about as sankies.[17] By referring to male resort workers as sanky-pankies, Sosúans see these men as prostituting themselves as well as sacrificing love for migration. The term is now loosely used throughout the Dominican Republic to refer to Dominican men who hit on tourist women—especially women older than they.

Female resort workers, too, undergo public scrutiny and risk being stereotyped as *putas* but usually from Dominicans outside of Sosúa, because Sosúans know that most of the women who clean, waitress, and cook in the hotels and other tourist businesses are from Sosúa, Puerto Plata, and other nearby towns. Sosúans also know that women who enter the sex trade are not from Sosúa but migrate from towns throughout the island (to protect their families left behind). To Dominicans outside of Sosúa, however, women's claims of working in Sosúa's hotels and restaurants can appear as "cover stories" for working in the sex trade. In fact, most of the sex workers I interviewed concealed their participation in the sex trade from their families and neighbors by creating "cover stories" about working in Sosúa's tourist hotels and restaurants.

History of Migration off the Island: "Headaches" for Dominicans Wishing to Migrate

The automatic eyebrow raising and speculation of Sosúans that suggest relationships between foreign tourists and Dominicans are *por residencia* result from the virtual impossibility of leaving the island legally without family members to sponsor migration. Responses to an Internet posting to the message board of a Dominican electronic newspaper in English, *Dominican One*, underscores just how difficult it is for Dominicans to enter the United States. Arnold, for example, queried, "Hi, I would like for my Dominican girlfriend to visit me in the United States for two weeks some time in the next year. How much of a big pain is this? She told me I needed to write her an invitation letter and she needed to get a passport. How hard is this and any headaches anyone here foresees?" (March 31, 2000). Two responses explained it would take a near miracle for Arnold's girlfriend to obtain a tourist visa: "No, no headaches. It just won't happen! Jesus Christ could not get a visa if he were Dominican! That is about how difficult it is" (March 31, 2000); and "Hahahahahahahahahahahaha" (April 2, 2000, from within the Dominican Republic). A third response hinted that the Dominican girlfriend might overstay her visa and that Arnold should not trust her motivations: "Want some good advice from someone who knows, don't bring her to the U.S. 'You will be sorry,' move to the Dominican Republic with her instead" (April 2, 2000). Arnold's innocent question revealed him to be a novice about the difficulties facing Dominicans who want to travel or migrate to the United States.

Understanding why Dominican resort workers and sex workers might feign love and use marriage—or are perceived as feigning love and using marriage—as a way to get off the island calls for a brief discussion of the island's migration history. The past few decades of migration from the Dominican Republic to New York and the transnational cultural and economic flows between the two places (Georges 1990; Grasmuck and Pessar 1991; Guarnizo 1994) have informed a diasporic mentality in the Dominican Republic. There is little doubt that families with relatives in New York have benefited as one of Eugenia Georges's informants sums up: "In the Dominican Republic there are three kinds of people: the rich, the poor and those who travel to New York" (1990:196). And of course, there is a fourth group: families who rely on remittances sent from family members abroad.[18]

Dominicans started using migration as a means to social mobility following the isolationist years under the dictator Trujillo (from 1930 to 1961), who restricted migration off the island. After Trujillo's assassination in 1961, restrictions on migration in both the Dominican Republic and the United States loosened. Sherri Grasmuck and Patricia Pessar argue that following the 1963 revolution, migration was "politically induced" by an "extremely unrestrictive immigration policy favored by the United States" which operated as a "safety-valve for political discontent" (1991:31). During these years of political unrest, Dominican migration to the United States increased from an average of 900 immigrants a year to 9,000 a year (Pessar 1995). Many of these early migrants had progressive ties and left disillusioned, or fearful, after the socialist Juan Bosch was overthrown by a U.S.-backed military coup in 1963. Out-migration to the United States significantly increased and complemented the model of economic development of the newly elected president, Balaguer, during his presidency of 1966 to 1978. (Balaguer, leader of the Reformist Party, was reelected in 1986 and remained in office until 1996.) Hurt by the Balaguer government's policy of keeping food prices artificially low, rural producers migrated to urban centers, where unemployment grew. Out-migration to the United States continued at an average rate of 12,000 a year during this period (Grasmuck and Pessar 1991). Following the deterioration of the national economy after 1974, and a rise in landlessness from the splintering of many smallholdings, both migrant and nonmigrant households experienced economic insecurity (Safa 1995). Migration permitted many families to hold onto a "middle-level status," while other nonmigrant families fell into poverty in the midst of a troubled economy (Georges 1990).

Without ties to New York or elsewhere, economic mobility is difficult—even for middle-class families—and, often, families end up just getting by and surviving. Low salaries are an obstacle to mobility for all classes, other than for the wealthy. Schoolteachers and office workers, for example, earn under 4,000 pesos a month (US$333.00). Consequently, many professionals with university degrees consider themselves both middle class and part of *los pobres* (the poor) at the same time. A social worker identified with two classes simultaneously: "My wife, a schoolteacher, and I have been working as professionals for twenty years. But do we own a house? Or a car? We Dominicans work until we die." He also recounted his parents' downward mobility: "My parents, who own a butcher shop, are old and should not be working. But they work every day, my father cutting meat and my mother stuffing sausage. They used to be middle class, but now with prices rising every day they are *pobres*."

Prices for basic foodstuffs, cooking gas, and gasoline continue to rise in the Dominican Republic. Two events in the spring of 2003—the collapse of a bank, Baninter, and the cost of hosting the Pan American Games—exacerbated an already deteriorating economy. Baninter's main owner, Ramon Báez Figueroa, was arrested for allegedly running a "bank within a bank" for more than a decade. The bank is reported to have lost $2.2 billion, a figure equal to 13 percent of the country's GDP. In the process, the peso has depreciated dramatically and the country's credit rating has been downgraded (Economist 2003).[19] In the midst of rising prices and a falling peso, the Dominican government (under President Hipolito Mejia) spent $175 million to host the Pan American Games in August 2003. Even though the Dominican government banned protests, demonstrators took to the streets to protest against the millions spent on athletic fields and facilities (Gonzalez 2003b). As Rev. Rogelio Cruz led a demonstration carrying the "torch of hunger" through Santo Domingo's poorest neighborhoods, the security chief for the games declared his troops would "rip the heads off" or "break the necks" of any protesters, and President Hipolito Mejia said he should be beaten (Gonzalez 2003a).

In this context of limited economic mobility and extraordinary obstacles to legal migration off the island, it becomes clear why Dominican migrants in Sosúa, most of whom do not receive remittances from family overseas, work so hard to establish transnational relationships with the tourist population. These transnational romantic ties act as surrogate family migration networks to access a middle-class lifestyle and its accompanying security. Without family members in New York or elsewhere to sponsor their legal migration, Dominicans who seek to migrate need other means of getting *fuera* (outside; off the island). Marriage to citizens of other countries is one surefire strategy.

Suspect Love

On account of the obstacles to legal migration, Dominican Sosúans consider the workers in several occupations as under suspicion for "performing" at being in love with tourists for money and visas: male sanky-pankies, male resort workers and activity directors, female resort workers, and female sex workers.

Sanky-Pankies

One of the first groups of Sosúans who were reputed to "perform" at being in love with tourists were the sanky-pankies. Those first called *sankies*, in the mid 1980s, were young men in their late teens and early twenties who worked on the beach renting jet skis, beach chairs, umbrellas, and the like. Their trademark was bleached dread locks, as well as tanned and toned bodies. Sankies were known for wooing white, female, middle-aged tourists. In this early stage of Sosúa's tourism development, many of the female tourists were French Canadian and Canadian. These men did not work for cash, as did female sex workers, but for gifts, meals, and other expenses at the discretion of the female tourists. Much like the "romance tourism" Pruitt and LaFont describe between Jamaican men and tourist women which unfolds through a "discourse of romance and long-term relationship" (1995: 423), sankies' skills often included treating the tourist women as "girlfriends." Romantic dinners, moonlight strolls, and lessons in dancing merengue at the nightclubs can be part of encounters between tourist women and *sankies*. But money also changes hands. French Canadian female tourists have described giving their Dominican "lovers" money (even though they did not ask for any) and clothes, as well as paying for meals and drinks (Herold et al. 1992). Female tourists do not perceive that they are "paying" for sexual services, however; they recount that "they fell in love with the men and the men fell in love with them" (Herold et. al. 1992:8). Similarly, Jacqueline Martis observed that men working in the sex trade in Saint Martin or Curaçao (with female tourists) were jockeying to "hook up with a woman who would take care of them and take them away from the island." They, like the sankies, "wanted to think of themselves as having a romantic liaison, not as prostituting" and thus referred to themselves as "players" (1999:211–12).

Few of these "original" sankies remain in Sosúa; they were successful at marrying female tourists and migrating to Canada. Sosúans report that most of these marriages ended in divorce, after the men received their citizenship. Today, there are a few high-profile men—allegedly some of the "original" sankies—who have returned from Canada. Now, in their late thirties and early forties, their profitable (and capital-intensive) motorcycle rental and beach equipment businesses stand as examples of what one can achieve through marriage and migration off the island.

Male Resort Workers and Activity Directors

In the light of the desperation some Dominicans feel to leave the island, and the difficulties they face in order to do so, it is easy to see why Sosúa's foreign tourists are a gold mine. Contact with foreigners distinguishes Sosúa's employment opportunities from those in other parts of the country. The actual job might be the same—waiting tables, bartending, or tending a cash register—but the chance to meet foreign tourists is a fringe benefit of working in the tourist sector, an investment of sorts, in the employee's future. The job of activity director, coveted by young Dominicans who seek either short- or long-term relationships with foreigners, perhaps best epitomizes the sexual or romantic promise of Sosúa. Usually young, energetic men (although there are some activity directors who are women) with self-taught skills in several languages, activity directors organize events for hotel guests, such as exercise classes, dance contests, and volleyball tournaments. Their reputation for romantic and sexual entanglements with female hotel guests is why Sosúans often call them sankies. As mentioned earlier, the two young Dominican men involved in the double wedding were both activity directors. One of the English women recalled how her soon-to-be husband greeted her and other guests with whom she was having a drink: "Hi. My name is Pablo and my job is to make your vacation fun" (Victoria 1994:44).

Hotel management, keenly aware of how highly valued these positions are, take advantage of willing young Dominicans. Some activity directors work for no wages during their "trial period," which might last a month or longer. The offers for dinner and nightclubbing, as well as gifts (some even continue to receive gifts from abroad long after tourists have returned home), showered on them by hotel guests give them the opportunity to elect to work for nothing and even continue to endure low wages later on. A Dominican manager at one of the largest all-inclusive hotels on the north coast smiled when I asked about the activity directors. "They have more contact with the guests than other staff," he said and laughed. "Thus, they are privileged." Norberto, the other young activity director who married in the double wedding, described getting many visa promises from hotel guests. But when, at the end of their vacation, the two English women promised that they would send airplane tickets so that Pablo and Norberto could come to England and meet the two women's families, Norberto "did not have many illusions," he said, "because there are many who say the same thing, but then nothing happens." "But," he added, "when I saw the ticket had arrived, I was convinced this thing was serious" (Victoria 1994:44).

Hugo, another activity director, left school at age 15 in Puerto Plata, where he lived with his family, to begin working in the resort complex at Playa Dorada, about 20 miles outside of Sosúa. "We are the heart of the hotel," he explained. "Without us, it would die; we keep the guests happy." Hugo has met a lot of women while working at the hotel: "We meet people all day. They come to us for everything, so we meet a lot of women from all over the world. I have many girlfriends in lots of countries. They send me things and come back on their vacations to visit me." This close contact can pay off. Hugo married a woman from England whom he met when she was a guest staying at the hotel. But "things did not work out." "My wife," he complained, "always wanted to know where I was going whenever I left the house." To make matters worse, he could not find a job. After living in England for nine months, he returned to the Dominican Republic. Now divorced, he is disillusioned with both living overseas and marriage. He is happy to be back at the hotel, meeting "a variety of women" who "spend their money on me."

At the time we spoke, he was not looking to marry—or to migrate off the island. Unlike his coworkers, he knew firsthand how difficult it is for Dominicans who are not fluent in English to live and to work in Europe. "You know everyone wants to go *fuera*—that's what I thought a few years ago. But it's a lie; it's not easy there. Sure you can make a lot more money there, if you can find a job." Hugo, like the female sex workers who have lived in Europe (whose stories I recount in Brennan 2004), has no more fantasies about life *fuera*. Yet it is unclear what caused him greater unease: marriage and monogamy or the experience of migration. "I don't want to be married—I can't go home to one woman in the house. I need to be free and loose, Dominican men are *machista*; we don't like to be reined in." Some migration scholars have documented threats to men's authority in the household through the migration process (Kibria 1993; Pessar 1995). Since men and women experience migration differently (Hondagneu-Sotelo 1994), marriage to foreign citizens presents even greater challenges during the migration process.

Female Resort Workers and Sex Workers

Consuelo, a 24-year old sex worker, walked around Los Charamicos clutching a pocket German-Spanish dictionary wherever she went. Having it with her at all times was a marker of prestige, allowing her to show off her envied ties to Europe. "I'm trying to learn German. I'm moving to Germany in the next few weeks to live with a German man I met here," she elaborated. She also was in the Codetel office at least once a day, sending or receiving faxes or telephoning Germany. She was able to pay for the calls with the money her German client-turned-boyfriend wired to her. Months later, she was still in town, running around making arrangements by fax and phone as urgently as if she were leaving the next day. Some of her coworkers dismissed her preoccupation with going to Germany as folly. Ani had known her for years, since they had worked together in a bar in Boca Chica.[20] "She was the same there—determined to get to Europe. She only sought out clients she thought could get her there." Ani laughed, "But look, she's still here. It does not work that way—it is not easy."

If it is "not easy" to get to Europe (or elsewhere off the island) by meeting foreign men, why do Dominican women such as Consuelo try so hard to do so? Sosúa as a tourist enclave operates much as urban spaces have in step migration. Consuelo, for example, sees migration to Sosúa as the first step toward marrying a foreign tourist, the only legal way she knows to obtain a visa to travel overseas. Without family in New York, women have a greater chance to get overseas by marrying a tourist than they do of obtaining a visa—legally—to the United States. In some ways, hanging out in the tourist bars in Sosúa is a better use of their time than waiting in line at the U.S. Consulate in Santo Domingo. Marrying a tourist can be seen as hitting the jackpot. This, in part, is why so many women who have never worked before in the sex trade decide to do so in Sosúa. Carla, a sex worker, illuminates why Sosúa draws women from all over the country: "We come here because we dream of a ticket." But without a visa, Dominicans cannot use the airplane ticket Carla describes.

Mari and Andrea: "No, it's not love"

The words *romance* and *love* are noticeably absent from female sex workers' and female resort workers' discussions of the "ideal" relationship with foreign tourists. Sex workers and resort workers are looking for *hombres serios*, not the loves of their lives. Fidelity, financial security, and a good future for their children are at the top of their wish lists. This is not to say that they do not also hope for romance. One Valentine's Day the tourist bars were abuzz with a striking mix of commercial and romantic desires. The sex workers were wishing one another a happy Valentine's Day, and many expressed hopes that they might find romance that evening. Some had gone to the hair salon earlier in the day, while others put on their best outfits and took more time than usual with their makeup. One sex worker, who had stopped going to the bars because at the time she had been receiving large money wires from a client in Europe, reappeared to celebrate Valentine's Day. She explained that she wanted to hang out with her friends and maybe fulfill her dreams of "romance."

The hopeful pursuit of romance I witnessed on Valentine's Day was rare because, in sex workers' narratives, economic imperatives usually outweigh romantic dreams. There is an expected tradeoff between emotion-driven love for financial mobility. Both sex workers and resort workers candidly admit that they sacrifice romantic love for a better future. Mari, for example, has used both waitressing and the sex trade (when she was younger) to meet foreign men. As a waitress she met and married a German man and lived in Düsseldorf for a year and a half. Surprisingly, she returned to Sosúa because she hated Germany and, as she put it, did not "love him." Back in Sosúa, this time working in *promoción* (passing out flyers to tourists for clubs and restaurants), she met a Dutch man in his fifties. Still married, Mari planned to return to Germany to see her husband and then "take the train to Holland." I reasoned that since she had chosen to leave Germany and return to the Dominican Republic, it was possible that she was looking for romantic love, not just a visa to live in Europe. After all, she had expressly said she did not love her German husband. I was wrong. She and her friend Elena (also a former sex worker) shook their heads, frustrated by my naïveté, and carefully spelled out for me that Mari did not love either of these men. These relationships, they made clear, "are not really about love." Rather, "they are about thinking of your family and your future." Because the Dutch man appeared to have more resources than the German man, along with the fact that he treated her well, Mari believed he would make a better husband.

Another sex worker, Andrea, spent the night with her Dominican boyfriend—the man she "really loved"—on the eve of her departure for Germany to marry a German man who had been a client. When I dropped by the next morning to wish her well before she left for Germany, her Dominican boyfriend was still asleep. Stepping outside onto her porch (she lived on the second floor of a house her German boyfriend had been paying for), she explained she could not lie about her feelings for her soon-to-be husband: "No, it's not love." Yet with images of an easier life for her and her two daughters compelling her to migrate, she put love aside—at least temporarily. She went to Germany, married, brought her girls over, and settled into a new life.

Although Andrea's friends who remained behind in Sosúa saw Andrea as living out their dreams, her marriage was far from ideal. Four years later she was still in Germany, but she was trying to get a divorce. Much like Mari, Andrea had met another German man who had a better job—and more money. They planned to marry as soon as her divorce came through. I found out about Andrea's new pursuit from her cousin in Sosúa, to whom she sends money every month. Her cousin was puzzled when I asked whether Andrea was in love with her new boyfriend. "This new guy has more money." For Andrea, who wanted her children to grow up in comfort and to get a good education, love takes a backseat to financial concerns. Besides, a network of female family members, such as this cousin and her two children, depend on Andrea to send remittances. In this sense, her successful performance of being in love is directly tied to her family obligations. She was lucky enough to get off the island, and now she is expected to (and willingly does) help out the other single mothers in her family, her parents, and her good friends, including Elena. She has even sent new sneakers, jeans, and belts to a circle of her closest friends (all sex workers). With so many expectations and demands on Andrea, there is considerable pressure on her to keep her relationship afloat, no matter what.

Considering the benefits for family and friends, it is easy to see why Andrea's friends, while sporting new fashions from Germany, perpetuate the fiction that marriage in Europe is without significant conflict. Even though life in Europe—especially in Germany—can be isolating for Dominican sex workers, stories of women's migration, such as Andrea's, still manage to persuade women that tourists will be their ticket off the island. Like the sanitized narratives about Dominican migrants during the early years of migration to New York, the stories of sex workers who migrated to Europe have been greatly romanticized. Because migrating to Europe is a relatively new phenomenon, few former sex workers, like Mari, or resort workers, like Hugo, have returned to Sosúa to dispel the myths and gossip of an easy and fantasy-filled life *allá* (over there). Instead, sex workers and resort workers imagine lives of material comfort for themselves and, among the women, for their children.

"Love" in a Global World: New Transnational Courting Practices

Part of a day's work for sex workers and resort workers who are interested in getting off the island—or at least in receiving money wires—is keeping in contact with clients who are back home in Europe. Faxes and telephone calls are the primary ways they communicate. And Codetel (a telecommunications company) has assumed a starring role in the unfolding drama of these relationships. At the Codetel office in Los Charamicos (the "Dominican" side of Sosúa), received faxes are filed in accordion files under first or last names or a slew of other identifying characteristics. There are faxes for "Juana at Hotel Paraíso" or for "Carmen at the Anchor." The senders might have met the recipients at these places or believe that these women work there all the time. Usually written in English or broken Spanish, these faxes document that romantic/sexual encounters are a by-product of Sosúa's tourist trade.[21] Indeed, some days the files are literally bursting with faxes. Cell phone use is on the rise, and during my visits to the nightclubs in 2003, cell phones were a visible accessory—nearly everyone (men and women) sported one on his or her person. Whether the phones work is another thing entirely; many Sosúans buy minutes for their phones through phone cards, rather than keep ongoing accounts.

Unlike the love letters sex workers send their clients, the faxes sex workers receive usually convey some kind of news: when to pick up a money wire or details about the men's return visits to Sosúa. It is not possible to receive incoming calls at Codetel, so sometimes transnational "couples" use faxes to arrange times that the women will call the men from Codetel (usually paid for by money wires sent by the men) or to arrange times that men will call the women at a neighbor's house.[22] Some sex workers have become adept at capitalizing on the communication resources available to them, and, as a result, novices at navigating this transnational terrain come to them for advice.[23] Sex workers who are literate and have a proven track record of receiving money wires or faxes from clients are at the top of this hierarchy. Elena, for example, has given out a lot of advice, and she has even helped compose letters and faxes for women who were uncertain about what to do with the addresses, fax numbers, and telephone numbers clients gave them. She helped Carmen write a letter to a Belgian client who had sent her a money wire and then abruptly stopped corresponding with her. Carmen came to Elena because, at the time, Elena was living with a German expatriate resident, Jürgen, and was experienced, indeed successful, at transnational courting. Elena's advice was simple and centered on Carmen's "performance of love": "You have to write that you *love* him and that you miss him. Write that you cannot wait to see him again. Tell him you think about him every day." Following Elena's guidelines, Carmen composed the following letter that I helped her translate into English (his English was better than his Spanish):

> Dear ——,
> I have been thinking of you every day and have been waiting for a fax to hear how you are. I got your money wire, thanks. But I still want to see you.
> Please send me a fax at the following number ——, and if possible, a fax number where I can reach you.
> I miss you very much and think of you all the time. I love you very much. I wait to hear from you. I hope you come to visit again very soon.
> Many Kisses,[24]

Carmen never heard from this client again.

SINCE WOMEN ALWAYS CAN ENLIST THE HELP of more literate friends, being able to read and write is not a critical skill in transnational courting. Sensing which men are not already married, and are likely to continue corresponding and to return for future vacations (the most certain first step to receiving an invitation to visit Europe or Canada), often proves a more valuable—and elusive—skill. While sorting through all the pictures and letters of her European clients, Nanci, for example, commented on which ones seemed the most serious about keeping in touch. She pronounced several too "young" and thus not likely to follow through on the relationships. Nanci had honed her ability to detect which transnational suitors were worth pursuing during her four years in Sosúa. She had been receiving money wires on and off from five or six European men at the same time. Her many and varied transnational ties were envied and difficult to replicate, yet many tried. Stashed away in a spare pocketbook, Nanci kept a bundle of letters and faxes.[25] She also had photos—photos of the men back home and photos of her with the men during their vacations in Sosúa. Taped to her wall were photos of at least 15 different foreign men. Several of them had returned to Sosúa to see Nanci and expressed interest in bringing her to Europe and marrying her (one of whom she eventually married, and with whom she moved to Germany and had a baby—but he later abandoned them after they had decided to move back to Sosúa).

Even those sex workers who are veterans of transnational dating cannot easily predict their European clients' actions (or inaction). Yet some seem better able than others to assess the characters of the men. Nora, who has never received an international fax or letter, kept a German client's business card among her valuables. Even though the client promised he would fax her, he had not responded to the numerous faxes she sent him. Nevertheless, Nora clung to the card as if it were a winning lottery ticket. She could not seem to throw it away. In contrast, many of her coworkers quickly move on to cultivating new relationships when faced with their clients' lack of communication.

Conclusion: Marriage, "Papers," and Suspect Love

In Sosúa's tourist economy, marriage solves obstacles to migration from one country to another; marriage also secures migrants' futures once they are in new countries. In the Spanish movie *Flores de otro mundo* (Flowers from another world; 1999), for example, an Afro-Dominican woman works in Madrid for four years as a domestic, during which time she is often stopped on the street by the police. Without the right papers, she explains to her Spanish boyfriend with whom she and her children are living, she cannot get a good job. An outsider, especially someone whose dark skin makes her unable to conceal her "otherness," cannot, she cries, "break into the circle." The only solution is a wedding. Although this woman eventually falls in love with her Spanish boyfriend, and he with her, she initially moves in with him to bring her children to Spain from the Dominican Republic and to begin the application process for Spanish residency. Love was not on her agenda; her children were her only concern. As she put it, "It doesn't matter what happens to me."

Similarly, the rush to marry in February and March 1997, in cities that are popular migration destinations in the United States (New York City, Los Angeles, Boston, and cities in Texas), demonstrated the central role marriage plays in many migrants' settlement strategies. Fearing that new punitive immigration legislation would prevent them from obtaining citizenship in the future, thousands lined up for licenses and wedding ceremonies. Witnessing this marriage frenzy, a reporter for the *New York Times* questioned the newlyweds' motivation.

> Rarely has love been so suspect in New York City as in the last few days, with young men and women of foreign origin being stopped by imperfect strangers and asked whether it is their hearts or their wallets that are going pitter-pat. The reason for this is simple: at marriage bureaus across town, there are suddenly crushing lines of couples looking to sprint down the aisle. No one can swear why this is happening. But common sense suggests that illegal immigrants by the thousands are racing to marry American citizens in the hope—a misguided hope, some experts caution—that they can stave off deportation after a toughened immigration law goes into effect on April 1. (Haberman 1997)

As the reporter suspected, some of these marriages were of course not for love but for residency. I spoke with a Dominican woman in New York who had over-stayed her tourist visa and paid $5,000 to a Dominican-born man with U.S. citizenship to marry her. "It's a lot of money, but it's the only way I can stay here." The ceremony itself was bittersweet: "I was very depressed going through the ceremony. It was sad to have such a special ceremony with someone you do not love. But I need my papers for my daughter's future." As a single mother, she is lonely and hopes one day to marry a man for love. But for now, she has a husband solely for documentation purposes. He has kept his end of the agreement by showing up for the ceremony and their meetings with immigration officials. Her cousin was not so lucky: a

Puerto Rican man disappeared shortly after she paid him $2,500 (a down payment on his $5,000 fee) to marry her. These two cousins in New York are in the position to "buy" a marriage and thus secure their legal status in the migration process. Unlike sex workers and resort workers in Sosúa, when these cousins pursued marriage strategies, there was no hope or pretense of emotion-driven love or romance on their part or on the part of the men they were marrying. Their performances of love were only for the INS.

Sex workers and resort workers who feign love for an opportunity to get off the island are banking on the outcome that their marriages and migration will translate into mobility for them and their families. Because sex workers have been traveling to Europe to live with European boyfriends only over the past 10 to 12 years, this migration *por residencia* is still a relatively new phenomenon. It remains to be seen how many of these relationships last. These Dominican women and European men may or may not formally marry, move the women's children to Europe, or have children together. Stories abound of the failed marriages of men gossiped about as sankies who married Canadian women and migrated to Canada in the early and mid 1980s. Some of these men's pasts have become legendary. Young men inspired by their visible success hang out at the businesses these men have started (especially motorcycle rentals, a particularly macho enterprise). Their performances of love paid off. Similarly, the double wedding might have caused snickering and raised eyebrows over the authenticity of the Dominican men's emotional commitment to their English wives, but Sosúans also acknowledged that these men were "very lucky." With their marriage certificates to English citizens, they were steps closer to migrating—legally—to Europe.

Acknowledgments

This chapter is part of a larger research project on sex tourism in Sosúa, the Dominican Republic, that resulted in the publication of Brennan 2004. The book is based on anthropological field research I conducted in Sosúa in summer 1993, 1994–95, summer 1999, and January and July 2003. I owe a great debt to CEPROSH, a Dominican nongovernmental organization that conducts HIV education and outreach with female sex workers.

Notes

1. "Un Amor en el Caribe" (Victoria 1994) appeared in *Rumbo*, one the Dominican Republic's most well-respected news magazines.
2. Judith Butler's groundbreaking theorization on "performance" in relation to gender has become a central concept in gender studies. For this project I am interested in her writing on "gender parody," which we see, for example, in drag that "implicitly reveals the imitative structure of gender itself—as well as its contingency" (1990:137). If I were to write about a "love parody" in the Butlerian sense, however, I would be suggesting that there is no "original." Later in this chapter I further explore this idea of distinguishing the "real thing" from false, inauthentic, or fabricated "love."

3. Catherine Lutz summarizes James Averill's (1985) description of love in "American understandings" as "idealization of the other, suddenness of onset, physical arousal, and commitment to the other" (Lutz 1988:145). In Sosúa, local understandings of what I am calling "real love" mirror Averill's description.

4. L. A. Rebhun was also interested in how people "describe sentiment" but moved past "vocabulary to discourse: what people talk about in relation to sentiment, how they communicate, what they say, as well as what they leave unsaid and they act out in wordless practice" (1999:11).

5. Catherine Lutz writes about the attachment of local meanings to emotion in her research with the Ifaluk: "Emotion can be as a cultural and interpersonal process of naming, justifying, and persuading people in relationship to each other. Emotional meaning is then a social rather than an individual achievement—an emergent product of social life" (1988:5).

6. Analyzing exotic and erotic representations of the Pacific—such as in the movie *South Pacific*—Margaret Jolly examines how difference "stimulate[s] desire" (1997:100). Writing about Brazilian women, Angela Gilliam finds that part of the appeal of women characterized as exotic "rests within the unequal economic and social exchange between visitors and the places to which they travel as tourists" (2001:174).

7. Cities with foreign military bases are an exception. For example, see Moon 1997 on the sex trade that grew up around the U.S. military bases in South Korea, Enloe 1989 on the links between militarization and women's exploitation, and Sturdevant and Stoltzfus 1992.

8. For more on male sex work, see Mark Padilla's (2007) research on Dominican male sex workers and Gisela Fosado's (2003) on Cuban male sex workers

9. Mahler and Pessar discuss globalized hierarchies as operating "at various levels that affect an individual or group's social location" such that they "shape, discipline, and position people and the ways they think and act" (2001:446).

10. These Chinese women's transnational use of marriage, Constance Clark writes, has earned them a reputation similar to that of Sosúan sex workers as "gold diggers" searching for foreign "airplane tickets" (2001:105).

11. Constable describes how, for example, working-class or rural Filipinas' workdays may involve "a combination of hard work in shops, factories, or rice fields combined with domestic chores and responsibilities for an extended household" (2003:66).

12. Eva Ilouz (1997) explores the connections between romantic love and the marketplace (1997), pointing out that in many cultures marriage has long been a site for the exchange of wealth. She comments that until the beginning of the 20th century, marriage was considered by all classes except for those who could not afford a ceremony, "one of the most, if not the most, important financial operations of their lives" (9). Reality television shows—such as *For Love or Money*, in which participants have to perform love convincingly enough to win money—have certainly been crass pop cultural reminders that all marriages potentially contain transactional elements. In contrast, Laura Ahearn (2001) charts how Nepalese women's increased literacy has allowed them to seek love marriages—facilitated through love-letter writing—rather than "capture" or arranged marriages.

13. The November 1994 double wedding also was widely publicized in the British press. In the wake of these stories, another British woman came forward with a cautionary tale. Four years earlier, Sharon Kelly had met and married Rafael Gutiérrez, a Dominican tour company driver, after an eight-week courtship. They married in the Dominican Republic and then successfully applied for a British visa for Rafael. Soon after their move to Sharon's home in Norwich, Rafael expressed a desire to obtain a visa to visit the United States. Denied once, he applied again and received a tourist visa. He left England with a one-way ticket to the Dominican Republic via New York but not before emptying Sharon's bank account, maxing out her credit card, and stealing her most valuable jewelry. Although they spoke by telephone when he was in New York, as of November 1994 Sharon had not heard from Rafael since May 1992 (Hardy 1994).

14. Karen Kelsky explains that the term *yellow cab* was "allegedly coined by American men, [but] yellow cab was in fact invented and popularized by Japanese journalists to imply that Japanese women are, from a foreigner's perspective, 'yellow' and can be hailed as easily as a taxi" (1994:465).

15. Angela Gilliam (2001) and Susanne Thorbek (2002a, 2002b) examine the relationship between the colonial eroticization of non-European women and the contemporary exoticization of third-world sex workers. In particular, both authors consider the role the brutal display in Paris's Musée de l'Homme of Saartje Baartman (a young woman taken from what is now South Africa to be exhibited like an animal in Europe) has played in shaping colonial and contemporary views of black women's sexuality. Her body "was placed at the unsavory intersection of slavery, an Enlightenment classificatory system, and quasi-pornographic notions of medicine" (Gilliam 2001:179).

16. Men who are gossiped about as sankies do not use this term to describe themselves. Mark Padilla's (2007) findings in a research project with 200 male sex workers in Santo Domingo and Boca Chica suggest that only a small minority of those interviewed use this term to describe themselves. Rather, more commonly, the men pejoratively apply the term to others, and sometimes use it when ribbing one another. Padilla finds that the term carries less stigma than the terms *puta* or *prostituta* for female sex workers, because male sex work (with female clients) in comparison with female work seems less transgressive and more in line with norms of male gender and sexuality.

17. Activity directors organize social events for hotel guests, such as dancing lessons and sporting events.

18. Remittances to the Dominican Republic grew by 85 percent between 1996 and 2000. In 2000 remittances totaled approximately $1.7 billion, 80 percent of which came from Dominicans living in the United States (Latin Finance 2001).

19. When I started fieldwork in the Dominican Republic in 1993, the official bank rate was around 12 pesos to US$1. In the summer of 2003, the rate climbed to 33 pesos.

20. Boca Chica is another tourist beach town with a lively sex trade. It is on the south coast of the Dominican Republic, outside of the capital, Santo Domingo.

21. Sex workers usually do not receive faxes written in German or in languages other than English or Spanish. Their clients/boyfriends who do not speak any English or Spanish appear to have received help from friends in translating their faxes so that the Dominican women can read them.

22. Sex workers do not have access to phones at the boardinghouses; nor do they have phones, other than cell phones, in their apartments or houses.

23. Although there are new cyber cafes in El Batey, e-mail is not—yet—a form of communication between sex workers and their clients. Since literacy is low among sex workers, and their familiarity with computers is nonexistent, it is not likely that this will become a widely used form of communication.

24. For more on letter writing between clients and sex workers, see *Hello My Big, Big Honey*, a collection of love letters that foreign men have sent Thai "bar girls" in Bangkok (Walker and Ehrlich 1992).

25. With only a third-grade education, Nanci could not read or write. To correspond with her suitors, she sought the help of more literate sex workers.

References

Ahearn, Laura M.
   2001 Invitations to Love: Literacy, Love Letters, and Social Change in Nepal. Ann Arbor: University of Michigan Press.

Altman, Dennis
  2001   Global Sex. Chicago: University of Chicago Press.
Appadurai, Arjun
  1990   Disjuncture and Difference in the Global Cultural Economy. Public Culture 2(2):1–24.
  1996   Modernity at Large: Cultural Dimensions of Globalization. Vol. 1. Minneapolis: University of Minnesota Press.
  2000   Grassroots Globalization and the Research Imagination. Public Culture 12(1):1–19.
Averill, James, R.
  1985   The Social Construction of Emotion: With Special Reference to Love. *In* The Social Construction of the Person. K. J. Gergen and K. E. Davis, eds. New York: Springer-Verlag.
Brennan, Denise
  2004   What's Love Got to Do with It? Transnational Desires and Sex Tourism in the Dominican Republic. Durham: Duke University Press.
Bruner, Edward M.
  1999   Return to Sumatra: 1957, 1997. American Ethnologist 26(2):461–477.
Butler, Judith
  1990   Gender Trouble: Feminism and the Subversion of Identity. New York: Routledge.
Chant, Sylvia, and Cathy McIlwaine, eds.
  1998   Three Generations, Two Genders, One World: Women and Men in a Changing Century. New York: Zed Books.
Clark, Constance D.
  2001   Foreign Marriage, "Tradition," and the Politics of Border Crossings. *In* China Urban: Ethnographies of Contemporary Culture. Nancy N. Chen, Constance D. Clark, Suzanne Z. Gottschang, and Lyn Jeffry, eds. Pp. 104–122. Durham: Duke University Press.
Constable, Nicole
  2003   Romance on a Global Stage: Pen Pals, Virtual Ethnography, and "Mail-Order" Marriages. Berkeley: University of California Press.
Economist
  2003   Swindled. June 14.
Enloe, Cynthia
  1989   Bananas, Beaches and Bases: Making Feminist Sense of International Politics. Berkeley: University of California Press.
Fanon, Frantz
  1967   Black Skin, White Masks. New York: Grove Press.
Fosado, Gisela
  2003   A Woman's Journey into the World of Male Sex Work. *In* Contemporary Cuba. Denise Blum and Peter McLaran, eds. Lantham, MD. Rowan & Littlefield.
Georges, Eugenia
  1990   The Making of a Transnational Community: Migration, Development and Cultural Change in the Dominican Republic. New York: Columbia University Press.
Gilliam, Angela M.
  2001   A Black Feminist Perspective on the sexual Commodification of Women in the New Global Culture. *In* Black Feminist Anthropology: Theory, Politics, Praxis, and Poetics. I. McClaurin, ed. New Brunswick, NJ: Rutgers University Press.
Gonzalez, David
  2003a Back Talk: Protesting through the Streets. New York Times, August 10: Sec. 8, p. 11.
  2003b Pan American Games: Games Lift Spirits in Santo Domingo. New York Times, August 8:D1.

Grasmuck, Sherri, and Patricia R. Pessar
1991   Between Two Islands: Dominican International Migration. Berkeley: University of
       California Press.
Guarnizo, Luis Eduardo
1994   Los Dominicanyorks: The Making of a Binational Society. ANNALS 553:70–83.
Haberman, Clyde
1997   Green Cards and Vows of Marriage. New York Times, February 21:A32.
Hamilton, Annette
1997   Primal Dream: Maculinism, Sin and Salvation in Thailand's Sex Trade. *In* Sites of
       Desire, Economies of Pleasure: Sexualities in Asia and the Pacific. L. Manderson and
       M. Jolly, eds. Pp. 145–165. Chicago: University of Chicago.
Hardy, Frances
1994   How I Bitterly Regret My Paradise Marriage. London Daily Mail, November
       18:20–21.
Herold, Edward, et al.
1992   Canadian Tourists and Sex Workers in the Dominican Republic. Paper presented at the
       conference Culture, Sexual Behavior, and AIDS, Amsterdam, July 24–26.
Hochschild, Arlie Russell
1983   The Managed Heart. Berkeley: University of California Press.
Hondagneu-Sotelo, Pierrette
1994   Gendered Transitions: Mexican Experiences of Immigration. Berkeley: University of
       California Press.
Illouz, Eva
1997   Consuming the Romantic Utopia: Love and the Cultural Contradictions of Capitalism.
       Berkeley: University of California Press.
Jolly, Margaret
1997   From Point Venus to Bali Ha'i: Eroticism and Exoticism in Representations of the
       Pacific. *In* Sites of Desire, Economies of Pleasure. L. Manderson and M. Jolly, eds. Pp.
       99–122. Chicago: University of Chicago Press.
Kelsky, Karen
1994   Intimate Ideologies: Transnational Theory and Japan's "Yellow Cabs." Public Culture
       6:465–478.
Kempadoo, Kamala
1998   The Migrant Tightrope: Experiences from the Caribbean. *In* Global Sex Workers:
       Rights, Resistance, and Redefinition. Kamala Kempadoo and Jo Doezema, eds. Pp.
       124–138. New York: Routledge.
Kibria, Nazli
1993   Family Tightrope: The Changing Lives of Vietnamese Americans. Princeton: Princeton
       University Press.
Latin Finance
2001   Reliance on Remittances. Dominican Republic: A Diversifying Economy. Supplement.
       November:32.
Lutz, Catherine
1998. Unnatural Emotions: Everyday Sentiments on a Micronesian Atoll and Their Challenge
       to Western Theory. Chicago: University of Chicago Press.
Mahler, Sarah J., and Patricia R. Pessar
2001   Gendered Geographies of Power: Analyzing Gender across Transnational Spaces.
       Identities 7(4):441–459.
Martis, Jacqueline
1999   Tourism and Sex Trade in St. Maarten and Curacao. *In* Sun, Sex, and Gold: Tourism
       and Sex Work in the Caribbean. K. Kempadoo, ed. Pp. 201–215. Lanham, MD:
       Rowman & Littlefield.

Moon, Katherine
  1997   Sex among Allies: Military Prostitution in U.S.-Korea Relations. New York: Columbia
         University Press.
Padilla, Mark B.
  2007   Caribbean Pleasure Industry: Tourism, Sexuality, and AIDS in the Dominican Republic
         (Worlds of Desire: The Chicago Series on Sexuality, Gender and Culture). Chicago:
         University of Chicago Press.
Pessar, Patricia R.
  1995   On the Homefront and in the Workplace: Integrating Immigrant Women into
         Feminist Discourse. Anthropological Quarterly 68(1):37–47.
Pruitt, Deborah, and Suzanne LaFont
  1995   For Love and Money: Romance Tourism in Jamaica. Annals of Tourism Research
         21(2):422–440.
Rebhun, L.A.
  1999   The Heart Is Unknown Country: Love in the Changing Economy of Northeast Brazil.
         Stanford: Stanford University Press.
Safa, Helen
  1995   The Myth of the Breadwinner: Women and Industrialization in the Carribbean.
         Boulder, CO: Westview.
Stoler, Ann
  1997   Educating Desire in Colonial Southeast Asia: Foucault, Freud and Imperial Sexualities.
         In Sites of Desire, Economies of Pleasure. L. Manderson and M. Jolly, eds. Pp. 27–47.
         Chicago: University of Chicago Press.
Sturdevant, Saundra Pollock, and Brenda Stoltzfus, eds.
  1992   Let the Good Times Roll. New York: New Press.
Thorbek, Susanne
  2002a The European Inheritance: Male Perspectives. In Transnational Prostitution: Changing
         Global Patterns. Susanne Thorbek and Bandana Pattanaik, eds. Pp. 24–41. New York:
         Zed Books.
  2002b Introduction. In Transnational Prostitution: Changing Global Patterns. Susanne
         Thorbek and Bandana Pattanaik, eds. Pp. 1–9. New York: Zed Books.
Victoria, Lorena S.
  1994   Un Amor en el Caribe. Rumbo, November 21:42–46.
Walker, Dave, and Richard Ehrlich
  1992   Hello My Big Big Honey: Love Letters to Bangkok Bar Girls and Their Revealing
         Interviews. Bangkok: Dragon Dance Publications.

11

Romancing the Club
Love Dynamics between Filipina Entertainers and GIs in U.S. Military Camp Towns in South Korea

Sealing Cheng

Love . . . is always an interrogation—a series of questions about the self and the other.
>   —Peggy Phelan (1993:21)

Work You need many boyfriends in the club. Otherwise, no one will buy you drinks.
>   —Anna, 18-year-old runaway Filipina entertainer

Play Well, it's a game that we play. You know, you have got what these women want and they have what we want.
>   —Roy, 34-year-old GI (staff sergeant, U.S. Forces in Korea)

This chapter examines the discourse of romantic love in the negotiations and identity construction between service providers and customers in an industry known for the sexual objectification of Asian women—clubs in the R&R (rest and recreation) industry for U.S. military in South Korea (henceforth "Korea"). In Korea, these clubs are found around U.S. military camp towns (*gijichon*) that constitute pockets of U.S.-dominated territories in the Korean nation. The ethnographic discussion here has three purposes. The first is to illustrate how "love" enters into the gijichon club industry between the Filipina entertainers and their GI boyfriends and how this cross-cultural "game of love" works in a situation of dislocation and a meeting of social and economic unequals. For GIs away from home, the illusion of intimacy enfolds their interactions in the club and their everyday lives in gijichon. It analyzes how political economy is "implicated in the production and reproduction of desire and is implicated in even the most minute and intimate levels of interaction" (Constable 2003:143). A second purpose is to analyze why "love" is an important discursive instrument for the Filipina entertainers to manage their labor and their vulnerabilities in an exploitative situation. In this sense, love is a "weapon of the weak" for female entertainers. The third purpose is to throw into relief the blurry lines between play and nonplay in the game of love, and the potential of "love" going beyond its intended performativity to have unpredictable emotional consequence on its players.

Love in R&R

Talking about love in any R&R industry for the U.S. military may seem ironic if not superfluous. R&R is frequently equated with military prostitution and considered contiguous with war rapes and sexual slavery, as exemplified by the issue of Comfort Women. The deployment of female sexual services for military men has been analyzed as an effect of aggressive male sexuality legitimized by military hypermasculinity (Enloe 1983, 1989, 2000; Harrison 2003; Higate 2003). Studies by political scientists and concerned critics (Enloe 1989; Moon 1997; Sturdevant and Stoltzfus 1993; Cummings 1992) on U.S. military prostitution are premised on exposing how masculinist state projects rely on the mobilization of women's bodies. The issue has become increasingly emotive and politically sensitive as challenges to the American political and military role in the Asia Pacific region have escalated. Furthermore, since the late 1990s, antitrafficking activists and policy makers have drawn increasing attention to the migration of women from developing countries into these R&R venues, condemning military presence for generating the demand for "trafficked women" and in the process condemning the military and war as institutionalized gender violence for the reproduction of state and capital on a global scale. In this period also nongovernmental organizations (NGOs) and the media have criticized the United States for its involvement in the trafficking of women for the purpose of sexual enslavement.[1] In this light, the image of burly young American men in uniforms sexually overpowering helpless third world women makes the notion of love—with its connotation of romance and mutuality—unthinkable.

While indebted to the cogent analyses of gender ideology and violence in military institutions cited earlier, this chapter departs from this body of research by looking at the everyday interactions between military men and women entertainers in an R&R industry since the late 1990s. Specifically, it explores the discourses and experiences of romantic love between Filipina entertainers and their regular GI patrons who meet in their displacement in Korea between 1998 and 2000. As such, it examines the importance of love as a discursive and emotional site for the exercise of individual agency and the interactive creation of social reality in the context of globalization. The presence of U.S. military in Korea and the entry of Filipinas as entertainers to serve this military are the products of different stages and types of globalizing dynamics—the former a result of the Korean War maintained by cold war politics, the latter a result of Korea's state-initiated globalization project in the 1990s and the discrepancy in economic developments between Korea and the Philippines in the past two decades. Thus, U.S. soldiers and Filipina entertainers meet in Korea in a radicalized power relationship layered by colonial history, the R&R entertainment industry, and labor migration in Asia.

The political economy of Asia Pacific has placed the United States, Korea, and the Philippines in a hierarchical relationship and their nationals as consumers, mediators, and service providers in gijichon, respectively. Love becomes the fulcrum where work, play, and identity intersect for Filipinas and their regular GI patrons in gijichon clubs. As a marginal site in the transnational field, gijichon is what Gloria Anzaldua calls the "borderland," where "two or more cultures edge each other, where people of different races occupy the same territory, where under, lower, middle and upper classes touch, where the space between two individuals shrinks with intimacy" (1987:3). The interactions between American soldiers and Filipina entertainers in gijichon thus provide a microscopic view of the political economy of desires in Asia Pacific.

Love in the Political Economy of Desires

Love is both a discourse for strategic articulation and an emotion that defies calculation. It is certainly not my claim that love is the great equalizer that could erase the power differentials between Filipina entertainers and their GI customers. Rather, I try to show that love is an integral aspect of the on-going negotiations within this power relation in a site of displacement, examining the discourse of romantic love between Filipina entertainers and GIs as what Lila Abu-Lughod and Catherine Lutz term "pragmatic acts and communicative performances." As they explain:

> The focus on discourse allows not only for insight into how emotion, like the discourse in which it participates, is informed by cultural themes and values, but also how it serves as an operator in a contentious field of social activity, how it affects a social field, and how it can serve as an idiom for communicating, *not even necessarily about feelings* but about such diverse matters as *social conflict, gender roles, or the nature of the ideal or deviant person.* (Abu-Lughod and Lutz 1990:11; emphasis added)

Hence, I explore the discourse of love as a social practice, negotiated and reproduced in the politics of desire in gijichon. "Politics of desire" here refers to the negotiation of desire within the webs of significance of gender, ethnicity, and class, shaped by the politico-economic context of the Philippines and the United States (cf. Constable 2003). In turn, we should view their manipulation and pursuit of love as commentaries on local and regional hierarchies (Tsing 1993). These "border crossings" thus comprise multiple "sites of creative cultural production" (Rosaldo 1989:208). Individual articulations of the emotion of love and subsequent maneuvers of these articulations challenge, and are circumscribed by, these social and cultural constructions.

Game

Self-representation and negotiations over money and sex converge in what entertainers and GIs refer to as "the game," with its participants as "players" and the "being played." The rules and logic of the game are culturally informed and contextually manipulated. Its players draw on the rhetoric and symbols of romantic love for often imperfect performances as well as the construction of their own experiences. L. A. Rebhun, in her study of the centrality of *amor* as a romantic passion and a sentiment of social affiliation in Caruaru in Northeast Brazil, argues that "emotional style may vary with the type of economy" (1999:85). The style of love between the Filipinas and their regular GI patrons is also specific to the political economy of gijichon, constituting a particular discourse of morality and pattern of intimacy.

The following account of the "game of love" is necessarily a counternarrative to previous studies of military prostitution and antitrafficking discourses that emphasize the victimhood of women. It brings out the importance of looking at the everyday life of marginal groups who have little access to institutional and political channels of redress. Where there is little space for political organizing or collective actions, it is all the more important to attend to the mundane aspects of life to understand their social and cultural agency—exercised as challenge and as attempts to transform their subordination (Scott 1987). Love is therefore a "weapon of the weak" for these Filipina entertainers.

This chapter draws on ethnographic fieldwork in two major U.S. military camp towns in Korea in 1998–2000, followed by a short visit to the Philippines in May 2000. Though my research is focused on the Filipinas, I made much effort to meet with their GI customers/boyfriends. Previous studies of military prostitution have largely neglected the soldiers as part of the equation,[2] perpetuating assumptions about the essential nature of sex workers' clients, reinforcing the idea of a "natural" male sex drive that has necessitated prostitution. GIs are an important part of the Filipinas' lives in Korea—as customers, boyfriends, friends, potential husbands, and passports out of poverty. Any consideration of the lives of Filipina entertainers in these GI clubs thus calls for a more nuanced understanding of the perspective of GIs and their interactions with the women.

R&R and Gijichon

GI clubs in Korea, Japan, the Philippines, and Vietnam are the progeny of a global network of U.S. military bases formed for the containment of communism as well as to preserve U.S. geopolitical interests in Asia Pacific in the postwar era. GI clubs are part of the R&R system that has been set up to provide the recreation that is necessary for the GIs to preserve their military effectiveness.[3] Those stationed onshore have access to the R&R facilities around their bases, while those who are offshore get to have their R&R when they pay their port calls in cities such as Hong Kong. Prostitution has been a key component of these R&R sites.

In 2000, there were 37,000 U.S. military personnel in Korea. This number was reduced by 9,154 as of May 2006 as part of the restructuring of U.S. forces in the Pacific (Department of Defense 2007). The structure of the R&R industry in gijichon is as follows. At the top level are clubs and bars that have female entertainers who would accompany a customer for the price of a "ladies" drink; sexual services may be provided for an additional payment, darts and pool are almost ubiquitous in these clubs, and the kind of music played in each club attracts particular clientele (from country music to hip hop). Far less glamorous is the street-level prostitution that usually relies on pimps (usually older gijichon women) to solicit clients on the streets for a "short-time" and the temporary wives who accompany servicemen during their tours of duty. In 1996, women from Russia and the Philippines and other third world countries were brought in, usually on one-year contracts, to fill the vacancies left by Korean women in the clubs. A few years later, as more and more of these Filipinas left the clubs either by running away or having GIs buy their contracts, many of them started living in rented accommodations as GIs' "wives."[4] (By around 2001 a street in one gijichon came to be called "Filipina lane.") Not all of these relationships result in legal marriages, even though some couples do end up marrying in Korea, in the Philippines, or in the United States. To my knowledge, four out of the 33 Filipinas I interviewed in Korea subsequently married GIs.

Stepping off the base almost immediately brings a GI into a jungle of clubs with scantily clad Asian women eager to shower their attention on any man for the price of a drink. While some GIs go in groups to play pool or darts, a visitor walking alone sends a clear message that he needs a woman. As soon as he enters a club, an entertainer will greet him and take him to his table. His drink order will be taken and the entertainer will provide him with company if he buys her ladies' drinks at $10 each (all dollar amounts in this chapter are in U.S. dollars)—much more expensive than the $2 beer the GI could get for himself. If the man desires continued company, he will have to buy more drinks. What the entertainer will do in exchange depends on the customer, the club, and the woman, as well as her need to fulfill any drinks quota that day—she might just sit next to him, perform a small dance, or dance provocatively, rubbing herself against the man's private parts before requesting a drink.

Club owners' observation that GIs favor Filipinas over Korean women has been confirmed by many of the GIs I spoke with.[5] As aliens in a foreign land and English speakers, GIs and Filipinas find it easier to identify with each other; also, as a result of a century of American colonialism and neo-colonialism in the Philippines, they share more in terms of culture and values.

The GI

In anti-American nationalist discourses around these R&R towns, GIs are unambiguously constructed as the embodiment of the foreign masculine thrust.[6] Academic analysis of military prostitution has largely focused on the voice of the women and identified their oppression and sufferings as the result of masculinist state projects, and their prostituted bodies as a symbol of the dominated nation (Moon 1997; Sturdevant and Stoltzfus 1993). This perspective gives a valid account of gendered structural oppression in the current political order. Yet how adequate is this perspective in understanding power relations and domination on the level of everyday practice when GIs, the supposed "perpetrators" or embodiment of these women's oppression, are not included in the analysis? To take one step away from this essentialization, I offer a brief examination of the social construction of GI as a category.

GIs are an ambiguous construction in American society and in American foreign policy.[7] They may be condemned as drunkards and sex-craved young lads who would be fighting in the streets if not for the army, or they may be hailed as patriots and freedom fighters that champion noble causes—in keeping with *Time* magazine's naming the GI as Person of the Year in 1950 and 2003 and one of the "Heroes and Icons" of the 20th century in 1999. "GI" commonly refers to the enlisted men rather than the officers; they are seen as working-class men rather than college graduates who tend to be ethnic minorities who "did not make it" (except for the army) and underachieving white people.

This idea that military recruits are marginal members of U.S. society may be a more a middle-class American construction than a reflection of reality. Recent statistics from the Department of Defense on the education attainment as well as ethnic make-up of active duty personnel of the U.S. military, supplemented by some of their personal accounts that I have collected, show that though GIs may not be "the best," they are not the "rejects" of society either.[8] Many of the enlistees join for the pay and benefits and recruiting resources that surpass civilian jobs. Some enlist for the college funds provided by the "GI Bill," and many immigrants join for the accelerated naturalization process the military offers. It is important to note that when these "perks" shrank in the late 1970s, the quality of new recruits fell.[9] Joining the army may actually be the best option out of many, rather than a "last resort."

Because the two Koreas are still technically at war, a GI's assignment to Korea is considered a "hardship" tour, where no government sponsorship for family members is provided.[10] The tour normally lasts for one year. The short duration of the assignment seems to justify the absence of any program that might help with the GIs' integration into the host country—there are no language-skills training and no briefing session on the social and cultural make-up of the country. Commonly and unofficially, the little they have heard about Korea is about the cheap sex available (cf. Bickford 2003).

Most of the GIs I talked with believed they were in Korea to prevent North Korean aggression. Though none of them considered patriotism a reason for enlisting, their identity as soldiers of the U.S. Forces in Korea was important to their sense of masculinity as an American male—the "GI Joe" identity. In addition, whatever their marginality may be in the United States, their identity as Americans was doubly confirmed on their posting to Korea by their race and by their job as GIs—an African American GI said that in Korea he felt more American, because he was immediately recognized as such.

In the clubs, the popularity of a man usually declines with the hard cash he possesses, especially with low-ranking privates. High-ranking GIs with a handsome salary could buy multiple drinks for an entertainer as well as her co-workers and are greeted most enthusiastically in the clubs. Those who refuse to buy the women drinks are often teased with the name "Cheap Charlie." This is a challenge to masculine pride that many young GIs find hard to deal with, and many Filipinas are familiar with the power of such tactics to get more out of the men.

Though virility is an important tenet in hegemonic masculinity, particularly so in the military, one GI who fulfilled the stereotype and frequented the clubs for sex drew disapproval from his fellow soldiers. Carl, a 20-year-old GI, talked about the "loser" in his company.

He was a virgin when he first came. When he first arrived, he said he would not go to those bars, that he won't be paying the girls or doing that. But in less than two weeks, he was going down there every night by himself. Usually people go in groups to have drinks, but going alone means it's something else you are looking for. I used to go alone. He spends all his money on the women, all he does is to drink and get women, we all think that he is a loser, he doesn't do anything except going downrange. . . . (Does he do well in the army?) No, he doesn't. He is a real loser.

This description of the "loser" may resemble popular portrayals of the bawdy GI,[11] yet his excessive and solitary indulgence in alcohol and women met with strong disapproval from his peers. Key to the designation of "loser" in Carl's description is the loss of control (over his sexuality, alcohol consumption, and money) and the defiance to the group. A man's apparently successful and continuous indulgence in aggressive sexuality to the exclusion of other ideal masculine qualities, such as discipline and comradeship, may mark him as a "loser" in the military.

The Filipinas

According to some Korean and international activists, these Filipino women have been "trafficked" into sexual slavery since 1996. This shift took place within the political economy of Korea's development in Asia. Korean women working in gijichon have earned such derogatory terms as "Western whore" and "Western Princess," referring to their selling their bodies as well as their nation to "the West"—with specific reference to the United States. In the 1990s, Korea's rapid economic advancement led to a shortage of Korean women to serve the American soldiers because of both the stigma and the relatively low income, necessitating the importation of women from the third world to fill these vacancies. This importation reflects the larger labor demand situation in Korea. Since the 1980s the government has sanctioned the importation of limited numbers of cheap foreign laborers to take up the "dangerous, dirty, and difficult" jobs abandoned by Korean nationals.

In the Philippines overseas employment has been essential to keeping the economy afloat since the mid 1970s. The Philippine government estimated that, in 2006, there were about 8.23 million overseas Filipinos in more than 193 countries; 3.8 million were overseas workers, and 874,792 were classified as irregulars (POEA 2006). Their remittances amounted to $10.69 billion in 2005, constituting more than 10 percent of Gross National Product (BLES 2006). Women have become the majority in the outflow of labor since the 1990s.[12] They leave mainly to work overseas as entertainers, domestic helpers, and nurses. Many of the "entertainers" end up working in the sex industry and have been identified by some NGOs and supragovernmental organizations as victims of "trafficking." In the many NGO and news reports I have seen on the subject "trafficked" women are consistently portrayed as innocent and powerless victims.

The Filipinas I met with in gijichon are between the ages of 17 and 35, most of them in their early twenties. Only a few of them have worked in a club before coming to Korea. Some have had no working experience, while those with working experience have worked in factories or in sales. The reasons they cited for coming to Korea include to make money for one's family and oneself, to see the world, and to show one's independence.

The women are usually in Korea on one-year contracts. Before 1999, women were promised a job as a waitress, a dancer, or a guest relations officer, but most of the women who have arrived since 2000 have had auditions for jobs as "entertainers" in which they were required to pose in bikinis. In general, by the time they arrived in Korea, these women had a vague idea of what their jobs would entail but few understood the exact nature of their working conditions—both because managers try to conceal the truth and because each club has different requirements. The women were all aware, however, that some parts of their migration and their job were illegitimate, because their agents had told them to tell immigration officers that they were leaving the Philippines as tourists, and because they had made a detour to Hong Kong or Bangkok, where they obtained their entertainer visas rather than in the Philippines.

Most of the Filipinas in question here enter Korea on E-6 entertainer visas and most are brought by the Korea Special Tourist Association made up of gijichon club owners and registered with the Ministry of Culture and Tourism. The organization was originally set up for the distribution of duty-free alcohol in the clubs. All the establishments catering to the military clientele are designated as foreigners-only and officially not accessible to Korean nationals.

UPON ARRIVAL, THE FILIPINA WOMEN must surrender their passports to the club owners, who keep them and at least part of the women's salaries until they leave Korea, to prevent them from running away. Most of the contracts the women sign are effectively void. Half of the $600 salary goes to their managers, and they may not get the two days off promised in their contract. They are required to entertain the GI customers by getting them to buy as many $10 ladies' drinks as possible, and they receive $2 for every $10 drink a customer buys them. Club owners can arbitrarily prohibit the women from taking days off or fine them for a variety of reasons, such as not fulfilling the drinks quota, trying to run away, or not behaving in a particular way. VIP rooms are found in some clubs and customers may take a woman into the room (with her consent) for around half an hour if he buys her four drinks. Sexual services including hand jobs and blow jobs may be provided on the premises. A customer may pay a "bar fine" to take a woman out of the club. Varying with the time of the month (more expensive on pay days) and the length of time desired, "bar fines" range from $100 to $300. The women usually get 20 to 40 percent of the money. Whatever happens in the VIP room or on a "bar fine" outing is subject to negotiation between the woman and the customer, or, in the words of many Filipinas, "It's up to you."

Filipina entertainers frequently asserted that their work was voluntary. Katie, for example, said "it's up to you" whether or not you prostitute yourself and that the women always had the choice of running away—as she herself had done. Similarly, women who went on a bar fine with GIs might run off at any time before sex. Janet said that "it's up to you" whether or not you perform a blow job for the customer in a VIP room. Many women did complain about the pressures club owners exerted on them to increase sales. But most preferred to see themselves as autonomous agents exercising control over their bodies and sexuality, contradicting the many activist discourses that stress these women's powerlessness.

Love as an Emotion Discourse in Gijichon Clubs

As in the entertainment industry for men in Japan, money and women are connected in gijichon nightlife, where they represent and structure the recreation men pursue.[13] Yet, unlike in the high-class hostess club Allison (1994) studied in Tokyo, sexual posturing and flirtation are often not confined to the clubs in gijichon, where there is a greater tendency for both sexes to extend the illusion of intimacy exhibited in the clubs to everyday reality.[14] In addition to the dimension of class, one important reason for this difference is the temporary dislocation from home that allows individual Filipinas and GIs greater freedom to flirt with such illusions. The effects of these relationships often reverberate beyond the physical boundaries of gijichon to the transnational flows of money and people. Mediated by the idioms of romantic love, money and sex are not a matter of simple transaction in gijichon clubs. In a context where "boyfriends" have become synonymous with "customers," "I-love-you" a daily utterance, and marriage proposals a weekly occurrence, relationships in gijichon clubs assume a complexity that challenges a dichotomous "male domination-female subordination" model put forward in most prostitution studies (Barry 1984; Hoigard and Finstad 1986; Jeffreys 1997; O'Connell-Davidson 1998).

The Possibility of Intimacy

In gijichon clubs regular patrons provide a stable source of income, as well as social and emotional support for the entertainers. Because of the exploitative working conditions in the clubs and the absence of channels of redress about employers' abuses, the Filipina entertainers are eager to wield influence over their customers whose number, loyalty, and generosity determine their well-being. And because of the potential for material and social advancement the women perceive in this hard-earned opportunity overseas compared with the generally humdrum reality at home, the romantic love rhetoric is important to them on three different levels—as a means of getting financial and material assistance, as a means of getting social support and respect as an individual, and, and as a means of securing a future through marriage. These goals might overlap or they might be realized separately. But key to the attainment of these goals is the women's "labor of love."

In the words of Carl, a GI who spent the first six months of his time and salary in the clubs in search of a girlfriend before giving up, "You see, they either make you feel pity for them, or make you feel special, or make you think that you are going to get something." Carl's insight points to three common tropes used by women to gain their customers' patronage: their own powerlessness, their customers' individuality, and the prospect of sex. These might operate separately but more frequently are combined to structure the illusion of intimacy in gijichon clubs.

The personalization of relationships in gijichon club relies on the creation of the potential of a relationship beyond the mediation of money. To this end, altruistic ideals of both friendship and romantic love are mobilized. A concatenation of lies, truths, and partial truths permeate relationships between entertainers and their regulars. To maintain their appeal, Filipina entertainers lie about their age, their virginity, their boyfriends, their marital status, and the number of children they have.

In gijichon, GIs often offer Filipinas gifts to usher a relationship from the commercial to the personal realm. Gifts from GIs range from such mundane objects as lotion, clothes, shampoo, medicine, phone cards, and fruit, snacks, and other food to luxury goods such as stereo cassette players and gold necklaces bought on base. When a GI invites a Filipina to lunch, she might bring two or three of her friends along. Such material and financial support is crucial to the well-being of the Filipinas. It is also important to recognize the affective dimension of these gifts. Much like the gifts Chinese cadres in Yunxiang Yan's (1996) study bestowed on their clients to maintain their loyalty and support, these gifts and favors are also offered within the context of a power relationship that nonetheless recognizes the importance of affective engagement—in this instance, the friendship of the Filipinas. In effect, it is a friendship between the "haves" and the "have-nots" gendered between the American GIs and Filipina entertainers. Very often, these gifts may also be "the props of a love affair" functioning as a means of legitimation (Frank 1998:188).

Many Filipinas adorned their rooms with stuffed toys, baseball caps, flowers that had been hung to dry, and other gifts from their customers. Like the pictures of family and friends they also put up, these were mementos of their identities beyond the "buy-and-sell" relationships in the clubs, and of their connections with places and possibilities beyond gijichon.

This discourse of romantic love imbricated with its material manifestation allows the women to deny or delay sex by calling for further demonstrations of love. "You would be my boyfriend, but we need to know each other. If you want me, you wait." Meanwhile, more gifts and drinks could be extracted. The successful entertainers are the "top drinkers," and usually the ones who manage to lead several men to believe that they are the "real" boyfriends.

The notion of romantic love constitutes mutuality and reciprocity between self and other. The romantic script also directs gender-appropriate "give-and-take" beyond the mutual exchange of the "I-love-you" utterance—the man protects and supports the woman materially, while the woman offers herself sexually. Hence, what is being given and taken differs between men and women. While utterance itself becomes a kind of music (Barthes 1978),[15] the exchange in the name of the utterance gives substance and maintains the discourse of romance, building links of obligation and emotional attachment in gijichon clubs—and sometimes beyond.

The Demand for Faithfulness

The common knowledge that promises should not be taken seriously qualifies the interactions in a club as "play." Yet, one important feature in this play of romantic love is that the ideal of faithfulness became built into the interactions and operated as a form of control, in particular on the GIs. For example, Wendy took a picture of Justin and showed it to other Filipinas, telling them he was her boyfriend—thus circumscribing his behavior in gijichon clubs. Others tried to spread such information by word of mouth, hoping to claim ownership over certain customers/boyfriends. While such ownership was generally respected, fights over customers/boyfriends were common.

Unfaithfulness was also common, despite these patrols. GIs' confessions to their girlfriends usually followed the same narrative: after a fight with their girlfriend, they went drinking in another club and bar fined another woman. Most of the women chose to show their magnanimity and forgiveness, tipping the balance of power toward themselves by manipulating the "guilt" of the men. Shirley said she was hurt when she found out that her boyfriend had paid the bar fine for another woman. One of the first questions she asked him after learning of the betrayal was, "How much did you pay for her bar fine?" When he said $300, she replied, "$300! You paid her $300? Why did you do that to me?"

In a context where money was a proof of love—or where economic and emotional intimacies were interdependent—infidelity was compounded by the sex act and the transfer of money. Regardless of the woman's emotional devotion, the need to police unfaithfulness was significant to her pride as well as her material well-being. While the Filipina "girlfriends" could often explain their behavior of intimacy with other men as part of their jobs—and the logic sometimes went, "If you give me more money, I need not be doing this"—the "boyfriends" had no similar excuse and were subject to the control of the ideal of "faithfulness."

Heather Montgomery finds that Thai children in prostitution are able to manipulate their Western clients into becoming fictive kin, committing them to responsibilities and obligations toward their families (Montgomery 1996:86–90). Just as the Thai children came to see prostitution as an economic exchange mediated through kinship ties rather than as a shameful vice, the Filipinas adopted gendered discourses in romantic love to negotiate their relationship with GI customers, mitigating the stigma of prostitution. If sex took place, it was at least based on "feelings" (of affection and gratitude), if not love.

Playing with Love

No GI visits a club in search of love. Love is the game GIs play in the clubs for fun and sex. This game of love is far more than a "romantic exercise" (Allison 1994:75–76).[16] The Filipinas' job is to play the game of love. Conversations constitute an important part of the interactions between GIs and the Filipinas, allowing the women to generate and participate in an illusion of intimacy, to pose as women who are both sexually available and vulnerable, persuading faithful and continual patronage of the GIs. The lines between play and nonplay, however, often blur in the process.

After the first six months of his stay in Korea, Carl finally chose to remain celibate—casting aside the struggle between the insincere relationship with "drinkie girls" who were easily accessible and the (potentially) sincere relationship with "GI girls," who were virtually inaccessible. This yearning for authenticity despite the availability of sex reveals a desire for recognition of oneself as a distinct individual—more than, in Carl's words, "just a customer." And such a yearning is not exclusive to inexperienced young GIs like Carl.

Both Justin and Roy were divorced and in their thirties. They enjoyed having fun and meeting the many women in the clubs. With the ladies' drinks they could afford to buy, they decided which women they talked to, and for how long. In gijichon clubs they paid "to be the king of the night" and be free from "the fear of rejection." "Back in the States," Roy said, "when I go to a bar, I have to get up and go to a girl. Here, I just have to sit down and they come to me. And they are mostly very beautiful women." Roy said he disliked American women, particularly those in the army because they were "not very feminine." He found Korean entertainers too materialistic and rather passive in bed: "Filipino women are less inhibited. Some are even more aggressive, I would say. Like this woman in M— Club. It was my first time in there and as soon as I got in, she took my hand, found the most secluded corner there was, and she was on top of me before I knew it." Roy did not use a condom and was "sweating bullets" in fear of contracting sexually transmitted diseases for the next few days after the encounter. Nonetheless, the reversal of gender dynamics in sex pleased him.

> Author: And you liked it?
> Roy: [Rolled his eyes.] Oh, yes. I did. It's good to have someone else take the initiative.
> Justin: It's every man's dream.
> Roy: Yes, because you don't have the fear of rejection. She is there doing it to you.

The relief from gaining a woman's approval and the pleasure of being "done to" instead of "doing it" have been cited as the common appeal of commercial sex to men (Allison 1994:124–141). In this instance of interracial sex, the masculine ego of the man found an extra boost in the willing submission of the exotic Filipina whose femininity and erotic appeal outbid her American and Korean counterparts. Roy, who insisted that he was only into fun and not love, turned out to be concerned not only about the sex but also about how "special" he was to the woman: "She told me that she didn't do it to everyone—it's just because she likes me that she does it with me. Well, I don't know if that is true. But the other night, I did sit there and observe her, and she didn't do it with other customers." The woman's utterance about liking him was important to Roy.[17] He was happy to confirm that she did not do the same thing to other men. Had Roy been concerned only about the sex, he would not have felt the need to return to verify the exclusiveness of his "privilege."[18] The affection that the woman declared for him, to his relish, marked his distinction from "everyone."

Defining Love

The discourse of love is a chief driving force in the economics and interpersonal dynamics of gijichon clubs. A GI's telling a woman "I love you" in an attempt to get her into bed is as much a part of the game as the woman's saying the same thing in the hope of getting a share of his pay check. That this is a game, however, does not mean there is no love—it is just a different type of love. The "love" that Roy felt for Lilly did not oblige him to answer her plea for an air ticket back to the Philippines. (And Lilly used her request as a last means to get money from Roy. Her air ticket had already been paid for by her club owner.)

> Roy: There is a difference between loving somebody and being in love with somebody.
> Justin: [Nodded.] Loving someone is different from being in love with somebody.
> Author: You have to explain this to me, I don't quite understand.
> R: You see. The English language is not very good for expressing ideas of love. In some other languages they have more terms for it. But we just have "love." Loving someone means you care about her, you are concerned about her, but you come first. But being in love with someone means that you put the other person's welfare first. That's the difference.
> J: It means [being] willing to sacrifice for someone.
> R: Yes, so I love many people but I come first before these people. I love Lilly, I am concerned about her, but I come first.
> J: You love someone—you have good sex. You are in love with someone—you make love.

Justin's last statement sums up the two different forms of love and the kinds of sex that each entails. The distinction lies in the relative weight that the self and the other carries. It confirms that, even in gijichon clubs, "love" is always a part of sexual encounters.

Serious Play

Yet despite the apparent distinction Justin outlined, emotions often turn out to be much more complex and difficult to contain. In fact, Justin himself crossed the line by "falling in love," and subsequently marrying, a 22-year-old entertainer whom he initially intended only to be part of his nightlife in gijichon.

> I did not expect it to happen either. . . . At first I made it very clear to her that there would be no commitment and I was there just for fun. But later, I started to see her more and we talked more, and in late February, I started to get more serious. She passed some of my little tests. I wouldn't be played. I told her, you don't have to go into the VIP rooms, it's not in your contract, and

anything that happens in that room is what you want to happen. If you want to be with me, you decide what you let happen in there. I don't want to hear that when we are married, "See, that's sergeant XX's wife. She used to work in a club and she used to do this and this with me." I said I don't want to hear anything like that if she becomes my wife. *I told her that to help her get some control of her situation, to help her look into the future.* And I think it helped her a lot. . . . She lost many customers because of me, because she refused to do what they asked her to. And the customers would ask for their money back. Sometimes [when] a customer would pay her to go out, she would pretend to be sick, go home early and then called me up. Then I would come and meet her. They [the guys] paid for me to go out with her. [He sounded very proud of that.] (My emphasis)

Justin explained why he had fallen in love with Wendy: "She really opens up her innermost thoughts to me." The search for authenticity of experience that is "every-where manifest in our society" (MacCannell 1973:589) is all the more pronounced in a context where "love" could be mere performance for material ends. Wendy's revelation of what Justin believed to be her most private thoughts marks a significant departure from the "game." It ushers Justin from the performative and therefore inauthentic "front" to the "back" (Goffman 1959), where the intimate "truth" lies. This privileged status became the basis for intimacy and commitment. In this brief summary of his relationship with Wendy, Justin outlines the negotiation of gender identities as a process within the discourse of romantic love in gijichon clubs. His words are consistent with Katherine Frank's argument that a clear distinction be-tween "real" and "faked" emotional involvement is difficult for women and men alike. Both parties participate in a performance of intimacy that involves self-repre-sentations in which "the phantasmatic and the real can be intricately intertwined" (1998:197).

Through the dynamics of interaction, this discourse of love circulates in gijichon, creating a network of men and women connected by "love"—a sentiment without a singular definition that thus ranges from a sense of social affiliation to passionate and altruistic devotion. Much is being exchanged in the name of "love" as emotional, economic, and social intimacies develop in gijichon. As such, the emotion discourse of love both constructs one's experience in gijichon and generates social reality.

The following case study situates the emotion discourse and its negotiation in the tensions between individual desires and family obligations, gender ideals and realities in the transnational context of Korea, the Philippines, and the United States.

Mary: Learning to Love, Dying for Love

Mary was a 28-year-old single parent who had left her three children in the care of her mother in the Philippines. She ran away from her violent husband and worked as an entertainer in the Philippines until she became pregnant with her third child. In April 1999 she went to Korea. Beginning in May we met and talked on the telephone regularly. When she returned home in May 2000, I met her and her family at the Centennial Airport in Manila and spent the next eight days with her. At our first meeting, Mary told me about her "boyfriends" and I asked whether she wanted to marry a GI. She did not know, she said. But any uncertainty that existed then had been dispelled completely by the end of a year in Korea. In time, Mary had come to recognize the many benefits marrying an American GI could bring to her and her family. Thus, she did not fail to leave Korea without securing a fiancé, who was to visit her family in the Philippines three weeks later.

At one of my first meetings with her, Mary told me about the three men she was seeing in Korea; one was her "real boyfriend," the other two were "just boyfriends." "But," she said, "I am still a virgin in Korea." Seized by my fascination with the sudden utterance of the word "virgin," I missed the subtle play Mary was engaged in by qualifying such a state with the geographical condition of "in Korea." The fact that she was a mother completely escaped me. I asked naïvely, "Really?" She responded, "In Korea, yes! I haven't slept with anyone yet!" Seeing my bewilderment, she added "I have a kid, remember?"[19]

SUCH PLAY ON THE FEMININE IDEAL of virginity and purity, which commands particular reverence among people with a strong Roman Catholic upbringing, is a common practice among Filipinas. There are basically two different, but related, ways in which Filipinas "play" with this ideal. One is illustrated by Mary's story, in which juxtaposing the ideal with her behavior may amount to a blatant contradiction to attain a comic, ironical, even subversive effect, while asserting her subscription to the ideal. Virginity becomes renewable as Mary appropriates the moral ideal through the effect of qualification ("in Korea"). The other way is to identify oneself as committed to such moral values and thus to demand respect and or pity and in doing so to protect or advance one's interests. In both cases, the women show a strong awareness of the strength of these dominant ideals along with an emotional, even if not literal, adherence to it. The strength of the purity ideal also hinges on its association with ideals about romantic love and related ideas of loyalty and monogamy. Unlike what is commonly perceived of the sex industry, these ideas feature significantly in these women's interactions with their customer/boyfriends.

Mary told me her one and only true love was a 19-year-old black GI named Jamie, and he was the only one with whom she had had sex ("I just want to have sex with one man; I want to be faithful"), even though she was going out with another GI and had a fiancé who had returned to the United States. Copulation set the boundary for faithfulness for most of the entertainers. Being physically intimate with other men, calling them "boyfriends," flirting with them, even going into a VIP room with a man for 20 minutes amounted to a behavior that fitted inside that boundary. Such a redefinition of codes of intimacy often became a bone of contention between the women and their boyfriends—contributing partly to the volatility of relationships in gijichon.

"It's a new GI. We are finished. It hurts," Mary told me on the phone one day in January 2000, referring to an army woman Jamie said he had met. I visited her the next day. In Mary's room, which she shared with Jenny at the back of the club, Mary and I sat on her bed as she told me, crying, what happened. Her coworkers, Jenny and Helen, as well as Helen's GI boyfriend were also there, all of them throwing in an occasional comment without offering much consolation. Then she proceeded to tear down from the wall the sketches scripted with "Love you 4 ever," a picture of her with Jamie, as well as her entire collection of stuffed toys, including the one that Jamie gave her when they first met. She picked up the big stuffed seal, threw it onto the floor, and kicked it while wailing and yelling, "I love him. I still love him." Typical of Mary, she giggled in between her frenzy, as if uncomfortable with her own anger. She took out a box containing all the notes and letters and photos from Jamie. She showed me a letter that said they had been together for three weeks, that he was serious, and that he did not want any more games and asked Mary to be serious too. On a small piece of paper was written "MARRY ME?" In fact, Jamie had given Mary an engagement ring three months into their relationship. He had further suggested that he would help her three children, her brother, and her parents to immigrate to the United States. Back then, Mary agreed to my suggestion that it would be "a dream come true."

The relationship had lasted for more than seven months and Mary could think of only one reason for the break-up:

> Maybe it's because I have a small mouth, maybe that woman has a big mouth. I can only take in a little bit [of his penis]. I can still hold his dick with my hand. But I want to give him satisfaction. . . . I really want to. I was so nice to him. I cook for him. I lost customers because of him. He gave me everything I wanted. He supported me. $100, sometimes $200 a month.

Mary rarely initiated talk about sex except in jokes. But this was no joke. Whether or not Jamie's being sexually unsatisfied was the true reason for their break-up, Mary's words reveal how intent she was on satisfying him. She never insisted that Jamie use a condom and started to take oral contraceptives only when I offered to accompany her to the pharmacy. Not only did Mary try to uphold the romantic ideal of faithfulness to Jamie (which she believed GI girls were incapable of), but she was eager to demonstrate her capacity to satisfy him domestically (cooking for him) and sexually.

Despite her love for Jamie, Mary finally agreed to marry Larry, a GI of Italian descent, because her family was opposed to having a black man in the family, and, furthermore, Jamie had been expelled from the army for misconduct and had returned to the United States, where he remained unemployed. I learned about Mary and Larry's decision to marry one afternoon when I met Mary outside the U.S. Embassy. She had come with Larry so that he could get the necessary papers for marriage. I was surprised at the news because Mary never talked much about Larry, except that there was "a white guy" who had been very nice to her even when Jamie left her.

Author: Do you love him?

Mary: No. (She turned and sniggered, as if I just said something silly)

A: Ha? So why are you marrying him? [I laughed.]

M: Because he gives me what I want.

A: And that is . . . ?

M: Money.

A: And . . . ?

M: [The opportunity] to go to the States.

Mary had repeated that she could not have sex with someone she did not love. Through another skillful play on ideas about female purity, romantic love, and the ideal of sex within marriage, Mary managed to refuse sex to Larry while she continued to lay claims to his financial support as a fiancé.

Mary: He even asked if I have slept with Jamie. And I said yes. I said yes, I gave myself to him.

A: And he doesn't mind?

M: Maybe he doesn't, but he accepts [it].

A: Why did you tell him?

M: Because he asked.

A: You could have said no.

M: I just wanted to tell the truth. I said I did.

A: And he accepts that you are not sleeping with him now?

M: Hmm, yes. Because I said, you know, OK, no more, I can't sleep with you before we are married after what [has] happened between me and Jamie, I don't want to do it again. . . . Even though you have spent a lot of money on me, I couldn't sleep with you.

A: Has he slept with another Filipina?

M: No.

A: So he has never had sex after coming to Korea?

M: He told me no. I think he is a virgin again.

A: A virgin?

M: Yes, again.

A: A virgin in Korea?

M: Yes.

I have to marvel at Mary's flexibility in kneading cultural and gender ideals to fit with her scheme of things. By portraying herself as a selfless romantic who "gave" herself to a man she truly loved but who had abandoned her, she assumed the image of a woman who has been disillusioned by men's love. She used this "trauma of love" to justify her refusal of sex to Larry. Mary's portrayal of herself also put Larry in the position of a suspect who might inflict further trauma, possibly calling for further demonstration of his "true love." Reminding Larry that the financial assistance she needed from him was not a sufficient reason for him to demand sex from her,

Mary reiterated that sex was not for sale despite her job. It was like saying that she had learned her lesson with men, and now, sex was, in Mary's delaying tactic with Larry, only sanctioned by the marital contract. Like many other Filipinas, Mary was making use of the image of the Philippines as a religious and conservative country to back up her claims that she would not have sex again before getting married. Portraying herself as the forsaken heroine of a tragic love tale, she had succeeded in representing herself as a victim of both economic and emotional woes who was not ready to compromise her moral values. And how much appeal did that have on the male ego of a young American GI to further pledge his love and support?

Faithfulness, honesty, understanding, and sacrifice are not only ideals of romantic love that these women merely "play" with to advance their interests. The frequency with which these ideas came up in their descriptions of themselves and others, as well as in their interactions with men, showed that these were important tenets in their social and cultural world. They also struggled constantly to adapt their actions to these ideals. At times the women boldly asserted their success, at other times they clearly revealed a sense of guilt and loss.

Mary explained to me more than once that her plan to marry Larry was tied to her plans for her family. She wanted to marry a man who could help bring good fortune to her family. She would get her three children and her 17-year-old brother to the United States once she was married. Mary wanted her brother to join the U.S. Army—to be a GI—so that they could both help with the family in the Philippines. She had largely given up the dream of marrying Jamie because of her family's opposition and the more promising future that Larry offered. She was aware that she knew little about Larry but was confident that marrying an American man would open doors to the land of riches for her family. She said she would divorce Larry after she received her U.S. citizenship. Meanwhile, Mary continued to indulge in her fruitless romance with Jamie in secret.

During a telephone conversation following our meeting in front of the U.S. Embassy, I asked whether Larry had given her an engagement ring. Mary said indifferently, "Yes, he said he would. But I don't care. I can live without a ring." I was thinking of how Mary had put family interest and preference before her own when she suddenly said, "I am sorry I am just using my brain now. . . . I mean I am sorry for my attitude now, that I am only using my brain."

Author: Oh, using your brain, and not your heart?
Mary: Not my heart. Yes. Not my heart.
A: What would you do if you were using your heart?
M: [Giggled for a while.] Maybe I am gonna kill myself? Ha ha ha.
A: Why?
M: 'Cuz it's hard for me. [She sounded as though she was sobbing but also laughed out aloud.]

It was typical of Mary to laugh while voicing her woes. Accounts of her problems were always checked by uneasy chuckles every now and then. The laughter might have been a kind of safety valve for her sense of helplessness but also for her sense of guilt. She would ask me, after telling me all her "plans," whether I thought that she was "bad." She was aware that her scheming was "bad" or morally regrettable, yet it had all been dictated by the "brain." The "brain" had come to stand for her family responsibilities, hard work, and calculations; the "heart" for her desires for love, romance, and freedom. In this confession, Mary expressed how she had subordinated her "self" to her roles as mother and daughter. A sobbing laugh or laughing sob becomes more comprehensible in the context of such tensions.

Back in the Philippines, in the presence of her family, she continued to exchange with pledges of love and longing on the telephone with Larry, repeating "I love you" or "I miss you" with a clear expression of weariness, preceded and followed by urgent requests for money. Her loathing for Larry seemed to grow with the vehemence of her complaints about him in front of her family, who approved of this marriage despite their rejection of Jamie. Mary made no attempt to hide the fact that she was marrying Larry as a sacrifice for the family.

"I don't know. Maybe *I will learn to love him*. I will try" (emphasis added). This was probably the most positive statement Mary made about her marriage plans with Larry. I was intrigued by Mary's idea of "learning" to love, which contrasted sharply with her belief in romantic love—like the love she had for Jamie that could not be explained. Listening together to Bryan Adams's "(Everything I do) I do it for you" in a karaoke in Olongapo, out of a compelling skepticism about romantic love rather than any urge to persuade, I said to Mary while her eyes were transfixed on the screen,

> Author: Don't believe this.
> M: What?
> A: That someone would die for you because of love.
> M: Why?
> A: Do you think someone would really do that?
> M: [Removed her gaze from the screen and turned to me] Yes. I will! [Pause. She relaxed her straightened back and collapsed against the sofa, her gaze returned to the screen as the song was coming to an end.] But I don't know if Jamie will.

Fenella Cannell (1998) has also found this distinction between "true love" and "learnt love" among the lowland Filipino women in Bicol. The phrase "only learnt love" is used to emphasize one's reservations about being joined with a spouse and one's reluctant obedience to the family. This "narrative of reluctance" constructs the value and power of the woman over her family and her spouse by turning herself into a "forced gift": "However great the degree of compulsion, and however powerful the notion that children owe obedience to their parents, the acts of obedience themselves obligate others, compelling recognition, a kind of return gift" (Cannell 1998:46). Mary's marriage plan should not be considered merely as an act of female self-abnegation for the family. She was operating in a gender system in which she recognized her opportunities and constraints as a woman and proceeded to construct her value as such.

Larry did visit Mary in the Philippines and stayed with her family for 20 days in May 2000. He left and continued to apply for Mary to join him in Korea as a fiancée. But five months later, he stopped sending her money after learning from other Filipinas that Mary cheated on him. Mary was suddenly flung into despondence with the departure of Larry. But her last words to Larry were, "I never loved you. I just wanted your money. And you've given me so much money, but I never slept with you. So who's the loser, eh?"

The narrative of reluctance with Larry over sex together with this ultimate denial of love had allowed Mary to claim her triumph over him when the marriage plan fell through. She refused to be the victim. It did not mean, however, that her conditions of subordination were altered. Prospects for alleviating her family burden were smashed along with the wedding bells.

Love as Weapon of the Weak

Helen found it amusing to list the multiple functions of her GI "boyfriends": "They do your laundry [on the base], they buy you phone cards, buy you food, take you out, buy you drinks and gifts. And they give you money!" Yet often their support could be mobilized only within an illusion of intimacy and sexual possibility. When asked if she felt that she was "playing" the GIs, Helen answered adamantly, "Yes. Because our owner is using us, so we are using them [the GIs] too. Our owner is making money with us, so we have to use them to make money too."

Among many of the Filipinas, there was a poignant awareness that the club owners and managers are exploiting them. They are also keenly aware of the power differentials between their American male customers and themselves, and between the United States and the Philippines. They are the "have-nots" in each of these relations. Such awareness is the basis for their emotional manipulation of their GI customers. In other words, their oppression becomes a source of their power. The awareness of their own subordination allowed the Filipinas to see their emotional manipulation of the GIs as a compensation for their powerlessness.

James Scott (1987) coined the phrase "weapon of the weak" out of his study of Malaysian peasants to describe how class struggle can take place on an everyday level, and how the poor refuse to accept the terms of their subordination. Erik Cohen argues that Thai women working in tourist-oriented bars are skilled in manipulating the ambiguity in their relationships with foreign men to assume a position of dominance, a capacity he calls "the power of the weak" (1986:124).

Love serves as a "weapon of the weak" for these Filipinas who draw on the symbols and rhetoric of love as a moral framework to negotiate their subordination and pursue their projects of aspiration. As migrant sex workers who have no official channels of redress for the human rights violations that take place daily in the club, they focus their energies on turning love into a source of power. In other words, where the state and the market fail them, love gives them hope.

Conclusion

Many Filipino women promised themselves that they would not get emotionally in-volved in Korea—they went to make money and as such should use their brains and not their hearts. Yet almost all of them leave Korea with tales of forsaken love. Most GIs have heard about the cheap sex available in Korea before they arrive, but many of them will spend months of time and salary looking for "love" in the clubs. For the Filipinas, poverty and the lack of opportunities at home have made working overseas a kind of privilege. While Korean women have turned away from gijichon and GIs, Filipino women continue to entertain visions of the United States as a land of op-portunities and riches where personal and familial dreams may come true. Attraction to GIs can hardly be separated from a more deep-rooted admiration for the country these men belong to and symbolize. The GIs are, in relation to the Filipinas, in a rare position to take as well as give. The amount of attention and sense of power as a man and as an American they can enjoy in these foreign towns far exceeds what can be found at home. "They are after just one thing," GIs and Filipinas frequently accuse each other: To the men, the women are interested only in money; to the women, the men want only sex. Yet human desires are rarely as simple and straightforward as that. Through their common desires for recognition, affection, and intimacy, Fili-pinas and GIs negotiate their own aspirations and longing with and through each other. But as Anna Tsing reminds us: "The kiss crosses cultures, proving mutual rec-ognition. Yet mutual is not symmetrical" (1993:213). The asymmetry, however, does not prevent the Dayak women Tsing studied from claiming control, knowledge and status in their stories of "alien romance." These stories also serve as a critical com-mentary on gender and regional hierarchies. Read in the larger political economy, they challenge the feminization of Asia and the exoticization of Asian women that have been part of conventional Western knowledge (Tsing 1993:213–229). Simi-larly, the love stories of Filipina entertainers that cross national and ethnic borders also defy the analytic boundaries of a culture (Rosaldo 1989). By making the choice to migrate, they have landed themselves in the "borderlands." For the Filipinas, giji-chon is the "borderland" between the Philippines and the United States, between the past and the future, between familial responsibilities and personal freedom, between uncertainty and security, and between accepting one's weakness and transforming it within the current order of things. Their agency must be recognized without neglect-ing the constraints of power and knowledge. Their creative projects of self-definition in their "labor of love" are but an expression of their awareness of the multiple pos-sibilities in this marginal space and time.

As this chapter points out, on a structural level, the club is the venue where female company and bodies are accessible either visually or physically at a price. This idea is built into the R&R industry in the Asia Pacific, where the masculine desires of American soldiers are entertained by Asian women. On the level of erotic economy, underlying this commercial exchange is the mutual participation in the romantic parable of discovery and conquest of the American (white) explorer who is rewarded with an alien lover, submissive and devoted. The projection of Western men's erotic and romantic fantasies onto the Asian women reached a peak with the stationing of U.S. troops in the Pacific.[20] The sexy docility in the Western image of Asian woman is further reproduced through sex tourism and mail-order bride brochures and websites.[21] On the level of everyday life, the commodification of intimacy and sexuality in the clubs threatens to undermine the personhood and individuality of the Filipinas as well as the GIs. "Love" and "marriage" become platforms for individuals' search for assurances and stability at a site strongly marked by the stigma of prostitution and personal vulnerabilities. "Love" personalizes the commercial exchange in the clubs with its claims of "authenticity," making it more acceptable to the parties involved, but also impacts on the subjective experiences of the individuals (Frank 1998; Rebhun 1999).

Notions of intimacy and love are commonly considered to be elusive at best if not downright irrelevant in the sex industry (Barry 1984, 1995; Brown 2000; O'Connell-Davidson 1998). The divergent forms that have developed in the industry make any generalization about relationships between service providers and their clients difficult. This chapter suggests that in understanding the sex industry, we need to recognize the actors as "persons"—rather than enclose them in their institutional identities as "punter," "GI," "prostitutes" and "trafficked women"—for that is how they understand themselves and on that premise engage in social interactions. It is only in such light that we can have a more nuanced understanding of identity, power, difference, and desires.

Notes

1. For example, the Fox News I-Team Report "U.S. Military Supported Sex Trafficking," broadcast in March 2002 led a group of Congress members to demand that the U.S. Department of Defense investigate and take drastic actions on the problem. The article "Filipinas in Prostitution around U.S. Military Bases in Korea: A Recurring Nightmare" by Jean Enriquez (2000) of Coalition Against Trafficking in Women-Asia Pacific is circulated globally and cited by a variety of reports on the trafficking of Filipina into U.S. military camp towns (see *www.catwinternational.org*). Two Korean organizations have produced reports that describe these Filipinas as "victims of trafficking" and at least partly hold the U.S. military responsible. See KCWU 1999; Saewoomtuh 2000.
2. Rather than examining GIs as persons, the media have often exclusively identified them as drunk and rowdy "clients"—as in the documentary *Camp Arirang* (1995), directed by Diana S. Lee and Grance Yoon Kyung Lee, for the Fox News report in March 2002.
3. Moon 1997 demonstrates how R&R facilities in Korea have been maintained and operated under the continuous negotiations between the U.S. and Korean governments.
4. For discussion of the relationships between runaway Filipinas who became "wives" to GIs in military camp towns, see Yea 2004.
5. The appeal of Russian women is less prevalent and seems to lie with younger GIs rather than the older and more senior ones. One 37-year-old GI explained to me, "We don't like the Russians. We were brought up that way." His words show how cold war politics has shaped individual desires.
6. In Korea, references to GIs among female activists rarely deviate from the paradigm of criminals and sex maniacs, "Because they frequently commit crimes against Koreans, the U.S. solders [sic] are also viewed as beasts who cannot control their sexual urges, as sexual

perverts who stagger around from abuse of recreational drugs and alcohol, or men who perceive women only as potential sex partners" (KCWU 1996:15). See also a campaign against U.S. military prostitution in the Philippines on the website of PREDA Foundation, *www. preda.org/navyback.htm.*

7. "GI" (government issue) was stamped on cartons of supplies sent out by the U.S. government during the World War II. The American soldier further made fame in the Korean War. In 1951, "GI Joe" was Man of the Year in *Time* magazine (January 1, 1951), praised for his valiant defense against communism. Though officially excised by the army as an unfavorable characterization, "GI" has continued to be widely used in American society and the media.

8. The job of an enlistee is generally comparable to a civilian job not requiring college education. We should determine the "social and economic marginality" of GIs on this basis. DMDC /1996 statistics for fiscal year 1996 show that out of 373,473 applications, there were 179,133 accessions (48 percent); 89 percent of these enlistees were between the age of 18 and 24. The same report also shows that enlisted men actually have a significantly higher proportion of high school graduates or equivalent compared to civilians in similar age range.

9. The situation improved only with major government initiatives to enhance recruiting programs and substantially increase pay and benefits (DMDC 1997).

10. In September 2000, there were only 5,798 command-sponsored dependents in Korea with a military strength of 36,565. In Japan, there were 40,188 command-sponsored dependents with a military strength of 40,189 (U.S. Department of Defense 2000).

11. For example, in the Fox News report in March 2002, a reporter went undercover as someone interested in buying sex and spoke with off-duty GIs in the club areas. The report portrayed these GIs bragging about their sexual ventures and knowledge in the clubs.

12. The ratio of women increased from 30 percent in 1975 to 51 percent in 1991 and 60 percent in 1994 (Gonzalez 1998).

13. In Anne Allison's (1994) study of a Tokyo hostess club, she points out how the packaging of women serves as a currency to flatter and build the male image for corporate executives and, as such, a woman functions as a status symbol. Woman and status are not as clearly related in the relatively egalitarian model of gijichon clubs, which have similar prices for drinks and bar fines. In this context, the man becomes the status symbol. A GI's rank and resources have important bearing on his appeal in the clubs. Entertainers are highly aware that sergeants make better customers than privates because of their higher income.

14. In the club Allison studied, the official club line does not allow liaisons between customers and hostesses. If a liaison occurs, the woman must leave her job in the club (1994:75).

15. "The figure of "I love you" refers not to the declaration of love, to the avowal, but to the repeated utterance of the love cry" (Barthes 1978:67).

16. Allison describes the flirtations between the Japanese corporate patrons of the hostess club she studied and the hostesses as a "romantic exercise" rather than a sexual or emotional one. In the words of a customer whom she interviewed, "If he still wants sex, there are places to go for that, too" (1994:127–128).

17. Roy's and Justin's comparison of "non-feminine" American woman and the "ultra-feminine" Asian women who are simultaneously "sexually aggressive" is similar to the rhetoric of sex tourists that O'Connell-Davidson studied in the Dominican Republic. She argues that these are men who try to reclaim the "natural" male rights they have lost in the extension of universal rights to women and persons of color and are "sexually hostile men" (2001:6). Key to O'Connell-Davidson's understanding of these men's patronage of sex tourism is the eroticized reclamation of male rights in the sex industry generated by global inequalities (13). The possibility that pleasure could be derived otherwise, such as from the woman's recognition of oneself as a unique individual worthy of affection, is not recognized.

18. Roy's return was important to the whole story, whether it was fabricated or not. I have no

way to find out the woman's motive. Roy was leaving Korea soon after he met this woman, and his departure prevented any further development in their relationship. I could only guess that because of his age, Roy looked like a high-ranking sergeant and thus potentially a good customer. The possibility of "love-at-first-sight" aside, the woman might have provided the "freebies" in the Maussian tradition of the gift that would bind Roy into a relationship of patronage. If the story or the detail was fabricated, it would still support my argument on the importance of self-affirmation for Roy in the sexual encounter.

19. When we first met she told me she had only one child. Six months later, she told me she had lied, and that she actually had three children. She did not want other people to know that she had so many children, worried that it might put some customers off. I interpreted the revelation as a sign of her growing trust of me.

20. Musical productions like *Madame Butterfly*, *Miss Saigon*, and *South Pacific* are but one of the many representations of this exotica.

21. We have been reminded, however, that such images of Asian women rarely go unchallenged by the "alien lovers" themselves; see Cohen 1982,1986; Odzer 1992; Tsing 1994; Constable 2003.

References

Abu-Lughod, Lila, and Catherine Lutz
  1990   Language and the Politics of Emotion. Cambridge: Maison des Sciences de l'Homme and University of Cambridge Press.
Allison, Anne
  1994   Nightwork: Sexuality, Pleasure, and Corporate Masculinity in a Tokyo Hostess Club. Chicago: University of Chicago Press.
Anzaldua, Gloria
  1987   Borderlands/La Frontera: The New Mestiza. San Francisco: Spinsters/Aunt Lute.
Barry, Kathleen
  1984   Female Sexual Slavery. Englewood Cliffs, NJ: Prentice-Hall.
  1995   The Prostitution of Sexuality. New York: New York University Press.
Barthes, Roland
  1978   A Lover's Discourse: Fragments. New York: Penguin Books.
Bickford, Andrew
  2003   See the World, Meet Interesting People, Have Sex with Them: Tourism, Sex, and Recruitment in the U.S. Military. American Sexuality Magazine 1(5). Electronic document, *http://nsrc.sfsu.edu/HTMLArticle.cfm?Article=113&PageID=8&SID=E4F9C1 566920220006B04542679162F4, accessed May 4, 2005.*
Brown, Louise
  2000   Sex Slaves: The Trafficking of Women in Asia. London: Virago.
Bureau of Labor and Employment Statisics, Department of Labor and Employment, Manila, Philippines (BLES)
  2006   LABSTAT Updates, October, 2006. Vol. 10, No. 26. Electronic document, *www.bles. dole.gov.ph/download/vol10_26.pdf*, accessed August 1, 2007.
Cannell, Fenella
  1998   Power and Intimacy in the Christian Philippines. New York: Cambridge University Press.
Cohen, Erik
  1982   Thai Girls and Farang Men: The Edge of Ambiguity. Annals of Tourism Research 9(3):403–428.

1986   Lovelorn Farangs: The Correspondence between Foreign Men and Thai Girls. Anthropological Quarterly 59:115–127.

Commission on Filipinos Overseas
    2002   Handbook for Filipinos Overseas. 6th edition. Manila, Philippines: Commission on Filipinos Overseas.

Constable, Nicole
    2003   Romance on a Global Stage: Pen Pals, Virtual Ethnography, and "Mail Order" Marriages. Berkeley: University of California Press.

Cummings, Bruce
    1992   Silent But Deadly: Sexual Subordination in the Korean Relationship. *In* Let the Good Times Roll. S. P. Sturdevant and B. Stoltzfus, eds. Pp. 169–175. New York: New Press.

U.S. Department of Defense,
    2007   Inspector General Report on Force Structure Changes in the U.S. Pacific Command— Roles and Responsibilities of Headquarters and Support Functions. US Department of Defense.

Defense Manpower Data Center (DMDC)
    1996   Active Duty Workforce Profile. March 31. Electronic document, http://cs.itc.dod.mil/files/content/ALLPublic/Workspaces/, accessed May 4, 2001.
    1997   Active Duty Workforce Profile. March 31. Electronic document, http://cs.itc.dod.mil/files/content/ALLPublic/Workspaces/, accessed May 4, 2001.

Enloe, Cynthia H.
    1983   Does Khaki Become You? The Militarisation of Women's Lives. London: Pluto Press.
    1989   Bananas, Beaches and Bases: Making Feminist Sense of International Politics. London: Pandora.
    2000   Maneuvers: The International Politics of Militarizing Women's Lives. Berkeley: University of California Press.

Enriquez, Jean
    2000   Filipinas in Prostitution around U.S. Military Bases in Korea: A Recurring Nightmare. Electronic document, *www.catw-ap.org/filipinas.htm*, accessed August 1, 2007.

Frank, Katherine
    1998   The Production of Identity and the Negotiation of Intimacy in a "Gentleman's Club." Sexualities 1:175–201.

Goffman, Erving
    1959   The Presentation of Self in Everyday Life. New York: Anchor Books.

Gonzalez, Joaquin Lacero
    1998   Philippine Labour Migration: Critical Dimensions of Public Policy. Singapore, Institute of Southeast Asian Studies.

Harrison, Deborah
    2003   Violence in the Military Community. *In* Military Masculinities: Identity and the State. Paul R. Higate, ed. Pp. 71–90. Westport, CT: Praeger.

Higate, Paul
    2003   Revealing the Soldier: Peacekeeping and Prostitution. American Sexuality Magazine, vol. 1. Electronic document, http://nsrc.sfsu.edu/HTMLArticle.cfm?Article=111&PageID=8&SID=61735F7D6C566894E5598052FCABBC85, accessed May 4, 2007.

Hoigard, Cecilie, and Liv Finstad
    1986   Backstreets: Prostitution, Money and Love. State College: Pennsylvania State University Press.

Jeffreys, Sheila
    1997   The Idea of Prostitution. North Melbourne, Vic., Australia: Spinifex.

Korea Church Women United Counselling Center for Migrant Women Workers (KCWU)
   1999   Fieldwork Report on Trafficked Women in Korea. Seoul: Korea Church Women
          United.
MacCannell, Dean
   1973   Staged Authenticity: Arrangements of Social Space in Tourist Settings. American
          Journal of Sociology 79:589–603.
Montgomery, Heather
   1996   Public Vice and Private Virtue: Child Prostitution in Pattaya, Thailand. PhD
          dissertation, Department of Anthropology, Cambridge University.
Moon, Katharine H. S.
   1997   Sex among Allies: Military Prostitution in U.S.-Korea Relations. New York: Columbia
          University Press.
O'Connell-Davidson, Julia
   1998   Prostitution, Power and Freedom. Ann Arbor: University of Michigan Press.
   2001   The Sex Tourist, the Expatriate, His Ex-Wife and Her "Other": The Politics of Loss,
          Difference and Desire. Sexualities 4:5–24.
Odzer, Cleo
   1994   Patpong Sisters: An American Woman's View of the Bangkok Sex World. New York:
          Blue Moon Books, Arcade Publishing. Distributed by Little, Brown, and Co.
Philippine Overseas Employment Administration (POEA)
   2006   OFW Global Presence: A Compendium of Overseas Employment Statistics.
Phelan, Peggy
   1993   Unmarked: The Politics of Performance. New York: Routledge.
Rebhun, L. A.
   1999   The Heart Is Unknown Country: Love in the Changing Economy of Northeast Brazil.
          Stanford: Stanford University Press.
Rosaldo, Renato
   1989   Culture and Truth: The Remaking of Social Analysis. Boston: Beacon.
Saewoomtuh
   2000   Recruitment of Foreign Women into S. Korea's Sex Industry: A Focus on Filipino
          Women. In Proceedings for the international conference Redefining Security. Okinawa.
Scott, James
   1987   Weapons of the Weak: Everyday Forms of Peasant Resistance. New Haven: Yale
          University Press.
Sturdevant, Saundra Pollock, and Brenda Stoltzfus
   1993   Let the Good Times Roll: Prostitution and the U.S. Military in Asia. 1st edition. New
          York: New Press, Distributed by Norton.
Tsing, Anna Lowenhaupt
   1993   In the Realm of the Diamond Queen: Marginality in an Out-of-the-Way Place.
          Princeton: Princeton University Press.
U.S. Department of Defense
   2000   Worldwide Manpower Distribution by Geographical Area. Washington: Department of
          Defense.
Yan, Yunxiang
   1996   Flow of Gifts: Reciprocity and Social Networks in a Chinese Village. Stanford:
          Stanford University Press.
Yea, Sallie
   2004   Runaway Brides: Anxieties of Identity among Trafficked Filipina Entertainers in South
          Korea. Singaporean Journal of Tropical Geography 25(2):180–197.

12

Love at First Site?
Visual Images and Virtual Encounters with Bodies

Nicole Constable

This chapter takes the conceptual pairing of love and globalization as a point of departure for exploring some of the ways in which new global technologies—such as the Internet—are linked to intimate experiences of everyday life. Whereas globalization is commonly equated with large-scale, unidirectional, homogenizing economic, political, and cultural processes, it has also drawn anthropological attention to its more subtle and localized and multidirectional cultural flows, disjunctures, fragmentation, and flexibility (Appadurai 1996; Ong 1999). Love, in contrast, brings to mind emotions, feelings, or experiences that may be romantic, conjugal, or platonic but are often thought of as private, personal, and intimate. A vast scholarly literature debates the origins, forms, and historical and geographical flows of the concept of love (e.g., Ahearn 2001; Giddens 1992; Jankowiak 1995; Rebhun 1999). Whereas it might be argued that anthropologists have been slow to consider the connections between love and globalization, the conjoined topics are often alluded to in other guises. The rapidly growing body of scholarship on contemporary patterns of gendered migration and mobility—of nannies, nurses, spouses, sex tourists, and sex workers—points to the multiple connections between globalization and the production, commodification, and consumption of caring and of sexual, domestic, emotional, and conjugal intimacies of various sorts (e.g., Brennan 2004, Choy 2003, Constable 1997, 2003, 2005; Ehrenreich and Hochschild 2003; Parrenas 2001). Such studies point to the intimacies of mobility and migration and to the connection between globalization and love in the broader sense.

The Internet fuels and facilitates growing opportunities for intimate social relationships that reach well beyond familiar localized terrains. Whereas some scholars point to the "positive effects of networks and their benefits for democracy and prosperity," others see "a darker outcome in which individuals are trapped and ensnared in a 'net' that predominantly offers new opportunities for surveillance and social control" (Kollock and Smith 1999:4), or identify ways in which the Internet's immediacy and speed "do not lead to great community and friendship" but to "bitter misunderstandings" (Inayatullah and Milojevic 1999:77). Among men and women who seek to meet marriage partners from geographically distant parts of the world, the Internet has become both an indispensable tool in establishing new relationships and a new context in which tensions and misunderstandings occur. Conjugal unions are the stated goal of those who seek marriage partners on-line, but "love" is a more complicated matter. Conjugal and romantic love between spouses is commonly viewed by U.S. men who seek foreign spouses through the Internet as an anticipated outcome and a necessary ingredient of marriage. However, as I have argued elsewhere (Constable 2003:chap. 5), love can be understood differently, as something that is optional or acquired through time, by their prospective spouses.

In this chapter, rather than focus narrowly on Western notions of romantic or conjugal love, I consider a broader range of global intimacies that are linked to the search for marriage partners. This includes conjugal love in the narrower sense but also ideas about bodily attraction and sexuality. I ask how bodies and sexual/emotional/marital relations are established, understood, and expressed on the Internet and how this relates to or differs from other contexts of the so-called real world. My main focus is on the relevance of bodies as images and bodies as matter in the virtual world and in the real world.

This chapter draws from research I conducted from 1998 to 2002 among Chinese women, Filipinas, and U.S. men who sought marriage partners through correspondence. The research was conducted on-line in virtual spaces of the Internet, and in "real life" (IRL) as I interviewed and met women and men in China, the Philippines, and the United States. In the course of the research I met face-to-face with dozens of women and men who were involved in correspondence relationships, and I met and communicated on-line with hundreds more. Initially I wrote to about 40 Filipinas and 40 Chinese women whose names were listed by Internet introduction agencies. I introduced myself as a woman researcher who sought to understand women and men's reasons for trying to meet foreign marriage partners and their experiences. I subsequently met many of these women in Beijing, Shenzhen, Manila, Cebu, and Butuan, and they introduced me to others they knew who were also involved in correspondence relationships. My relationship with several of these women continued over several years on-line and in person. As a researcher, I gained permission to join four private Internet lists for men who had or who sought Chinese or Filipina fiancées or wives. I got to know about 30 men through repeated private Internet communications and met about 20 men in person (Constable 2003: chap. 2).

My wider project was an ethnographic critique of academic studies, popular media images, and antitrafficking representations of "mail-order" brides, catalogues, and marriages that depict foreign women as commodities who—desperate for opportunities that are unavailable in their impoverished homelands—are said to "sell" themselves to first world men who seek to "buy" wives. Whereas women are commonly, stereotypically, and simplistically depicted as either innocent victims of trafficking or as hyper-agents who are desperate to come to the West, men are—in equally simplistic terms—commonly depicted as losers in the U.S. marriage market who seek submissive foreign women as maids, sex partners, or obedient wives. Although there may be elements of truth in such stereotypes, too often they are based on limited knowledge of failed and abusive relationships that have caught the eye of activists and the popular media. Critics of mail-order marriages can be faulted for reproducing simplistic images and caricatures, and for paying too little attention to women's and men's actual experiences, choices, and desires. Moreover, they often overlook the ways in which political economy and power are intertwined with cultural constructions of pleasure, love, and desire (Constable 2003).

This chapter draws from Appadurai's ideas about the global cultural economy as a "complex, overlapping, disjunctive order" involving new cultural landscapes of people, ideas, images, technology, and capital—or what he calls ethnoscapes, ideoscapes, mediascapes, technoscapes, and financescapes—that serve as building blocks for newly imagined worlds (1996:32–33). Internet-mediated global marriage-scapes involve fluid interconnections between people, technology, and images that allow women and men from geographically distant regions of the world to imagine and seek out new global experiences and relationships. Cyberspace offers new imaginings and new opportunities for escape from local marital constraints, yet the options have limits and the possibilities are not equally available to all.

Cyberspace is an arena that reflects and reproduces certain preexisting global inequalities and social realities. I largely agree with the observation that, "despite the hype of cyberspace as 'unmarked' territory, we are nonetheless mapping this frontier with the same categories of distinction that we have used to map modern reality" (O'Brien 1999:88). In contrast to the notion that bodies are invisible, absent, or immaterial in the virtual world, offering endless utopian possibilities, research on correspondence courtship and marriage suggests that bodies are very much present in cyberspace and that they most often continue to be imagined in highly conventional racial and gendered terms. Moreover, unlike MUDs (multi-user domains) that may assume fantasy lives that are self-contained within Internet-defined fantasy spaces (Featherstone and Burrows 1995; Kollock and Smith 1999:7), correspondence relationships are usually premised on the assumption that virtual experiences and real life can intersect. Too much doubt placed on the expectation that represented and imagined bodies in cyberspace correspond to bodies in real life becomes the basis for ending the correspondence. Thus I argue against interpretations of the Internet as overly liberatory and disembodied, yet at the same time I do not want to create the impression that on-line embodiment is overly fixed or predetermined or that it does not allow for new sorts of imaginative possibilities.

In the first section of this chapter, I briefly consider the growing role of the Internet in the United States and the global business of romance, and I question the notion of the Internet as a utopian and democratic medium. I then go on to describe and analyze an array of on-line encounters with bodies, faces, or body images that appear in various arenas of virtual space and at various stages of the correspondence process. I consider particular disjunctures, as bodies and photographic images are presented, maneuvered, and (mis)read by women and men, and as women's and men's intimate imaginings, fantasies, and experiences conflict and differ across cyberspace and real life. Finally, I discuss the value and the risk of focusing narrowly on bodies and technology in the study of correspondence relationships. I consider how technologically mediated bodily images and global intimacies may expand the bounds of what is considered acceptable or appropriate off-line in "real life" but may also point to important structural and cultural difficulties in translating virtual bodily experiences and fantasies into actual relationships on the ground. Despite its increased inclusiveness, the growing opportunities it offers for various forms of pleasure, and the multiplicity of forums in which to express opposed voices, the "global technological democracy" continues nonetheless to work at some cross purposes with the desires of those who seek to create better lives for themselves in the real world.

Internet Technology and the Business of Romance

In and beyond the United States, Internet technology has fueled a boom in matchmaking, dating, and introduction services. New digital landscapes attract a growing number of domestic and international clients, women and men, gay and straight, and people of an ever-wider range of socioeconomic classes. Increasingly, for example, there exist services that are aimed at assisting single, wealthy, professional men and women in U.S. cities whose career tracks have not allowed them the time and opportunity to meet partners locally. Advertisements for such services (which include lunch dates, circular dinners, and 30-minute dates) can typically be found in airline and business magazines. Other types of matchmaking agencies specialize in arranging introductions between heterosexual expatriate men (less often women) with compatriots in China, India, or elsewhere, publicizing their services in foreign-language or expatriate newspapers. Another type of service, that which is most relevant here, specializes in introducing never-married or divorced U.S. men (or men from other Western or English-speaking countries) who are dissatisfied with Western or U.S. women and who generally seek more "traditional" wives with "old-fashioned" family values" from other regions of the world, particularly Asia, Eastern Europe and the former Soviet Union, and Latin America (see *www.goodwife.com*).

By the mid 1990s the technology aimed at introducing U.S. men to prospective foreign partners had changed radically. Whereas printed catalogues ("mail-order catalogues") that were delivered by postal service were the main communiqué of the 1980s are still available for subscription today, they were quickly superseded in popularity by Internet-based agencies and websites. In mid March 1998 Robert Scholes (1999) located 153 international introduction services on *www.goodwife.com*; by August 2000 I located 350 (Constable 2005:170). These agencies, it should be noted, market themselves to "marriage-oriented" Western men who are seeking like-minded "life partners" from other regions of the world. They thus aim to distinguish themselves from sites associated with sex work, sex tourism, or escort services. Typically, the U.S. men range from so-called blue-collar working-class occupations to upper-middle-class professionals; the women span an even broader socioeconomic spectrum.

The Internet has fueled a boom in the possibilities for meeting people and developing platonic, romantic, and sexual relationships of various sorts, but does this make it the "technological global democracy" that some have envisioned? As I have discussed elsewhere (Constable 2003:60–61), the imagined Internet community of men and women involved in correspondence marriages and the wider community of observers, friends, compatriots, and kin may participate in various parts of the global ethnoscape and may even express themselves freely and sometimes anonymously. But they do not do so on equal terms. The moderators of certain chat groups, news-groups, and listservs often restrict membership. Filipinas, for example, are listed as prospective spouses by introduction agencies, and they may belong to an Internet list reserved for "wives" of U.S. men, but I found them to be virtually nonexistent among the participants in an Internet discussion about the ills and virtues of "mail-order brides" that included mainly men from the U.S. and the Philippines. Partici-pating on the Internet requires access to technology that is still available to only a fraction of the world's population. Even once such access is gained, specific Internet terrains reflect specific and restricted access to power. As Sara Keisler reminded us in the 1990s, "only a minority of U.S. families are connected to the Internet, and just a tiny percentage of the world's population has been on line even once" (1997:ix).

Nonetheless, because of the boom in numbers of Internet international mar-riage introduction businesses during the past decade, the opportunities for Chinese women, Filipinas, and women of various nationalities to be listed on introduction websites, and to participate on "friend finder" discussions have grown phenomenally. The listings of Western and non-Western men have also increased, as have, presum-ably, the number of members subscribing to receive such services. The sheer growth in number of participants, as well as the variety of "respectable" types of introduc-tion services available to members of the U.S. computer-literate elite or mainstream middle-class may eventually decrease the stigma that was once widely—and is still to some degree—associated with meeting a foreign partner through correspondence. What was once popularly seen as a desperate act of alienated and old-fashioned men who were unsuccessful at finding marriage partners on the local market, and that required subscriptions to catalogues delivered by mail in plain brown wrap-pers, can now be recast as part of a much more widespread, respectable, modern, high-tech, and even stylish solution for singles of various types and ages. That men (and women) today can privately peruse thousands of listings, that they need not pay or join to see the initial listings, that they can invisibly send their subscription payments with credit card numbers over the Internet makes it a more attractive and enticing opportunity than the cumbersome, time-consuming, and shrouded practice of sending off for printed catalogues by mail.

Over the past decade, the Internet has had a very immediate impact on Chinese women's opportunities to communicate with men from other countries.[1] For urban Chinese women in the people's Republic of China who have access to the Internet through school or work, and the growing few who have access through their own computers at home, meeting someone through the Internet is not entirely differ-ent from other means of introduction that have also become popular in the past two decades in urban areas. Agencies directed at introducing local urban men and women or introducing local women to overseas Chinese or foreign men are varia-tions on local approaches to matchmaking. In China, introduction agencies carry little of the stigma associated with the notion of "mail-order bride" agencies in the

United States, and unlike in the Philippines, the derogatory term "mail-order bride" was, as of 2003, yet unknown. Since China's "opening up" to the rest of the world—beginning in the early 1980s—Chinese women have gradually come to represent a small but growing percentage of non-Western women listed on Internet websites. International introduction agency offices located in China sometimes offer Chinese women clients access to e-mail, translation services, and options for sending and receiving messages through the office staff. When e-mail messages are received at a local office, the staff prints them out and notifies the clients by telephone.[2]

Linked to the colonial, military, and postcolonial relationship between the United States and the Philippines, Filipinas, until the last decade, have been by far the largest nationality represented in international introduction agency catalogue listings. More recently, as observations of introduction websites clearly show, listings of women from Eastern Europe and the former Soviet Union have been the fastest growing in number. Whereas the Internet has likely played a major role in attracting Chinese women to international Internet introductions and correspondence, by the late 1990s I met only a few Filipinas who had originally met their partners through the Internet. At that time, the vast majority had been listed in printed catalogues and had begun their correspondences through the postal service. Whereas Chinese women I met considered the Internet the preferred mode of communication, it played a less exclusive and significant role among Filipinas, many of whom still commonly exchanged letters by mail. In 1999 and 2000 I met many Filipinas who had not met their pen pals through the Internet but who later wrote to them from Internet cafes. Although the cost was low by U.S. standards, many still considered it prohibitively expensive. Some men sent their partners money to cover the fees. A few women had a foreign partner who paid to install telephone lines in their rural homes, and I knew of a few women in committed relationships whose fiancés had bought them computers so they could communicate regularly by e-mail while they tolerated long separations or awaited visas or emigration, but such cases were exceptional.[3]

Internet Bodies and Real Lives

Many older well-known writings about the Internet either ignore or deny the existence or the relevance of bodies in digital space. In Howard Rheingold's now classic book, for example, he describes his first encounters in real life (IRL) with members of his virtual community named the WELL. "It was one of the oddest sensations in my life. I had contended with these people, shot the invisible breeze around the invisible water cooler, shared alliances and formed bonds, fallen off my chair laughing with them, become livid with anger at some of them. But there wasn't a recognizable face in the house. I had never seen them before" (1993:2). Despite falling off his chair laughing and becoming livid with anger, Rheingold writes that "people in virtual communities do just about everything people do in real life, *but we leave our bodies behind. You can't kiss anybody, and nobody can punch you in the nose*" (1993:3; emphasis added).

Whereas Rhinegold seems unaware of how his own bodily reactions suggest that bodies are not simply left behind, and he seems to overlook the link between bodies and related social identities, many other authors have expressed optimism that new technologies would allow for a variety of postgendered possibilities, the stripping away of physical markers, an escape from mind/body or nature/culture dualism, and transcendence of the human body (Featherstone and Burrows 1995; Haraway 1991; Plant 1995). Other scholars, more recently, have observed a variety of ways in which identity markers such as race, gender, status, and age continue to carry great relevance on-line (Burkhalter 1999; Ebo 1998; O'Brien 1999; Wilson and Peterson 2002). O'Brien observes a certain "wishful thinking" in writing that suggests that cyberspace can be "a realm in which physical markers such as sex, race, age, body type and size will eventually lose salience as a basis for the evaluative categorization of self / other" or will "lose their cognitive-emotive grip" and that the mind will float "free of corporeal existence" (1999:77). With regard to gender identities, she argues—within the United States—that, far from becoming irrelevant on the web, where the opportunity exists for people to freely invent and explore new identities,   strict binary gender distinctions are more often reproduced on-line in very pronounced ways, even among those experimenting with on-line "cross dressing" where gendered divisions, she argues, become ever more binary and stereotypical rather than fluid and imaginative. She concludes that "whatever the bandwidth, whether it be the telephone or on-line text, when we interact with another with whom we do not have physical contact, we proceed as if they were embodied. . . . To do so we must conjure an image of them. Gender—based on a conventional male-female binary—is the primary dimension by which we do so" (100). Along a similar vein, in his study of race on-line, Byron Burkhalter found that in the absence of visual clues, words, attitudes, and beliefs are often used to infer racial identity and physical characteristics (1999).

Correspondence courtship—an extreme example to be sure—further illustrates some of the ways in which highly gendered and raced discourses are often expressed, presumed, accepted, and reproduced on-line, off-line, and in the intersecting spaces between the two. In the case of correspondence courtship, faces and bodies—and by extension the gender and racial/national identities assumed to accompany them—are often placed quite literally front and center and are therefore difficult to dismiss or to ignore. That is not to say that bodies are everything, or that on-line embodiment is fixed or cannot be manipulated, but that the existence of bodies within this context is rarely forgotten or overlooked. The most common first encounter at the Internet introduction website is between a man looking at his computer screen to find a partner and the small thumbnail photographs of women who are prospective pen pals. During the 1990s, these photographs of Filipinas and Chinese women were highly reminiscent of passport or school yearbook photographs, usually depicting a smiling frontal view of a woman's face and shoulders.[4] Over the past several years photographs have become larger and are complemented by a wider array of larger and often more glamorous photographs of women in various contexts and poses that are usually available after one has joined or subscribed to the agency's on-line introduction services. The thumbnail photographs, however, are most likely the first, the most immediate, and the best-known images encountered through introduction websites and catalogues, and they have received by far the greatest attention in critical studies of printed "mail-order bride" catalogues (e.g., Halualani 1995; Robinson 1996; Tolentino 1996; Tsing 1993; Villapando 1989; Wilson 1988).

There are a variety of other ways in which bodies and body images can be encountered in the course of cyberspace correspondence relationships. In his infamous on-line and printed guidebook for men who seek brides through the Internet, for example, Gary Clark advises men to think very carefully about the sort of woman they want to marry. He cautions them to think about whether they really want a wife who will make other men drool, or whether they prefer a woman who does not draw too much male attention. "Once you have the physical side of things handled, [then] you need to turn your attention to everything else" (1998:36). Clark alludes briefly to men's appearance before attending in far more detail to women's: "You [men] don't have to be rich, young, or thin to marry a foreign woman 20 or more years younger than yourself who is absolutely beautiful. It helps if you're not terribly ugly, but I've seen some amazing looking women married (and happily so) to some pretty un-amazing looking men" (34). He urges men to use a "visualization tool." He recommends that they collect photographs of women—ideally full-body or nude shots from men's magazines such as Playboy—and that they pin up the photograph of their ideal type where they will see it often, such as next to their computers so that they will recognize the right one when they see her. "After you've collected enough samples, sit down and sort through them very carefully. If you are honest with yourself, you'll find one picture that comes closer than any of the others in depicting the physical characteristics of the woman you want. These should be general characteristics; facial type, build type, hair, skin, and eye color, etc. If you prefer smaller breasts, don't use a picture of someone with double Ds" (35). Describing his own situation, he writes, "I used a fully nude poster of a beautiful Oriental woman and pinned it to the wall just above my computer monitor." Although he had no specific "oriental" nationality in mind to begin with, because he had this image next to his computer, he notes that "it's probably no accident that the woman I married is Chinese" (36).

The poster of a nude Asian woman who embodied the characteristics he sought in prospective partners, hung just above his computer monitor so he could look at it and imagine the women he corresponded with, vividly illustrates the importance of gender and race as marked on real bodies imagined across cyberspace. Yet Clark's detailed focus on race and body types (and my selective focus on this aspect of his work) may risk overemphasizing the importance of appearance within the wider process of correspondence courtships. Although race or nationality is clearly linked in many men's minds with desired notions of femininity, many of the men I encountered on-line and off-line also made a concerted effort to downplay the importance of the body, or at least to hold off on the final judgment about "chemistry" until after a sense of rapport and compatibility had been established. That is not to say that they would write to women whose photographs they found unattractive, but none admitted to adopting Clark's approach, and some initiated correspondence with women who had not posted photographs at all or who they considered less attractive.

Simon,[5] a 50-year-old U.S. investment banker who married a 43-year-old Chinese high school teacher, was one of many men I got to know on-line who said that he sought to meet partners through Internet introduction and correspondence at least in part because that method would allow him to focus first and foremost on a woman's personality and character. As Simon explained, "I wouldn't marry someone I couldn't love. . . . This time around I wanted to do my first 'screening' based on the practical aspects of a long term relationship" (Constable 2003:127). He was interested in Chinese women, he explained, because of what he saw as the "old fashioned feminine characteristics," such as devotion to family, softness, kindness, and virtue, that they use to describe themselves on-line. He wrote to several women whose postings had caught his attention, including one woman who was "older and not as gorgeous as the rest, but whose face had a lot of character." Her photograph was "not-so-hot" but once they got into Internet correspondence, "the relationship took off." In person, she "bowled" him over and they "jelled right away."

Kevin is another U.S. man now married to a Chinese woman. He sought to meet someone through correspondence so that he would have the opportunity to build the relationship on a foundation of practical compatibility. As Kevin explained to me in an e-mail message, he had "been married before under the guise of Love. Both [marriages] fell apart because of our strong physical attraction instead of [concern for] the deeper person." Like Simon, he aimed to find a partner he found physically attractive, but he made a conscious attempt to give priority to other considerations.

Yet even in the absence of photographs, or with an emphasis on personality and compatibility, gender and race/nationality cannot be dismissed. They are among the first things a man believes that he "knows" about a prospective partner before he initiates any communication, and they are most often assumed to be connected, as in Simon's conflation of Chinese women, with certain feminine characteristics. Whereas Simon's statements about Chinese women can be understood as linked to essentialized cultural assumptions about traditional or learned feminine qualities, other men's statements suggested more racially based—innate or biological—assumptions about "Asian," "Oriental," or Chinese femininity. Occasionally Internet correspondences forced men and women to reconsider their naïve or stereotypical assumptions about race/nationality and gender. This reconsideration occurs, for example, when a woman expresses herself more assertively than is expected of an "Asian woman," or when a man reacts in ways that call into question women's assumptions about the open-mindedness and modernity of "Western men."

Internet Deception

Despite recent suggestions that people may be more truthful on-line than off (Thompson 2004),[6] Internet deception is always a possibility, and Internet relationships and romances are no exception (Donath 1999; Van Gelder 1996). In this regard, the electronically mediated situation is not entirely different from its earlier incarnation of postal correspondence. Contemporary tales of photographs and mis-leading images circulated on-line are strikingly reminiscent of the tales of early 20th-century Korean and Japanese picture brides who had seen a handsome but distant young fiancé's photograph, only to discover upon arrival in the United States and meeting her aged spouse that the photograph had been taken decades earlier. A con-temporary item of folklore that circulates on this topic among both U.S. men and Chinese women involved in correspondence relationships is of the prospective part-ner who sends a deceptive photograph—perhaps that of a fashion model scanned from a magazine—instead of his or her real self. At the arranged meeting time at the airport, expecting a dashing model-like partner, the man or woman walk on by and refuse to meet.

One very famous U.S. case of Internet deception in the mid 1980s, was that of Joan, a supposedly disabled woman, who was in fact a male New York psychothera-pist named Alex (Van Gelder 1996). This case, first written about in *Ms.* magazine in 1985, has been much commented on. Rheingold describes the sense of outrage that followed the revelation of Joan's identity among the women of the group who had developed an intimate on-line friendship with her (1993:165). Again, Rheingold mentions little or nothing of bodies in real life, and he uses this example to illus-trate the point that there is "no shield for deceit" in the Internet community (165). O'Brien, in contrast, highly attuned to gendered bodies and sexuality, points to a number of factors that help explain some of the women's sense of betrayal, and their feeling that they were victims of "ultimate deceit" and "mind rape." As she explains, Alex and Joan "were the hub of an intense on-line community of on-line friends and lovers" (1999:88). Although no one had met Joan in person reportedly because of her severe physical disabilities, she had on-line affairs with women and also was the confidante of women who were intimately involved with Alex in real life. "Alex often flew the women that he met on-line to New York for weekend frolics in the real flesh. Inevitably, these women, who were usually friends of Joan, would go on-line with her and share the details of their IRL encounters with Alex" (88). Whereas Rheingold plays down the existence of real bodies relationships in the Joan/Alex story, O'Brien highlights how they are interconnected with real-life actions and with assumed gendered bodies and identities (see also Stone 1995).

The Joan/Alex story, like the following Internet encounter between a Chinese woman and a man she referred to as a "sex man," illustrates conflicts between fic-tional/fantasy identities and desires in cyberspace and identities and expectations that are more closely linked to expectations in the real world. The examples that follow point to collisions, confrontations, and intersections between on-line and off-line fantasies, desires, and spaces, but it is important to stress that they do not point to rigid dichotomies between on-line and off-line, so-called real and virtual spaces (Wilson and Peterson 2002:456).

A divorced Chinese woman in her forties who I met in Beijing explained that she had hoped to meet a marriageable Western man. She described her shock and embarrassment soon after joining a (free) international friend-finder group when she received an e-mail letter from a "sex man."[7] She was appalled because the man wrote "all about his sexual desires in his first letter." She was upset but also intrigued. Rather than ignore him, she wrote back to "tell him off" and to explain that this was no way to meet a partner or to begin a relationship. She then engaged in an e-mail exchange with him for several days—perhaps in an effort to reform him or out of curiosity and intrigue—before she finally gave up. It is important to note that, as she explained, in real life she would not have "felt safe" with this (presumed) Western man, who did nothing but write of his sexual fantasies and desires, and she would certainly never have agreed to meet him in person, but on the Internet she felt it was different. Without the Internet, such an interaction could not have occurred. Especially interesting about this example is the way in which the man's and the woman's objectives clash but momentarily intersect: whereas she approached the Internet as a way to pursue a possible long-term relationship in real life, he seemed to approach it (at least in part) as a context within which to live out his sexual fantasies with Chinese women. This example, like others that follow, reflect a diversity of expectations and interpretations that exist in relation to the circulation of embodied and disembodied selves.

The story of Lu, another Chinese woman who sought a foreign marriage partner, points to a more subtle and cross-culturally complex example of technologically enhanced bodies, cultural misunderstandings, and what I have interpreted as an unintended deception. In 1999 Lu was in her late forties and had a white-collar job in a Beijing geological firm. I first spotted her listing on kiss.com, a marriage-oriented Internet introduction service. I had been struck by her listing because her age was posted as 48, but her photograph depicted a very attractive, young, sexy woman with a guitar whom I would have guessed to be in her early twenties. The woman looked to me like a music star and the photograph like a music CD cover. I wrote to Lu, but she did not write back. It was therefore a great coincidence when Lu's coworker Moira, to whom I had also written and who had agreed to meet me in Beijing, introduced me to Lu. Moira—who had not posted her photograph but was represented by a silhouette of a sexy generic Chinese woman—felt very competitive with Lu. She was upset because Lu's "art photo" (a professional glamor photograph) had attracted a lot of attention. Moira complained that many of the men who initially wrote to both of them developed greater interest in Lu because her photograph was more beautiful than the more natural shots that Moira had later sent of herself. Seeking my opinion on whether Lu's photograph looked anything like the "real person," Moira arranged for me to meet Lu face-to-face.

Later on, when I got to know Lu, she shared many of her Internet experiences with me. She and Moira poked fun at some of the men who, unaware that they compared notes, told them both, "You are the only one"; at the middle-aged man who had never lived apart from his mother; of the man who wanted Lu's dress size so that he could bring her a respectable wardrobe befitting a "business manager's date" when he came to visit. One day Lu met me alone for lunch and asked—perhaps in response to Moira's hints—whether there was any problem with using an "art photo" and whether I thought that Americans might be misled by it. As she explained, this genre is popular in China and no one, she insisted, would think that was how she really looked. I explained that, at the time, men might not understand because such glamor shots were not as widely known in the United States as they were among urban women in China, even though most Chinese consider them a "Western" style and practice. In the coming weeks she sent her pen pals "natural" shots of herself and most of them stopped writing. When she reported this development, she had another question: "Do American men care about women's bodies?" One reason for this concern, she explained, was that several years ago she had breast cancer and had undergone a mastectomy.

From the vantage point of the Internet, Lu's studio art photograph was easily consumed by U.S. men who were eager to meet an attractive and age-defying Chinese woman. Unlike the more blatant Chinese art or glamor photographs that depict fog rising from the ground, pink poodles, and false backdrops that most Western observers would probably identify as in some way "fake," Lu's picture was far subtler and carried few clues that it did not represent her as she really appeared. When this particular illusion or fantasy was defied, the interest of many of her pen pals waned. Liu's deception was unintentional, but it points nonetheless to a technologically mediated cultural disjuncture, a misunderstanding of bodies across the transnational space of correspondence courtships, one that is made possible by the global flow of various technologies including Western-style fashion photography and globally circulating images from glamor magazines (Adrian 2003).

Yanyi's Kiss

Yanyi was one of several women I met through kiss.com in 1999.[8] Her thumbnail photograph depicted the face of a pretty young woman with wavy hair, wide eyes, and, as one of my Chinese friends put it, someone who did not look entirely Chinese. The listing followed a regular format: Age: 32; Country: China; City: Shenzhen; Height: 5'0; Weight: 95 lbs.; Religion: unspecified; Smokes: no; Drinks: no; Children: no; Education: university; Profession: other; Marital Status: never married. Such was the information that a man looking for a pen pal would have seen. Of all the women with whom I communicated, Yanyi was the friendliest and the most outgoing and expressive. Her correspondences with me conveyed a sense of her warmth, honesty, and trustworthiness, feelings that she may well also have conveyed to her male pen pals.

In her thirties and still unmarried, Yanyi was considered by Chinese standards "over the hill." She was educated and worked as a manager for an international consulting firm in Shenzhen. At the time she earned a very respectable salary by local terms, about US$700 a month. At work, she had her own office and there she had free use of a computer that she could use after hours or when work was slack. When we first met, she had recently ended an intense and difficult relationship with an Australian man, Russ, she had initially met through the Internet. She explained to me that I was the only one with whom she could talk honestly about the experience. Her family had intensely disliked Russ and disapproved of their relationship, so it was impossible to talk with them about it. After several hours together, we stopped by her office and she gave me a pile of printouts of Internet correspondences (a pile a foot high of single-spaced and double-sided e-mail messages). For the next 12 hours I read and took notes. Striking to me at the time was how within the course of their six-month correspondence Russ began to express his deep feelings of love for her, to write her poetry, to refer to her as "my dear wife," and to express a variety of sexual fantasies. The messages covered a wide range of topics, and the couple got to know about many aspects of each other's lives. They exchanged photographs. They had fights and disagreements, most of which were satisfactorily resolved (Constable 2003:149–150).

In the course of their correspondence, Russ's e-mail messages became sexually explicit and very intimate. At the time, I was somewhat uncomfortable reading them and was surprised that Yanyi had not filtered them out.[9] I took only sparse and general notes on the more sexual topics in her pile of e-mail messages. I was mainly interested at the time in getting a more general sense of the unfolding of a correspondence relationship, and I was struck at how their relationship became increasingly intimate (both emotionally and sexually). I was also interested to see Yanyi's responses shift between assertively putting him in his place (especially when he made what she considered racist generalizations about the Chinese), playful and teasing expressions of shyness, active pleasure and participation, and amusement. References to body parts, underwear sniffing, body hair, erections, and sexual wetness were mainly initiated by Russ, but Yanyi played a surprisingly active and seemingly comfortable part in much of the sexual aspect of their Internet courtship.

I took detailed notes on one message that seemed far less risqué to me but bothered Yanyi a lot and provoked a very strong response from her. In his message, Russ fantasized about meeting in person at the train station and about their first long, wet, and passionate lingering kiss. No doubt imagining the real world rather than the virtual one, Yanyi was awakened from her reverie and answered very frankly that she would "turn purple with embarrassment" if he were to try such a thing. Russ, perhaps not understanding the difference between this rather tame fantasy and his others, in turn replied that if she did not kiss him upon his arrival, he would turn right back around and leave, or that perhaps he ought to cancel his plans to visit altogether. Yanyi tried to reason with him and replied, "You know, maybe it's our cultural shortcoming—we [Chinese] don't address sweetly, hug, kiss, or touch so much to show our feelings or intimacy as do people in Western cultures. (That's why I don't know if I can give you a deep long kiss as the first hello right in public)" (Constable 2003:150). In a later message, revealing his effort to understand the situation but also demonstrating his incomprehension of the contemporary situation in China, Russ wrote to her of a "true story" of a Chinese couple who had kissed in public and were caught by a Chinese Communist Party member. As he reported, the couple was arrested and the woman was sentenced to eight years and the man to two years of hard labor.

As it turned out, in hindsight, their exchange about the kiss was telling. Russ was extremely self-centered and completely insensitive to Yanyi's personal, professional, and familial situation. From the moment he arrived in China, he expected her to support him financially and to place him at the center of her life. Russ also had fairly severe physical and emotional problems that Yanyi had learned about in the course of their correspondences, but that she had not fully understood. As she explained, in retrospect she should have broken up with him much earlier, but by the time she had learned enough about him, it was already too late. Their Internet relationship had already crossed a line of intimacy that made it very difficult for her to back away.

This vignette illustrates both the possibilities for bodily pleasure through the Internet, and the voluntary if not equal participation of a man and woman in a physical and emotional relationship in virtual space. Yet it also illustrates the way in which Internet fantasies and experiences cannot easily be transplanted into real life. Russ's insensitivity to the norms of public and private, on-line and off-line sexual expressions in China were a clear source of conflict, but only among many others. What had "worked" for six months of daily—and often numerous times daily—communication over the Internet would, Yanyi agreed, not likely have survived an initial face-to-face courtship. This example, that of the Chinese woman and the "sex man," and that of Lu's photograph point to the conflicts—and the blur—between supposedly "real" and "fictitious" sites and experiences, or those that are aimed at fantasy and performance and those aimed at "real life" experiences and relationships, but also to the added component of cross-cultural misunderstandings that can be exacerbated through a communicative medium that conveys a sense of virtual and real intimacy. In the context of Internet courtship, I would argue that bodies are fantasized and projected, changing and in flux, near or far from consciousness in any particular communication, but they are always part of the picture.

Conclusion

In my earlier work on correspondence courtship and marriage, I intentionally shifted my analysis away from "mail-order-bride catalogues" and images of women's bodies for several reasons. One was that preexisting studies of "mail-order brides" tended to focus primarily or exclusively on catalogues. They made little or no reference to the real-life experiences of the women and men involved in correspondence marriages, other than the occasional mention of the most sensationalized media cases. Another reason is that such studies placed far too much attention on women as sexual objects, sexual images, or sexual fantasies of Western men. Most of the photographs that Chinese women and Filipinas post of themselves on introduction websites, as noted earlier, resemble yearbook or passport photographs and show women who are clean-cut and straitlaced. Many men, moreover, aim to distance themselves from women who are or might be considered sexually promiscuous, aiming instead to find "traditional wives" with "old-fashioned family values" (see also Wilson 1988).[10] My purpose is not to deny the existence of racialized sexual stereotypes or sexual fantasies as an important factor in correspondence relationships but to counterbalance these important issues with some of the less well known and equally important aspects of correspondence courtship and marriage.

This chapter is an effort to shift and refocus my earlier study of correspondence courtship and marriage to the depiction and perception of bodies and the intersections between bodies and bodily experiences in virtual space on the Internet and in real life. Distinctions can perhaps be made between three levels of bodily representations and experiences: (1) the photographs and written descriptions of bodies on the Internet; (2) the physical or embodied responses to Internet representations; and (3) face-to-face interactions that highlight the potential ruptures and disjunctures between Internet and real-life bodies and experiences. My intent has been to show some of the uncomfortable tensions between the intersecting realms of cyberspace and so-called real life, or what might better be seen as on-line/off-line intersections. Part of the tension and also the appeal of the Internet are derived from the fact that it is a tool that creates an increasingly efficient time/space compression, rendering it possible for more people to communicate faster and to establish broader social contacts than would otherwise be possible through simple print medium and the postal service. Yet a problem arises in relation to the different purposes for which the Internet can be used. Is it a space in which to express one's fantasies with anyone who is willing (and economically privileged enough) to partake and respond with little interference from the real world, or is it a space in which to pursue real and fundamental goals IRL? A common understanding of the "ground rules" becomes ever more difficult as a wider array of people, with different goals, objectives, and aspirations, in different parts of the world, participate in such global marriage-scapes.

Despite the reproduction of particular structural inequalities, the opportunity for correspondence courtships and marriages provide Chinese women and Filipinas (and women from certain other parts of the world as well) with new opportunities for mobility and pleasure. Although a narrower focus on bodily images and experiences that are linked to the Internet clearly runs the risk of once again reifying the body, race, and sexuality at the expense of other issues, it does not lead to an altogether different argument. The Internet has led not only to the creation of new and more widely available opportunities for men and women from different parts of the world to meet, correspond and sometimes marry; it also contributes to the possibilities for bodily pleasure and also to the risks associated with mobility across virtual and real social terrains.

Notes

1. The Internet has also had a huge impact on Chinese popular and political culture in general, opening up new spaces for artists, writers, activists, and ordinary people that are at least temporarily outside of the government's official gaze.
2. Unlike U.S. men who typically join the agency and never actually go to the agency's office or headquarters, and never meet its staff face-to-face, several Chinese women I knew in Beijing visited a particular agency's office regularly, knew the staff, and had the opportunity to meet other clients.
3. At the time of my research, wireless mobile telephones were not common in the Philippines. Since then they have become more popular, and the cost of international calls and

text messaging has dropped, contributing to the growing popularity of this mode of communication (see Pertierra et al. 2002).

4. In the late 1990s photographs depicted some marked stylistic differences between women of different nationalities. In photographs, Filipinas and Chinese women generally appeared to be more conservative and clean-cut than Eastern European women, who, on the whole, dressed and posed in seemingly more explicitly sexy and provocative ways.

5. All names of individuals encountered in the course of on-line and off-line research are pseudonyms.

6. Thompson reports on Jeffrey Hancock's study of 30 undergraduates at Cornell University who "mishandled the truth in one quarter of all face-to-face conversations, and in a whopping 37 percent of phone calls. But when they went into cyberspace . . . only 1 in 5 instant messaging chats contained a lie, and barely 14 percent of e-mail messages were dishonest" (2004:24).

7. The manager of a Chinese agency suggested that such experiences are less common in subscription-type introduction agencies (such as her own) because such men could not maintain their reputations. She would warn the women she knew, she said, about men who seemed to want a "sexual vacation" rather than a "lifetime partner." Payment of subscription fees seemed to suggest to her a greater commitment to pursuing a "real" relationship.

8. For a fuller description of Yanyi's relationship with Russ, see Constable 2003:146–151. Here, the story is abbreviated and refocused on the issue of bodies, the Internet, and their off-line meeting.

9. Many Chinese women I met were very frank in raising sexual topics that they said they would not discuss with friends and family. My identity as a "Western" woman, informed by their view of Westerners as notoriously open about sex, no doubt contributed to their openness.

10. Women also pay close attention to the verbal and visual clues from men. Chinese women, for example, often avoided or ceased correspondence with men who exposed tattoos, posed without shirts or in singlets, or had unattractive facial hair.

References

Adrian, Bonnie
  2003   Framing the Bride: Globalizing Beauty and Romance in Taiwan's Bridal Industry. Berkeley: University of California Press.
Ahearn, Laura
  2001   Invitations to Love: Literacy, Love Letters, and Social Change in Nepal. Ann Arbor: University of Michigan Press.
Appadurai, Arjun
  1996   Modernity at Large: Cultural Dimensions of Globalization. Minneapolis: University of Minnesota Press.
Brennan, Denise
  2004   What's Love Got to Do with It? Transnational Desires and Sex Tourism in the Dominican Republic. Durham: Duke University Press.
Burkhalter, Byron
  1999   Reading Race On-line: Discovering Racial Identity in Usenet Discussions. *In* Communities in Cyberspace. Marc A. Smith and Peter Kollock, eds. Pp. 60–75. New York Routledge.
Choy, Catherine C.
  2003   Empire of Care: Nursing and Migration in Filipino American History. Durham Duke University Press.

Clark, Gary
   1998   "Your Bride Is in the Mail": How to Find the Bride You *Really Want* by Corresponding
          with Ladies in Foreign Countries. Las Vegas: Words That Work Publications.
Constable, Nicole
   1997   Maid to Order in Hong Kong: Stories of Filipina Workers. Ithaca: Cornell University
          Press.
   2003   Romance on a Global Stage: Pen Pals, Virtual Ethnography, and "Mail Order"
          Marriages. Berkeley: University of California Press.
   2005   A Tale of Two Marriages: International Matchmaking and Gendered Mobility. *In*
          Cross-Border Marriages: Gender and Mobility in Transnational Asia. Nicole Constable,
          ed. Pp. 166–186. Philadelphia: University of Pennsylvania Press.
Donath, Judith
   1999   Identity and Deception in the Virtual Community. *In* Communities in Cyberspace.
          Marc A. Smith and Peter Kollock, eds. Pp. 29–59. New York: Routledge.
Ebo, B. L.
   1998   Cyberghetto or Cybertopia? Race, Class, and Gender on the Internet. Westport, CT.:
          Praeger.
Ehrenreich, Barbara, and Arlie Russell Hochschild, eds.
   2003   Global Woman: Nannies, Maids, and Sex Workers in the New Economy. New York:
          Metropolitan Books.
Featherstone, Mike, and Roger Burrows
   1995   Cultures of Technological Embodiment: An Introduction. *In* Cyberspace, Cyberbodies,
          Cyberpunk: Cultures of Technological Embodiment. M. Featherstone and R. Burrows,
          eds. Pp. 1–20. Thousand Oaks, CA: Sage.
Giddens, Anthony
   1992   The Transformation of Intimacy: Sexuality, Love, and Eroticism in Modern Societies.
          Stanford: Stanford University Press.
Halualani, Rona Tamiko
   1995   The Intersecting Hegemonic Discourses of an Asian Mail-Order Bride Catalog:
          Philipina "Oriental Butterfly" Dolls for Sale. Women's Studies in Communication
          118(1):45–64.
Haraway, Donna
   1991   Symians, Cyborgs and Women: The Reinvention of Nature. London: Free Association
          Books.
Inayatullah, Sohail, and Ivana Milojevic
   1999   Exclusion and Communication in the Information Era: From Silences to Global
          Communication. *In* Woman@Internet: Creating New Cultures in Cyberspace. Wendy
          Harcourt, ed. Pp. 76–87. New York: Zed Books.
Jankowiak, William, ed.
   1995   Romantic Passion: A Universal Experience? New York: Columbia University Press.
Keisler, Sara
   1997   Preface. *In* Culture of the Internet. Mahwah, NJ: Lawrence Erlbaum Associates.
Kollock, Peter, and Mark A. Smith
   1999   Communities in Cyberspace. *In* Communities in Cyberspace. Marc A. Smith and Peter
          Kollock, eds. Pp. 3–28. New York: Routledge.
O'Brien, Jodi
   1999   Writing in the Body: Gender (Re)production in On-line Interaction. *In* Communities
          in Cyberspace. Marc A. Smith and Peter Kollock, eds. Pp. 76–104. New York:
          Routledge.
Ong, Aihwa
   1999   Flexible Citizenship: The Cultural Logic of Transnationality. Durham: Duke University
          Press.

Parrenas, Rhacel Salazar
  2001   Servants of Globalization: Women, Migration, and Domestic Work. Stanford: Stanford
         University Press.
Pertierra, Raul, Eduardo F. Ugarte, Alicia Pingol, Joel Hernandez, and Nikos L. Dacanay
  2002   Txt-ing Selves: Cellphones and Philippine Modernity. Manila: De La Salle University
         Press.
Plant, Sadie
  1995   The Future Looms: Weaving Women and Cybernetics. *In* Cyberspace, Cyberbodies,
         Cyberpunk: Cultures of Technological Embodiment. M. Featherstone and R. Burrows,
         eds. Pp. 45–64. Thousand Oaks, CA: Sage.
Rebhun, L. A.
  1999   The Heart Is an Unknown Country: Love in the Changing Economy of Northeast
         Brazil. Stanford: Stanford University Press.
Rheingold, Harold
  1993   The Virtual Community: Homesteading in the Electronic Frontier. New York:
         Addison-Wesley.
Robinson, Kathryn
  1996   Of Mail-Order Brides and "Boys' Own" Tales: Representations of Asian-Australian
         Marriages. Feminist Review 52 (Spring):53–68.
Scholes, Robert
  1999   The "Mail Order Bride" Industry and Its Impact on U.S. Immigration. *In* International
         Matchmaking Organizations: A Report to Congress (Appendix A). Electronic
         document, *www.uscis.gov/files/article/MobRept_AppendixA.pdf*, accessed July 7, 2007.
Stone, Allucquere Rosanne
  1995   The War of Desire and Technology at the Close of the Mechanical Age. Boston: MIT
         Press.
Thompson, Clive
  2004   The Honesty Virus. New York Times Magazine, March 21:24–28.
Tolentino, Roland B.
  1996   Bodies, Letters, Catalogs: Filipinas in Transnational Space. Social Text 48:49–76.
Tsing, Anna Lowenhaupt
  1993   In the Realm of the Diamond Queen: Marginality in an Out-of-the-Way Place.
         Princeton: Princeton University Press.
Van Gelder, Lindsey
  1996   The Strange Case of the Electronic Lover. *In* Computerization and Controversy.
         Charles Dunlop and Robert Kling, eds. Pp. 533–546. San Diego: Academic.
Villapando, Venny
  1989   The Business of Selling Mail-Order Brides. *In* Making Waves: An Anthology of
         Writings by and about Asian American Woman. Asian Women United of California,
         eds. Pp. 318–327. Boston: Beacon.
Wilson, Ara
  1988   American Catalogues of Asian Brides. *In* Anthropology for the Nineties. Johnetta Cole,
         ed. Pp. 114–125. New York: Free Press.
Wilson, Samuel M. and Leighton C. Peterson
  2002   The Anthropology of On-line Communities. Annual Review of Anthropology
         31:449–467.

Contributors

Elizabeth Bernstein is Assistant Professor of Sociology and Women's Studies at Barnard College, Columbia University. She is the author of *Temporarily Yours: Sexual Commerce in Post-Industrial Culture* (University of Chicago Press, 2007) and co-editor of *Regulating Sex: The Politics of Intimacy and Identity* (Routledge, 2004). Her research interests include sexuality and the state; sexual commerce; the sociology of the body, sex, and gender; and feminist methods.

Denise Brennan is Associate Professor of Anthropology in the Department of Sociology and Anthropology at Georgetown University. She is the author of *What's Love Got to Do with It?: Transnational Desires and Sex Tourism in the Dominican Republic* (Duke University Press, 2004). Currently she is writing a book on the recovery and resettlement process of trafficked persons, tentatively titled *Life after Slavery: Creating Home/Returning Home*. Her research interests include human trafficking, the global sex trade, migration, women's labor, and Latin America and the Caribbean.

Sealing Cheng is Henry Luce Assistant Professor in the Women's Studies Department at Wellesley College. Her work has appeared in the following journals: *Health and Human Rights, International Feminist Journal of Politics, East Asia,* and *Asia-Pacific Viewpoint*. She is currently working on a manuscript titled "Transnational Desires: Filipina Entertainers in US Military Camp Towns in South Korea." Her research interests include sexuality, prostitution, migration, trafficking, and human rights and she has conducted research in South Korea, the Philippines, Hong Kong, and Shanghai.

Nicole Constable is a Professor in the Department of Anthropology at the University of Pittsburgh. Her geographical areas of specialization are Hong Kong, China, and the Philippines. Her publications include: *Maid to Order in Hong Kong: Stories of Filipina Workers* (Cornell University Press, 1997), *Romance on a Global Stage: Penpals, Virtual Ethnography, and Mail Order Marriages* (University of California Press, 2003), and *Cross-Border Marriages: Gender and Mobility in Transnational Asia* (University of Pennsylvania Press, 2004).

Katherine Frank is a cultural anthropologist, currently an SSRC Sexuality Research Postdoctoral Fellow in the Sociology Department at the University of Wisconsin-Madison, and a Faculty Associate in Cultural Anthropology at the College of the Atlantic. She is the author of *G-Strings and Sympathy: Strip Club Regulars and Male Desire* (2002), and co-editor of *Flesh for Fantasy: Producing and Consuming Exotic Dance* (2006). She has also written on eating disorders, gender, pornography, feminism, and monogamy.

Carla Freeman is an Associate Professor of Women's Studies and Anthropology at Emory University. Her recent publications include a book, *High Tech and High Heels in the Global Economy: Women, Work, and Pink Collar Identities in the Caribbean* (Duke University Press, 2000), and several journal articles on gender, globalization, labor, and identity in the Caribbean. She is interested in the culture and political economy of globalization; feminist anthropology; "modernity" and its relationship to development; and the Caribbean region.

Jennifer S. Hirsch is Associate Professor of Sociomedical Sciences at Columbia University. She is the author of *A Courtship after Marriage: Sexuality and Love in Mexican Transnational Families* (University of California Press, 2003) and co-editor of *Modern Loves: The Anthropology of Romantic Love and Companionate Marriage* (University of Michigan Press, 2006). Her major research interests include gender; sexuality and HIV; US-Mexico migration; and the comparative anthropology of love.

Marcia C. Inhorn is a Professor of Public Health and Anthropology at the University of Michigan. She has conducted research on infertility and the new reproductive technologies in Egypt, Lebanon, United Arab Emirates, and Arab America. She's the founding editor of the *Journal of Middle East Women's Studies* and an associate editor of *Global Public Health*. Her books include: *Infertility and Patriarchy* (University of Pennsylvania Press, 1996) and *Local Babies, Global Science* (Routledge, 2003), and she is co-editor of *Infertility around the Globe* (University of California Press, 2002) and *The Anthropology of Infectious Disease* (Routledge, 1997).

Miguel Muñoz-Laboy is Assistant Professor of Sociomedical Sciences at Columbia University. His work has appeared in journals such as *Sexualities* and the *American Journal of Public Health*. His major research interests include gender, sexuality and health among ethnic minority youth in the urban United States, and male bisexuality and HIV prevention.

Mark B. Padilla is an Assistant Professor of Public Health and Adjunct Assistant Professor of Anthropology at the University of Michigan. He is author of the book *Caribbean Pleasure Industry: Tourism, Sexuality, and AIDS in the Dominican Republic* (University of Chicago Press, 2007), and his work has appeared in the journals *Social Science and Medicine*, *Journal of Homosexuality*, and *Archives of Sexual Behavior*. His research and writing focuses on structural approaches to health, gender and sexuality, and the HIV/AIDS epidemic in Latin America and the Caribbean.

Richard G. Parker is Professor and Chair of the Department of Sociomedical Sciences and Director of the Center for Gender, Sexuality and Health at Columbia University. His publications include *Bodies, Pleasures and Passions: Sexual Culture in Contemporary Brazil* (Beacon Press, 1991), *Beneath the Equator: Cultures of Desire, Male Homosexuality, and Emerging Gay Communities in Brazil* (Routledge, 1999), *Framing the Sexual Subject: The Politics of Gender, Sexuality and Power* (University of California Press, 2000), and *Culture, Society and Sexuality, 2nd edition* (Routledge, in press). He is a founding editor of the journal, *Culture, Health and Sexuality*, and the editor-in-chief for *Global Public Health*.

Heather Paxson is an Assistant Professor in the Department of Anthropology at the Massachusetts Institute of Technology. She is the author of *Making Modern Mothers: Ethics and Family Planning in Urban Greece* (University of California Press, 2004). Her recent research is an ethnographic project on the making, marketing, and eating of artisanal cheeses in the US and Europe.

L. A. Rebhun is currently Research Affiliate in Yale University's Department of Anthropology. She is the author of *The Heart is Unknown Country: Love in the Changing Economy of Northeast Brazil* (1999) and co-author of *Alcohol and Homicide: A Deadly Combination of Two American Traditions* (1995). Her major research interests include child survival, economic development, social change, globalization, and gender/sexuality in Latin America and the Caribbean.

Robert E. Sember is a South African researcher and artist. His interests include sexual rights, arts-based activism, and the political economy of HIV/AIDS. He has taught at the Mailman School of Public Health at Columbia University and in the School of the Arts at UCLA. He is a member of the sound arts collective Ultra-red, which has exhibited and performed across the United States and internationally.

Saskia E. Wieringa is a member of the Faculty of Social and Behavioural Sciences at the Amsterdam School for Social Science Research. Major recent publications include: *Sexual Politics in Indonesia* (Palgrave/MacMillan, 2002), *Female Desires* (co-edited with Evelyn Blackwood, Columbia University Press, 1999) and *Tommy Boys, Lesbian Men and Ancestral Wives* (with Ruth Morgan, Jacana Publishers, 2005). Dr Wieringa has worked extensively on issues of gender planning, women's empowerment, and women's organizations.